COMPREHENSIVE GUIDE TO PHARMACEUTICAL REGULATORY SCIENCE

DR. K. NAGASREE, DR. KONDA SHRAVAN KUMAR, DR. K. N. V. RAO

Made with ♥ on the Notion Press Platform
www.notionpress.com

Contents

Comprehensive Guide To Pharmaceutical Regulatory Science

Dr. K. Nagasree
Associate Professor,
Department of Regulatory Affairs,
Samskruti College of Pharmacy,
Ghatkesar, Hyderabad, Telangana, India
Dr. Konda Shravan Kumar
Principal,
Samskruti College of Pharmacy,
Ghatkesar, Hyderabad, Telangana, India
Dr. K. N. V. Rao
Principal,
Nalanda College of Pharmacy,
Charlapally, Nalgonda, Telangana, India
Editor
Dr. A. Muralidhar Rao
Principal,
St. Mary's College of Pharmacy,
Secunderabad, Telangana, India

Published by Notion Press
Notion Press, Inc.
800, West El Camino Real #180,
California, USA 94040
Notion Press Media Pvt Ltd
#7, Red Cross Road,
Egmore, Chennai, Tamil Nadu 600008
Email ID: publish@notionpress.com
Phone Number: +91 44 46315631

Introduction to Pharmaceutical Regulatory Science

1.1 Overview of Pharmaceutical Regulatory Science

Pharmaceutical regulatory science is a multidisciplinary field that focuses on ensuring the safety, efficacy, and quality of pharmaceutical products through regulatory processes. It involves a detailed understanding of the drug development process and the various regulatory requirements that must be met in different countries to market pharmaceutical products. Regulatory science is crucial in ensuring that medicines, biologics, medical devices, and other healthcare products meet the appropriate standards to protect public health. This field combines scientific principles with legal and regulatory frameworks to guarantee that drugs are safe and effective for their intended use.

1.1.1 Definition of Pharmaceutical Regulatory Science

Pharmaceutical regulatory science refers to the study and application of regulatory policies and procedures to the development, approval, and marketing of pharmaceutical products. It includes the regulation of drug products throughout their lifecycle, from research and development (R&D) to clinical trials, manufacturing, marketing, and post-market surveillance. This field is governed by national and international regulations that set the standards for drug safety, quality, and efficacy.

The regulatory processes are designed to ensure that new drugs, biologics, and medical devices meet the required safety and efficacy standards before they are available for use in the market. Regulatory science also involves maintaining an understanding of evolving scientific advancements, new methodologies in testing, and the changing legal frameworks that govern the industry. Regulatory scientists must navigate a complex system of regulations, guidelines, and international agreements to facilitate the approval of new drugs and therapies while ensuring that the public is protected from unsafe or ineffective treatments.

Key components of pharmaceutical regulatory science include:

- Regulatory submission processes: Involves the submission of data, including preclinical, clinical, and manufacturing information, to regulatory bodies such as the FDA (Food and Drug Administration), EMA (European Medicines Agency), or PMDA (Pharmaceuticals and Medical Devices Agency).
- Drug approval pathways: Regulatory science involves understanding the different pathways for drug approval, including fast track, orphan drug status, and conditional approval, which may vary by jurisdiction.
- Compliance with regulations: It ensures that pharmaceutical companies adhere to good manufacturing practices (GMP), good clinical practices (GCP), and other regulatory standards to ensure drug quality.

Pharmaceutical regulatory science is a dynamic field, adapting to changes in scientific knowledge, technological advances, and emerging healthcare needs. It plays a critical role in safeguarding public health by ensuring that drugs and medical devices are safe, effective, and of the highest quality.

1.1.2 Scope of Regulatory Affairs in Drug Development

The scope of regulatory affairs in drug development is vast and covers all stages of the pharmaceutical product lifecycle, from initial discovery through post-marketing activities. Regulatory affairs professionals work closely with researchers, clinicians, manufacturing units, and government agencies to ensure compliance with laws and regulations throughout the development process. Regulatory affairs are critical at every stage, from the discovery of a new drug to its approval, market entry, and monitoring after it is released.

1.1.2.1 Drug Discovery and Preclinical Development

The regulatory process begins with the drug discovery phase, where new chemical entities (NCEs) or biologics are identified. At this stage, regulatory requirements focus on preclinical studies, which involve testing the drug on animal models to assess safety, toxicity, and pharmacokinetics. Regulatory authorities such as the FDA require substantial preclinical data before allowing clinical trials to begin. The submission of an Investigational New Drug (IND) application is essential to receive permission to conduct human clinical trials.

During preclinical development, regulatory bodies evaluate:

- Toxicology studies: These studies are necessary to identify the potential harm a drug may cause when used in humans.
- Pharmacokinetics: Understanding how the body absorbs, distributes, metabolizes, and excretes the drug.
- Pharmacodynamics: Understanding the drug's effect on the body, including the mechanism of action.

The regulatory authorities carefully review this data to ensure the drug is safe for initial human testing. Regulations also ensure that the drug development follows ethical guidelines, protecting both the animal and human subjects involved in the studies.

1.1.2.2 Clinical Development and Approval

Once preclinical data is accepted, clinical trials can proceed. Clinical development involves multiple phases:

- Phase I: The first-in-human studies, focusing on safety and pharmacokinetics in a small group of healthy volunteers.
- Phase II: Tests for the drug's efficacy and optimal dosage in patients with the condition.
- Phase III: Large-scale trials to confirm the drug's efficacy and monitor adverse effects.

During this phase, pharmaceutical companies must submit New Drug Applications (NDAs), where they present the clinical trial data to regulatory authorities. Regulatory agencies review the data for safety, efficacy, and overall benefit-risk balance before approval.

1.1.2.3 Post-Market Surveillance

Even after a drug is approved and reaches the market, regulatory affairs continue to play a role. Post-marketing surveillance, or Phase IV studies, monitors the drug's long-term effects and detects any rare side effects that might not have been identified during clinical trials. Regulatory bodies may require companies to conduct additional studies or implement risk management strategies if new safety concerns arise.

The scope of regulatory affairs extends into managing pharmacovigilance activities, which involves tracking adverse events and ensuring that timely actions are taken to mitigate risks. Regulatory bodies like the FDA and EMA mandate the submission of periodic safety update reports (PSURs) to keep track of the safety profile of marketed drugs.

1.1.2.4 Regulatory Compliance and Global Regulations

Regulatory affairs are not confined to a single country; drugs must comply with regulations across different jurisdictions. Pharmaceutical companies must navigate complex global regulations to market their products worldwide. This includes understanding requirements for drug submissions, manufacturing standards, and labeling rules across markets in the U.S., EU, Japan, Canada, and other countries.

Countries such as the U.S. follow FDA regulations, while the EU operates under the European Medicines Agency (EMA). Both agencies regulate drug submissions, clinical trial designs, and manufacturing standards but may have different timelines, requirements, and processes. The Common Technical Document (CTD) has been developed to harmonize submission requirements across different regulatory bodies and is widely used for submitting drug information globally.

Pharmaceutical regulatory science also ensures that the drug manufacturing process adheres to Good Manufacturing Practices (GMP). This includes inspecting facilities, reviewing manufacturing protocols, and ensuring compliance with international quality standards to ensure the final product is consistently produced and controlled.

1.1.3 Importance of Regulatory Affairs in Ensuring Drug Safety and Efficacy

Regulatory affairs play a critical role in ensuring that pharmaceutical products are both safe and effective for human use. They act as a safeguard, ensuring that new drugs meet stringent safety and efficacy standards before they reach the market. Regulatory professionals, in collaboration with scientists, clinicians, and regulatory bodies, are responsible for ensuring that all stages of drug development, including preclinical studies, clinical trials, and post-marketing surveillance, comply with legal and ethical standards. This process is vital to public health and ensures that only those drugs that provide a net benefit to patients are approved for use.

Safety Assurance

One of the primary goals of regulatory affairs is to guarantee that drugs do not pose unnecessary risks to patients. This is achieved through the careful evaluation of toxicology studies and clinical trial data to assess potential harmful effects. Regulatory bodies, such as the FDA and EMA, require comprehensive preclinical data on the pharmacological and toxicological properties of a drug to assess its safety before it can proceed to human trials. Clinical trials (Phase I-III) further evaluate the drug's safety profile, ensuring that adverse effects are minimized, and appropriate risk management strategies are in place.

During clinical trials, regulatory authorities require continuous monitoring of adverse events to determine the safety of the drug in larger and more diverse populations. They also mandate that pharmaceutical companies report any serious side effects, enabling them to make informed decisions about whether the benefits outweigh the risks. Post-market surveillance (Phase IV) plays a key role in identifying long-term side effects and rare adverse events that were not detected during clinical trials. This ongoing monitoring ensures that any new risks are promptly addressed through safety updates, recalls, or labeling changes.

Efficacy Assurance

Regulatory affairs also play a crucial role in ensuring that a drug is effective in treating the intended condition. Regulatory bodies carefully evaluate clinical trial data to confirm that the drug demonstrates the claimed therapeutic effects. Regulatory authorities review the clinical endpoints (i.e., the specific outcomes that measure the drug's effectiveness) to ensure that they are scientifically valid and clinically relevant. The efficacy of a drug is not only assessed based on the results from controlled trials but also through its effectiveness in real-world clinical settings, as reported by healthcare professionals and patients.

Ensuring the efficacy of a drug also includes verifying that the claims made by the manufacturer are scientifically substantiated. Regulatory professionals are responsible for ensuring that the labeling, packaging, and marketing materials of the drug do not exaggerate its therapeutic benefits and provide clear, evidence-based information on how the drug should be used, potential side effects, and any contraindications.

Through stringent regulatory processes, regulatory affairs help maintain public trust in the pharmaceutical industry by ensuring that only those drugs that have demonstrated both safety and efficacy are allowed to enter the market.

1.1.4 Role of Regulatory Bodies in Drug Approval

Regulatory bodies are the central authorities responsible for overseeing the approval and market access of pharmaceutical products. Their primary role is to ensure that drugs are safe, effective, and of high quality before they are introduced to the public. These organizations establish and enforce regulatory standards that guide drug development, clinical trials, manufacturing, labeling, and post-marketing surveillance. Regulatory agencies also act as intermediaries between pharmaceutical companies and the government, providing clear guidance on legal requirements while protecting public health.

Drug Evaluation and Approval

One of the most important roles of regulatory bodies is to evaluate and approve drugs before they are marketed. The process begins when a pharmaceutical company submits an application for a new drug, which includes all the data collected during the preclinical and clinical trial phases. Regulatory bodies, such as the U.S. FDA, the European Medicines Agency (EMA), and the Japanese PMDA, review this data to determine whether the drug meets safety, efficacy, and quality standards.

These agencies evaluate the risk-benefit ratio of a drug based on the clinical trial data and other available scientific evidence. The regulatory body must determine whether the drug offers sufficient benefit to patients to justify the potential risks associated with its use. This evaluation process also includes assessing whether the drug's manufacturing process meets the required Good Manufacturing Practices (GMP) to ensure consistent production of high-quality products. The approval process is rigorous, with regulatory bodies scrutinizing all aspects of drug development and ensuring that the public's health is safeguarded.

Regulatory Guidance and Standards

Regulatory bodies play a pivotal role in setting the standards for drug development, clinical trials, and post-market surveillance. They provide detailed guidance documents and regulations that outline the specific requirements for drug development, clinical trial designs, and reporting of adverse events. These guidelines help pharmaceutical companies navigate the complex regulatory landscape and ensure compliance with the necessary laws and regulations.

For example, the FDA issues guidance documents on the design of clinical trials, including the required study populations, endpoints, and statistical analysis methods. Similarly, the European Medicines Agency provides guidelines on the development of biologic drugs and the approval of orphan drugs for rare diseases. Regulatory bodies also establish standards for drug labeling, which must include essential information such as dosage instructions, contraindications, and potential side effects. These standards ensure that healthcare providers and patients have the necessary information to use the drug safely and effectively.

Post-Market Surveillance and Safety Monitoring

Once a drug is approved, regulatory bodies continue to monitor its safety and effectiveness through post-market surveillance. This phase, also known as Phase IV, involves the ongoing collection and analysis of data regarding the drug's real-world performance. Regulatory agencies require pharmaceutical companies to submit periodic safety update reports (PSURs) and conduct additional studies to assess long-term safety. If new safety concerns arise after the drug is on the market, regulatory agencies can issue safety warnings, require additional labeling changes, or even withdraw the drug from the market if necessary.

In addition to monitoring adverse drug reactions, regulatory bodies also oversee the implementation of risk management plans, which include strategies to mitigate potential risks associated with the drug. This includes ensuring that healthcare professionals are properly educated on the drug's safety profile and that patients are informed of any potential risks before starting treatment.

Global Coordination and Harmonization

Regulatory bodies also play a significant role in global drug approval processes by engaging in regulatory harmonization efforts. Organizations like the International Council for Harmonisation of Technical Requirements for Pharmaceuticals for Human Use (ICH) work to create standardized guidelines and regulatory requirements for drug approval across different regions. By working together, regulatory bodies can streamline the drug approval process, reduce duplication of efforts, and ensure that drugs are evaluated using consistent criteria worldwide. This collaboration helps to ensure that drugs can be marketed in multiple countries, improving global access to safe and effective medicines.

In conclusion, regulatory bodies are central to the approval, monitoring, and ongoing safety of pharmaceutical products. They ensure that drugs meet stringent standards for safety, efficacy, and quality while guiding the industry through complex regulatory processes. Their role in drug approval is vital for maintaining public health and ensuring that patients receive effective and safe treatments.

This expanded text now includes detailed explanations for the specified subsections without using bold or highlighted words in the middle of the paragraph, adhering to your request for improved readability. Let me know if you need further adjustments!

1.2 Regulatory Authorities and Agencies

Regulatory authorities are essential to the pharmaceutical industry as they set the standards and guidelines that ensure the safety, efficacy, and quality of drug products. These organizations oversee the entire lifecycle of pharmaceuticals, from development to post-market surveillance. National regulatory bodies are responsible for implementing regulations within their respective countries, ensuring that pharmaceutical companies meet the required standards before drugs can be marketed to the public. Some of the most influential regulatory bodies worldwide include the U.S. FDA, the European Medicines Agency (EMA), the Japanese Pharmaceuticals and Medical Devices Agency (PMDA), and Health Canada.

1.2.1 National Regulatory Bodies

National regulatory bodies play a vital role in the drug approval process within their respective countries. These agencies are responsible for reviewing drug submissions, conducting inspections, and monitoring the safety and quality of pharmaceutical products. Some of the key responsibilities of national regulatory bodies include evaluating clinical trial data, setting manufacturing standards, approving new drugs, and ensuring the safety of marketed products through post-market surveillance.

1.2.1.1 Food and Drug Administration (FDA), USA

The **Food and Drug Administration (FDA)** is one of the most well-known regulatory bodies globally, primarily responsible for overseeing the safety and efficacy of drugs, biologics, medical devices, food, and cosmetics in the United States. Founded in 1906, the FDA is a part of the U.S. Department of Health and Human Services (HHS). Its primary mission is to protect public health by ensuring that drugs and medical products are safe, effective, and manufactured to the highest quality standards.

Role and Function of the FDA

The FDA is responsible for regulating and approving pharmaceuticals for human use, including prescription and over-the-counter (OTC) drugs. The agency's role extends beyond drug approval to include monitoring the production, distribution, labeling, and advertising of these products. The FDA is tasked with enforcing regulations on the clinical testing of drugs, ensuring compliance with Good Manufacturing Practices (GMP), and conducting inspections of pharmaceutical facilities.

One of the FDA's most important functions is to ensure that all drugs, biologics, and medical devices are safe and effective for use before they are made available to the public. The agency reviews clinical trial data, assesses potential risks and benefits, and grants approval based on the available scientific evidence.

Drug Approval Process

The FDA follows a structured and rigorous process for the approval of new drugs. The process begins with the submission of an **Investigational New Drug (IND)** application, which allows clinical testing of a new drug in humans. The clinical trial process is divided into several phases:

- **Phase I**: Focuses on the safety and pharmacokinetics of the drug in a small group of healthy volunteers.
- **Phase II**: Assesses the drug's effectiveness and dosage in patients with the target condition.
- **Phase III**: Confirms the drug's efficacy and safety in a larger group of patients, often in a randomized, controlled trial.

Once these phases are successfully completed, the pharmaceutical company submits a **New Drug Application (NDA)** to the FDA for review. The NDA includes all clinical trial data, manufacturing information, proposed labeling, and details about the drug's safety and efficacy. The FDA reviews the data and makes a determination on whether the drug can be approved for marketing in the U.S.

FDA Guidelines and Regulations

The FDA provides comprehensive guidance to the pharmaceutical industry on drug development, clinical trials, and manufacturing. These guidelines help ensure that pharmaceutical companies comply with federal regulations and meet the FDA's requirements for safety and efficacy. Some key regulations enforced by the FDA include:

- **Good Clinical Practice (GCP)**: The FDA ensures that clinical trials follow ethical standards and protect the rights of participants. This includes requirements for informed consent, institutional review board (IRB) approval, and the monitoring of adverse events.
- **Good Manufacturing Practice (GMP)**: The FDA enforces GMP standards to ensure that drugs are consistently produced and controlled to meet quality standards. This includes inspections of manufacturing facilities and oversight of the production process.
- **Labeling and Advertising Regulations**: The FDA also regulates drug labeling and advertising to ensure that consumers and healthcare providers have accurate, clear, and truthful information about the drug's uses, risks, and benefits.

Post-Market Surveillance

Even after a drug has been approved by the FDA, the agency continues to monitor its safety and effectiveness through post-market surveillance. This is known as **Phase IV** monitoring, and it includes tracking adverse events and ensuring that the drug continues to meet safety standards once it is in widespread use. The FDA has a **MedWatch** program for reporting adverse drug reactions and product defects, which helps healthcare providers and the public report any safety concerns related to a drug.

The FDA also has the authority to take regulatory action if new safety information arises. This could include requiring changes to a drug's labeling, restricting its use, or even withdrawing the drug from the market if necessary. The FDA's ongoing surveillance ensures that the public is protected from drugs that may pose unforeseen risks after their approval.

The FDA's Impact on Global Drug Development

While the FDA primarily regulates drugs within the United States, its influence extends worldwide. The FDA's approval process is considered one of the most rigorous in the world, and many countries use the FDA's standards and guidelines as a benchmark for their own drug approval processes. Furthermore, the FDA often works with other international regulatory agencies to harmonize drug approval requirements and facilitate the global exchange of pharmaceutical products.

The FDA's influence is also seen in its leadership role within the **International Council for Harmonisation (ICH)**, a global body that works to standardize drug development and approval processes across major markets. The FDA's global reach makes it a key player in ensuring that drugs meet the highest standards of safety and efficacy, not just in the U.S. but also in markets around the world.

1.2.1.2 European Medicines Agency (EMA), EU

The **European Medicines Agency (EMA)** is the regulatory body responsible for the scientific evaluation, supervision, and safety monitoring of medicines in the European Union (EU). Founded in 1995 and headquartered in Amsterdam, the EMA operates under the European Union's legal and regulatory framework, playing a pivotal role in protecting public health by ensuring that medicines are safe, effective, and of high quality. The EMA evaluates human and veterinary medicines and works closely with the **European Commission, European Parliament**, and national regulatory authorities to oversee drug approval and post-market surveillance in the EU member states.

Role and Function of the EMA

The EMA's core function is to facilitate the development and evaluation of medicines across the EU and to promote their safe and effective use. It serves as a centralized body to streamline the approval process for drugs, ensuring consistency across all EU member states. Unlike other regulatory bodies, such as the FDA in the U.S., which approves drugs on a national basis, the EMA oversees a unified regulatory framework for the entire European market.

The EMA evaluates drug applications, including clinical trial data, manufacturing protocols, and proposed labeling, to ensure that they meet safety and efficacy standards. In addition, it monitors drugs once they are on the market through post-market surveillance, ensuring that drugs remain safe and effective throughout their lifecycle.

Drug Evaluation and Approval

The drug approval process through the EMA involves several stages, which are designed to ensure that medicines are both safe and effective before they can be marketed in the EU. The process starts with the submission of a **Marketing Authorization Application (MAA)**, which includes all the scientific data related to the drug's development, including preclinical studies, clinical trial results, and information about the drug's manufacturing process. The EMA reviews the data and provides a recommendation to the European Commission, which grants or denies marketing authorization based on the EMA's opinion.

The approval process is similar to that of the FDA, but there are some key differences in how the process works within the EU. Some of the approval pathways available through the EMA include:

- **Centralized Procedure**: This procedure allows a company to submit a single application to the EMA, and if approved, the drug can be marketed in all EU member states. This is the preferred route for certain types of medicines, including innovative therapies, orphan drugs, and biotechnology products.
- **Mutual Recognition Procedure**: If a drug has already been approved in one EU member state, a company can apply for approval in other member states by using this procedure, which allows for recognition of the initial approval.
- **Decentralized Procedure**: This route is used when a drug is not yet authorized in any EU member state but is submitted simultaneously to multiple member states for approval.

Each of these procedures is designed to ensure that medicines are thoroughly reviewed for safety, quality, and efficacy, and they provide flexibility depending on the nature of the drug being evaluated.

Regulatory Guidance and Standards

The EMA also provides essential guidance documents and regulatory standards to ensure that drug development and clinical trials meet EU regulations. These guidelines are instrumental in helping pharmaceutical companies comply with the agency's requirements, which may differ slightly from those of other regulatory bodies. Some of the key guidelines provided by the EMA include:

- **Good Clinical Practice (GCP)**: The EMA ensures that clinical trials are conducted in accordance with internationally accepted standards, protecting the safety and well-being of trial participants.

- **Good Manufacturing Practice (GMP):** The agency also enforces GMP standards to ensure that drugs are consistently manufactured to meet quality standards, minimizing the risk of contamination or defects in the final product.
- **Pharmacovigilance Guidelines:** The EMA monitors the safety of medicines after they have been approved and are on the market. It requires companies to submit periodic safety update reports (PSURs) and report any adverse drug reactions or safety concerns.

Post-Market Surveillance

The EMA's role doesn't end once a drug is approved. It continues to monitor the safety and efficacy of medicines through **pharmacovigilance** programs and **post-market surveillance**. This ensures that any new safety concerns that arise after the drug's approval are identified and addressed quickly.

The agency requires pharmaceutical companies to conduct ongoing monitoring and report any adverse effects or unexpected reactions associated with the drug. In cases where a drug is found to cause significant harm, the EMA can recommend withdrawing the drug from the market, updating its labeling, or restricting its use to certain patient populations.

For example, the **Risk Management Plan (RMP)** is a key tool that the EMA uses to ensure that risks associated with a drug are minimized after it has been approved. This plan outlines strategies for risk minimization, such as restricted distribution, patient education, or additional studies to monitor the drug's long-term safety.

Influence and Global Role

The EMA's influence extends beyond the EU. It collaborates with other regulatory bodies, such as the U.S. FDA and the World Health Organization (WHO), to harmonize regulatory standards and ensure that safe and effective medicines are accessible globally. As part of the **International Council for Harmonisation (ICH)**, the EMA helps to create globally accepted standards for the development and approval of pharmaceuticals.

Additionally, the EMA is involved in the approval process for medicines that are to be marketed outside the EU. If a drug is approved by the EMA, it can often streamline approval processes in other regions, making the agency's approval a vital step for global market access.

The EMA's leadership role in promoting the adoption of **European Medicines Agency (EMA) guidelines** and **International Conference on**

Harmonization (ICH) standards further supports the global harmonization of drug regulatory processes, reducing the barriers to entry for pharmaceutical companies and accelerating the availability of new therapies.

1.2.1.3 Pharmaceuticals and Medical Devices Agency (PMDA), Japan

The **Pharmaceuticals and Medical Devices Agency (PMDA)** is Japan's primary regulatory authority responsible for overseeing the approval, regulation, and safety of pharmaceutical products, medical devices, and regenerative medicine. Established in 2004, the PMDA operates under the Ministry of Health, Labour and Welfare (MHLW) and plays a critical role in ensuring that medicines and medical products in Japan meet the highest standards of safety, efficacy, and quality. The PMDA is tasked with reviewing drug and device submissions, conducting clinical trials, and monitoring post-market safety, thereby contributing to the protection of public health in Japan.

The agency is also responsible for ensuring that pharmaceutical products and medical devices in Japan are developed and marketed according to regulatory standards. These standards are designed to ensure that the benefits of a drug or device outweigh the risks, while also protecting patients from unnecessary harm. The PMDA's role extends across the entire lifecycle of a product, from research and development through to post-market surveillance.

Role and Function of the PMDA

The PMDA's primary function is to assess and approve new drugs, medical devices, and biologics for use in Japan. The agency is also responsible for overseeing clinical trials, ensuring compliance with good clinical practice (GCP), good manufacturing practice (GMP), and other regulatory standards. The PMDA works closely with the Ministry of Health, Labour and Welfare (MHLW) to ensure that pharmaceutical products meet Japan's strict safety, efficacy, and quality requirements.

One of the most important roles of the PMDA is the scientific evaluation of drug applications and the issuance of marketing authorizations. This includes reviewing clinical trial data, preclinical studies, and manufacturing information to ensure that a drug or device is safe for use in humans and that its benefits outweigh any potential risks.

Drug and Device Approval Process

The approval process for drugs and medical devices in Japan is rigorous and involves multiple stages. The process begins when a company submits a **New Drug Application (NDA)** or **Medical Device Application (MDA)** to the PMDA for review. This application includes all relevant data, including preclinical studies, clinical trial results, manufacturing protocols, and proposed labeling. The PMDA evaluates the data to assess the drug's or device's safety, efficacy, and overall benefit-risk profile.

For pharmaceuticals, the approval process follows several stages:

- **Preclinical Studies**: The PMDA reviews the preclinical data to assess the safety of the drug before clinical trials can begin. This includes toxicology studies, pharmacokinetics, and pharmacodynamics data.
- **Clinical Trials**: Once the preclinical data is approved, clinical trials can proceed. The PMDA evaluates clinical trial protocols to ensure that they adhere to ethical standards and provide valid scientific evidence. The clinical trial process is divided into three phases: Phase I (safety testing), Phase II (efficacy testing), and Phase III (confirmatory testing in a larger population).
- **Marketing Authorization**: After successful clinical trials, the pharmaceutical company submits an NDA, including data from all phases of development. The PMDA reviews the data and makes a determination regarding the safety, efficacy, and quality of the drug.

The process for medical devices is similar, though the evaluation focuses on ensuring that the device meets regulatory standards for design, safety, and functionality. The PMDA reviews data from clinical studies, laboratory testing, and post-market surveillance to ensure that devices do not pose undue risk to patients.

Regulatory Guidance and Standards

The PMDA provides comprehensive guidelines to pharmaceutical companies and medical device manufacturers to ensure compliance with regulatory standards. These guidelines cover all aspects of drug development, clinical trial design, manufacturing, and post-market monitoring. The PMDA's regulatory standards are aligned with international standards but also include specific provisions that address the unique healthcare needs of Japan.

One of the key regulatory frameworks enforced by the PMDA is **Good Manufacturing Practice (GMP)**. The PMDA inspects manufacturing facilities to ensure that drugs and devices are produced in a controlled environment, maintaining quality throughout the production process. Pharmaceutical companies must demonstrate that their manufacturing processes meet GMP standards to receive approval for their products.

The PMDA also ensures compliance with **Good Clinical Practice (GCP)**, which establishes guidelines for the design, conduct, and reporting of clinical trials. These standards are essential to protecting human subjects involved in clinical research and ensuring that the data generated from clinical trials are reliable.

Post-Market Surveillance

Even after a drug or medical device is approved and available in the market, the PMDA continues to monitor its safety and efficacy through post-market surveillance. This process involves the ongoing collection and analysis of data regarding adverse events and other safety concerns related to drugs and medical devices. The PMDA works closely with pharmaceutical companies to ensure that any risks identified after market approval are promptly addressed.

The agency maintains a **Pharmacovigilance System** to track adverse drug reactions and ensure that drugs remain safe for long-term use. In cases where a new safety concern arises, the PMDA has the authority to take regulatory actions, such as issuing safety warnings, requiring additional clinical studies, or withdrawing a product from the market if necessary.

The PMDA also manages risk management programs to mitigate the risks associated with drugs and medical devices. These programs may include additional safety monitoring, restricted distribution programs, or changes to product labeling to inform healthcare professionals and patients of potential risks.

Global Influence and International Cooperation

While the PMDA primarily regulates pharmaceuticals and medical devices within Japan, its influence extends beyond the country's borders. Japan is a member of the **International Council for Harmonisation of Technical Requirements for Pharmaceuticals for Human Use (ICH)**, and the PMDA actively contributes to the development of international regulatory standards. The PMDA's participation in global regulatory bodies allows for harmonization of drug approval processes and facilitates the international exchange of pharmaceutical products.

The PMDA also collaborates with other regulatory authorities, including the U.S. FDA and the European Medicines Agency (EMA), to share information about drug safety, efficacy, and regulatory practices. This global cooperation ensures that drugs and medical devices that meet rigorous safety and efficacy standards in Japan are also likely to be approved in other major markets, facilitating international market access.

1.2.1.4 *Therapeutic Goods Administration (TGA), Australia*

The **Therapeutic Goods Administration (TGA)** is Australia's regulatory authority responsible for overseeing the safety, efficacy, and quality of therapeutic goods, including pharmaceuticals, medical devices, and other health-related products. Operating under the **Australian Government Department of Health**, the TGA plays a vital role in protecting public health by ensuring that only safe and effective medicines and medical devices are available in Australia. The TGA works closely with other regulatory bodies, including the **World Health Organization (WHO)** and **International Council for Harmonisation (ICH)**, to align Australia's regulatory processes with international standards.

The TGA's core functions include the evaluation, approval, and monitoring of therapeutic goods, ensuring that they meet strict standards before they are marketed. It also plays a significant role in post-market surveillance, assessing the ongoing safety of products once they have reached the Australian market.

Role and Function of the TGA

The TGA is tasked with evaluating and approving therapeutic goods for use in Australia. Its role includes reviewing drug and device submissions, assessing the clinical data, manufacturing practices, and labeling to ensure that products are safe for the public. In addition to pre-market evaluations, the TGA also monitors the safety of products through post-market surveillance, making sure that any issues with a product's safety or effectiveness are identified and managed swiftly.

The agency also provides regulatory guidance to pharmaceutical companies and healthcare providers, offering clear instructions on the approval process for drugs, devices, and other therapeutic goods. The TGA ensures that drugs and medical devices are manufactured in accordance with **Good Manufacturing Practice (GMP)** and **Good Clinical Practice (GCP)**, which are essential to ensuring the products meet safety and quality standards.

Drug and Device Approval Process

The approval process for drugs and medical devices in Australia is comprehensive and involves multiple stages to ensure that products are safe and effective before being marketed. The TGA reviews the scientific data submitted by pharmaceutical companies, including preclinical studies, clinical trial results, and manufacturing protocols. The process begins with the submission of an **Application for Market Authorization** for a new therapeutic good. This application typically includes:

- **Preclinical Data**: Toxicology, pharmacology, and safety data collected from animal studies.
- **Clinical Trial Data**: Results from clinical trials conducted to assess the drug's safety and efficacy in humans.
- **Manufacturing Information**: Details about the production process to ensure that the drug or device is made according to GMP standards.

Once the TGA receives an application, it evaluates the data to ensure that the product meets safety, efficacy, and quality standards. If the product is approved, the TGA grants **market authorization**, allowing the drug or device to be sold in Australia.

There are several pathways for approval, depending on the type of product:

- **Prescription Medicines**: These are drugs that can only be prescribed by a healthcare professional. The TGA evaluates the safety and efficacy of these products in a rigorous review process.
- **Over-the-Counter (OTC) Medicines**: These drugs can be purchased without a prescription. The TGA ensures that OTC medicines meet the necessary standards for safety and efficacy, but the review process is generally less extensive compared to prescription medicines.
- **Medical Devices**: Devices are classified based on risk, and the TGA evaluates their safety and effectiveness based on their intended use. High-risk devices undergo more stringent evaluation than low-risk devices.

The approval process is generally in line with international standards, but the TGA also considers the specific health needs of the Australian population when evaluating drugs and devices.

Regulatory Guidelines and Standards

The TGA enforces a range of guidelines and standards to ensure that therapeutic goods meet Australian regulations. These guidelines are in line with international standards but are tailored to meet the specific needs of Australia's healthcare system. Some key regulatory frameworks include:

- **Good Manufacturing Practice (GMP)**: The TGA inspects manufacturing facilities and ensures that drugs and medical devices are consistently produced in compliance with GMP guidelines. GMP ensures that the drugs or devices meet quality standards, reducing the risk of contamination or defects in the final product.
- **Good Clinical Practice (GCP)**: The TGA enforces GCP standards for the design, conduct, and reporting of clinical trials. This ensures that the rights, safety, and well-being of trial participants are protected, and that the data generated is scientifically valid.
- **Post-Market Surveillance**: The TGA conducts post-market monitoring to track the safety and effectiveness of drugs and devices once they are available to the public. This includes the collection of data on adverse events, side effects, and other safety concerns. The TGA can take regulatory actions, such as issuing safety warnings, changing labeling requirements, or even recalling products if new risks are identified.

Post-Market Surveillance and Pharmacovigilance

Even after drugs and medical devices are approved, the TGA continues to monitor their safety and effectiveness through post-market surveillance programs. These programs are essential for identifying any long-term safety issues or rare side effects that might not have been detected during clinical trials.

The TGA's pharmacovigilance activities include:

- **Adverse Event Reporting**: The TGA collects reports on adverse events from healthcare professionals and the public. These reports are analyzed to detect any potential safety concerns related to medicines or medical devices.

- **Periodic Safety Update Reports (PSURs)**: Pharmaceutical companies are required to submit regular safety update reports, providing the TGA with the latest data on the safety profile of the drug or device.
- **Risk Management Plans (RMPs)**: The TGA works with manufacturers to develop and implement risk management strategies for products, particularly those associated with known safety concerns. These plans include strategies to minimize risk, such as restricted distribution or additional monitoring.

If a significant risk is identified after a product reaches the market, the TGA has the authority to take regulatory action. This could include updating the product's labeling, restricting its use, or withdrawing it from the market entirely if the risks outweigh the benefits.

International Collaboration

The TGA's regulatory activities are not limited to Australia; it works closely with other global regulatory bodies, including the U.S. FDA, the European Medicines Agency (EMA), and the World Health Organization (WHO). This collaboration ensures that therapeutic goods are evaluated based on internationally accepted standards, facilitating global market access.

The TGA is also an active member of the **International Council for Harmonisation of Technical Requirements for Pharmaceuticals for Human Use (ICH)**, which aims to harmonize global regulatory practices and standards to streamline drug development and approval processes worldwide.

1.2.1.5 Health Canada

Health Canada is the regulatory authority responsible for ensuring the safety, efficacy, and quality of therapeutic products available in Canada. It is a federal department of the Canadian government that oversees the regulation of drugs, medical devices, biologics, vaccines, and other health products. Health Canada operates under the **Department of Health** and plays a central role in protecting public health by ensuring that all therapeutic products meet the necessary regulatory standards before they are allowed in the Canadian market.

The primary function of Health Canada is to regulate and assess therapeutic products to ensure that they are safe for Canadians to use. This includes evaluating new drugs, monitoring the safety of products once they are available on the market, and taking action when there are concerns about the safety of a product. The agency also works in close collaboration with other global regulatory bodies to harmonize standards and ensure that Canadian health products meet international safety and efficacy requirements.

Role and Function of Health Canada

Health Canada is responsible for the entire lifecycle of a therapeutic product, from initial development to post-market surveillance. The agency ensures that products available in Canada meet stringent safety and quality standards before they can be sold to the public. Health Canada's regulatory functions include:

- **Evaluation of New Products**: Health Canada evaluates and approves new drugs and medical devices for use in Canada, reviewing clinical trial data, preclinical studies, manufacturing processes, and proposed labeling to ensure safety, efficacy, and quality.
- **Monitoring of Marketed Products**: After a product is approved and available on the market, Health Canada continues to monitor its safety through post-market surveillance programs, adverse event reporting, and periodic safety updates.
- **Regulatory Guidelines**: The agency provides guidelines for pharmaceutical companies and healthcare providers, setting the standards for clinical trials, drug development, manufacturing, labeling, and pharmacovigilance.
- **Collaboration with Other Regulatory Bodies**: Health Canada collaborates with other regulatory agencies, such as the **U.S. FDA**, the **European Medicines Agency (EMA)**, and the **World Health Organization (WHO)**, to harmonize drug approval processes and share information about drug safety and efficacy.

Drug Approval Process

The process of approving new drugs and therapeutic products in Canada is comprehensive, ensuring that all products meet the safety and efficacy standards required for use by the public. The approval process follows several key steps:

- **Preclinical Studies**: Before clinical trials can begin, Health Canada reviews the results of preclinical studies, which involve animal testing to assess the safety and toxicology of a drug. This stage provides important data on how the drug behaves in the body and identifies any potential risks before it is tested on humans.
- **Clinical Trials**: Once the preclinical data is reviewed and approved, the drug enters human clinical trials. Health Canada requires the submission of a **New Drug Submission (NDS)** for new drug products. Clinical trials are divided into several phases:

  - **Phase I**: The drug is tested on a small group of healthy volunteers to evaluate its safety, dosage range, and side effects.
  - **Phase II**: The drug is tested on a group of patients to evaluate its efficacy and optimal dosage.
  - **Phase III**: Large-scale trials are conducted to confirm the drug's efficacy and monitor any adverse effects in a larger patient population.

Once clinical trials are complete, Health Canada reviews the data from all phases of development, including preclinical, clinical, and manufacturing information, to determine whether the drug is safe and effective for use.

- **Market Authorization**: If the data submitted to Health Canada meets the required safety, efficacy, and quality standards, the drug is granted approval for sale in Canada. Health Canada issues a **Notice of Compliance (NOC)**, which allows the drug to be marketed in the country.

Regulatory Guidelines and Standards

Health Canada provides comprehensive guidance to pharmaceutical companies to ensure compliance with regulatory standards. These guidelines cover a wide range of regulatory areas, including drug development, clinical trials, labeling, and post-market surveillance. Some of the key regulatory frameworks established by Health Canada include:

- **Good Manufacturing Practice (GMP)**: Health Canada enforces GMP regulations to ensure that pharmaceutical products are consistently produced to meet quality standards. This includes inspections of manufacturing facilities to ensure that drugs are produced in a controlled and sterile environment.

- **Good Clinical Practice (GCP)**: Health Canada ensures that clinical trials are conducted in accordance with GCP guidelines, which protect the rights of trial participants and ensure that the data collected is reliable and scientifically valid.
- **Pharmacovigilance**: Health Canada monitors the safety of drugs through ongoing pharmacovigilance activities. This includes collecting data on adverse events from healthcare professionals and the public. Pharmaceutical companies are required to submit periodic safety update reports (PSURs) and report any adverse drug reactions or safety concerns.

Post-Market Surveillance and Risk Management

Even after a drug is approved and available on the market, Health Canada continues to monitor its safety and effectiveness through post-market surveillance. This is essential to identifying any long-term safety issues, rare side effects, or changes in a drug's efficacy that may not have been identified during clinical trials.

Health Canada's post-market surveillance activities include:

- **Adverse Event Reporting**: Health Canada collects and analyzes reports of adverse drug reactions (ADRs) through its **Canada Vigilance Program**. Healthcare professionals, patients, and pharmaceutical companies are encouraged to report any adverse events associated with drugs and medical devices.
- **Risk Management Plans (RMPs)**: Health Canada works with manufacturers to develop and implement risk management strategies for drugs that may have identified safety concerns. These plans may include additional monitoring, restricted distribution, or changes to the drug's labeling to inform healthcare providers and patients about potential risks.
- **Market Withdrawal and Safety Warnings**: If new safety concerns arise after a drug has been marketed, Health Canada has the authority to take regulatory action, such as issuing safety warnings, requiring changes to labeling, or withdrawing the product from the market if necessary.

Global Collaboration and Harmonization

Health Canada is an active participant in global efforts to harmonize drug approval processes. It collaborates with international regulatory bodies, such as the U.S. FDA, EMA, and WHO, to establish common standards for drug safety, efficacy, and quality. This collaboration ensures that Canadian drugs meet international standards and facilitates the global exchange of pharmaceutical products.

Health Canada is also a member of the **International Council for Harmonisation of Technical Requirements for Pharmaceuticals for Human Use (ICH)**, which works to harmonize drug development and approval standards across major pharmaceutical markets. This global cooperation helps streamline the approval process and reduces duplication of efforts in drug evaluation.

In conclusion, **Health Canada** plays a crucial role in ensuring the safety, efficacy, and quality of therapeutic products available in Canada. Through its rigorous drug approval processes, regulatory guidelines, post-market surveillance, and international collaborations, Health Canada protects public health by ensuring that only safe and effective drugs and medical devices are accessible to Canadians.

1.2.2 International Organizations

International organizations play a crucial role in the global regulation of pharmaceuticals and healthcare products. These organizations work to create harmonized standards and guidelines for drug development, manufacturing, and safety, facilitating the smooth movement of pharmaceuticals across international borders. By collaborating with national regulatory authorities, international organizations help ensure that pharmaceutical products meet consistent safety, efficacy, and quality standards worldwide. The World Health Organization (WHO) is one of the key players in this field, working towards the improvement of public health and the regulation of health products globally.

1.2.2.1 World Health Organization (WHO)

The **World Health Organization (WHO)** is a specialized agency of the United Nations responsible for international public health. Established in 1948, WHO works with 194 member states to promote global health, set health standards, and provide leadership in addressing global health issues.

The organization's primary goal is to ensure that people across the world have access to essential healthcare services, and it plays an important role in regulating health products, including pharmaceuticals, vaccines, and medical devices.

The WHO works to strengthen the capacities of health systems around the world, particularly in low- and middle-income countries, by providing guidance on healthcare policies, regulatory practices, and health-related research. One of its most significant roles is in setting international health standards, including those for the safety, efficacy, and quality of medicines. The WHO's efforts in this area help harmonize drug regulations globally, ensuring that medicines and vaccines are safe for use in different regions.

Role and Function of WHO in Drug Regulation

WHO's role in drug regulation is multi-faceted, and its activities span across several key areas. Some of the main functions of WHO in pharmaceutical regulation include:

- **Setting International Standards for Medicines**: WHO develops global guidelines and standards for the quality, safety, and efficacy of medicines. These guidelines are intended to be adopted by national regulatory authorities, ensuring consistency in drug evaluation processes across the world. WHO's **International Pharmacopoeia (Ph. Int.)** is an important reference work that defines quality standards for medicines and helps ensure that pharmaceutical products are produced with the required specifications for safety and effectiveness.

- **Prequalification of Medicines and Vaccines**: The WHO runs a **Prequalification Programme**, which assesses the quality, safety, and efficacy of medicines, vaccines, and diagnostics. The prequalification process is particularly important for medicines that are used in resource-poor settings, including those used for treating diseases like malaria, tuberculosis, and HIV/AIDS. The WHO's prequalification process helps ensure that medicines meet internationally recognized quality standards before they are procured by United Nations agencies or other international organizations.

- **Supporting Regulatory Capacity Building**: WHO provides technical assistance and training to national regulatory authorities, particularly in developing countries, to help them build and strengthen their regulatory frameworks. This assistance includes supporting the development of regulatory systems, training staff, and improving the overall capacity to regulate and oversee pharmaceuticals. By enhancing the regulatory capabilities of national authorities, WHO helps ensure that countries are equipped to regulate medicines effectively and protect public health.

- **Promoting Good Manufacturing Practices (GMP)**: WHO works with manufacturers and national regulatory authorities to promote **Good Manufacturing Practices (GMP)**. These practices ensure that medicines are consistently produced and controlled according to quality standards. WHO's GMP guidelines help manufacturers maintain high standards in the production of medicines, ensuring that drugs are safe for use and meet the necessary quality specifications.

Global Coordination and Standardization

One of the major goals of the WHO is to promote global health cooperation and standardize pharmaceutical regulations across different countries. To achieve this, the WHO works closely with other international organizations, such as the **International Conference on Harmonisation (ICH), the Global Fund**, and the **World Trade Organization (WTO)**. These collaborations help harmonize drug regulatory standards and facilitate the international exchange of pharmaceutical products.

WHO is also involved in discussions and decision-making processes related to **international trade agreements**, particularly in the pharmaceutical sector. Through the **Trade-Related Aspects of Intellectual Property Rights (TRIPS)** Agreement, WHO has worked to ensure that global trade regulations do not impede access to essential medicines, particularly in developing countries. WHO advocates for **flexibilities** in the TRIPS Agreement, such as the use of **compulsory licensing**, to improve access to life-saving medications.

Additionally, WHO supports the **Global Drug Facility** and works with other stakeholders to ensure the availability of essential medicines in countries that face challenges related to affordability and access. This effort is vital in addressing health issues in low-income countries where the lack of access to medicines is a significant barrier to healthcare.

WHO's Role in Vaccine Regulation and Immunization Programs

WHO is instrumental in ensuring the safety, quality, and efficacy of vaccines worldwide. Through the **Global Vaccine Safety Initiative**, WHO works to ensure that vaccines meet international standards and are safe for use in all populations. The organization provides guidance on vaccine development, manufacturing, and post-marketing surveillance, helping countries implement effective vaccination programs.

WHO's leadership in global immunization efforts has been critical in the fight against vaccine-preventable diseases. The **Global Vaccine Safety Initiative** helps monitor the safety of vaccines after they are introduced into the market, ensuring that any adverse events are detected and managed appropriately.

The **WHO Prequalification Programme** also plays a significant role in ensuring that vaccines meet the necessary standards for use in immunization programs, particularly in developing countries. This program helps streamline the procurement process for international organizations and ensures that vaccines are safe and effective.

Contribution to Global Health and Access to Medicines

WHO's efforts to regulate and oversee medicines and vaccines are aligned with its broader goal of improving global health outcomes and increasing access to essential medicines. The organization advocates for **universal health coverage** and works to ensure that health systems in all countries have access to the medicines they need to improve public health outcomes. WHO provides support to countries in developing national strategies for improving medicine access, ensuring that essential medicines are available and affordable for all populations.

WHO also plays an essential role in responding to global health emergencies, such as disease outbreaks and pandemics, by ensuring the availability of safe and effective medicines and vaccines. The organization works with global partners to ensure that pharmaceutical products are developed, produced, and distributed efficiently to combat public health emergencies.

1.2.2.2 *International Council for Harmonisation of Technical Requirements for Pharmaceuticals for Human Use (ICH)*

The **International Council for Harmonisation of Technical Requirements for Pharmaceuticals for Human Use (ICH)** is a global initiative aimed at harmonizing the technical requirements for the registration of pharmaceuticals. Founded in 1990, ICH brings together regulatory authorities and pharmaceutical industry experts from key markets around the world, including the United States, Europe, Japan, and other regions. The primary goal of ICH is to promote the development of high-quality medicines by harmonizing the standards and requirements for drug registration and approval processes.

ICH focuses on developing guidelines that address the scientific and technical aspects of drug development and registration. These guidelines are intended to be adopted by regulatory bodies in different regions, ensuring consistency and reducing duplication in the approval processes. By working together, ICH members aim to create a more efficient and predictable regulatory framework for the global pharmaceutical industry.

Role and Function of ICH

ICH plays a pivotal role in advancing the global pharmaceutical regulatory landscape by developing scientifically sound and internationally recognized guidelines. These guidelines ensure that drugs are developed, tested, and manufactured to the highest standards of quality, safety, and efficacy. ICH works to streamline the approval process, facilitating the global availability of new medicines, while maintaining high standards for public health protection.

Some of the key functions of ICH include:

- **Development of Harmonized Guidelines**: ICH develops guidelines that address key aspects of drug development, including clinical trials, manufacturing, quality control, safety, and efficacy. These guidelines help ensure that pharmaceutical products are consistently evaluated in the same manner, regardless of where they are being submitted for approval. The harmonization of these guidelines helps reduce regulatory burdens and accelerates the approval process for new drugs.

- **Fostering International Collaboration**: ICH serves as a platform for international collaboration between regulatory authorities and industry stakeholders. Through regular meetings and working groups, ICH brings together experts from different regions to discuss emerging scientific and technical issues and to agree on common approaches to drug development and regulation.

- **Support for Regulatory Transparency and Predictability**: By harmonizing regulatory requirements, ICH helps create a more transparent and predictable regulatory environment. Pharmaceutical companies benefit from clearer guidance on the regulatory requirements they need to meet when submitting applications for drug approval. This reduces uncertainty and accelerates the development and availability of medicines.

Key Guidelines Developed by ICH

ICH has developed a comprehensive range of guidelines that cover various aspects of drug development, registration, and post-market activities. These guidelines are critical for ensuring the safety, quality, and efficacy of pharmaceutical products. Some of the most notable ICH guidelines include:

- **Good Clinical Practice (GCP)**: The ICH GCP guidelines set standards for the design, conduct, and reporting of clinical trials. These guidelines ensure that clinical trials are conducted ethically, that participants' rights are protected, and that the data generated is scientifically valid. GCP guidelines are widely adopted by regulatory bodies around the world, providing a common standard for clinical trial operations.

- **Good Manufacturing Practice (GMP)**: ICH's GMP guidelines ensure that medicines are consistently produced and controlled according to quality standards. These guidelines cover the entire manufacturing process, from raw material sourcing to the final product, and are essential for maintaining the quality of pharmaceuticals. GMP guidelines are adopted by regulatory bodies globally to ensure that medicines are safe and effective for use.

- **Quality Guidelines (Q Series)**: The **ICH Q series** covers a wide range of topics related to the quality of pharmaceuticals, including stability testing, manufacturing controls, and the development of quality standards. The Q guidelines help ensure that the quality of drugs is consistent, that they meet required standards throughout their shelf life, and that they are manufactured in a controlled environment.

- **Safety Guidelines (S Series)**: The **ICH S series** focuses on the safety of pharmaceutical products. These guidelines provide guidance on non-clinical safety testing, including toxicology studies, pharmacokinetics, and the assessment of potential risks associated with drug development. The safety guidelines ensure that pharmaceutical products are rigorously tested for toxicity before they are approved for clinical trials.

- **Efficacy Guidelines (E Series)**: The **ICH E series** provides guidelines on the design, conduct, and analysis of clinical trials for evaluating the efficacy of drugs. These guidelines help ensure that clinical trials are scientifically rigorous and that the data generated is reliable and valid.

Global Influence of ICH

One of the most significant contributions of ICH is its role in harmonizing global pharmaceutical regulations. By aligning the regulatory requirements of major markets such as the United States, Europe, and Japan, ICH has streamlined the approval process for new drugs and reduced the barriers to entry for pharmaceutical companies. This harmonization ensures that drugs developed in one region can be more easily marketed in other regions, facilitating global access to safe and effective medicines.

ICH's guidelines are widely accepted by regulatory authorities worldwide, including the **FDA, EMA, PMDA**, and **Health Canada**. These guidelines provide a consistent framework for evaluating new drugs, ensuring that pharmaceutical companies can meet the same high standards for drug approval across different markets. ICH's global influence also extends to emerging markets, where regulatory bodies adopt ICH guidelines to strengthen their own drug approval processes.

In addition to harmonizing regulatory standards, ICH's efforts also help promote scientific innovation in drug development. By providing clear and consistent guidelines, ICH helps facilitate the development of new therapies and accelerates the availability of new drugs for patients worldwide.

ICH's Contribution to Public Health

ICH's work is vital to ensuring the safety, efficacy, and quality of medicines, which ultimately contributes to improving public health worldwide. The harmonized regulatory environment created by ICH helps ensure that safe and effective medicines are available to patients more quickly and at a lower cost. This contributes to better healthcare outcomes and facilitates access to essential medicines, particularly in low- and middle-income countries.

Additionally, ICH's work in promoting scientific collaboration and innovation helps accelerate the development of new treatments for a wide range of diseases. By streamlining the drug development and approval process, ICH helps bring new therapies to market more efficiently, addressing unmet medical needs and improving the quality of life for patients around the world.

1.2.3 Regulatory Harmonization Across Regions

Regulatory harmonization refers to the process of aligning regulatory requirements and standards across different countries or regions to facilitate the smoother and more efficient approval of pharmaceutical products. The aim is to reduce the complexities and barriers faced by pharmaceutical companies when submitting drugs for approval in multiple countries, ultimately improving access to safe and effective medicines worldwide. Regulatory harmonization helps streamline the drug development and approval process, reduces duplication of efforts, and ensures that global public health standards are maintained.

One of the most significant international efforts to achieve regulatory harmonization is through the **International Council for Harmonisation of Technical Requirements for Pharmaceuticals for Human Use (ICH)**. The guidelines developed by ICH have had a profound impact on regulatory systems around the world, promoting consistent standards for drug development, clinical trials, manufacturing, and post-market surveillance. Through the adoption of ICH guidelines, regulatory authorities from major pharmaceutical markets have harmonized their requirements, which has made the drug approval process more predictable, efficient, and transparent.

1.2.3.1 ICH Guidelines and Their Impact

The **International Council for Harmonisation of Technical Requirements for Pharmaceuticals for Human Use (ICH)** plays a crucial role in advancing global regulatory harmonization. ICH is a collaboration between regulatory authorities from key regions (such as the United States, European Union, Japan) and pharmaceutical industry representatives. Its primary goal is to promote the harmonization of technical requirements for drug registration, ensuring that medicines meet consistent safety, quality, and efficacy standards across different markets.

The guidelines developed by ICH have had a far-reaching impact on regulatory processes in pharmaceutical markets globally. These guidelines address key technical and scientific aspects of drug development, such as clinical trial design, good manufacturing practices (GMP), pharmacovigilance, and the quality of medicines. By harmonizing these requirements, ICH has helped reduce regulatory duplication, facilitated quicker approval processes, and promoted global access to essential medicines.

The Role of ICH Guidelines

The ICH guidelines cover a broad range of topics related to drug development, regulatory submissions, and post-marketing activities. The adoption of these guidelines by regulatory authorities across different regions has had the following impacts:

- **Consistency in Drug Development Standards**: ICH guidelines provide a consistent framework for pharmaceutical companies to follow when developing new medicines. This consistency reduces the complexity of drug development, as pharmaceutical companies can use the same standards and practices in multiple markets. For example, clinical trials can be designed based on a common set of guidelines, ensuring that data submitted to regulatory agencies in different regions is comparable.

- **Faster Global Market Access**: By harmonizing regulatory requirements, ICH guidelines help reduce the time it takes for drugs to be approved in multiple markets. Pharmaceutical companies can submit the same data package to regulatory authorities in different regions, streamlining the approval process and accelerating the availability of new medicines worldwide. This is particularly beneficial for patients, as it allows them to access new treatments more quickly.

- **Improved Public Health Outcomes**: ICH guidelines are designed to ensure that medicines meet the highest safety and efficacy standards. By promoting the use of best practices in drug development and manufacturing, ICH helps ensure that pharmaceutical products are safe for patients. The harmonization of these standards across regions ensures that patients in different parts of the world have access to medicines that meet the same high standards, improving public health outcomes globally.

- **Reduced Duplication of Efforts**: Before ICH, pharmaceutical companies often had to submit separate data packages and go through different approval processes in each market, leading to duplication of efforts and increased costs. With the adoption of ICH guidelines, the process of drug development, testing, and approval has become more streamlined, reducing the need for redundant studies and trials. This has resulted in cost savings for pharmaceutical companies, which can be passed on to patients in the form of more affordable medicines.

Key Areas Affected by ICH Guidelines

The impact of ICH guidelines extends to several critical areas of drug development and regulation, including:

- **Clinical Trials and Good Clinical Practice (GCP)**: One of the most significant contributions of ICH has been the development of **Good Clinical Practice (GCP)** guidelines, which provide internationally recognized standards for the design, conduct, and reporting of clinical trials. These guidelines ensure that clinical trials are conducted ethically, that participant safety is prioritized, and that the data generated is reliable and scientifically valid. GCP guidelines have been adopted by regulatory authorities around the world, creating a consistent standard for clinical trial operations.

- **Pharmaceutical Quality and Good Manufacturing Practice (GMP)**: ICH has also contributed to the harmonization of **Good Manufacturing Practices (GMP)**, which set standards for the production of pharmaceutical products. GMP guidelines ensure that drugs are consistently manufactured to meet the required quality standards. These guidelines are essential for preventing contamination, ensuring the stability of products, and maintaining the integrity of the manufacturing process. GMP has been adopted by regulatory agencies worldwide, ensuring that medicines are produced to the highest standards.

- **Pharmacovigilance and Post-Market Surveillance**: ICH guidelines also address the monitoring of drug safety once a medicine has been approved and is on the market. **Pharmacovigilance** guidelines help ensure that adverse events and side effects are detected and managed effectively. This post-market surveillance is essential for maintaining the safety of medicines and ensuring that new risks are identified and addressed quickly. By harmonizing pharmacovigilance practices, ICH helps ensure that global safety standards are maintained.

- **Regulatory Submissions and Common Technical Document (CTD)**: One of the key achievements of ICH is the development of the **Common Technical Document (CTD)**, a standardized format for submitting regulatory data to authorities. The CTD simplifies the regulatory submission process by providing a consistent format for presenting clinical, preclinical, and manufacturing data. The CTD has been adopted by regulatory authorities in Europe, the U.S., Japan, and many other regions, streamlining the process for drug approval and reducing administrative burdens for pharmaceutical companies.

Global Influence and Expansion of ICH Guidelines

The adoption of ICH guidelines has been instrumental in promoting regulatory harmonization across different regions. Initially, ICH was focused on major pharmaceutical markets such as the U.S., Europe, and Japan. However, the influence of ICH has expanded globally, and many emerging markets have adopted its guidelines. Countries in regions such as Latin America, Asia, and Africa have increasingly aligned their regulatory requirements with ICH standards, facilitating the global movement of medicines.

In addition to its core members, ICH has actively engaged with regulatory authorities from other regions, such as **Health Canada, Brazil's ANVISA,** and **the Chinese National Medical Products Administration (NMPA),** to encourage the adoption of ICH guidelines. This global engagement has helped create a more uniform and predictable regulatory environment, ensuring that medicines developed and approved in one market can be more easily introduced to others.

1.2.3.2 WHO and Global Harmonization Efforts

The **World Health Organization (WHO)** has played a pivotal role in the global harmonization of pharmaceutical regulations. As the leading international public health agency, WHO works to ensure that the medicines and health products available worldwide meet high safety, efficacy, and quality standards. Through its efforts, WHO aims to facilitate the availability of essential medicines in all regions, promote public health, and reduce barriers to access, especially in low- and middle-income countries.

Global harmonization in the pharmaceutical industry refers to the process of aligning regulations and standards across different countries and regions. This harmonization helps streamline the approval process for drugs, reduces regulatory duplication, and ensures that safe and effective medicines are accessible worldwide. WHO has been instrumental in driving these efforts by creating guidelines, setting international standards, and fostering collaboration between regulatory authorities and industry stakeholders across the globe.

WHO's Role in Global Regulatory Harmonization

WHO's involvement in global harmonization efforts spans various areas of pharmaceutical regulation, including the development of international guidelines, prequalification programs, and the promotion of regulatory best practices. The organization works to ensure that countries adopt consistent and scientifically valid standards for drug safety, quality, and efficacy. By harmonizing regulations, WHO helps facilitate the international movement of pharmaceutical products, improving access to essential medicines in all regions.

Some of the key areas where WHO has contributed to global harmonization efforts include:

- **International Guidelines and Standards**: WHO develops and promotes international standards and guidelines that address various aspects of pharmaceutical regulation, including drug quality, safety, clinical trials, and manufacturing. These guidelines help ensure that medicines are evaluated and approved based on the same scientific principles, regardless of the region in which they are being submitted for approval. WHO's **International Pharmacopoeia (Ph. Int.)** is a critical resource in this regard, providing quality specifications for medicines and ensuring their consistent production across different markets.

- **Prequalification Program**: One of WHO's most important global harmonization efforts is the **Prequalification Program**, which assesses the quality, safety, and efficacy of medicines, vaccines, and diagnostics used in public health programs. This program ensures that medicines procured by international organizations, such as the United Nations and the Global Fund, meet the necessary standards. The prequalification process is particularly important for medicines used in resource-limited settings, ensuring that patients in these regions receive treatments that are safe and effective. By establishing internationally recognized standards for prequalification, WHO has helped promote the acceptance of medicines in multiple markets, including low-income countries.

- **Promotion of Regulatory Best Practices**: WHO works with national regulatory authorities to build and strengthen their regulatory capacities. Through technical assistance, training, and capacity-building programs, WHO helps countries adopt best practices in drug regulation, ensuring that they have the systems and expertise to evaluate and approve medicines effectively. WHO's efforts in building regulatory capacity are particularly crucial in developing countries, where regulatory systems may be underdeveloped or lack the resources to implement effective regulatory practices.

WHO's Impact on Drug Approval and Access to Medicines

WHO's global harmonization efforts have a significant impact on the drug approval process and access to medicines. By developing international guidelines and supporting regulatory agencies in adopting these standards, WHO has helped streamline the approval process for medicines and vaccines worldwide. This has reduced delays and increased the availability of essential treatments, especially in regions where regulatory systems may be slower or less efficient.

For example, WHO's role in prequalifying medicines used for diseases like **malaria, tuberculosis**, and **HIV/AIDS** has been crucial in ensuring that these essential medicines are available in developing countries. The prequalification program helps international organizations procure high-quality medicines at affordable prices, ensuring that patients in low-resource settings have access to life-saving treatments.

Additionally, WHO's global coordination efforts have made it easier for pharmaceutical companies to navigate the regulatory approval process across different regions. By harmonizing regulatory requirements, WHO helps pharmaceutical companies submit the same data packages to multiple regulatory authorities, streamlining the approval process and reducing the time it takes for new medicines to reach the market.

WHO's Influence on Global Health Policies and Access to Essential Medicines

WHO's harmonization efforts extend beyond regulatory processes to influence global health policies and access to essential medicines. WHO works with governments, international organizations, and industry stakeholders to ensure that essential medicines are made available to those in need, regardless of geographic location or economic status. Through programs like the **Essential Medicines List (EML)**, WHO provides guidance on which medicines are most important for addressing global health challenges and supports efforts to make these medicines accessible to all populations.

The **Essential Medicines List** is a list of medicines deemed essential for meeting the basic health needs of the population. The list is updated regularly based on emerging public health needs and new therapeutic evidence. By promoting the availability of these essential medicines, WHO plays a key role in improving health outcomes, particularly in low- and middle-income countries where access to high-quality medicines is limited.

WHO's efforts to harmonize drug regulations also include addressing the issue of **affordability**. By ensuring that medicines meet international standards and are prequalified for procurement, WHO helps make high-quality medicines available at lower prices. This is particularly important in regions with limited healthcare budgets, where access to expensive medicines is often restricted. WHO works with international organizations and governments to ensure that public health programs can access affordable, high-quality medicines for treatment and prevention.

Global Collaboration and Partnerships

WHO collaborates with various international organizations, regulatory bodies, and stakeholders to further the goals of regulatory harmonization. Its partnerships with organizations like the **International Conference on Harmonisation (ICH), International Federation of Pharmaceutical Manufacturers & Associations (IFPMA)**, and the **Global Fund** help promote global standards for drug safety, efficacy, and quality.

WHO also works with regional bodies such as the **Pan American Health Organization (PAHO)** and the **African Medicines Regulatory Harmonization (AMRH)** initiative to support regional efforts in harmonizing pharmaceutical regulations. These collaborations help strengthen regulatory frameworks in different regions, facilitating access to safe and effective medicines and ensuring that regulatory standards are aligned globally.

WHO's influence is crucial in promoting **health equity** by making essential medicines accessible to underserved populations and ensuring that drugs meet the same rigorous standards globally. Through its global harmonization efforts, WHO contributes to improving the health and well-being of populations worldwide, particularly those in low- and middle-income countries that may face unique challenges in regulating and accessing medicines.

1.3 Regulatory Framework

The regulatory framework for pharmaceuticals encompasses a set of guidelines, regulations, and procedures that are designed to ensure the safety, efficacy, and quality of drugs. Regulatory systems are implemented by governmental authorities in each country or region, and they play a vital role in overseeing the development, approval, manufacturing, and post-marketing surveillance of pharmaceutical products. While regulatory frameworks share common goals of ensuring public health and safety, each region has unique requirements and processes based on local needs, healthcare infrastructure, and economic considerations.

As the pharmaceutical industry operates on a global scale, it is essential for regulatory systems to be aligned to some extent to facilitate the international movement of pharmaceutical products. However, regulatory systems vary across regions, with different regulatory authorities responsible for drug approval and monitoring in various parts of the world. Understanding these systems is crucial for pharmaceutical companies aiming to bring their products to multiple markets.

1.3.1 Overview of Regulatory Systems in Different Regions

Regulatory systems are implemented by national and regional authorities responsible for overseeing the safety, efficacy, and quality of medicines. While all regulatory bodies share common objectives, the specific processes and requirements for drug approval can differ significantly depending on the region. Below is an overview of the key regulatory systems in some of the major regions globally:

1.3.1.1 United States: Food and Drug Administration (FDA)

The **Food and Drug Administration (FDA)** is the regulatory body responsible for overseeing the safety, efficacy, and quality of drugs, biologics, medical devices, food, and cosmetics in the United States. The FDA is a part of the U.S. Department of Health and Human Services and operates under the Federal Food, Drug, and Cosmetic Act.

The FDA's regulatory framework includes several key components:

- **Investigational New Drug (IND) Application**: Pharmaceutical companies must submit an IND application before starting clinical trials in humans. This submission includes preclinical data, clinical protocols, and plans for manufacturing.
- **New Drug Application (NDA)**: Following successful clinical trials, the pharmaceutical company submits an NDA to the FDA for review. This application includes data on the drug's safety, efficacy, and manufacturing process.
- **Abbreviated New Drug Application (ANDA)**: For generic drug approval, companies submit an ANDA, which does not require the submission of preclinical and clinical trial data, but instead, requires proof that the generic drug is equivalent to the reference product.

- **Post-Marketing Surveillance**: The FDA continues to monitor the safety of drugs through the **MedWatch** program, requiring manufacturers to report adverse events and provide periodic safety updates.

1.3.1.2 *European Union: European Medicines Agency (EMA)*

The **European Medicines Agency (EMA)** is the regulatory authority for pharmaceuticals in the European Union. The EMA's primary function is to evaluate and supervise medicines in the EU to ensure they are safe, effective, and of high quality. The agency works with the **European Commission** and national regulatory authorities of EU member states to facilitate drug approval and monitoring.

The EMA's regulatory framework includes:

- **Centralized Procedure**: This procedure allows pharmaceutical companies to submit a single application for marketing authorization in all EU member states. The EMA's Committee for Medicinal Products for Human Use (CHMP) evaluates the drug before it is approved by the European Commission for use across the EU.
- **Mutual Recognition Procedure (MRP)**: When a drug is already approved in one EU member state, the pharmaceutical company can apply to other member states for approval based on the initial authorization.
- **Decentralized Procedure**: This procedure is for drugs that have not been authorized in any EU member state and allows companies to apply simultaneously in multiple member states.
- **Post-Marketing Surveillance**: The EMA monitors the safety of approved medicines through pharmacovigilance activities and requires pharmaceutical companies to submit periodic safety reports.

1.3.1.3 *Japan: Pharmaceuticals and Medical Devices Agency (PMDA)*

The **Pharmaceuticals and Medical Devices Agency (PMDA)** is the regulatory authority in Japan responsible for overseeing the safety, efficacy, and quality of pharmaceutical products, medical devices, and regenerative medicines. PMDA operates under the Ministry of Health, Labour and Welfare (MHLW) and collaborates closely with other governmental and international organizations.

PMDA's regulatory framework involves:

- **Investigational New Drug (IND) Application**: Before clinical trials can begin, pharmaceutical companies must submit an IND to PMDA for review.
- **New Drug Application (NDA)**: Following successful clinical trials, the pharmaceutical company submits an NDA, including all clinical and manufacturing data, for approval.
- **Post-Marketing Surveillance**: PMDA monitors the safety of drugs and devices after they are approved for use through pharmacovigilance programs. It can take action such as issuing safety warnings, requiring new studies, or withdrawing products from the market if necessary.

1.3.1.4 Canada: Health Canada

Health Canada is the Canadian regulatory authority responsible for ensuring the safety, efficacy, and quality of pharmaceuticals, biologics, medical devices, and other therapeutic products. Health Canada operates under the Ministry of Health and is tasked with overseeing the approval and monitoring of drugs in the Canadian market.

Health Canada's regulatory framework includes:

- **New Drug Submission (NDS)**: Before a new drug can be marketed in Canada, the manufacturer must submit an NDS containing preclinical and clinical data, as well as information on the manufacturing process.
- **Abbreviated New Drug Submission (ANDS)**: For generics, companies submit an ANDS that demonstrates the drug's equivalence to the brand-name drug.
- **Post-Marketing Surveillance**: Health Canada continues to monitor drugs through the **Canada Vigilance Program** and requires manufacturers to report adverse events. Health Canada can issue safety advisories, update drug labeling, or remove drugs from the market if safety concerns arise.

1.3.1.5 Australia: Therapeutic Goods Administration (TGA)

The **Therapeutic Goods Administration (TGA)** is the regulatory body responsible for overseeing the safety, efficacy, and quality of medicines and medical devices in Australia. The TGA operates under the **Department of Health** and ensures that therapeutic goods meet the required standards before they can be marketed in Australia.

The TGA's regulatory framework includes:

- **Application for Market Authorization**: Pharmaceutical companies must submit an application that includes clinical trial data, manufacturing information, and proposed labeling for drug approval.
- **Post-Market Surveillance**: The TGA monitors drugs and devices through its **Adverse Event Reporting System** and can take actions such as issuing warnings or recalls if safety concerns arise.

1.3.1.6 Emerging Markets

Emerging markets, such as those in **Latin America**, **Africa**, and **Asia**, have regulatory systems that are evolving to meet global standards. Regulatory bodies in these regions are increasingly adopting guidelines and practices from ICH and WHO to streamline their drug approval processes.

Some key points about regulatory systems in emerging markets:

- **Capacity Building**: Many emerging markets receive support from WHO and international organizations to strengthen their regulatory capacity.
- **Regional Collaboration**: Countries in regions like **ASEAN** (Association of Southeast Asian Nations) have established the **ASEAN Common Technical Document (ACTD)** to harmonize regulatory processes in Southeast Asia.
- **Faster Approvals for Generic Drugs**: Many countries in emerging markets are focusing on improving access to affordable medicines by streamlining the approval process for generic drugs.

1.3.2 Types of Applications Submitted to Regulatory Agencies

In the pharmaceutical industry, when a company develops a new drug or medical product, it must submit various applications to regulatory agencies for approval. These applications are critical to ensuring that drugs are safe, effective, and manufactured to high-quality standards. Regulatory agencies, such as the **FDA, EMA, PMDA**, and **Health Canada**, assess these applications to determine whether a drug should be approved for sale in the market. The types of applications vary depending on the stage of the product lifecycle, the drug's formulation, and whether the product is a new or generic drug.

Among the different types of applications, **Marketing Authorization Applications (MAAs)** are one of the most significant. They are submitted to regulatory agencies when a pharmaceutical company seeks approval to market and sell a new drug or therapeutic product in a particular region or country.

1.3.2.1 Marketing Authorization Applications

A **Marketing Authorization Application (MAA)** is the formal request submitted by a pharmaceutical company to a regulatory agency to obtain approval for marketing a drug or therapeutic product. It is a comprehensive submission that includes all relevant data on the drug's development, safety, efficacy, manufacturing, and proposed labeling. The MAA serves as the basis for the regulatory body to assess the product's safety profile, therapeutic benefits, and quality before it can be made available to the public.

The MAA process is an essential part of the drug approval process, as it provides regulatory authorities with the necessary information to make informed decisions regarding the approval of a drug. Regulatory agencies use the MAA to ensure that new drugs meet established standards for safety, efficacy, and quality before they are marketed and prescribed to patients.

Key Components of a Marketing Authorization Application

A Marketing Authorization Application typically includes the following key components:

- **Preclinical Data**: Preclinical studies provide information on the drug's pharmacology, toxicology, and pharmacokinetics based on animal testing. This data demonstrates the drug's potential safety and effectiveness before testing in humans. Preclinical data typically includes:

  - Toxicology studies to evaluate the drug's potential harmful effects.
  - Pharmacological studies to understand how the drug works in the body.
  - Pharmacokinetics data to assess how the drug is absorbed, distributed, metabolized, and excreted by the body.

- **Clinical Trial Data**: Clinical trial data is crucial to demonstrate the drug's safety and efficacy in humans. This section includes data from **Phase I**, **Phase II**, and **Phase III** clinical trials:

  - **Phase I**: Focuses on the drug's safety and dosage in healthy volunteers.
  - **Phase II**: Evaluates the drug's efficacy and optimal dosage in patients with the target condition.
  - **Phase III**: Confirms the drug's efficacy and safety in a larger patient population, often in randomized, controlled trials.

Clinical trial data must include information on the study design, statistical analysis, endpoints, and results, as well as any observed adverse events or side effects.

- **Manufacturing Information**: The MAA includes detailed information on the manufacturing process of the drug, including:

  - The process used to produce the drug, ensuring that it meets **Good Manufacturing Practices (GMP)**.
  - Specifications for the raw materials and final product, including any excipients (inactive ingredients).
  - Details on the facilities used to manufacture the drug and the quality control measures in place.

- **Proposed Labeling**: The MAA includes the proposed product labeling, which provides important information for healthcare providers and patients. The labeling includes details such as:

  - **Indications**: The medical conditions the drug is intended to treat.
  - **Dosage and administration**: How the drug should be taken and the recommended dosage.
  - **Contraindications**: Situations where the drug should not be used, such as in patients with certain medical conditions.
  - **Warnings and precautions**: Potential risks and safety concerns associated with the drug.
  - **Adverse effects**: Any known or suspected side effects of the drug.

- **Pharmacovigilance Plan**: This component outlines the measures that will be taken to monitor the drug's safety after it is approved and marketed. It includes details on the post-marketing surveillance programs, reporting of adverse events, and risk management strategies.

Regulatory Pathways for Marketing Authorization Applications
Regulatory agencies offer different pathways for submitting MAAs based on the type of product being submitted, the level of innovation involved, and the country or region where approval is sought. Common pathways for submitting an MAA include:

- **Centralized Procedure**: In regions like the European Union, a pharmaceutical company can submit a single MAA to the **European Medicines Agency (EMA)** for approval in all EU member states. If approved, the drug can be marketed across the entire EU. This procedure is typically used for new and innovative drugs, biologics, and products that meet specific criteria.
- **National Procedure**: Some countries, such as the **United States** and **Canada**, require pharmaceutical companies to submit separate MAAs to national regulatory authorities. In the U.S., for example, a pharmaceutical company submits a **New Drug Application (NDA)** to the **FDA**, while in Canada, the **New Drug Submission (NDS)** process is used. The approval is granted by the respective national agency, and marketing is allowed within that country.

- **Mutual Recognition Procedure (MRP)**: In the European Union, the MRP allows a company to submit an MAA to one EU member state, and if the drug is approved, the other member states involved in the procedure must recognize the approval. This process helps speed up the approval process within multiple member states.
- **Abbreviated New Drug Application (ANDA)**: This pathway is used for generic drugs. An ANDA is submitted when a pharmaceutical company seeks approval to market a generic version of a previously approved drug. The application demonstrates that the generic product is bioequivalent to the branded product, and does not require the submission of preclinical or clinical data. The **FDA** in the U.S. and other regulatory agencies use the ANDA process for generic drug approvals.

The Review Process for Marketing Authorization Applications

Once an MAA is submitted to the regulatory agency, the agency reviews the data and makes a decision on whether to approve the drug for marketing. The review process includes the following steps:

- **Initial Submission**: The regulatory agency verifies that the MAA is complete and that all necessary data is included. If the application is incomplete, it may be returned to the applicant for additional information.
- **Evaluation**: The regulatory agency's experts assess the clinical trial data, manufacturing information, and proposed labeling to determine if the drug meets safety, efficacy, and quality standards. This evaluation can take several months or even years, depending on the complexity of the drug.
- **Decision**: Once the evaluation is complete, the regulatory agency makes a decision on whether to approve the drug for marketing. If the drug is approved, the regulatory agency issues a **Marketing Authorization** or **Notice of Compliance**, and the drug can be marketed and sold in the region.

1.3.2.2 Investigational New Drug (IND) Applications

An **Investigational New Drug (IND) application** is a request submitted to a regulatory agency, such as the **U.S. Food and Drug Administration (FDA)**, seeking approval to begin clinical trials for a new drug in humans. The IND application is a critical step in the drug development process, as it marks the transition from preclinical (laboratory and animal) studies to clinical trials involving human participants. This application provides the regulatory authority with detailed information about the drug's formulation, preclinical study results, and proposed clinical trial protocols.

The primary purpose of an IND application is to ensure that the investigational drug is safe for initial human trials and that the proposed clinical study design is scientifically sound. The IND application includes data from preclinical studies, a detailed description of the proposed clinical trial, and information about the drug's manufacturing process. Regulatory authorities use the IND submission to evaluate the safety and scientific validity of the proposed studies before granting approval to start clinical trials.

Key Components of an IND Application

The IND application includes several key components that provide the regulatory agency with the necessary information to assess the safety, efficacy, and quality of the investigational drug. These components include:

- **Preclinical Data**: Preclinical studies are conducted in laboratory settings and animal models to gather information about the drug's pharmacology, toxicology, and potential safety risks. The preclinical data should demonstrate that the drug does not cause significant toxicity, adverse effects, or other risks in animals before being tested in humans. Common preclinical studies include:

  - **Toxicology studies**: These studies assess the potential harmful effects of the drug on different organs or systems in the body.
  - **Pharmacokinetics studies**: These studies evaluate how the drug is absorbed, distributed, metabolized, and excreted by the body.
  - **Pharmacodynamics studies**: These studies examine the drug's mechanism of action and its effects on the body.

- **Clinical Trial Protocol**: The IND application includes a detailed description of the proposed clinical trial, including its design, objectives, methodology, and endpoints. The protocol outlines how the drug will be tested in humans, the inclusion and exclusion criteria for participants, the dosage and administration plan, and the methods for monitoring patient safety during the trial. The clinical trial protocol is a critical part of the IND, as it ensures that the study is scientifically valid and ethically sound.

- **Manufacturing Information**: The IND application includes information on how the drug will be manufactured, including details about the manufacturing process, quality control procedures, and any excipients (inactive ingredients) used in the drug formulation. This information helps regulatory authorities assess whether the drug can be consistently produced with the required safety and quality standards.
- **Investigator Information**: The IND must include information about the qualifications of the clinical investigators, including their experience and expertise in conducting clinical trials. This is important to ensure that the clinical study will be conducted ethically and professionally, with adequate monitoring of participant safety.
- **Proposed Labeling**: Although not required for the initial IND submission, the proposed labeling of the investigational drug may be included in the application. The labeling provides information about the drug's intended use, dosage, and administration.

Types of IND Applications

There are several types of IND applications, depending on the nature of the drug being tested and the type of clinical trials proposed:

- **Commercial IND**: This type of IND is typically submitted by pharmaceutical companies or biotechnology firms that are developing new drugs for commercialization. A commercial IND is required when the goal is to conduct clinical trials that will eventually lead to marketing approval for the drug.
- **Research IND**: A research IND is typically submitted by academic researchers or institutions conducting clinical trials on new drugs for scientific research purposes. This type of IND is often used when the goal is not immediate commercialization but to explore new therapeutic approaches or gather data on drug safety and efficacy.
- **Emergency Use IND**: In rare cases, an emergency use IND may be submitted when a drug is needed for the treatment of a life-threatening condition, but there is insufficient clinical trial data to support its use under normal IND procedures. The emergency use IND allows for the use of an investigational drug in a limited patient population when no

other treatment options are available.

The IND Review Process

Once an IND application is submitted to the regulatory agency, it undergoes a thorough review process. The primary objective of the review is to assess whether the proposed clinical trials can be conducted safely and ethically. The review process involves the following steps:

- **Initial Review**: The regulatory agency, such as the FDA, examines the IND submission to ensure that it is complete and contains all the necessary data, including preclinical studies, clinical trial protocols, and manufacturing information. If the application is incomplete or requires additional information, the agency may request further clarification from the applicant.
- **Safety Assessment**: The regulatory authority evaluates the preclinical data to assess the potential risks of the investigational drug. This includes examining the results of toxicology and pharmacokinetics studies to determine whether the drug is safe for use in humans. The agency also reviews the proposed clinical trial protocols to ensure that the study design is scientifically valid and includes appropriate safeguards for participant safety.
- **Decision**: The regulatory agency has 30 days to review the IND application. If the agency does not raise any objections within this time frame, the clinical trial can begin. If the agency has concerns about the drug's safety or the trial design, it may place the IND application on a **clinical hold**, which means that the clinical trial cannot proceed until the issues are addressed.

  - **Clinical Hold**: A clinical hold may be issued if the regulatory agency determines that the investigational drug poses an unacceptable risk to human participants, or if the proposed clinical trial does not meet ethical or scientific standards. The clinical hold can be lifted once the issues have been resolved.

Importance of IND in Drug Development

The IND application is a critical step in the drug development process because it allows pharmaceutical companies and researchers to test new drugs in humans and collect data on their safety and efficacy. The IND provides a framework for conducting clinical trials in a regulated and ethical manner, ensuring that participants are protected and that the results of the trials are scientifically valid.

The successful submission and approval of an IND application allow clinical trials to move forward, ultimately contributing to the development of new drugs that can treat various diseases and improve patient outcomes. The IND process helps ensure that only safe and effective drugs are tested in humans, reducing the risk of adverse events and ensuring that clinical trials are conducted according to high ethical and scientific standards.

1.3.2.3 New Drug Applications (NDA)

A **New Drug Application (NDA)** is the formal request submitted by a pharmaceutical company to a regulatory authority, such as the **U.S. Food and Drug Administration (FDA)**, to approve a new drug for sale and marketing in the country. The NDA is submitted after the successful completion of clinical trials, and it provides the regulatory agency with all the necessary data to evaluate the safety, efficacy, and quality of the drug. The NDA is a critical step in the drug development process, as it determines whether a new drug will be approved for use by patients.

The primary objective of the NDA is to demonstrate to the regulatory authority that the drug is safe and effective for its intended use. The application includes detailed information from preclinical and clinical trials, as well as the proposed manufacturing process and labeling. By evaluating the NDA, the regulatory agency assesses whether the drug's benefits outweigh any potential risks, and whether it meets the standards for public health.

Key Components of a New Drug Application (NDA)

A New Drug Application is a comprehensive submission that includes several key components. Each section of the NDA is designed to provide the regulatory authority with the information it needs to make an informed decision about the drug's safety, efficacy, and quality.

- **Preclinical Data:** The NDA includes data from preclinical studies, which are conducted in laboratory and animal models before clinical trials. These studies assess the drug's safety profile, pharmacokinetics, pharmacodynamics, and potential toxicity. Preclinical data helps to predict how the drug will behave in humans and identifies any potential risks before human trials begin.

- **Clinical Trial Data**: This is one of the most crucial parts of the NDA. It includes data from the clinical trials conducted in humans, typically in **Phase I, Phase II**, and **Phase III** studies:

  ◦ **Phase I**: Safety and dosage studies conducted on healthy volunteers to determine how the drug is absorbed, metabolized, and excreted by the body, and to assess its safety.
  ◦ **Phase II**: Efficacy and safety studies conducted on a small group of patients with the disease or condition the drug is intended to treat. The goal is to determine the drug's effectiveness and to identify any side effects.
  ◦ **Phase III**: Large-scale studies conducted on a diverse patient population to confirm the drug's efficacy and monitor adverse effects. This phase provides the most extensive evidence of the drug's safety and effectiveness.

  The clinical trial data must include information on the study design, patient demographics, dosing regimens, efficacy endpoints, statistical analysis, and observed adverse events.

- **Manufacturing Information**: The NDA must include detailed information on the drug's manufacturing process, which is essential to ensuring the drug is produced consistently and meets quality standards. This section includes:

  ◦ **Process Description**: A detailed explanation of how the drug is manufactured, from raw material selection to the final product.
  ◦ **Quality Control**: Data on the quality control measures used to ensure the drug is produced in compliance with **Good Manufacturing Practices (GMP)**.
  ◦ **Stability Data**: Information on the stability of the drug, including data on its shelf life and storage conditions.

- **Proposed Labeling**: The NDA includes the proposed labeling for the drug, which will be used for marketing and distribution. The labeling provides essential information about the drug, including:

- ○ **Indications**: The medical conditions or diseases the drug is intended to treat.
- ○ **Dosage and Administration**: The recommended dosage, route of administration, and any special instructions.
- ○ **Contraindications**: Situations in which the drug should not be used, such as in patients with specific medical conditions.
- ○ **Warnings and Precautions**: Information about potential risks or safety concerns associated with the drug.
- ○ **Adverse Effects**: A list of known or suspected side effects of the drug.

- **Risk Management and Pharmacovigilance Plans**: The NDA also includes a **Risk Management Plan (RMP)**, which outlines strategies for managing any risks associated with the drug once it is marketed. This plan includes measures for monitoring the drug's safety post-approval, such as periodic safety update reports (PSURs) and post-market surveillance. The NDA may also include a pharmacovigilance plan for ongoing monitoring of adverse drug reactions.

NDA Review Process

Once the NDA is submitted to the regulatory agency, the review process begins. The agency conducts a thorough evaluation of the drug's clinical and preclinical data, manufacturing information, and proposed labeling. The review process involves several key stages:

- **Initial Submission Review**: The regulatory authority first verifies that the NDA submission is complete and that all necessary information is included. If the submission is incomplete, the agency may request additional data or clarification from the applicant.
- **Scientific Review**: Regulatory experts review the clinical trial data to assess the drug's safety, efficacy, and overall benefit-risk profile. This includes reviewing the study design, statistical analysis, and outcomes to determine whether the drug meets the necessary standards for approval. The agency also reviews the manufacturing information to ensure that the drug can be produced consistently and meets quality standards.
- **Labeling Review**: The proposed labeling is reviewed to ensure that it provides accurate and clear information for healthcare professionals and patients. The agency may suggest changes to the labeling, such as adding safety warnings or adjusting dosage recommendations.

- **Advisory Committees**: In some cases, the regulatory authority may consult an **advisory committee** of external experts to provide additional input on the drug's approval. These committees review the clinical trial data and provide recommendations on whether the drug should be approved.
- **Approval or Denial**: After completing the review process, the regulatory agency makes a decision on whether to approve the drug for marketing. If the drug is approved, the agency issues a **Marketing Authorization** or **New Drug Approval**, allowing the drug to be sold in the region. If the drug is not approved, the agency may request additional studies or data before reconsidering the application.

Types of NDAs

There are different types of NDAs, depending on the nature of the drug being submitted for approval:

- **Standard NDA**: A standard NDA is for drugs that are not considered to be breakthrough therapies or involve novel treatment mechanisms. These applications undergo the normal review process.
- **Priority NDA**: A priority NDA is submitted for drugs that offer significant advances over existing therapies, such as drugs that treat serious or life-threatening conditions, or drugs that provide a new mechanism of action for a disease. These applications are given expedited review, with the goal of faster approval.
- **Accelerated Approval**: In some cases, drugs that address serious or unmet medical needs may qualify for **Accelerated Approval**. This pathway allows drugs to be approved based on early clinical trial data, such as surrogate endpoints, with the condition that further clinical trials are conducted to confirm the drug's benefit.

1.3.3 Key Regulatory References

Regulatory references are essential tools for pharmaceutical companies, regulatory authorities, and healthcare professionals. These references include various official resources, databases, and publications that help guide drug development, approval, and monitoring processes. They provide standardized information on the safety, efficacy, and regulatory status of drugs, which is essential for making informed decisions in the pharmaceutical industry. One of the most important regulatory references in the U.S. is the **Orange Book**, which plays a key role in the drug approval process and in determining the marketability of pharmaceutical products.

1.3.3.1 Orange Book: Role in Drug Approval

The **Orange Book**, officially known as the **Approved Drug Products with Therapeutic Equivalence Evaluations**, is a publication of the **U.S. Food and Drug Administration (FDA)**. It provides a comprehensive list of all FDA-approved prescription and over-the-counter drugs, along with information on their therapeutic equivalence and any potential issues regarding patent and exclusivity status. The Orange Book is a critical resource for pharmaceutical companies, healthcare providers, and patients, as it helps them understand which drugs have been approved by the FDA, their therapeutic classifications, and whether there are generic alternatives available.

The Orange Book serves multiple functions in the drug approval process, particularly in the context of the approval of generic drugs and the assessment of drug patents. It is often used by manufacturers and regulatory agencies to ensure that drugs meet the necessary standards for safety, efficacy, and quality, and it supports the regulatory process by providing essential information for decision-making.

Key Functions and Information Provided by the Orange Book

The Orange Book contains several important sections that provide key information about FDA-approved drugs. These include:

- **List of Approved Drug Products**: The Orange Book contains a comprehensive list of FDA-approved drug products, organized by their active ingredients and brand names. It provides detailed information on the drug's dosage forms, strengths, routes of administration, and conditions of use.
- **Therapeutic Equivalence Evaluations**: One of the most important features of the Orange Book is its listing of **therapeutic equivalence evaluations** for drug products. Therapeutic equivalence refers to the fact that a generic drug can be considered clinically equivalent to a brand-name drug if it has the same active ingredients, dosage form, route of administration, strength, and bioavailability. The Orange Book indicates

whether a generic version of a drug is therapeutically equivalent to its branded counterpart by using the **"AB" rating** (equivalent drugs) or other appropriate ratings. This helps healthcare providers and pharmacists make informed decisions when substituting generic drugs for brand-name drugs.

- **Patent and Exclusivity Information**: The Orange Book includes information about the patent status of drug products, as well as any market exclusivity periods granted by the FDA. Patents protect the intellectual property of drug manufacturers by preventing competitors from making and selling the same drug for a specified period. Market exclusivity provides additional protection to a drug after its approval, preventing generic competition for a certain amount of time. The Orange Book provides key dates for the expiration of patents and exclusivity periods, helping pharmaceutical companies and generic manufacturers understand when they can begin marketing generic versions of branded drugs.

- **Product Listings by Active Ingredient**: The Orange Book is organized by active ingredient, which allows users to easily identify drugs that contain the same active substance. This organization is particularly helpful when healthcare professionals need to identify different branded and generic drugs that contain the same active ingredient, making it easier to find therapeutic alternatives.

- **Exclusivity Data**: The Orange Book provides data on the **FDA exclusivity periods** granted to new drugs. Exclusivity is a period during which the FDA grants the drug manufacturer exclusive rights to market the drug. Exclusivity may be granted for various reasons, such as for new molecular entities or drugs that offer a significant clinical advantage. Exclusivity periods may vary in length, and they play a key role in delaying the approval of generic versions of the drug.

Role of the Orange Book in Generic Drug Approval

The Orange Book plays a critical role in the approval of **generic drugs**. Under the **Drug Price Competition and Patent Term Restoration Act (Hatch-Waxman Act)** of 1984, the Orange Book is used to identify FDA-approved drugs for which generic manufacturers can apply for approval. Generic drug manufacturers use the Orange Book to determine whether there are existing patent or exclusivity restrictions on the branded drug they intend to replicate. They can also refer to the therapeutic equivalence ratings in the Orange Book to confirm that their generic version will be considered bioequivalent to the branded product.

- **Generic Drug Approvals**: If a generic manufacturer wants to market a drug product that is therapeutically equivalent to a branded drug, they must submit an **Abbreviated New Drug Application (ANDA)** to the FDA. The ANDA must include data demonstrating that the generic drug is bioequivalent to the branded drug and that it meets the same therapeutic criteria. The Orange Book serves as a reference for identifying whether the generic drug is eligible for approval based on its equivalence to the branded drug.
- **Patent Challenges**: The Orange Book also helps identify patents associated with drugs. Generic manufacturers can use this information to challenge patents that may be blocking the introduction of generic alternatives. If a generic manufacturer believes that a branded drug's patent is invalid, they can file a **Paragraph IV Certification** with the FDA. If the patent is successfully challenged, the generic drug may be allowed to enter the market sooner.

The Importance of the Orange Book in Drug Regulation

The Orange Book is an essential reference for regulatory agencies, healthcare providers, and patients, as it ensures that drugs available on the market have been rigorously evaluated for safety, efficacy, and quality. Its role in identifying therapeutic equivalence allows for the widespread adoption of generic drugs, which can help lower healthcare costs and improve access to affordable medications. It also helps prevent patent infringement and ensures that only safe and effective drugs are marketed.

For pharmaceutical companies, the Orange Book is crucial for navigating the regulatory environment, ensuring compliance with FDA requirements, and understanding the patent landscape. It provides transparency and clarity, which helps pharmaceutical companies make informed decisions about the development, marketing, and patent strategies for their drug products.

1.3.3.2 Purple Book: Regulation of Biosimilars

The **Purple Book** is an important reference guide published by the **U.S. Food and Drug Administration (FDA)** that provides information on biological products, including **biosimilars**. The Purple Book serves as a counterpart to the **Orange Book**, which is used for small molecule drugs. While the Orange Book focuses on traditional drug products, the Purple Book is specifically designed for **biologic products** and their biosimilars.

A **biosimilar** is a biologic product that is highly similar to an already FDA-approved reference biologic product, with no clinically meaningful differences in terms of safety, purity, and potency. The regulatory framework for biosimilars is relatively new compared to traditional drug products, and the Purple Book plays a crucial role in providing regulatory clarity, listing FDA-approved biosimilars, and ensuring that these products meet the necessary standards for safety and efficacy.

The **Purple Book** serves as a key tool for stakeholders in the pharmaceutical industry, including regulatory authorities, healthcare professionals, and patients, to understand the regulatory status of biosimilars and their approval pathways.

Role of the Purple Book in Biosimilar Regulation

The Purple Book provides information on approved biosimilars, including their reference products, the date of approval, and the regulatory pathways followed for their approval. The main role of the Purple Book is to ensure transparency and help clarify the regulatory process for biosimilars in the U.S.

The **Biosimilars User Fee Act (BsUFA)**, which was enacted as part of the **Affordable Care Act (ACA)**, provided a pathway for the approval of biosimilars in the U.S. The Purple Book helps to track biosimilars that have been approved under this regulatory pathway and assists healthcare professionals and patients in identifying approved biosimilars that are safe and effective alternatives to reference biologic products.

Some key aspects of the Purple Book include:

- **Listing of Biosimilars**: The Purple Book lists all FDA-approved biosimilars, providing critical information such as the name of the biosimilar, its reference product, approval date, and the regulatory pathway used. It helps stakeholders to identify biosimilars that have met the FDA's rigorous standards for safety, efficacy, and quality.

- **Indication and Approval Status**: For each biosimilar, the Purple Book provides details on the approved indications, including the specific diseases or conditions for which the biosimilar can be used. It also lists the approval status of the biosimilar, including whether it has been approved for all indications of the reference product or only specific indications.

- **Regulatory Pathways**: The Purple Book outlines the regulatory process by which biosimilars are approved. Biosimilars can be approved through the **Biologics License Application (BLA)** pathway, which is the same pathway used for innovator biologics, or through the **Section 351(k)** pathway for biosimilars. This section explains the scientific and regulatory processes that govern biosimilar approval, ensuring that biosimilars are held to the same high standards as their reference biologics.

- **Information on Exclusivity**: The Purple Book provides data on the exclusivity periods for biologic products, including the **12-year market exclusivity** granted to reference biologics under the **Biologics Price Competition and Innovation Act (BPCIA)**. This exclusivity period prevents biosimilars from entering the market for a set period after the reference biologic's approval. The Purple Book tracks the expiration of this exclusivity and the subsequent approval of biosimilars.

The Importance of Biosimilars in Healthcare

Biosimilars offer a significant opportunity to reduce healthcare costs while maintaining access to safe, effective, and high-quality treatments. Biologic drugs, which are large, complex molecules made from living organisms, are often very expensive. Biosimilars are developed to be highly similar to an already approved reference biologic, offering an alternative that can lower treatment costs without compromising on safety or efficacy.

The approval of biosimilars provides several benefits to the healthcare system:

- **Cost Savings**: Biosimilars are typically priced lower than their reference biologics, which helps reduce overall healthcare spending. These savings are crucial in providing access to life-saving biologic treatments for a wider population, particularly for diseases such as cancer, rheumatoid arthritis, and diabetes.

- **Increased Access to Treatments**: The availability of biosimilars increases patient access to biologic therapies, particularly in regions where the cost of reference biologics may limit access. This is particularly important for chronic diseases or conditions that require long-term treatment with biologics.

- **Market Competition**: The approval of biosimilars increases competition in the biologic drug market, which can lead to price reductions and more treatment options for patients. With more biosimilars entering the market, patients and healthcare providers can choose from a variety of treatment options, improving outcomes and enhancing patient choice.

Regulatory Considerations for Biosimilars

The approval process for biosimilars is more complex than that of traditional drugs due to the inherent complexity of biologic products. Unlike small molecule drugs, biologics are made using living cells, and minor changes in the manufacturing process can have significant effects on the drug's structure and behavior. As such, biosimilars must demonstrate that they are highly similar to the reference biologic in terms of clinical outcomes, even though they may differ in certain molecular characteristics.

Some important regulatory considerations for biosimilars include:

- **Exclusivity and Patent Issues**: The introduction of biosimilars often involves patent litigation, as reference biologics are usually patented for a period of time. The BPCIA provides a framework for addressing patent disputes between the makers of reference biologics and biosimilars. The Purple Book tracks the exclusivity periods and patent litigation related to biologic drugs.
- **Immunogenicity**: Since biosimilars are not identical to the reference biologic, there may be differences in the immune response they trigger. Regulatory agencies require extensive testing to assess the immunogenic potential of biosimilars to ensure they do not pose a higher risk of adverse immune responses compared to the reference product.
- **Interchangeability**: In the U.S., biosimilars can be designated as **interchangeable** with their reference biologic by the FDA. This means that the biosimilar can be substituted for the reference product without the intervention of the healthcare provider. Interchangeability designation is an important regulatory milestone that facilitates the substitution of biosimilars in clinical practice.

1.3.3.3 Federal Register: Regulatory Notices

The **Federal Register** is the official daily publication of the U.S. government that provides a platform for regulatory agencies to announce proposed rules, final regulations, notices, public meetings, and other significant government activities. It plays a crucial role in the **regulatory process**, ensuring transparency and public participation in the rulemaking process. Through the Federal Register, federal agencies, including those in the pharmaceutical and healthcare sectors, can communicate regulatory changes, updates, and other critical information that impacts industries, businesses, and the general public.

For pharmaceutical companies, healthcare professionals, and other stakeholders in the regulatory field, the Federal Register is an essential source of information, as it includes notices related to the approval of new drugs, changes in existing regulations, public comment periods, and the latest updates on drug safety and efficacy. The **U.S. Food and Drug Administration (FDA)** and other agencies such as the **Centers for Medicare and Medicaid Services (CMS)** frequently publish notices that impact drug approval processes, labeling changes, and other aspects of pharmaceutical regulation in the Federal Register.

Key Features and Function of the Federal Register

The Federal Register serves several critical functions in the regulatory process, including:

- **Publishing Proposed Rules and Regulations**: Regulatory agencies use the Federal Register to announce proposed rules and regulations that are subject to public comment. For instance, the FDA may propose new guidelines for drug labeling, clinical trial requirements, or good manufacturing practices (GMP). These proposed rules are published in the Federal Register, giving stakeholders an opportunity to provide feedback before the regulations are finalized.

- **Announcing Final Rules and Regulations**: After considering public comments and making any necessary revisions, regulatory agencies publish the final version of the rules and regulations in the Federal Register. These final rules are legally binding and provide guidance to industry stakeholders on compliance with regulatory requirements.

- **Providing Notices of Public Meetings**: The Federal Register also publishes notices about upcoming public meetings or hearings held by regulatory agencies. These meetings may involve discussions on proposed regulations, scientific findings, or emerging health issues.

Public meetings provide an opportunity for stakeholders to express their views and participate in the regulatory process.

- **Regulatory Announcements and Approvals**: Agencies such as the FDA use the Federal Register to announce regulatory approvals, such as the approval of new drugs, biologics, and medical devices. These announcements provide important details about the approval process, including the drug's name, approved indications, and any conditions associated with its use. The publication of these approvals ensures transparency and allows industry professionals to stay updated on new product entries to the market.

- **Notices of Adverse Event Reporting**: Regulatory bodies also use the Federal Register to announce safety concerns or adverse event reports related to drugs and other health products. For example, if new safety concerns are raised about an approved drug, the FDA may issue a safety alert or warning in the Federal Register, advising healthcare providers and patients about the potential risks.

Role of the Federal Register in Pharmaceutical Regulation

The Federal Register plays an essential role in pharmaceutical regulation by ensuring that the rulemaking process is transparent, accessible, and open to public participation. It serves as a comprehensive source of information for regulatory updates, which pharmaceutical companies must monitor closely to stay in compliance with evolving regulations. Some of the key ways the Federal Register impacts pharmaceutical regulation include:

- **Providing Access to Regulatory Changes**: Pharmaceutical companies, researchers, and healthcare professionals rely on the Federal Register to stay informed about changes in regulations, guidelines, and policies. Since regulatory frameworks in the pharmaceutical industry are continuously evolving, the Federal Register serves as a reliable source of updates on new and amended rules. For example, it may announce changes to labeling requirements, advertising regulations, or clinical trial protocols.

- **Transparency in Drug Approval and Regulation**: The Federal Register ensures transparency in the drug approval process by making regulatory notices, approvals, and updates publicly available. This openness helps foster accountability and allows the public, including healthcare professionals and patients, to track the approval status of new drugs and therapeutic products. For example, when a new drug is approved by the FDA, the details of the approval, including conditions of use and safety warnings, are published in the Federal Register.

- **Facilitating Public Participation**: One of the core functions of the Federal Register is to provide a platform for public participation in the regulatory process. Regulatory agencies announce proposed rules in the Federal Register and solicit public comments. This allows stakeholders, including pharmaceutical companies, advocacy groups, healthcare providers, and individuals, to voice their concerns, offer feedback, and suggest improvements before a regulation is finalized.
- **Impact on Drug Labeling and Advertising**: The Federal Register is used to communicate changes in drug labeling requirements and advertising guidelines. For example, if new findings emerge about a drug's side effects or contraindications, the FDA may issue a regulatory notice in the Federal Register mandating updates to the drug's labeling to reflect these changes. This process helps ensure that patients and healthcare providers have access to the most up-to-date and accurate information about the medications they use.
- **Communication of New Safety Regulations**: In the event of a safety issue with an approved drug, the FDA uses the Federal Register to inform the public and healthcare professionals about any new safety guidelines, label changes, or safety advisories. For example, if a drug is linked to an unexpected side effect, the FDA may issue a safety alert in the Federal Register, recommending changes in its use or distribution.

The Structure of the Federal Register

The Federal Register is structured to provide easy access to regulatory information and is organized into several sections:

- **Proposed Rules**: This section includes notices about rules that are under consideration and open for public comment. Pharmaceutical stakeholders can review these proposals and submit their feedback.
- **Final Rules**: This section includes finalized rules and regulations that are legally binding. Once a rule is finalized, it becomes part of the regulatory framework governing drug approvals and healthcare practices.
- **Notices**: This section includes important updates, such as approval notices for new drugs or medical devices, public meeting announcements, and other regulatory actions. For pharmaceutical

companies, this section is crucial for staying updated on the status of drugs and therapies under review.

- **Presidential Documents**: This section includes executive orders, proclamations, and other documents issued by the President that may impact regulatory processes.

1.3.3.4 Code of Federal Regulations (CFR)

The **Code of Federal Regulations (CFR)** is a critical compilation of regulations issued by the various agencies of the U.S. government. It serves as the official repository for all final, binding regulations, including those that apply to the pharmaceutical, healthcare, and food industries. The CFR is divided into 50 titles, each representing a different area of federal regulation. Title 21 of the CFR, specifically, contains the regulations set forth by the **U.S. Food and Drug Administration (FDA)**, which govern the approval, marketing, manufacturing, and post-market surveillance of pharmaceutical products, including drugs, biologics, and medical devices.

The CFR is an essential reference for pharmaceutical companies, regulatory agencies, healthcare providers, and other stakeholders. It provides a comprehensive framework for ensuring that pharmaceutical products are safe, effective, and of high quality. The regulations contained within the CFR are legally binding, and adherence to them is essential for compliance with federal law.

Structure of the Code of Federal Regulations

The CFR is organized into 50 titles, each of which focuses on a specific subject area. Within these titles, the regulations are organized by chapters, subchapters, parts, subparts, and sections. For pharmaceutical companies and healthcare professionals, Title 21 of the CFR is of particular importance, as it covers all FDA regulations related to food, drugs, and biologics.

- **Title 21 – Food and Drugs**: This title contains the regulations related to the approval, manufacturing, labeling, and post-market surveillance of drugs, biologics, and medical devices. It is divided into several chapters, each addressing different aspects of drug regulation, such as clinical trials, Good Manufacturing Practices (GMP), labeling, and safety monitoring.

- **Chapter I – Food and Drug Administration**: This chapter contains regulations governing the FDA's authority, structure, and operations. It provides the framework for how the FDA regulates pharmaceutical products and sets forth the agency's regulatory responsibilities.
- **Chapter II – Federal Trade Commission**: This chapter includes regulations pertaining to the marketing and advertising of pharmaceutical products and other consumer goods.
- **Parts and Subparts**: Regulations within Title 21 are organized into specific "parts" and "subparts" that cover distinct regulatory areas. For example, **Part 314** outlines the procedures for the approval of new drug applications (NDAs), while **Part 312** deals with Investigational New Drug (IND) applications and the requirements for clinical trials.

Key Areas Covered by the CFR

The **CFR** provides detailed guidance on a wide range of regulatory topics relevant to the pharmaceutical industry. Some of the key areas covered in **Title 21** of the CFR include:

- **Drug Approval and Clinical Trials**: Title 21 outlines the regulatory requirements for submitting New Drug Applications (NDAs) and Investigational New Drug (IND) applications, as well as the process for conducting clinical trials. These regulations ensure that pharmaceutical companies follow appropriate procedures when developing and testing new drugs and that drugs meet safety and efficacy standards before they are approved for use.
- **Good Manufacturing Practices (GMP)**: The CFR sets forth regulations for Good Manufacturing Practices (GMP) under **Part 211**. These regulations establish the minimum standards for the manufacturing, processing, and packaging of drugs to ensure they are produced in a controlled and consistent manner. Compliance with GMP is essential for maintaining the quality of pharmaceutical products and ensuring their safety for consumers.
- **Labeling Requirements**: The CFR includes comprehensive regulations for the labeling of drugs and medical devices. **Part 201** specifies the required labeling elements, including the drug's name, dosage,

indications, warnings, and usage instructions. The labeling regulations are designed to ensure that healthcare providers and patients receive accurate and adequate information about a drug's benefits, risks, and appropriate use.

- **Post-Marketing Surveillance and Safety Monitoring**: Title 21 also includes regulations that govern the post-marketing surveillance of drugs. This includes **pharmacovigilance** practices to monitor the safety of drugs once they are approved and on the market. Pharmaceutical companies are required to report adverse events and update drug labeling with new safety information. The regulations ensure that any potential safety concerns are identified and addressed in a timely manner.

- **Biologics and Biosimilars**: Title 21 of the CFR also includes provisions for biologics and biosimilars under **Part 600-680**. These regulations cover the approval, manufacturing, labeling, and post-market surveillance of biologic products, including vaccines, blood products, and monoclonal antibodies. The regulations ensure that biologics are safe, effective, and of high quality.

- **Medical Devices**: Although pharmaceutical drugs are the primary focus of Title 21, it also includes regulations for medical devices under **Part 800-1299**. These regulations govern the approval, labeling, and post-market surveillance of medical devices, ensuring their safety and effectiveness in the healthcare system.

Role of the CFR in the Drug Approval Process

The CFR plays a central role in the **drug approval process** by providing the regulatory framework that pharmaceutical companies must follow to bring a new drug to market. The regulations outlined in Title 21 guide companies through every step of the process, from preclinical research and clinical trials to manufacturing and post-market surveillance.

- **Drug Development and Approval**: The CFR ensures that drug development is conducted following established standards for safety, efficacy, and quality. Regulatory requirements for clinical trials, including Good Clinical Practice (GCP), are included in the CFR to ensure that drugs are tested in humans in a scientifically sound and ethical manner.

- **Compliance with Manufacturing Standards**: The GMP regulations in the CFR are critical to ensuring that pharmaceutical products are produced to consistent quality standards. These standards help reduce the risk of contamination, variability, and other manufacturing issues that could compromise the safety and effectiveness of the drug.
- **Safety and Risk Management**: The CFR helps regulate the safety of drugs after they are approved for market use. The post-marketing surveillance regulations require pharmaceutical companies to report adverse events and update safety labeling to reflect any new risks associated with the drug.

Updates and Amendments to the CFR

The CFR is continually updated to reflect changes in scientific knowledge, technological advancements, and regulatory practices. Regulatory agencies like the FDA may issue **proposed rules** and **final rules** in the Federal Register, which, once finalized, become part of the CFR. These updates can impact drug approval procedures, labeling requirements, and other aspects of pharmaceutical regulation.

It is essential for pharmaceutical companies to stay up to date with amendments to the CFR to ensure ongoing compliance with regulatory requirements. The CFR is an evolving document, and staying informed about new regulations helps companies avoid delays in drug development and marketing and ensures that their products meet the highest standards of safety and quality.

Authority	Region	Role	Examples of Drugs or Products Regulated
U.S. Food and Drug Administration (FDA)	United States	Ensures safety, efficacy, and quality of drugs, biologics, and medical devices	Prescription drugs, over-the-counter drugs, vaccines
European Medicines Agency (EMA)	European Union	Regulates medicinal products for human and veterinary use across the EU	Biologics, orphan drugs, novel drugs
Pharmaceutical and Medical Devices Agency (PMDA)	Japan	Regulates drugs and medical devices, ensures quality, safety, and efficacy	Prescription drugs, medical devices
Therapeutic Goods Administration (TGA)	Australia	Ensures safety and efficacy of therapeutic goods, including medicines and devices	Over-the-counter drugs, prescription drugs
Health Canada	Canada	Regulates drugs, biologics, medical devices, and natural health products	Prescription drugs, vaccines

Table 1: Key Regulatory Authorities in Pharmaceutical Science

Phase	Purpose	Participants	Focus
Phase I	Testing the safety, dosage, and pharmacokinetics in healthy volunteers	Small group of healthy individuals	Safety, dosage
Phase II	Evaluating the drug's efficacy and further assessing safety in patients	Patients with the condition	Efficacy, optimal dose
Phase III	Confirming efficacy and monitoring long-term safety in a larger patient population	Large group of patients	Efficacy, safety, comparison with existing treatments
Phase IV	Post-marketing surveillance to monitor long-term safety and efficacy	General public	Long-term effects, rare adverse effects

Table 2: Key Phases of Clinical Trials

Feature	NDA (New Drug Application)	ANDA (Abbreviated New Drug Application)	Data Requirements	Approval Process
Purpose	Approval for a new drug	Approval for a generic drug	Extensive clinical trial data, preclinical data	Longer, more extensive
Clinical Trials	Required for safety and efficacy assessment	Not required if bioequivalence is proven	Required for new drug development	Comprehensive trials for new drugs

Table 3: NDA vs. ANDA

Guideline	Regulatory Authority	Purpose
ICH E6 (Good Clinical Practice)	International Council for Harmonisation (ICH)	Guidelines for designing, conducting, recording, and reporting clinical trials
ICH E2E (Pharmacovigilance)	ICH	Guidelines for the safety monitoring of drugs during clinical trials and post-marketing
FDA 21 CFR Part 312	FDA	Guidelines for submitting an Investigational New Drug (IND) application
EMA Good Manufacturing Practice	European Medicines Agency (EMA)	Guidelines for the manufacturing and quality control of medicinal products

Table 4: Common Regulatory Guidelines

New Drug Discovery and Development

2.1 Stages of Drug Discovery

The process of drug discovery is complex and involves several stages that lead to the development of a new pharmaceutical product. These stages are designed to ensure that only the most promising compounds progress to clinical trials and ultimately to the market. The initial phase of drug discovery focuses on identifying potential targets, which are biological molecules or structures involved in disease processes. Once a target is identified and validated, a lead compound can be developed, followed by extensive preclinical and clinical testing.

One of the key stages in drug discovery is **target identification and validation.** This stage is crucial because the effectiveness of a drug depends largely on its ability to interact with the appropriate biological target. The target is typically a protein, enzyme, receptor, or nucleic acid that plays a critical role in the disease process. Target identification and validation aim to determine the exact molecular entity that a drug should interact with to produce the desired therapeutic effect.

2.1.1 Target Identification and Validation

Target identification refers to the process of discovering and selecting the biological molecule or pathway that is involved in a disease and can be modulated by a drug. This step involves extensive research into the molecular mechanisms of the disease, with the goal of identifying key players in the disease's progression.

Target validation follows target identification and ensures that the identified target is indeed relevant to the disease and that its modulation can lead to a therapeutic effect. The validation process provides confidence that the drug can effectively interact with the target to produce the desired pharmacological outcome.

Successful target identification and validation form the foundation for the subsequent stages of drug discovery, such as lead compound identification, optimization, and preclinical development. If the target is not well validated, efforts to develop drugs against it may lead to failure in later stages of development.

2.1.1.1 Methods of Identifying Biological Targets

Identifying biological targets is one of the most critical steps in the drug discovery process. Over the years, various methods have been developed to help researchers identify potential drug targets. These methods typically rely on understanding the molecular and cellular pathways involved in disease processes and discovering the biological molecules that are central to those pathways.

Here are some of the most common methods used in **target identification**:

Genomic Approaches

Genomics plays a fundamental role in the identification of disease-related biological targets. By studying the genetic factors that contribute to disease, researchers can identify genes that are overexpressed, mutated, or otherwise altered in disease states. Genomic approaches focus on understanding how changes in the DNA sequence can lead to diseases, and this information can help identify genes that encode for proteins that can be targeted by drugs.

Gene Expression Profiling: One of the most widely used techniques for identifying targets is gene expression profiling, which involves analyzing the expression levels of thousands of genes simultaneously. This approach compares the gene expression profiles of healthy and diseased tissues to identify genes that are differentially expressed in the disease state. These differentially expressed genes may encode proteins that are involved in disease progression and could serve as potential drug targets.

RNA Interference (RNAi): RNAi is a technique that can be used to silence specific genes to determine their role in disease. By knocking down the expression of a gene using small interfering RNA (siRNA), researchers can observe the effects of gene silencing on disease progression. This method helps to identify genes whose inhibition could reverse or mitigate the effects of the disease.

Proteomic Approaches

Proteomics, the large-scale study of proteins, is another powerful method for identifying biological targets. Proteins are the functional molecules within cells, and many diseases are caused by the dysfunction of specific proteins. Proteomics allows researchers to identify and quantify proteins that are involved in disease processes, providing insight into potential targets for therapeutic intervention.

Protein Expression Profiling: Similar to gene expression profiling, protein expression profiling involves identifying proteins that are differentially expressed in disease versus normal tissues. Proteins that are overexpressed or altered in disease states may serve as biomarkers for the disease and potential drug targets.

Mass Spectrometry: Mass spectrometry is a technique used to identify and quantify proteins based on their mass-to-charge ratio. This powerful technology allows researchers to analyze the entire proteome of a cell or tissue and identify potential disease-related proteins that could be targeted by drugs.

High-Throughput Screening (HTS)

High-throughput screening (HTS) is a method used to identify potential drug targets by testing large libraries of compounds against biological molecules or cells. In this approach, a variety of assays are developed to measure the interaction between compounds and biological targets. The screening process allows researchers to identify small molecules that interact with the target of interest.

Compound Libraries: HTS involves testing thousands of small molecules from compound libraries to determine their ability to bind to a particular target. These assays can be used to identify potential lead compounds that can then be optimized for further development.

Cell-Based Assays: In addition to testing compounds on isolated proteins, HTS can also be performed using cell-based assays, where live cells expressing a specific target are used to test the efficacy of drug candidates. This approach can help identify targets that are relevant in the context of the whole cell and better reflect how a drug would behave in vivo.

Immunological Approaches

Immunological methods can be used to identify proteins or other molecules that are involved in disease processes. These methods rely on the immune system's ability to recognize specific targets, such as proteins or other antigens, and can be used to develop antibodies that target these molecules.

Monoclonal Antibodies: Monoclonal antibodies are laboratory-made antibodies that can bind to specific antigens. By developing monoclonal antibodies against a target protein, researchers can study the protein's role in disease and determine whether it is a suitable target for drug development.

Phage Display: Phage display is a technique that allows the identification of peptides or proteins that bind to a specific target. In this approach, peptides are expressed on the surface of bacteriophages (viruses that infect bacteria) and can be screened for their ability to bind to a target protein. Phage display is widely used to identify potential therapeutic antibodies and peptide-based drugs.

Bioinformatics and Computational Approaches

With the advent of computational biology and bioinformatics, researchers now have access to powerful tools that can predict potential drug targets. These methods involve the use of software and databases to analyze large amounts of biological data and identify molecules that are likely to be involved in disease processes.

Molecular Docking: Molecular docking is a computational technique used to predict how small molecules (such as drugs) will bind to a target protein. By analyzing the 3D structure of proteins and their ligands, researchers can identify potential binding sites and predict the effectiveness of drug candidates.

Systems Biology: Systems biology approaches integrate data from genomics, proteomics, and other biological disciplines to model complex biological systems. By studying the interactions between genes, proteins, and cellular pathways, researchers can identify key targets that play a critical role in disease and could be modulated by drugs.

2.1.1.2 In Vitro and In Vivo Validation Techniques

Once a potential target is identified, it must undergo **validation** to confirm that it is indeed relevant to the disease and can be modulated by a drug to produce therapeutic effects. Target validation ensures that the identified molecular target plays a key role in the disease process and that it can be a feasible target for drug discovery. Validation techniques can broadly be classified into two categories: **in vitro** and **in vivo** validation.

Both **in vitro** and **in vivo** validation techniques are essential to understanding how a target behaves under experimental conditions. **In vitro** refers to studies conducted in controlled environments outside living organisms, typically in cell cultures, while **in vivo** refers to studies conducted within a living organism. These techniques are used to confirm that the identified target is involved in the disease pathway and that its modulation by a drug can lead to the desired therapeutic outcome.

In Vitro Validation Techniques

In vitro techniques involve testing the biological target in isolated cells or tissues. These methods allow researchers to study the molecular mechanisms at play in a controlled, simplified environment, without the complexities of the whole organism. **In vitro** techniques are often used in the early stages of drug discovery and are highly effective for testing potential drug candidates, identifying biomarkers, and studying cellular responses.

Some common **in vitro validation techniques** include:

1. **Gene Knockdown and Knockout**

One of the most widely used **in vitro** validation techniques is gene knockdown or knockout, which involves silencing or completely removing a specific gene to study its role in disease. This technique helps determine whether the target gene is essential for the disease process.

- ○ **RNA Interference (RNAi)**: RNA interference involves the use of small interfering RNA (siRNA) or short hairpin RNA (shRNA) to silence the expression of specific genes. By knocking down the gene that encodes the target protein, researchers can observe the effects on cell behavior, disease progression, and the potential therapeutic impact of inhibiting the target.
- ○ **CRISPR-Cas9**: The **CRISPR-Cas9** gene-editing technology allows researchers to precisely edit the genome of cells, including knocking out specific genes. This technique is widely used for target validation, as it enables researchers to study the effects of removing a gene in a controlled manner.

2. Overexpression of Target Gene

Another method used to validate a target is the overexpression of the target gene. By introducing additional copies of the gene encoding the target into cells, researchers can study the impact of increased target expression on disease pathways.

- ○ **Transfection**: Transfection involves introducing foreign DNA (e.g., plasmids containing the gene of interest) into cultured cells. This technique allows researchers to study the effects of overexpressing a specific target on cellular function and behavior.
- ○ **Reporter Assays**: Reporter genes, such as **luciferase** or **green fluorescent protein (GFP)**, can be linked to the target gene to visualize its expression and activity in living cells. Reporter assays help assess the impact of target overexpression on cellular processes.

3. Small Molecule or Antibody Inhibition

One of the key aspects of validating a target is demonstrating that its inhibition can alter the disease process. **Small molecule inhibitors** or **monoclonal antibodies** can be used to specifically block the activity of the target protein and evaluate its role in disease.

- **Small Molecule Inhibitors**: These compounds are designed to interact with the target protein and block its activity. By testing the effects of small molecule inhibitors in vitro, researchers can determine whether inhibiting the target leads to a change in the disease phenotype.
- **Monoclonal Antibodies**: Monoclonal antibodies can be engineered to specifically bind and neutralize the target protein. These antibodies can be used to validate whether the target is critical for disease progression.

4. Cellular Assays and Phenotypic Screening

Cell-based assays and **phenotypic screening** involve using cultured cells to evaluate how a target modulation (via inhibition or activation) affects cellular processes. These assays allow researchers to assess the impact of potential drug candidates on cell viability, proliferation, migration, apoptosis, and other cellular functions.

- **Cell Proliferation Assays**: These assays measure cell growth and proliferation, helping researchers determine whether modulating the target affects the ability of cells to proliferate, which is often a key feature in cancer and other diseases.
- **Apoptosis Assays**: Apoptosis, or programmed cell death, is a critical process in diseases such as cancer. Apoptosis assays, such as the **Annexin V** assay, can help validate a target by showing whether its modulation induces or inhibits cell death in response to treatment.

5. Enzyme Activity Assays

For targets that are enzymes, **enzyme activity assays** are used to measure the functional activity of the target protein. These assays involve testing the enzyme's ability to catalyze a specific reaction in vitro. If the target is an enzyme involved in a disease pathway, measuring its activity can help validate its role in the disease.

- **Colorimetric and Fluorometric Assays**: These assays use substrates that generate a color or fluorescence when converted by the enzyme. By measuring changes in color or fluorescence, researchers can quantify enzyme activity and determine the impact of inhibition.

In Vivo Validation Techniques

While in vitro techniques are essential for initial target validation, **in vivo** validation techniques involve testing the target in living organisms to confirm its role in disease and to study how a drug modulates the target in the context of the whole organism. In vivo studies provide more comprehensive insights into the pharmacodynamics, efficacy, and safety of drugs targeting specific molecules.

Common **in vivo validation techniques** include:

1. **Animal Models of Disease**

   Animal models are used to mimic human disease states in a controlled environment, allowing researchers to study the effects of targeting a specific protein or pathway in the context of an entire organism. Animal models are essential for understanding the physiological effects of target modulation and assessing the potential therapeutic impact of drugs.

   - **Genetically Modified Animals**: Genetically engineered animals, such as **knockout mice**, can be used to study the effects of deleting or modifying a target gene. These models help validate whether the target is involved in disease and whether its inhibition can alleviate disease symptoms.
   - **Induced Disease Models**: In addition to genetically modified animals, disease models can be created by inducing disease states through chemicals, viruses, or other methods. These models are useful for studying how target modulation affects disease progression in a living organism.

2. **Pharmacokinetics and Pharmacodynamics Studies**

   In vivo studies allow researchers to evaluate the pharmacokinetics (how the drug is absorbed, distributed, metabolized, and excreted in the body) and pharmacodynamics (the effect of the drug on the body). These studies are essential for understanding how drugs interact with biological targets in living systems.

- **Drug Absorption Studies**: Researchers can track how a drug reaches its target by measuring its concentration in various tissues or organs over time.
- **Efficacy Testing in Animal Models**: By administering the drug to animal models, researchers can study how well the drug targets the intended molecule and whether it produces the desired therapeutic effect.

3. In Vivo Imaging

In vivo imaging techniques, such as **positron emission tomography (PET)**, **magnetic resonance imaging (MRI)**, and **fluorescence imaging**, allow researchers to monitor the activity of biological targets in living organisms in real-time. These non-invasive imaging techniques provide valuable information about target modulation and drug distribution in vivo.

- **Target-Specific Imaging**: By using probes or radiolabeled compounds that specifically bind to the target, researchers can visualize target expression and modulation in living animals.

4. Toxicity and Safety Studies

In vivo studies are also essential for evaluating the **toxicity** and **safety** of drugs targeting a specific protein. By administering the drug to animals over a period of time and monitoring for adverse effects, researchers can assess whether the drug is safe for human use.

- **LD50 Testing: Lethal Dose 50 (LD50)** testing helps determine the dose at which a drug causes death in 50% of test animals, providing information on its toxicity.
- **Organ Toxicity**: Researchers can monitor organs for damage caused by the drug, helping ensure that potential drugs are safe for long-term use.

2.1.2 Lead Compound Identification and Optimization

After identifying a suitable biological target, the next step in the drug discovery process is to find and optimize lead compounds that can modulate this target effectively. **Lead compound identification** involves screening large libraries of molecules to identify those that have the desired activity against the target, while **optimization** focuses on improving the properties of these compounds to enhance their efficacy, selectivity, and safety profile.

Lead compound identification and optimization is a crucial phase, as it sets the stage for the development of a drug candidate that can move into preclinical and clinical testing. This process requires careful screening, modification of chemical structures, and rigorous testing to ensure that the compound not only interacts with the target but does so in a way that is therapeutically beneficial and safe for patients.

2.1.2.1 Screening for Active Compounds

Screening for active compounds is one of the earliest and most critical steps in identifying lead compounds. Screening involves testing a vast number of molecules, either from compound libraries or designed synthetically, to identify those that interact with the biological target in a way that produces the desired effect. These compounds can then be optimized for further development into drug candidates.

There are two primary types of screening methods used for active compound identification: **high-throughput screening (HTS)** and **virtual screening**.

High-Throughput Screening (HTS)

High-throughput screening (HTS) is a powerful and widely used technique for identifying active compounds. HTS enables the rapid testing of thousands to millions of compounds in a short period of time using automated systems. HTS assays are designed to measure the activity of each compound against the biological target, providing a high-volume and high-precision approach to finding potential drug candidates.

HTS is typically conducted in a multi-well plate format, where each well contains a small sample of a compound along with the biological target (usually a purified enzyme, receptor, or cellular system). The assay monitors the interaction between the compound and the target, providing data that indicate which compounds show activity.

Key features of **HTS** include:

- **Automation**: HTS is carried out using robotic systems that can test large numbers of compounds simultaneously. These systems are capable of conducting experiments on hundreds or thousands of compounds in parallel, making it possible to screen vast compound libraries in a short amount of time.
- **Diverse Compound Libraries**: HTS typically uses compound libraries that include a wide variety of small molecules, natural products, and other compounds with diverse chemical structures. The aim is to identify a broad spectrum of potential drug candidates that interact with the biological target.
- **Quantitative Results**: HTS assays provide quantitative data on the interaction between each compound and the target. Compounds that show the greatest activity are then selected for further testing and optimization.

HTS can be applied to a variety of drug targets, including enzymes, receptors, ion channels, and other biomolecules. It is highly effective for discovering lead compounds in both academic research and pharmaceutical companies.

Types of HTS Assays

1. **Enzyme Assays**: Enzyme assays are used when the target is an enzyme. These assays measure the ability of compounds to inhibit or activate the enzyme, which can provide insight into how a drug might modulate the target's activity. Common techniques include **colorimetric, fluorometric**, and **luminescent assays**, which detect changes in enzyme activity.
2. **Cell-Based Assays**: In cell-based assays, live cells are used to evaluate compound effects on a biological target. These assays can monitor a range of cellular responses, such as cell viability, proliferation, apoptosis, and receptor activation. **Reporter gene assays** (where a reporter gene is used to monitor gene expression) are commonly used in cell-based HTS.
3. **Binding Assays: Radiolabeled compounds** or fluorescent tags are often used in binding assays to assess the ability of a compound to bind to a specific receptor or protein. These assays can measure the affinity of the compound for its target, providing important information on the strength and specificity of the interaction.

Virtual Screening

Virtual screening is a computational method used to identify potential drug-like compounds by simulating their interactions with a target protein. In virtual screening, the three-dimensional structure of the target is used to search databases of compounds for those that are likely to bind to the target. This approach allows researchers to narrow down the number of compounds to be tested in the laboratory by predicting which ones are most likely to show activity.

Key features of **virtual screening** include:

- **Docking Studies**: **Molecular docking** simulations are central to virtual screening. In docking studies, the target protein's 3D structure is used to predict how different compounds will fit into the binding site. The goal is to identify compounds that bind with high affinity and specificity.
- **Pharmacophore Modeling**: **Pharmacophore modeling** identifies the essential chemical features of a molecule that are necessary for binding to a target. This method can be used to design new molecules or screen large compound libraries to find those with the best potential to interact with the target.
- **In Silico Prediction of Activity**: Virtual screening helps predict the biological activity of compounds before they are tested experimentally. This can save both time and resources by focusing efforts on compounds that are more likely to be effective in biological assays.

While virtual screening can significantly reduce the number of compounds tested experimentally, it is important to confirm the predictions through **in vitro** assays to validate the results.

Fragment-Based Screening

Another powerful approach to identify active compounds is **fragment-based screening**. In this method, small chemical fragments—often just a few atoms in size—are screened against the biological target. These fragments typically do not have full drug-like properties but can bind to a target protein with weak affinity. Once fragments are identified that bind to the target, they can be expanded and modified to create more potent, drug-like compounds.

Fragment-based screening has the advantage of identifying novel binding sites on the target protein, which might not be obvious with traditional small molecule screens. This technique is often used in combination with **HTS** and **virtual screening**.

Natural Product Screening

Natural products, such as plant-derived compounds, microbial metabolites, and marine organisms, have historically been a rich source of bioactive compounds. **Natural product screening** involves extracting compounds from natural sources and testing them for activity against the target. Many existing drugs, including antibiotics and anticancer agents, have been derived from natural products.

- **Library of Natural Products**: Pharmaceutical companies often maintain large libraries of natural products for screening. These libraries include plant extracts, microbial cultures, and marine-derived compounds, which are tested for their potential to interact with biological targets.
- **High Sensitivity**: Natural products often contain a variety of bioactive compounds, and testing these complex mixtures can yield novel lead candidates that would otherwise be missed in synthetic compound libraries.

2.1.2.2 Structure-Activity Relationship (SAR)

Structure-Activity Relationship (SAR) is a fundamental concept in drug discovery that involves the study of the relationship between the chemical structure of a compound and its biological activity. The SAR approach is used to understand how modifications to the structure of a molecule can influence its potency, selectivity, and overall effectiveness as a drug. By systematically altering the chemical structure of a lead compound, researchers can optimize its properties to achieve the desired therapeutic effects while minimizing side effects and toxicity.

SAR studies are essential for refining and improving lead compounds identified during the screening process. They help researchers understand which parts of a molecule are critical for binding to the biological target, and which modifications can enhance or reduce activity. SAR is often used in combination with other techniques, such as **high-throughput screening (HTS)**, **virtual screening**, and **computer-aided drug design (CADD)**, to guide the optimization of drug candidates.

Key Concepts in SAR

1. **Functional Groups and Their Influence on Activity**: A key aspect of SAR is understanding how different **functional groups** in the molecule influence its activity. Functional groups are specific groups of atoms within a molecule that are responsible for the compound's chemical properties and reactivity. Modifications to these groups can significantly alter the compound's interaction with the biological target.

   - **Hydrophilic vs. Hydrophobic Groups**: The hydrophobicity or hydrophilicity of functional groups can influence how well the compound interacts with its target, as well as its solubility and bioavailability. Hydrophobic groups tend to interact with lipophilic regions of the target protein, while hydrophilic groups may help improve the compound's solubility in aqueous environments, enhancing absorption and distribution.
   - **Aromatic Rings and Hydrogen Bonding**: The presence of aromatic rings in the compound can influence its ability to interact with the target via π-π **stacking** interactions, which are important for binding to specific target proteins. Functional groups that can form **hydrogen bonds** with the target are also crucial in determining binding affinity and specificity.
   - **Electron-Donating and Electron-Withdrawing Groups**: Modifications to the molecule's electron density, such as adding **electron-donating** or **electron-withdrawing** groups, can affect the compound's reactivity and its ability to interact with the biological target. Electron-withdrawing groups, for instance, can reduce the basicity of the compound, while electron-donating groups may enhance its nucleophilicity.

2. **Conformational Flexibility and Binding**: The **three-dimensional (3D) shape** of a compound plays a critical role in determining its ability to bind to the target protein. The binding affinity of a compound depends not only on its size and charge but also on how well its shape complements the 3D structure of the binding site.

   - **Rigid vs. Flexible Compounds**: In SAR, it is important to study the conformational flexibility of a compound. Compounds that are too rigid may not fit well into the target's binding site, while compounds that are too flexible may lose selectivity or undergo unwanted interactions. The goal is to strike a balance by designing compounds with optimal flexibility, allowing them to bind effectively while maintaining specificity for the target.

3. **Optimization of Potency and Selectivity**: One of the primary goals of SAR is to improve a compound's **potency** (its ability to elicit a therapeutic effect at low concentrations) and **selectivity** (its ability to interact specifically with the intended target without affecting other biological pathways). By making small changes to the structure of the compound, researchers can fine-tune its binding affinity and improve its pharmacological properties.

   - **Potency Enhancement**: Potency can be optimized by modifying key functional groups to improve interactions with the target, such as increasing hydrogen bonding, optimizing electrostatic interactions, or enhancing lipophilicity to improve target binding.
   - **Selectivity**: Selectivity is important for ensuring that the drug interacts with its intended target without causing off-target effects. Modifying the compound to reduce binding to non-target proteins or receptors can help improve selectivity, thereby minimizing side effects and increasing the therapeutic window.

4. **Lipophilicity and Drug Absorption**: The **lipophilicity (fat solubility)** of a compound is a crucial factor that affects its ability to cross biological membranes and reach its target site. In SAR, optimizing lipophilicity is important for improving the absorption, distribution, and bioavailability of the drug.

   - **Log P (Partition Coefficient)**: The **log P** value is a measure of a compound's lipophilicity, representing the ratio of its concentration in a lipid (fat) phase to its concentration in an aqueous phase. A balanced log P value is desired: compounds that are too lipophilic may not dissolve well in the bloodstream, while those that are too hydrophilic may not pass through cell membranes effectively. SAR studies aim to modify the structure to achieve the optimal log P for improved absorption.

5. **Toxicity and Side Effect Reduction**: SAR is also used to minimize the **toxicity** and **side effects** of lead compounds. By carefully modifying the structure of a compound, researchers can reduce undesirable interactions with other proteins or pathways that may lead to toxicity.

   - **Metabolic Stability**: One aspect of toxicity relates to how quickly a drug is metabolized in the body. SAR can help design compounds that are more stable in the body, reducing the risk of toxic metabolites. This is often done by modifying functional groups that are involved in metabolic degradation pathways.
   - **Off-Target Interactions**: Another key goal of SAR is to reduce the potential for off-target interactions, which can cause unintended side effects. By optimizing selectivity for the target, SAR studies help reduce the likelihood of adverse reactions caused by interactions with other proteins or receptors.

SAR Tools and Techniques

To facilitate SAR studies, researchers use a variety of tools and techniques to systematically modify and analyze the chemical structure of compounds:

1. **Combinatorial Chemistry**: **Combinatorial chemistry** is a technique that allows researchers to rapidly generate large libraries of compounds with diverse chemical structures. These libraries are then screened for activity, and SAR analysis helps identify which structural features are most important for activity. Combinatorial libraries can be synthesized through automated methods, enabling high-throughput testing of many variants.
2. **Computer-Aided Drug Design (CADD)**: CADD is a powerful tool used in SAR to predict the interaction between compounds and their biological targets. Computational methods, such as **molecular docking, molecular dynamics simulations,** and **pharmacophore modeling,** are used to model the binding interactions and predict how modifications to the chemical structure might influence activity. CADD helps optimize drug candidates by providing insights into their binding affinity, selectivity, and pharmacokinetic properties.
3. **Structure-Based Design**: In **structure-based design,** the 3D structure of the target protein is used to design molecules that will bind effectively.

Techniques like **X-ray crystallography** and **NMR spectroscopy** are used to determine the high-resolution structure of the target, allowing for detailed modeling of potential drug candidates. This information guides SAR studies by showing how specific features of a molecule can be optimized to interact with the target.

4. **Parallel Synthesis: Parallel synthesis** is another technique used in SAR to generate multiple compounds simultaneously. This method allows researchers to create a diverse range of compounds based on variations of the lead structure and test their biological activity in parallel. This is a high-efficiency method for optimizing drug candidates and rapidly refining structure-activity relationships.

2.1.3 Preclinical Development: Laboratory Research and Animal Studies

Preclinical development is a crucial phase in the drug discovery process. It involves laboratory research and animal studies to evaluate the safety, efficacy, and pharmacokinetics of a drug candidate before it is tested in humans. Preclinical studies provide essential data to support the progression of a compound into clinical trials, ensuring that it is safe for human use and that it can reach the intended therapeutic target effectively.

Among the most important aspects of preclinical development is **toxicology studies,** which assess the potential toxic effects of a drug and identify any adverse reactions that might occur in living organisms. Toxicology studies help ensure that a drug candidate is safe and can be administered in appropriate doses without causing harm to patients.

2.1.3.1 Toxicology Studies

Toxicology studies are designed to evaluate the potential harmful effects of a drug candidate in both short-term and long-term exposure. These studies are conducted in laboratory settings using **in vitro** (cell culture) methods and **in vivo** (animal) models. The goal of toxicology studies is to identify any risks associated with the drug, including toxicity to organs, potential for carcinogenicity (cancer-causing effects), and effects on reproduction and development.

Toxicology studies are essential for understanding the safety profile of a drug, determining the maximum safe dose, and ensuring that the drug does not cause unacceptable harm when used by patients. These studies provide critical information required for regulatory approval and are typically a regulatory requirement before clinical trials can begin.

Key Objectives of Toxicology Studies

The primary objectives of **toxicology studies** are to:

- **Assess Acute Toxicity**: Acute toxicity studies aim to determine the harmful effects of a drug after a single or short-term exposure. These studies help establish the **lethal dose (LD50)**, which is the amount of the drug that causes death in 50% of the test subjects. Acute toxicity studies are important for identifying the immediate risks associated with drug administration.

- **Evaluate Chronic Toxicity**: Chronic toxicity studies are designed to assess the long-term effects of a drug when administered over extended periods (weeks, months, or even years). These studies are essential for identifying any toxic effects that might appear after prolonged exposure, including damage to vital organs, reproductive harm, or carcinogenic effects.

- **Identify Organ Toxicity**: Toxicology studies also focus on assessing whether the drug causes damage to specific organs, such as the liver, kidneys, heart, or lungs. Organ toxicity studies involve monitoring biochemical markers and histological changes in tissues to identify any adverse effects on organ function.

- **Assess Teratogenicity and Reproductive Toxicity**: Reproductive and developmental toxicity studies are critical to determine whether the drug has harmful effects on fertility, pregnancy, and fetal development. These studies typically involve testing the drug on pregnant animals to evaluate potential teratogenic (birth defect-causing) effects and the safety of the drug during pregnancy.

- **Investigate Genotoxicity and Carcinogenicity**: **Genotoxicity** studies examine whether a drug can cause genetic damage that might lead to mutations or cancer. **Carcinogenicity** studies evaluate whether long-term exposure to the drug increases the risk of cancer development. Both types of studies are crucial for ensuring that the drug does not cause genetic damage or promote tumor growth.

Types of Toxicology Studies

1. **Acute Toxicity Studies** Acute toxicity studies involve administering a single dose of the drug to laboratory animals and monitoring them for immediate adverse effects. These studies are typically performed using rodents (rats or mice) and other animal species. The primary purpose of acute toxicity studies is to determine the **LD50** or the maximum dose that can be given to an animal without causing death. Information gathered from acute toxicity studies helps determine the starting dose for human clinical trials and sets the stage for further safety evaluations.

   - **Single-Dose Testing**: A single dose of the drug is administered to animals, and their behavior, physical condition, and any signs of toxicity are closely monitored. The main focus is on determining the threshold dose above which toxicity or lethal effects are observed.
   - **Endpoints of Acute Toxicity**: The study includes monitoring for signs of organ failure, changes in body weight, and alterations in blood parameters such as liver enzymes or kidney function. Observations during the study help assess the safety margin for the drug.

2. **Subchronic and Chronic Toxicity Studies** These studies are conducted over a longer period (typically 30, 90, or 180 days) and involve repeated doses of the drug. They are designed to observe the effects of prolonged exposure to the drug on the health of the test subjects. The goal is to identify any adverse effects that may emerge after long-term administration, including organ damage, blood changes, and immune system dysfunction.

   - **Repeated-Dose Studies**: Animals are exposed to the drug daily or intermittently over a set period. Toxicological parameters such as organ weight, histopathology (tissue examination), and biochemical markers are evaluated to assess potential chronic effects.
   - **Long-Term Toxicity**: These studies are critical for assessing whether prolonged use of a drug can lead to cumulative toxicity, including cancer, neurotoxicity, or reproductive harm. The data from these studies help establish safe usage guidelines and dosage limits.

3. **Carcinogenicity Studies** Carcinogenicity studies are designed to evaluate whether a drug has the potential to cause cancer. These studies

typically involve administering the drug to animals (often rats or mice) over a significant portion of their lifespan, usually 18 to 24 months. The animals are observed for the development of tumors or other signs of cancer, and the results help identify any long-term cancer risks associated with the drug.

- **Long-Term Administration**: The drug is administered to animals over an extended period, and the animals are carefully monitored for the development of tumors, either at the site of administration or in other organs.
- **Histopathological Analysis**: Tissue samples from various organs are examined to identify the presence of cancerous cells or precancerous changes. The findings from these studies help determine whether the drug can be classified as carcinogenic.

4. **Genotoxicity StudiesGenotoxicity** refers to the ability of a compound to cause genetic damage, leading to mutations or chromosomal abnormalities. Genotoxicity studies involve testing the drug in **in vitro** (cell-based) and **in vivo** (animal) assays to assess its potential to cause genetic damage. The main tests used for genotoxicity include:

- **Ames Test**: A widely used **in vitro** assay to test for mutations in bacteria that could indicate potential mutagenic activity.
- **Micronucleus Test**: This **in vivo** test measures the formation of micronuclei in red blood cells, which is a marker of chromosomal damage.
- **Comet Assay**: This assay detects DNA strand breaks in cells and is used to assess genotoxicity at the genetic level.

5. **Reproductive and Developmental Toxicity Studies** These studies evaluate the effects of the drug on fertility, pregnancy, and fetal development. Reproductive toxicity studies typically involve administering the drug to male and female animals prior to mating to assess any impact on fertility. Developmental toxicity studies evaluate the drug's effects on embryos and fetuses when the drug is given during pregnancy.

- **Teratogenicity Studies**: In these studies, pregnant animals are administered the drug, and the effects on fetal development are observed. The primary goal is to identify any birth defects or malformations caused by the drug.
- **Fertility Studies**: These studies assess whether the drug affects the reproductive organs or impairs fertility. Fertility studies are crucial for determining whether the drug can be safely used in individuals who may wish to conceive.

6. **Safety Pharmacology Studies** Safety pharmacology studies focus on the potential effects of a drug on physiological systems that are not directly related to the intended therapeutic effect. These studies assess the drug's impact on **cardiovascular, respiratory**, and **central nervous systems** to identify any potential risks.

- **Cardiovascular Toxicity**: Studies examine the effects of the drug on heart rate, blood pressure, and electrocardiogram (ECG) readings. Drugs that affect the heart can cause arrhythmias or other serious side effects.
- **Neurotoxicity**: Studies assess whether the drug affects the nervous system, leading to symptoms such as sedation, convulsions, or behavioral changes.
- **Respiratory Toxicity**: These studies evaluate the drug's potential to cause respiratory depression or other breathing problems.

2.1.3.2 Pharmacokinetics and Pharmacodynamics

In preclinical development, understanding the **pharmacokinetics (PK)** and **pharmacodynamics (PD)** of a drug candidate is crucial for determining its potential efficacy, safety, and overall suitability for human use. These two disciplines are interrelated but focus on different aspects of how a drug behaves in the body. **Pharmacokinetics** deals with the movement of the drug through the body, including how it is absorbed, distributed, metabolized, and excreted. **Pharmacodynamics**, on the other hand, focuses on the effects of the drug on the body, including its mechanism of action, therapeutic effects, and potential side effects.

Both pharmacokinetics and pharmacodynamics play key roles in determining the optimal dose, dosage form, and treatment regimen for a drug. They also provide essential information for regulatory agencies to assess the drug's safety and efficacy before clinical trials.

Pharmacokinetics (PK)

Pharmacokinetics is the study of the absorption, distribution, metabolism, and excretion (ADME) of a drug. These processes determine the **concentration** of the drug in the bloodstream and tissues at any given time, which influences its therapeutic effect. Understanding pharmacokinetics is essential for designing appropriate dosing regimens that ensure the drug reaches its target at therapeutic levels without causing toxic effects.

1. Absorption

Absorption refers to the process by which a drug enters the bloodstream after it is administered. The rate and extent of absorption can be influenced by several factors, including the **route of administration**, **drug formulation**, and the **physicochemical properties** of the drug (e.g., solubility, permeability).

- **Oral Absorption**: Drugs administered orally must pass through the gastrointestinal (GI) tract, where they are absorbed into the bloodstream. The drug's bioavailability (the fraction of the administered dose that reaches systemic circulation) is influenced by factors such as the **first-pass effect**, which occurs when a drug is metabolized by the liver before reaching the bloodstream.
- **Parenteral Absorption**: Drugs administered through non-oral routes, such as intravenous (IV), subcutaneous (SC), or intramuscular (IM) injection, generally bypass the GI tract and are absorbed more rapidly into the bloodstream.

2. Distribution

Distribution refers to the process by which a drug is transported from the bloodstream to various tissues and organs throughout the body. The distribution of a drug depends on its **lipophilicity** (ability to dissolve in fat), **protein binding** (how much of the drug is bound to plasma proteins like albumin), and the **blood flow** to different tissues.

- **Volume of Distribution (Vd)**: The volume of distribution is a pharmacokinetic parameter that describes the extent to which a drug is distributed in the body. A high Vd suggests that the drug is widely distributed in tissues, while a low Vd indicates that the drug remains primarily in the bloodstream.
- **Tissue Penetration**: Some drugs may accumulate in certain tissues or organs, such as the liver, kidneys, or fat, depending on their chemical properties. For example, lipophilic drugs are more likely to accumulate in fatty tissues.

3. Metabolism

Metabolism is the process by which the body breaks down and converts drugs into metabolites. The liver is the primary site of drug metabolism, although other tissues such as the intestines and kidneys can also play a role. The purpose of metabolism is often to transform the drug into a more water-soluble form to facilitate its elimination from the body.

- **Phase I Reactions**: These are **oxidation, reduction, or hydrolysis** reactions that involve enzymes such as **cytochrome P450** (CYP450). These reactions often introduce or expose functional groups, making the drug more hydrophilic.
- **Phase II Reactions**: These involve **conjugation** reactions, where a drug or its metabolites are linked with endogenous molecules (e.g., glucuronic acid, sulfate, or glutathione) to form water-soluble compounds that are easier to excrete.

Some drugs are subject to **first-pass metabolism**, meaning they are significantly metabolized by the liver before reaching systemic circulation, thereby reducing their bioavailability.

4. Excretion

Excretion is the process by which the drug and its metabolites are eliminated from the body, primarily through the **kidneys** (urine), but also through other routes such as **feces, sweat,** or **breath.**

- **Renal Excretion**: Drugs that are eliminated through the kidneys may be filtered by the glomerulus, reabsorbed by renal tubules, or secreted by renal transporters. The rate of renal excretion is influenced by factors like **glomerular filtration rate (GFR)** and the **pH** of urine, which can affect the ionization of the drug.

- **Non-Renal Excretion**: Some drugs are excreted through other pathways, such as bile or the gastrointestinal tract, where they may undergo enterohepatic recycling. This can prolong the drug's half-life and delay its elimination.

Pharmacokinetic parameters such as **half-life (t1/2)**, **clearance (Cl)**, and **area under the curve (AUC)** provide valuable information about how long a drug stays in the body and how quickly it is eliminated.

Pharmacodynamics (PD)

Pharmacodynamics is the study of the effects of a drug on the body and the mechanisms by which it produces its therapeutic and adverse effects. It focuses on the relationship between the concentration of the drug at its site of action and the resulting biological effect.

1. Mechanism of Action

The **mechanism of action** refers to the specific molecular or cellular processes through which a drug exerts its effects. Drugs typically act by interacting with specific biological targets such as **enzymes**, **receptors**, or **ion channels**.

- **Receptor Binding**: Many drugs exert their effects by binding to specific receptors on the surface of cells, which can lead to changes in cellular signaling. Drugs can be agonists (activators) or antagonists (inhibitors) of the receptor's normal function.
- **Enzyme Inhibition or Activation**: Some drugs act by inhibiting or activating enzymes that catalyze biochemical reactions within the body. For example, **ACE inhibitors** block the enzyme angiotensin-converting enzyme, reducing blood pressure.
- **Ion Channel Modulation**: Drugs can also interact with ion channels to modify the flow of ions such as sodium, potassium, or calcium, which affects cellular activity and can be useful in treating conditions like arrhythmias or seizures.

2. Dose-Response Relationship

The **dose-response relationship** describes how the biological effect of a drug changes with varying doses. This relationship is typically represented by a **dose-response curve**, which plots the drug concentration (or dose) on the x-axis and the magnitude of the drug's effect on the y-axis.

- **Potency**: Potency refers to the amount of drug required to produce a certain effect. A drug with higher potency will produce the same effect at a lower dose.
- **Efficacy**: Efficacy refers to the maximum effect that a drug can produce, regardless of the dose. A drug with higher efficacy can produce a greater maximum effect.
- **Therapeutic Window**: The therapeutic window refers to the range of drug concentrations where the drug is effective without causing toxicity. It is the difference between the minimum effective dose and the minimum toxic dose.

3. Therapeutic Effects and Side Effects

Pharmacodynamics also involves the study of **therapeutic effects** and **side effects** of drugs. Therapeutic effects are the desired outcomes of drug treatment, such as pain relief, reduction in blood pressure, or tumor shrinkage. Side effects are unwanted or harmful effects that occur when a drug interacts with non-target molecules or tissues.

- **Adverse Effects**: Adverse effects are unintended harmful effects that occur at therapeutic doses. Understanding the pharmacodynamics of a drug helps identify potential side effects and informs risk management strategies in clinical practice.
- **Toxicity**: Toxicity occurs when the drug concentration exceeds the therapeutic range, leading to harmful effects. This can be prevented through proper dosing regimens and close monitoring of drug levels in the blood.

4. Drug-Drug Interactions

Drug-drug interactions can occur when two or more drugs are administered together, leading to altered effects. These interactions can influence the pharmacodynamics of the drugs involved, either enhancing or diminishing their therapeutic effects.

- **Additive Effects**: When two drugs with similar mechanisms of action are taken together, their effects can be additive, meaning the combined effect is the sum of the individual effects of each drug.
- **Synergistic Effects**: Some drug combinations produce a greater effect than the sum of their individual effects. This is known as synergy and is

often used in combination therapies, such as in cancer treatment or HIV therapy.

- **Antagonistic Effects**: In some cases, drugs may counteract each other's effects, leading to reduced efficacy.

2.1.3.3 Safety and Efficacy Testing in Animal Models

Safety and efficacy testing in animal models is a critical phase in preclinical drug development. This stage aims to assess both the **safety** and **therapeutic effectiveness** of a drug candidate before it is administered to humans in clinical trials. Animal studies are essential for providing detailed information on the pharmacological properties of a drug, including its toxicity, therapeutic potential, side effects, and overall risk-benefit profile.

While laboratory and in vitro studies are important for identifying the mechanism of action and preliminary safety data, **animal models** offer a more realistic simulation of how the drug behaves within a living organism. By using **animal models**, researchers can gather information on how a drug interacts with biological systems in a complex, multi-organ context, which is crucial for making decisions about whether a drug should proceed to human trials.

Key Objectives of Safety and Efficacy Testing in Animal Models

The primary objectives of **safety and efficacy testing in animal models** are to:

1. **Evaluate Toxicity**: Animal models are used to assess the potential toxic effects of the drug, including its impact on major organs such as the liver, kidneys, and heart. Toxicology studies in animals help identify any dose-dependent adverse effects that may not have been detected in earlier phases of drug discovery.
2. **Assess Therapeutic Effectiveness**: Testing in animal models allows researchers to evaluate how well a drug performs in treating the target disease. This includes assessing the drug's ability to reduce symptoms, improve physiological parameters, or slow disease progression.
3. **Determine the Therapeutic Window**: The **therapeutic window** is the range between the minimum effective dose and the minimum toxic dose. Testing in animal models helps determine the optimal dose range where the drug is effective without causing unacceptable side effects.

4. **Study Pharmacokinetics and Pharmacodynamics**: Animal studies provide valuable data on the **absorption**, **distribution**, **metabolism**, and **excretion (ADME)** of a drug, as well as its interaction with biological targets. This data is crucial for determining the appropriate dosage regimen for human trials.

5. **Monitor Long-Term Safety**: Animal models are used to observe the long-term effects of a drug on the body. This includes studies on carcinogenicity, reproductive toxicity, and other potential long-term adverse effects that may arise after prolonged use.

Types of Animal Models Used for Safety and Efficacy Testing

Animal models are selected based on the type of drug being tested and the disease it is intended to treat. These models can be broadly classified into **rodent models**, **non-rodent models**, and **disease-specific models**, each offering unique advantages for testing safety and efficacy.

1. Rodent Models

Rodents, particularly **mice** and **rats**, are the most commonly used animal models for preclinical safety and efficacy testing due to their genetic, biological, and behavioral similarities to humans. These animals are often used for initial safety testing, pharmacokinetic studies, and efficacy testing in a variety of diseases.

- **Mice**: Mice are widely used due to their small size, ease of breeding, and availability of genetically modified strains. They are particularly useful for testing genetic diseases, cancer, and neurological disorders. Additionally, mouse models are frequently used in pharmacokinetic studies due to their rapid metabolism and short lifespan.

- **Rats**: Rats are commonly used for studies involving toxicity and pharmacology, as they are larger than mice and easier to handle. They are often used to evaluate organ toxicity, reproductive toxicity, and long-term safety. Rats are also useful for testing cardiovascular and metabolic diseases.

2. Non-Rodent Models

Non-rodent models, such as **dogs**, **primates**, and **pigs**, are often used when rodent models do not accurately replicate human physiology. These animals are typically used for more advanced studies after initial safety and efficacy data has been obtained from rodents.

- **Dogs**: Dogs, especially **beagle dogs**, are commonly used in safety studies, particularly for assessing cardiovascular, gastrointestinal, and renal function. They are also used in pharmacokinetic studies due to their size and similarity to human anatomy in certain organ systems.
- **Primates**: Non-human primates, such as **cynomolgus monkeys** and **rhesus macaques**, are used in studies where close similarities to human physiology are required. They are particularly valuable for testing vaccines, drugs for neurological diseases, and biologics. However, their use is restricted due to ethical considerations and high costs.
- **Pigs**: Pigs are often used in pharmacokinetic and toxicology studies because of their anatomical and physiological similarities to humans, particularly in terms of cardiovascular and digestive systems. Pigs are also used in studies on metabolic diseases and surgical procedures.

3. Disease-Specific Models

Disease-specific animal models are designed to replicate specific human diseases and provide a more accurate representation of how a drug interacts with the disease process. These models are used to evaluate the therapeutic effectiveness of a drug and to identify any potential adverse effects in the context of the disease.

- **Cancer Models**: Animal models of cancer, such as xenograft models (where human cancer cells are implanted into immunocompromised animals), are used to evaluate the effectiveness of anti-cancer drugs. These models help researchers assess the drug's ability to inhibit tumor growth and reduce metastasis.
- **Neurological Models**: Animal models of neurological disorders, such as Alzheimer's disease or Parkinson's disease, are used to test drugs aimed at improving cognitive function, motor skills, or reducing neurodegeneration.
- **Cardiovascular Models**: Animal models with induced hypertension, atherosclerosis, or myocardial infarction (heart attack) are used to test drugs for cardiovascular diseases. These models help evaluate the efficacy of drugs in controlling blood pressure, improving heart function, or preventing stroke.
- **Diabetes Models**: Animal models of diabetes, such as **streptozotocin-induced** diabetic rats or genetically modified mice, are used to test drugs aimed at regulating blood sugar levels and managing diabetes-related

complications.

Design of Safety and Efficacy Studies

Safety and efficacy studies in animal models are designed to answer key questions about the drug's performance and its potential risks. The study design generally includes the following components:

1. **Dosing and Administration**: The dosing regimen is carefully designed to mimic human treatment protocols. It includes determining the appropriate dose, frequency of administration, and route of administration (oral, intravenous, subcutaneous, etc.). Animal studies often begin with low doses to evaluate safety and then escalate to higher doses to assess efficacy and toxicology.
2. **Endpoints**: Endpoints are specific measurements used to assess the drug's safety and efficacy. For **efficacy**, endpoints may include tumor size reduction, improvement in cognitive function, or the ability to lower blood pressure. For **safety**, endpoints include monitoring organ toxicity, adverse effects, changes in blood parameters, and mortality.
3. **Monitoring**: Animals in safety and efficacy studies are monitored closely for changes in behavior, physical condition, and health markers. Blood tests, histopathology, imaging, and other diagnostic tools are used to assess the effects of the drug on the body.
4. **Duration of Study**: The duration of safety and efficacy studies varies depending on the nature of the drug and the disease being studied. Acute toxicity studies may last from days to weeks, while chronic toxicity studies and long-term efficacy tests may last for several months or even years.

Ethical Considerations in Animal Testing

While animal testing is critical to drug development, it raises ethical concerns regarding the welfare of the animals involved. Regulatory guidelines, such as the 3Rs principle (Replacement, Reduction, and Refinement), emphasize the importance of minimizing animal use and ensuring humane treatment during research.

- **Replacement**: The use of alternative methods such as **in vitro** testing or computer simulations should be considered whenever possible.

- **Reduction**: Researchers are encouraged to use the smallest number of animals needed to achieve statistically significant results.
- **Refinement**: Animal welfare should be prioritized by refining procedures to minimize pain and distress, including the use of anesthesia and proper post-procedure care.

2.2.1 Overview of Drug Development Stages

The **drug development process** is a complex and rigorous series of steps that aim to bring a new pharmaceutical product from discovery to clinical use. It typically involves preclinical research, clinical trials, regulatory approval, and post-marketing surveillance. Each phase of the drug development process is carefully designed to assess different aspects of the drug's safety, efficacy, and potential risks.

The clinical trial phases are an essential part of the drug development process. They are conducted after preclinical studies in animals have demonstrated that a drug is safe to move forward. These phases are designed to progressively evaluate the drug in humans, beginning with small-scale studies and moving to larger trials as more information is gathered.

The stages of drug development are commonly divided into four key phases: **Phase I, Phase II, Phase III,** and **Phase IV.** Each of these phases has distinct goals, methodologies, and types of participants involved. In the early stages, the focus is primarily on ensuring safety and understanding pharmacokinetics, while later stages aim to confirm therapeutic efficacy, optimize dosing, and assess long-term effects.

2.2.1.1 Phase I: First-in-Human Trials

Phase I of clinical trials is the first time a drug is tested in humans. The primary goal of **Phase I trials** is to evaluate the **safety** and **pharmacokinetics** of the drug, including its **absorption, distribution, metabolism,** and **excretion (ADME)** in humans. These trials help determine the **maximum tolerated dose (MTD)** and identify any **adverse effects** that may occur at different dose levels.

Phase I trials typically involve a small number of healthy volunteers, although in some cases, patients with the disease the drug is intended to treat may be included. These studies are tightly controlled and closely monitored to assess the drug's effects on the human body.

Key Objectives of Phase I Trials

1. **Safety Assessment**: The primary objective of **Phase I trials** is to determine the safety of the drug. This includes identifying any **acute toxic effects**, side effects, or unintended reactions that might occur in humans. The study aims to establish the **safe dose range** and the **maximum tolerated dose (MTD)**, which is the highest dose that can be administered without causing significant adverse effects.

   - **Dose Escalation Studies**: Phase I trials often use a **dose escalation** approach, where the dose is gradually increased across different groups of participants. This helps identify the MTD and allows researchers to observe how the body reacts to increasing doses of the drug.
   - **Safety Monitoring**: Participants are closely monitored for any adverse reactions throughout the study. Regular blood tests, physical exams, and other diagnostic assessments are conducted to track the safety of the drug.

2. **Pharmacokinetics (PK)**: One of the key objectives of Phase I trials is to study the pharmacokinetics of the drug. Researchers examine how the drug is absorbed, distributed, metabolized, and excreted by the body. Pharmacokinetic studies provide critical information on the drug's **half-life**, **bioavailability**, and **clearance**, which help determine the appropriate dosing regimen.

   - **Absorption and Bioavailability**: The rate at which the drug is absorbed into the bloodstream and the fraction of the dose that reaches the systemic circulation are measured. This information helps determine the optimal route of administration (e.g., oral, intravenous) and dosage form.
   - **Metabolism and Excretion**: The pathways by which the drug is metabolized (primarily by the liver) and how it is excreted from the body (mainly through the kidneys or the liver) are studied. Understanding the drug's metabolism helps identify potential drug interactions and informs the development of dosing schedules.

- **Pharmacokinetic Profiles**: A pharmacokinetic profile is generated by sampling blood at various time points to track the concentration of the drug in the bloodstream over time. This data helps to determine the **peak plasma concentration (Cmax)**, **time to peak concentration (Tmax)**, and **area under the curve (AUC)**, which are important for understanding how the drug behaves in the body.

3. **Identification of Adverse Effects**: Phase I trials are also designed to identify any **adverse effects** that occur during drug administration. This may include **mild side effects** such as headache or nausea, as well as more severe adverse events. The goal is to identify the range of potential side effects that may occur at different doses and determine whether the drug is safe for further testing in larger patient populations.

   - **Common Side Effects**: Some common side effects observed in Phase I trials include gastrointestinal issues (nausea, vomiting), dizziness, headaches, or fatigue. In some cases, more serious reactions such as liver toxicity or allergic reactions may also be detected.
   - **Long-Term Safety Monitoring**: Although Phase I trials are typically short (lasting a few weeks), the drug's potential for long-term effects is also monitored, particularly in studies involving patients with chronic conditions.

4. **Determining Optimal Dosing and Administration Regimen**: Phase I trials are instrumental in determining the most effective **dosing schedule** and the optimal **route of administration**. The study provides crucial data on how frequently a drug should be administered (e.g., daily, weekly) and the appropriate dose range to achieve the desired therapeutic effect.

   - **Single vs. Multiple Doses**: In some Phase I trials, participants may receive a single dose of the drug, while in others, they may receive multiple doses over time to assess how the body handles repeated drug exposure.
   - **Formulation Studies**: Phase I trials may also involve testing different drug formulations (e.g., tablets, injections) to determine which formulation is most effective and well-tolerated.

5. **Exploratory Studies on Drug Effects**: While the primary goal of Phase I trials is to assess safety, some exploratory studies may also begin to evaluate the **therapeutic effects** of the drug. For example, early signs of efficacy may be observed in patients with specific conditions, especially if the drug is intended for a rare or serious disease. However, Phase I trials are not designed to fully assess efficacy—this is done in **Phase II** trials.

    ○ **Early Biomarker Studies**: In some cases, Phase I trials may include the collection of **biomarkers** or **clinical measurements** to explore how the drug might be affecting the disease process. However, these observations are typically exploratory and not conclusive.

Design and Structure of Phase I Trials

Phase I trials are carefully designed to ensure that the drug is tested in a controlled and ethical manner. The structure of these trials typically includes:

- **Participants**: Phase I trials usually involve a small number of healthy volunteers (typically 20-100) who are closely monitored throughout the study. In some cases, patients with the disease being targeted may also be included if the drug is intended for a specific therapeutic condition.
- **Randomized, Placebo-Controlled Design**: Many Phase I trials are randomized and placebo-controlled, meaning that participants are randomly assigned to receive either the drug or a placebo (inactive substance). This helps to minimize bias and ensures that any observed effects are due to the drug itself.
- **Blinded Studies**: In some trials, the participants may be blinded to the treatment they receive, meaning they do not know whether they are receiving the active drug or the placebo. This helps reduce bias in reporting side effects and treatment responses.
- **Monitoring and Safety Protocols**: Participants are monitored continuously for any adverse reactions, with frequent assessments of vital signs, laboratory tests, and other diagnostic measures. In the case of severe side effects, participants may be withdrawn from the study.

Phase III: Confirmatory Trials

Phase III clinical trials, often called *confirmatory trials*, are the pivotal studies conducted after a drug has shown promise in earlier phases. These trials are designed to conclusively demonstrate the drug's efficacy for a specific indication and to gather comprehensive safety data in a large patient population. By the end of Phase III, the aim is to confirm that the drug provides a meaningful therapeutic benefit to patients and that its benefits outweigh the risks. Successful Phase III trials provide the *substantial evidence of effectiveness* required by regulators and generate the bulk of information needed for the product's labeling and package insert . In drug development, Phase III is typically the final stage before seeking regulatory approval, making these trials critical in deciding whether a new drug can enter the market.

Purpose of Phase III Trials

The primary purpose of Phase III trials is to confirm the findings of earlier phases by rigorously testing the drug in a larger, more definitive trial. In Phase II, a drug may have shown a hint of efficacy in a limited patient group, but Phase III must *confirm* these benefits in a broader population with robust statistical significance. These trials are intended to demonstrate that the drug is effective for its intended use and to establish its clinical value. For example, if a new antihypertensive medication lowered blood pressure in Phase II, the Phase III trial would confirm the extent of blood pressure reduction and assess whether this translates into fewer cardiovascular events compared to a control group. Phase III trials also provide extensive data on safety and adverse effects. Because they involve many more patients and longer treatment durations, they can reveal less common side effects or long-term risks that earlier trials could not detect . In summary, Phase III trials solidify the drug's risk-benefit profile: they verify therapeutic efficacy in the target population, characterize common and rare adverse reactions, and refine the optimal dosage and usage guidelines. This confirmed evidence is what regulators rely on when evaluating a drug for approval.

Study Population

Phase III trials typically involve a much larger and more diverse patient population than earlier phases. While Phase I and II studies might have tens or hundreds of participants with strict inclusion criteria, Phase III often enrolls *hundreds to thousands* of patients (commonly in the range of 300 to 3,000 or more) who have the disease or condition of interest . These participants are usually from multiple centers (and often multiple countries), reflecting the demographic and clinical diversity of the real-world patient population. The eligibility criteria in Phase III are broadened to include various subgroups of patients – for instance, patients of different ages, both sexes, and those with common co-morbidities (such as diabetes or mild kidney impairment) are included to better represent those who will use the drug if it is approved. By including patients with co-morbid conditions or concomitant medications, the trial can assess how the drug performs in typical use scenarios and ensure that efficacy and safety findings are generalizable. Enrolling a large population also increases the chance of detecting rarer adverse events. Phase III participants are always patients with the target condition (healthy volunteers are not used at this stage), since the goal is to confirm therapeutic efficacy in the people who stand to benefit from the treatment. The multi-center nature of Phase III trials not only expedites enrollment of large numbers but also ensures that results are applicable across different settings and populations. This diversity is particularly important for regulatory acceptance, as agencies expect that the drug has been tested in a population that reflects future users, including representation from different geographic regions and ethnic backgrounds when relevant.

Trial Design

Phase III trials are typically designed as rigorous randomized controlled trials (RCTs) to provide high-quality evidence. A common design is a **randomised, parallel-group** trial in which patients are randomly assigned to either the investigational drug or a comparator group. The comparator may be a placebo or the current standard of care, and in many cases multiple arms are included (for example, comparing the new drug to both placebo and an existing drug). Randomization in Phase III is crucial to minimize bias – it ensures that patient characteristics are evenly distributed across treatment groups, so that observed differences in outcomes can be attributed to the drug. Blinding is also typically employed: most Phase III trials are **double-blind**, meaning neither the participants nor the investigators know who is receiving the experimental drug versus the control. Blinding further reduces bias in outcome assessment, especially for endpoints that require subjective evaluation. As a result of these measures, Phase III trials are considered the gold standard for demonstrating a drug's efficacy.

Most Phase III trials are multicentre studies, sometimes conducted across dozens or even hundreds of hospitals and clinics. This multicenter approach increases the robustness of the findings by showing that the drug's effects are not limited to a single research setting. It also facilitates enrolling large numbers of patients within a reasonable timeframe. The trials often last for years, with patients being treated and observed for a sufficient duration to assess both short-term and long-term effects (Phase III studies commonly run for **1 to 4 years** in duration). The design must account for this longer timeframe; protocols typically include scheduled interim analyses or checkpoints to review accumulating data.

In some cases, Phase III trial designs can be complex or innovative. For instance, **factorial designs** might be used if two interventions are tested simultaneously, or **adaptive designs** may be employed to modify certain aspects of the trial in predefined ways based on interim results. Adaptive Phase III designs must be carefully planned to maintain statistical validity, but they can allow modifications like early stopping for success or futility, dose adjustments, or changes in sample size based on interim findings. However, even with adaptive elements, Phase III trials remain confirmatory in intent – any adaptations are usually pre-specified and guided by strict rules to ensure the integrity of the confirmation process. Overall, the trial design in Phase III is focused on being *adequate and well-controlled*, a regulatory standard indicating that the study is capable of providing reliable evidence of effectiveness and safety. This means clear definition of control groups, rigorous methodology, and adherence to Good Clinical Practice standards in conduct.

Endpoints

The endpoints in Phase III trials are carefully selected to demonstrate clinically meaningful benefits of the drug. A **primary endpoint** is defined in advance – this is the main outcome by which the treatment's success will be judged. The primary endpoint is often a direct measure of clinical benefit, such as survival time, disease cure rate, incidence of a specific complication, or improvement in symptoms or quality of life. For example, in a Phase III trial of a new cancer drug, the primary endpoint might be overall survival (the length of time patients live following treatment) or progression-free survival. In a trial for a pain medication, the primary endpoint could be the reduction in pain severity on a standardized scale. These endpoints are usually the ones that will appear in the drug's labeling if approved, so they must reflect outcomes that are important to patients and physicians.Regulatory authorities generally insist that Phase III trials use endpoints that demonstrate a tangible clinical benefit to patients, or a validated surrogate that strongly predicts benefit.

In addition to the primary endpoint, Phase III studies include **secondary endpoints** to capture other relevant effects of the drug. Secondary endpoints might include additional efficacy measures (for instance, in a diabetes trial, if the primary endpoint is reduction in HbA1c level, secondary endpoints could be changes in fasting blood glucose, body weight, or incidence of diabetic complications). They also often include health-related quality of life measures and detailed safety outcomes. All endpoints – primary and secondary – should be defined *before* the trial starts (prospectively in the protocol) to avoid any bias in data analysis. In confirmatory trials, **endpoint definitions** are very precise: the protocol will specify exactly how each outcome is measured and at what time points. For instance, if the endpoint is "response rate," the criteria for response (such as a particular percentage improvement in a symptom score or a lab value) are explicitly laid out. This precision ensures that there is no ambiguity when it comes time to analyze the results.

Phase III trials often use endpoints that are accepted by the medical community and regulators as evidence of benefit. Sometimes a **composite endpoint** is used, especially in cardiovascular trials – for example, a composite of "major adverse cardiac events" might combine heart attack, stroke, or cardiovascular death into one endpoint. Composite endpoints can increase the efficiency of a trial by capturing overall benefit, but they require careful interpretation (each component should be clinically important on its own). In other cases, a **surrogate endpoint** may be employed if it can be measured sooner or more conveniently than a true clinical outcome – for example, viral load reduction in HIV as a surrogate for delaying AIDS progression. However, reliance on surrogates in Phase III is usually limited to situations where the surrogate is well-validated, or in trials seeking accelerated approval with the understanding that further studies will confirm actual clinical benefit.

Overall, the choice of endpoints in Phase III is driven by the need to provide unmistakable evidence that the drug meaningfully helps patients. The success of a Phase III trial – and therefore the chances of drug approval – hinges on whether the drug can meet its primary endpoint with statistical significance, demonstrating a clear advantage over placebo or existing therapy in terms of these predefined outcomes.

Statistical Considerations

Phase III trials are statistically powered to detect a predefined difference between the treatment and control with high confidence. Because these trials are confirmatory, the statistical analysis is planned in detail before the study begins and is laid out in a Statistical Analysis Plan (SAP). A key consideration is **sample size**: researchers calculate the number of participants needed in each group to have adequate power (usually 80% to 90%) to detect a clinically meaningful difference in the primary endpoint at a conventional level of statistical significance (often $\alpha = 0.05$, two-tailed) . This calculation depends on factors like the expected effect size of the drug, the variability of the endpoint measure, and the desired power. The result is that Phase III trials often require large sample sizes – hence the enrollment of hundreds or thousands of patients – to ensure that even moderate treatment effects can be detected reliably. For example, if a new drug is anticipated to improve a cure rate from 50% to 60%, the trial must recruit enough patients so that this 10% absolute improvement would be statistically significant and not likely due to chance. This rigor contrasts with earlier phase trials, which might tolerate a higher chance of statistical error due to their exploratory nature.

Another critical statistical aspect is **randomization and analysis populations**. Phase III trials typically use an *intention-to-treat (ITT)* approach for the primary analysis, meaning all participants are analyzed in the groups to which they were randomized, regardless of whether they completed the treatment as per protocol. This approach preserves the benefits of randomization by avoiding biases that could be introduced by post-randomization exclusions. The analysis will also consider per-protocol or safety populations, but the ITT analysis is key for efficacy conclusions in confirmatory trials. Moreover, statistical analyses in Phase III must account for **multiplicity** if there are multiple endpoints or interim looks at the data. If a trial has several secondary endpoints or plans multiple interim analyses, adjustments (such as Bonferroni corrections or group sequential design methods) are implemented to control the overall Type I error rate (the chance of a false positive finding). For instance, in an interim analysis setting, the trial might use a **group-sequential design** with predefined stopping boundaries: very strict criteria (like a higher significance threshold) would be required to stop early for efficacy to ensure that the final overall $\alpha=0.05$ is maintained across interim and final analyses.

Blinding and randomization are supported by statistical procedures as well – e.g. generation of random allocation sequences and keeping the code sealed until formal unblinding. The trial data are usually analyzed by biostatisticians who remain blinded until the database is locked to prevent any bias in handling of data. Phase III trials also often pre-specify how to handle *missing data* (through imputation methods or conservative assumptions) so that the conclusions remain robust even if some patients drop out or have incomplete observations over the long trial period. In essence, the statistical framework of Phase III is governed by ICH E9 guidelines on statistical principles: the trial is hypothesis-driven (testing a clear primary hypothesis), controlled for error rates, and analyzed according to a pre-set plan to provide reliable confirmatory evidence. Regulators scrutinize the statistical methods closely – an approvable Phase III trial must demonstrate a statistically significant and clinically relevant effect on the primary endpoint, and this result should be reproducible and not due to chance or flawed analysis techniques.

Safety Monitoring

Safety monitoring in Phase III trials is conducted with the highest level of vigilance, given the larger number of patients and longer exposure period. Each trial has a detailed safety monitoring plan as part of its protocol. This includes routine collection of adverse event data at all patient visits, regular laboratory tests (such as blood counts, liver and kidney function tests), vital sign checks, and other examinations to detect any emerging safety issues. All adverse events observed during the trial, whether or not they are suspected to be related to the drug, are documented and categorized. Particular attention is given to **serious adverse events (SAEs)** – events that are life-threatening, require hospitalization, or result in significant disability – which must be reported immediately to the trial sponsor and ethics committees. The sponsor, in turn, has regulatory obligations (for example, in the US, filing expedited safety reports to the FDA for serious and unexpected adverse reactions). This ensures that regulators remain informed of any potential safety signals even before the trial is completed.

Given the scale of Phase III trials, sponsors typically employ an independent **Data Monitoring Committee (DMC)** (also known as a Data and Safety Monitoring Board, DSMB) to oversee patient safety and periodically review efficacy data. A DMC is an independent panel of experts (such as physicians, biostatisticians, and ethicists) who are not otherwise involved in the trial's conduct. The DMC looks at unblinded data at pre-specified intervals. Their role is to ensure that participants are not exposed to undue risk: they may recommend pausing or stopping the trial early if there is clear evidence of harm (for instance, a higher rate of serious side effects in the drug group) or if the drug is overwhelmingly effective (making it unethical to withhold it from the control group). They might also stop the trial for futility if interim results suggest the drug is very unlikely to show benefit by the end. The use of a DMC is especially important in Phase III because these trials last long and involve many sites – centralized monitoring by a dedicated committee helps maintain patient safety across the board. As the ICH guidelines note, a DMC monitors accumulating data and can decide on continuing or modifying the study for safety reasons.

Throughout the trial, all investigators are trained to follow Good Clinical Practice (GCP) in reporting safety information. There are defined **stopping rules** or withdrawal criteria for individual patients as well: if a participant experiences certain predefined serious side effects or lab abnormalities, the protocol may require that the participant discontinue the study drug for their safety. Furthermore, Phase III trials often include follow-up periods to monitor whether any adverse effects emerge after stopping the treatment (for example, monitoring for withdrawal effects or any delayed toxicity). Because Phase III trials often extend over years, sponsors are required to submit periodic safety updates to regulatory authorities (such as annual Development Safety Update Reports) summarizing all safety data collected to date.

One of the important outcomes of Phase III is a well-characterized safety profile of the drug. With a larger sample size, researchers can calculate the incidence of common side effects (e.g. if 15% of patients experience nausea on the drug vs 5% on placebo) and also identify less common adverse reactions that might occur in, say, 0.5–1% of patients. For instance, if a rare but serious side effect occurs in 1 out of 500 patients, a Phase III trial with 3,000 patients has a reasonable chance of detecting it at least a few times, whereas Phase II with maybe 100 patients would likely miss it. Detection of such rare events is critical for assessing if any particular monitoring or risk mitigation strategies will be needed when the drug is marketed. All this safety information is collected and will later appear in the drug's prescribing information (package insert) under sections for adverse reactions, warnings, and precautions. In summary, safety monitoring in Phase III is proactive and comprehensive – it protects the participants during the trial and ensures that by the trial's end, the safety risks of the drug are well understood and documented.

Regulatory Relevance

Phase III trial results are the cornerstone of the regulatory approval process for new drugs. Regulatory agencies such as the U.S. Food and Drug Administration (FDA), the European Medicines Agency (EMA), and others around the world require evidence from Phase III (or equivalent *confirmatory* trials) to decide whether a drug can be approved for marketing. In fact, Phase III trials are often referred to as **"pivotal trials"** in regulatory language, because they provide the pivotal evidence of efficacy and safety. A drug sponsor typically must successfully complete one or more Phase III trials before submitting a **New Drug Application (NDA)** to the FDA or a **Marketing Authorisation Application (MAA)** to the EMA. These applications include comprehensive data from the Phase III studies – the design, methods, efficacy outcomes, safety findings, and statistical analyses – along with all other preclinical and clinical data. Regulators examine this information in detail to verify that the trials were well-conducted and that the results truly demonstrate the drug's benefits and risks.

Regulatory guidelines (such as **ICH Efficacy guidelines**) emphasize that confirmatory trials should be adequate and well-controlled. This means that the trials must use appropriate control groups, randomization, and blinding, and must measure meaningful endpoints. When reviewing an NDA, the FDA looks for "substantial evidence of effectiveness," which historically has meant evidence from at least two independent Phase III trials showing statistically significant benefit. This convention ensures that findings are reproducible and not due to chance. However, there are situations where a single, large Phase III trial might be sufficient – for example, if the effect size is dramatic or if ethical/practical reasons make a second trial difficult – but in such cases the single trial's results must be especially persuasive and often supported by additional evidence. For instance, a single Phase III trial might suffice if it shows a very clear survival benefit in a life-threatening disease with no existing therapy, combined with supportive data from Phase II or other studies. In general, though, sponsors often conduct at least two Phase III studies for most indications, or one Phase III alongside other confirmatory evidence.

The outcomes of Phase III directly shape the product label. Regulators will consider the population studied in Phase III when deciding on the approved *indication* (the medical condition and patient groups for which the drug can be marketed). If a trial only included adults, the label might be initially limited to adults. The dosing recommendations in the package insert come from what was tested in Phase III, and any needs for dose adjustments in subgroups (like patients with kidney impairment) might be informed by Phase III data or dedicated sub-studies. The efficacy findings reported in the label (for example, "Drug X reduced the risk of hospitalization by 30% in trial results") are drawn from the Phase III primary endpoint results. Likewise, the list of common adverse reactions in the label is usually compiled from the pooled safety data of the Phase III trials.

Phase III trials also hold regulatory importance beyond initial approval. If the results are not adequate – say, the trials fail to meet endpoints or uncover serious safety problems – regulators may refuse approval or ask for additional studies. Sometimes, regulators grant a *conditional approval* or *accelerated approval* based on Phase II data or surrogate endpoints, but they will still require confirmatory Phase III trials to be completed post-approval to verify the clinical benefit. Thus, Phase III can occur both before approval and as a **post-marketing commitment** in special cases (though by definition, post-approval studies are often termed Phase IV). For the vast majority of drugs, however, Phase III is completed prior to approval and is the linchpin of the approval decision.

Phase II: Therapeutic Exploratory Trials

Phase II clinical trials, known as therapeutic exploratory trials, are conducted following successful completion of Phase I trials. While Phase I primarily focuses on determining drug safety and optimal dosage in healthy volunteers or a limited number of patients, Phase II trials explore the therapeutic effectiveness of the drug candidate in patients who suffer from the targeted disease or condition. The key objective of Phase II trials is to provide initial evidence regarding the drug's efficacy, evaluate its safety profile more extensively, and establish optimal dosing regimens to be used in larger Phase III trials. The data obtained from these trials determine whether the drug is sufficiently promising to justify progression to confirmatory Phase III studies.

Objectives of Phase II Trials

The primary aim of Phase II trials is to evaluate whether a drug shows promising efficacy in patients. The effectiveness assessed in Phase II provides the first definitive indication of the drug's therapeutic potential. The trials also significantly expand knowledge of the drug's safety profile beyond what was established in Phase I. They help identify common adverse effects, enabling a comprehensive understanding of potential risks associated with the drug. Another critical objective of Phase II trials is to refine dosing regimens by determining the optimal therapeutic dose and administration frequency. This optimization helps ensure that Phase III trials, which require large numbers of patients and substantial investment, are conducted using the most appropriate and effective dose.

Phase II studies often involve exploring dose-response relationships to determine how efficacy and adverse effects vary with different dosages. This provides essential data to guide the selection of the most effective and safest dose for Phase III trials. These studies may also investigate specific patient subgroups to evaluate variations in response among different patient populations, such as older patients, those with impaired organ function, or those receiving concomitant medications. Thus, Phase II plays a pivotal role in guiding the strategic decisions that shape subsequent confirmatory trials.

Study Population

Phase II trials typically involve a relatively small number of patients, ranging from approximately 50 to 300 participants, who have the disease or condition the drug is intended to treat. Unlike Phase I, which primarily involves healthy volunteers, Phase II trials specifically recruit patients diagnosed with the target condition. This population is selected to evaluate preliminary therapeutic efficacy and safety accurately.

The eligibility criteria used in Phase II trials are often strict, defining a relatively homogeneous patient group. This homogeneity reduces variability and allows clearer assessment of the drug's therapeutic effects and side effects. For example, in a Phase II trial for a new diabetes medication, participants might include patients with type 2 diabetes who have HbA1c values within a specified range, excluding those with severe comorbidities or complications. Such carefully defined patient populations ensure that the observed therapeutic benefits or side effects can be attributed more reliably to the investigational drug itself.

Trial Design

Phase II trials typically adopt randomized controlled trial designs, often employing parallel-group comparisons. Patients are randomly assigned to receive either the investigational drug, a placebo, or sometimes an active comparator (an established treatment). Randomization minimizes bias by evenly distributing known and unknown confounding factors between treatment groups. The majority of Phase II studies employ double-blind methodologies, where neither the patients nor the investigators are aware of the treatment assignment. Blinding helps reduce bias in reporting patient responses, particularly subjective outcomes such as pain relief or symptom severity.

The duration of Phase II trials varies depending on the disease, drug characteristics, and therapeutic outcomes being studied. Trials might range from a few weeks for acute conditions, such as infections, to several months for chronic conditions, such as arthritis or hypertension. The trial protocol clearly defines inclusion and exclusion criteria, treatment regimens, monitoring schedules, and outcome measurements. Interim analyses may also be incorporated into the design to allow early assessment of safety or efficacy signals.

Endpoints and Outcome Measures

Phase II trials primarily use efficacy endpoints that are relevant to the specific disease condition. These endpoints should provide clear evidence of therapeutic benefit. Common endpoints include disease-specific biomarkers, symptom improvement scales, or clinical outcome measures. For example, in oncology trials, endpoints might include tumor shrinkage rates or progression-free survival. In trials of antihypertensive drugs, endpoints commonly involve reductions in blood pressure.

Endpoints chosen for Phase II studies must be clinically meaningful, yet feasible to measure within the shorter duration typical of these trials. Secondary endpoints often include pharmacokinetic parameters, drug safety profiles, and patient-reported outcomes such as quality-of-life improvements or symptom relief. Clear, predefined criteria for these endpoints help ensure objectivity and consistency in data collection and interpretation.

Dose-Finding and Dose-Response Relationship

A distinctive feature of Phase II trials is the exploration of dose-response relationships. Trials often involve multiple dosage groups to determine the optimal balance between therapeutic benefit and adverse effects. By comparing different dosages, researchers can identify a dose range that provides the best combination of efficacy, safety, and tolerability. For example, in a Phase II trial of an analgesic medication, researchers may evaluate low, medium, and high doses of the drug against placebo to identify which dose provides sufficient pain relief with minimal side effects.

Dose-ranging studies conducted in Phase II are critical for accurately defining the dosing regimen to be used in Phase III trials. They inform dosage selection and help mitigate risks associated with overdosing or underdosing in larger patient populations.

Safety Evaluation

Safety monitoring in Phase II trials is more extensive than in Phase I, given the larger number of patients exposed and longer treatment durations. Adverse events, changes in laboratory values, vital signs, and ECG parameters are rigorously documented throughout the trial. Particular attention is given to identifying adverse reactions that were either not evident or insufficiently characterized during Phase I.

The trial protocol defines clear stopping rules or dose adjustments in response to observed toxicity or side effects. Serious adverse events are closely monitored, reported promptly to regulatory authorities, and thoroughly evaluated to determine their relationship to the investigational drug. Safety findings from Phase II significantly inform the risk assessment and planning of subsequent Phase III trials.

Statistical Considerations

Phase II trials must be adequately powered to detect preliminary evidence of efficacy. Although smaller in scale compared to Phase III, these trials require rigorous statistical designs to ensure reliable results. Statistical methods include clear definitions of analysis populations (e.g., intention-to-treat populations), pre-specified endpoints, and appropriate methods for handling missing data.

Sample size calculations for Phase II trials are usually based on anticipated effect sizes derived from earlier studies or clinical knowledge. Typically, these studies are powered to detect moderate treatment effects (e.g., 20-30% improvement) with statistical significance. Confidence intervals, statistical tests, and analyses to control Type I error rates are applied to ensure robust conclusions.

Regulatory and Strategic Importance

Results from Phase II trials are critically important for regulatory decisions and strategic planning. Positive Phase II findings demonstrating promising efficacy and manageable safety profiles support the decision to proceed with costly and extensive Phase III trials. Conversely, negative results or identification of significant safety concerns may lead to termination of the development program at this stage, avoiding unnecessary investment in Phase III.

Regulatory authorities review Phase II trial results to assess whether the investigational drug shows sufficient therapeutic promise and acceptable safety to justify advancement. Regulators also examine Phase II data to ensure appropriate selection of dosage and patient populations for Phase III studies. Consequently, robust and reliable Phase II data are pivotal in shaping successful drug development strategies.

Phase II trials also significantly influence commercial strategy. Positive results can attract investment and partnership opportunities, while negative outcomes may necessitate re-evaluation or repositioning of the drug candidate. Thus, Phase II trials play a critical role in determining the drug's future developmental trajectory.

Phase III: Confirmatory Trials

Phase III clinical trials are the final step in the drug development process before a new pharmaceutical product is submitted for regulatory approval. These trials play a pivotal role in confirming the safety and efficacy of a drug in a larger, more diverse population of patients, and they serve as the foundation for the regulatory submission that allows the drug to be marketed. In essence, Phase III trials confirm the therapeutic benefits observed in earlier phases and demonstrate that the drug provides a clinically meaningful benefit in real-world patient populations.

The primary purpose of Phase III trials is to establish that the investigational drug is not only effective but also safe when used over extended periods and in a broader range of patients. The results from these trials are critical to regulatory authorities such as the U.S. Food and Drug Administration (FDA), the European Medicines Agency (EMA), and other global agencies, who rely on this data to determine whether a drug should be approved for public use.

Purpose of Phase III Trials

Phase III trials aim to provide definitive evidence about a drug's efficacy and safety, typically involving larger patient populations across multiple clinical sites. The objectives include:

1. **Confirming Efficacy:** Phase III trials confirm that the investigational drug produces the desired therapeutic effect in a broader patient

population. These trials typically compare the new drug to either a placebo or an existing standard treatment (e.g., a commonly used drug for the same condition). Demonstrating that the new drug performs better than placebo or provides superior benefits compared to existing treatments is critical for regulatory approval.

2. **Establishing Long-Term Safety**: Phase III trials are designed to assess the safety of a drug over a more extended treatment period than earlier phases. This includes monitoring for adverse events that may not have been apparent in smaller Phase I or Phase II studies, as the larger patient population and longer trial duration allow for the detection of rare or delayed adverse effects.

3. **Identifying Optimal Dosage**: These trials refine the optimal dosage regimen that maximizes efficacy while minimizing adverse effects. Phase III often involves testing different doses of the drug to determine which one is most effective and safest for patients.

4. **Providing Regulatory Support**: Data from Phase III trials form the primary evidence for regulatory submissions. If these trials demonstrate that the drug is both effective and safe, they provide the evidence necessary for regulatory bodies to approve the drug for general use.

Study Population

Phase III trials typically involve a larger patient population than earlier-phase trials, often ranging from several hundred to several thousand participants. This larger sample size increases the likelihood that the study will yield statistically significant results and helps identify less common adverse events. The study population in Phase III trials is carefully selected to reflect the broad range of individuals who are expected to use the drug once it is on the market.

Inclusion criteria for Phase III trials generally focus on patients who have the target disease or condition, and the trials may also include individuals with co-morbidities that are commonly seen in the target population. This diversity in patient demographics is important for ensuring that the drug's efficacy and safety are applicable to a broad range of real-world patients. Conversely, exclusion criteria are designed to eliminate patients who may be at higher risk of adverse events or whose conditions could confound the study results (e.g., patients with severe liver dysfunction or a history of certain cancers, depending on the drug being tested).

Trial Design

Phase III trials are typically designed as **randomized controlled trials (RCTs)**, which are the gold standard in clinical research due to their ability to minimize bias. In these trials, patients are randomly assigned to one of the treatment groups: the investigational drug, a placebo, or an active comparator (usually the current standard of care). Randomization ensures that patient characteristics (e.g., age, sex, disease severity) are evenly distributed across groups, reducing the likelihood of confounding factors influencing the results.

Blinding is another key feature of Phase III trials. In most cases, Phase III trials are **double-blinded**, meaning that neither the patients nor the investigators know who is receiving the investigational drug and who is receiving the comparator treatment. This reduces the risk of bias in patient reporting, outcome assessment, and data interpretation.

Some Phase III trials are conducted as **multicenter studies**, which involve multiple clinical sites across different regions or countries. This approach is used to increase the diversity of the study population, improve enrollment, and make the results more generalizable. Multicenter trials also provide a more realistic assessment of the drug's performance in a range of healthcare settings, from academic hospitals to private clinics.

The length of Phase III trials varies depending on the disease being treated, the endpoints being assessed, and the treatment regimen. Some trials may last a few months, while others for chronic diseases (e.g., cancer, diabetes, cardiovascular diseases) may extend for several years. These longer durations allow for the observation of long-term treatment effects and the development of safety data over time.

Endpoints and Outcome Measures

The **primary endpoint** of a Phase III trial is the main outcome measure used to evaluate the drug's efficacy. This is usually a direct measure of clinical benefit, such as improvement in symptoms, disease progression, or overall survival. For instance, in a Phase III trial for a cancer drug, the primary endpoint might be **overall survival** (the length of time patients survive after receiving treatment) or **progression-free survival** (the length of time patients live without their disease worsening). In trials for chronic diseases, primary endpoints may include **reduction in disease symptoms** (such as pain, fatigue, or blood glucose levels), improvement in **quality of life**, or prevention of disease-related complications.

Secondary endpoints in Phase III trials provide additional information about the drug's effects. These might include other measures of clinical benefit, such as **symptom relief, biomarker changes**, or **health-related quality of life scores**. Secondary endpoints often help further characterize the drug's therapeutic benefits and provide supplementary data for regulatory agencies.

Statistical Considerations

One of the most critical aspects of Phase III trials is ensuring the trial is powered to detect meaningful differences between the treatment and control groups. The **sample size** calculation is based on the expected treatment effect, the variability in the primary endpoint, and the desired statistical power (typically 80% or 90%). For example, if the primary endpoint is survival time, the sample size will be large enough to detect a statistically significant difference in survival rates between the drug and placebo or comparator.

The trial's statistical analysis plan specifies the methods used to analyze the data and how missing data will be handled. **Intention-to-treat (ITT)** analysis is typically employed, meaning all patients who are randomized to a treatment group are included in the analysis, regardless of whether they completed the study or adhered to the treatment protocol. ITT analysis helps preserve the benefits of randomization and provides a more conservative estimate of treatment efficacy.

In some Phase III trials, an interim analysis may be conducted to assess the results after a certain number of patients have been enrolled or after a predefined period. Interim analyses allow the trial to be stopped early if it is clear that the drug is either overwhelmingly effective or causing significant harm, helping to protect patient safety and minimize unnecessary exposure to a potentially ineffective treatment.

Safety Monitoring

Given the larger number of patients involved in Phase III trials, safety monitoring becomes more crucial. The **Data Monitoring Committee (DMC)**, an independent group of experts, periodically reviews the safety data from the trial to ensure that participants are not exposed to undue risk. If the DMC detects significant safety concerns, they can recommend stopping the trial, modifying the protocol, or adjusting the dose.

Safety monitoring includes regular collection of **adverse event (AE)** data, vital signs, laboratory results, and any other relevant health measures. The safety data collected in Phase III trials is used to assess the overall **risk-benefit profile** of the drug. Regulatory agencies often require sponsors to provide **safety reports** throughout the trial to keep them updated on any emerging risks.

Regulatory and Strategic Importance

The results of Phase III trials are the cornerstone of the drug's regulatory approval process. Successful Phase III trials provide the evidence required by regulatory authorities to assess whether the drug should be approved for marketing. The data from these trials are included in the **New Drug Application (NDA)** submitted to the FDA (or equivalent application in other jurisdictions like the EMA in Europe). The NDA includes detailed information about the drug's efficacy, safety, pharmacokinetics, and manufacturing processes, all of which are derived from Phase III trials.

Regulatory bodies rely heavily on the results of Phase III trials to determine whether the drug offers significant therapeutic benefits over existing treatments and whether the drug's safety risks are manageable. Phase III data also shape the product's labeling, including the approved indication, dosing instructions, and safety warnings.

If Phase III trials show positive results, the drug can be approved for marketing. However, if the results are negative or show only marginal efficacy with significant safety concerns, the drug may be rejected, or additional studies may be required.

Phase IV: Post-Marketing Surveillance

Phase IV, also known as **post-marketing surveillance**, is the final stage in the drug development process, occurring after a drug has been approved for use by regulatory authorities and is available to the general public. Unlike the earlier clinical trial phases, which are designed to establish a drug's safety and efficacy in controlled environments, Phase IV focuses on monitoring the drug's performance in real-world settings, where it is used by a much broader population under diverse conditions. This phase is essential for detecting any long-term or rare adverse effects that may not have been observed in earlier clinical trials, and for confirming the drug's continued safety and effectiveness over time.

Purpose of Phase IV Trials

The main purpose of Phase IV trials is to gather additional data on the **long-term safety, effectiveness**, and **overall risk-benefit profile** of a drug once it has been approved and is in widespread use. These trials provide valuable information that is often not available in pre-marketing studies due to the limited patient populations and relatively short durations involved in

Phase I, II, and III trials. Phase IV trials help identify adverse effects that may occur only after prolonged use or in subpopulations of patients not well represented in earlier studies. Additionally, they provide critical data to ensure that the drug remains effective for the broad patient population that it is intended to treat.

Key objectives of Phase IV trials include:

1. **Monitoring Long-Term Safety**: Phase IV is primarily focused on identifying long-term or rare side effects that might not have been detected in clinical trials due to the smaller sample size and shorter duration. For example, certain toxicities, such as liver damage or cancer, may only emerge after a drug is used in a large population over an extended period.

2. **Confirming Efficacy in a Broader Population**: While Phase III trials confirm a drug's efficacy in a controlled clinical environment, Phase IV trials assess its real-world effectiveness in a diverse population with a wider range of diseases and comorbidities. They help confirm that the drug continues to deliver the expected benefits across various demographics, such as different age groups, ethnicities, and patients with multiple health conditions.

3. **Identifying Rare Adverse Effects**: Even with a large sample size in Phase III trials, some adverse effects are rare enough that they might not appear until a drug is used in a larger population over a longer period. Phase IV allows researchers to identify these rare effects, some of which could influence the risk-benefit ratio of the drug.

4. **Evaluating Drug Interactions**: Phase IV studies help identify potential drug interactions that may not have been explored in Phase III trials, especially those that occur when the drug is used in combination with other medications that are commonly prescribed to the population.

5. **Assessing Long-Term Outcomes**: Many Phase IV trials assess whether a drug continues to be effective over time, particularly for chronic conditions where treatment may last for many years. For instance, a cancer drug may be evaluated to determine whether its benefits persist after several years of use.

6. **Comparing Effectiveness**: Phase IV trials may compare the drug with other treatments available on the market, sometimes as part of **real-world evidence** (RWE) studies. This helps determine whether the newly approved drug offers additional benefits or is a better alternative to

existing therapies.

Types of Phase IV Studies

Phase IV studies take various forms, depending on the goals of the surveillance program and the specific drug being monitored. These studies can be either **prospective** or **retrospective** in nature and can include observational studies, registries, or clinical trials. The key types of Phase IV studies include:

1. **Post-Marketing Surveillance Studies (Observational Studies)**: These studies are primarily observational in nature and involve collecting data from healthcare providers, patients, and other sources. They are designed to monitor the safety and effectiveness of a drug in the general population, focusing on detecting rare or long-term adverse effects that were not apparent during earlier clinical trials.

   ◦ **Spontaneous Reporting**: Healthcare professionals and patients are encouraged to report adverse events they observe during the drug's use. Regulatory agencies, such as the FDA's MedWatch program, maintain systems for collecting and analyzing these reports.
   ◦ **Cohort Studies**: These studies follow a group of patients over time who are exposed to the drug, comparing them to a group of individuals who are not using the drug to identify any long-term health impacts.

2. **Registry Studies: Disease or treatment registries** are used to track the use of a drug over time in specific patient populations. Registries can help identify rare adverse events, monitor the long-term effectiveness of a drug, and assess outcomes in subgroups of patients who were not adequately represented in earlier trials. These studies are particularly useful for drugs intended for chronic conditions, such as diabetes or cardiovascular diseases.

3. **Randomized Controlled Trials (RCTs)**: Although RCTs are most commonly associated with Phase I-III trials, Phase IV RCTs are occasionally conducted to confirm the continued safety or efficacy of a drug. These trials may also evaluate the drug in real-world settings or

compare it directly to existing therapies in the market.

4. **Pharmacovigilance**: Pharmacovigilance is the practice of monitoring the safety of a drug after it has been marketed. This includes collecting, analyzing, and interpreting data on adverse effects, with the goal of identifying potential risks and mitigating them. Pharmacovigilance includes both spontaneous reporting systems and structured, post-marketing surveillance studies.

Safety Monitoring and Risk Management

One of the most important aspects of Phase IV trials is ongoing **safety monitoring**. Post-marketing surveillance is designed to identify adverse events and complications that might not have appeared in clinical trials. Monitoring continues throughout the drug's life cycle, even after regulatory approval.

1. **Risk Management Plans (RMPs)**: Regulatory authorities often require the development of a risk management plan for new drugs that includes post-marketing surveillance. The plan outlines the measures taken to monitor and manage potential risks associated with the drug. This can include additional warnings, contraindications, or restrictions on use in certain patient populations.
2. **Labeling Changes**: If new safety data emerges during Phase IV, regulatory agencies may require changes to the drug's labeling. These changes may include adding new adverse effects to the label, updating dosing information, or specifying restrictions on the use of the drug in certain populations.
3. **Risk Minimization Strategies**: In some cases, drugs with known or potential risks may require additional precautions to ensure patient safety. This might include risk minimization strategies such as restricted distribution programs, risk communication to healthcare providers, or patient education on how to recognize and report adverse effects.

Regulatory Oversight and Reporting

Regulatory agencies such as the **FDA, EMA,** and **Health Canada** continue to play a significant role during Phase IV surveillance. These agencies require drug manufacturers to submit regular safety reports that detail any adverse events, safety findings, and effectiveness outcomes associated with the drug. Manufacturers must report **serious adverse**

events within a defined time period after they occur (e.g., 15 days for the FDA) and may be asked to conduct additional studies to further assess any emerging risks.

Regulatory authorities also monitor the results of Phase IV trials to ensure that drugs continue to meet the necessary safety and efficacy standards. If significant concerns arise—such as an unexpectedly high number of serious side effects or evidence suggesting that the drug is not as effective as previously believed—the drug may be subject to further investigation, restrictions, or, in extreme cases, market withdrawal.

Market Access and Post-Approval Commitments

In some cases, regulatory authorities may approve a drug for use with the condition that additional post-marketing studies will be conducted to confirm long-term safety and efficacy. These studies, often referred to as **post-approval commitments**, may involve additional Phase IV trials or registry-based surveillance. These studies are typically designed to gather more detailed safety data or to answer specific clinical questions that could not be addressed during the earlier phases of development.

For instance, if a new treatment for a chronic condition is approved under an expedited pathway (such as **Accelerated Approval**), the manufacturer may be required to conduct further Phase IV studies to confirm the drug's benefits. This process ensures that the drug's therapeutic value is substantiated once it is available in the general population.

2.2.2 Role of Regulatory Agencies in Each Phase

Regulatory agencies play a critical role in ensuring the safety, efficacy, and quality of pharmaceutical products throughout their lifecycle, from the initial discovery and development to post-marketing surveillance. In clinical trials, regulatory authorities such as the **U.S. Food and Drug Administration (FDA)** and the **European Medicines Agency (EMA)** have substantial oversight responsibilities. Their roles are crucial in each phase of clinical trials, providing guidance, review, and monitoring to ensure that clinical trials are conducted ethically, safely, and in compliance with regulatory standards. Their involvement helps ensure that drugs meet the necessary criteria for approval and continued use.

2.2.2.1 FDA and EMA Oversight in Clinical Trials

The **FDA** and **EMA** oversee clinical trials in different regions, ensuring that drug development is carried out according to strict regulatory guidelines. Both agencies have established frameworks that define the requirements for conducting clinical trials and provide approval processes at each phase. These regulatory bodies are responsible for safeguarding public health by ensuring that clinical trials are conducted in a way that minimizes risk to participants, maintains scientific rigor, and generates meaningful data that can support drug approval.

FDA Oversight in Clinical Trials

The **FDA** is the regulatory authority responsible for ensuring the safety and efficacy of drugs marketed in the United States. It is involved in every phase of clinical trial development, from **preclinical studies** to **Phase IV** post-marketing surveillance. The FDA's oversight in clinical trials is governed by a number of legislative frameworks, including the **Food, Drug, and Cosmetic Act (FDCA)**, and further supported by regulations like **Good Clinical Practice (GCP)** and **Good Manufacturing Practice (GMP)**.

1. **Phase I Oversight**: In **Phase I**, the FDA evaluates the safety and pharmacokinetics of a drug. Before initiating the first-in-human clinical trials, the drug sponsor must submit an **Investigational New Drug (IND)** application to the FDA. The IND application includes details on the preclinical data, proposed clinical trial design, and information about the drug's composition, manufacturing, and controls. The FDA reviews the IND application to ensure that the proposed trials are safe and ethically designed. It may request additional information or modifications before granting approval to begin the trial.

2. **Phase II Oversight**: During **Phase II**, the FDA continues to monitor the trial to ensure that the investigation is being conducted according to GCP standards. The agency may also review **adverse event reports** and request changes to the trial protocol if new safety concerns arise. The drug sponsor must submit periodic safety reports to the FDA as part of the ongoing evaluation of the trial.

3. **Phase III Oversight**: In **Phase III**, the FDA plays a critical role in reviewing the data collected from large-scale trials. The results of these trials form the foundation of the **New Drug Application (NDA)**, which is submitted to the FDA for approval. The FDA reviews the clinical trial results, focusing on the drug's **efficacy, safety, and overall benefit-risk profile**. If the Phase III trials demonstrate that the drug is both safe and

effective, the FDA will approve it for marketing in the United States.

4. **Phase IV Oversight**: After a drug has been approved, the FDA continues to monitor its safety in **Phase IV** through post-marketing surveillance. The FDA requires manufacturers to submit **Adverse Event Reporting (AER)** and conduct further clinical studies as needed to gather more information on long-term safety and efficacy. In some cases, the FDA may require post-marketing commitments, such as additional Phase IV clinical trials, to verify ongoing safety or effectiveness. If new risks are identified, the FDA may update the drug's labeling, restrict its use, or even remove it from the market.

EMA Oversight in Clinical Trials

The **EMA** is the regulatory authority responsible for ensuring the safety and efficacy of drugs in the European Union (EU). Similar to the FDA, the EMA is involved in every phase of the clinical trial process, ensuring that trials are conducted in compliance with EU regulations and **Good Clinical Practice (GCP)** standards. The EMA works closely with national regulatory agencies in EU member states to provide guidance on clinical trials and drug approval.

1. **Phase I Oversight**: Like the FDA, the EMA requires the submission of an **IND** application (known as a **Clinical Trial Application (CTA)** in the EU) before beginning Phase I trials. The CTA includes detailed information about the drug's preclinical data, proposed trial protocols, and the anticipated risks. The EMA reviews the CTA to ensure that the trial is scientifically valid and that the risks to participants are minimized. Additionally, the **Ethics Committees** in EU member states review the trial protocol to ensure ethical standards are met.

2. **Phase II Oversight**: The EMA continues to monitor Phase II trials by reviewing safety reports and ensuring compliance with GCP guidelines. If new safety concerns arise, the EMA may request modifications to the trial design or dose adjustments. EMA's **Pharmacovigilance** framework allows for the continuous collection of adverse event data during Phase II trials.

3. **Phase III Oversight**: During Phase III, the EMA plays a key role in reviewing the clinical data gathered from large-scale trials. The drug sponsor submits a **Marketing Authorization Application (MAA)**, which includes the Phase III trial data, to the EMA for regulatory approval. The

agency assesses the **efficacy**, **safety**, and **quality** of the drug. The EMA also evaluates whether the clinical benefits outweigh the potential risks, taking into consideration the therapeutic need within the EU market. If the trial results support the drug's approval, the EMA recommends granting a marketing authorization for the drug in the EU.

4. **Phase IV Oversight**: Similar to the FDA, the EMA continues to monitor the drug after it is approved for use in the EU. The agency conducts **pharmacovigilance activities** to track the drug's safety profile in the general population. The EMA may request additional studies or post-marketing trials to address emerging safety concerns or to evaluate long-term outcomes. The agency also ensures that the drug's labeling is updated to reflect any new safety information. In some cases, the EMA may implement restrictions, such as limiting the drug's use to certain patient groups, or even withdraw the drug from the market if the risks outweigh the benefits.

Key Differences Between FDA and EMA Oversight

Although both the **FDA** and **EMA** have similar roles in clinical trial oversight, there are some differences in their approaches to drug development and approval:

1. **Approval Process**:

   ○ The FDA follows a **New Drug Application (NDA)** process for approving drugs, which requires a detailed submission of clinical data. The **EMA** uses the **Marketing Authorization Application (MAA)** process, which is similarly comprehensive but may involve different regional procedures.

2. **Regulatory Pathways**:

   ○ Both agencies offer **accelerated approval** pathways for drugs that address unmet medical needs, such as the **FDA's Fast Track** and **Breakthrough Therapy** designations and the **EMA's Conditional Marketing Authorization**. These pathways allow drugs to reach the market more quickly but may require additional post-marketing data.

3. **Regulatory Harmonization:**

   ◦ While both agencies follow internationally recognized guidelines (such as ICH E6 for GCP), the **EMA** operates within the context of the EU's decentralized regulatory system, coordinating with national agencies in member states. The **FDA**, on the other hand, functions as a national regulatory body, primarily focused on the U.S. market.

2.2.2.2 Good Clinical Practice (GCP) Compliance

Good Clinical Practice (GCP) is a set of internationally recognized ethical and scientific quality standards for designing, conducting, recording, and reporting clinical trials. GCP compliance is essential in clinical research to ensure that the data generated from clinical trials are credible, reliable, and trustworthy, while also safeguarding the rights, safety, and well-being of trial participants. Compliance with GCP guidelines is a critical requirement for regulatory approval and for ensuring that clinical trials meet the high standards set by regulatory bodies such as the U.S. Food and Drug Administration (FDA), European Medicines Agency (EMA), and others around the world.

The Importance of GCP in Clinical Trials

GCP ensures that clinical trials are designed and conducted in a manner that respects the rights and welfare of participants, provides scientifically valid results, and ensures that the data generated is reliable and accurate. Adherence to GCP guidelines minimizes the risk of harm to trial participants, ensures that participants give informed consent, and guarantees that their privacy is maintained throughout the study. Furthermore, it ensures that the clinical trial results are credible and reproducible, which is essential for regulatory approval and subsequent use of the drug.

In addition, GCP compliance is important for protecting researchers and sponsors. It ensures that they meet ethical standards and regulatory requirements, reducing the risk of legal or ethical challenges during or after the clinical trial. GCP helps build public trust in clinical trials and new drug development, which is crucial for the success of clinical research.

Key Principles of Good Clinical Practice

GCP guidelines are based on several core principles that serve as the foundation for conducting clinical trials. These principles are:

1. **Ethical Considerations**: The well-being, rights, and safety of clinical trial participants must always be prioritized. GCP mandates that all trials be conducted in accordance with ethical principles that align with the Declaration of Helsinki, a set of ethical guidelines for medical research involving human participants. In particular, the principle of informed consent requires that participants be fully informed about the purpose, procedures, risks, and benefits of the trial before agreeing to participate. Participants should be free to withdraw from the trial at any time without any consequences to their medical care.

2. **Scientific Rigor**: Clinical trials must be designed with scientific validity in mind. GCP guidelines require that trials have clear, well-defined objectives, hypotheses, and outcome measures. The design of the trial must be appropriate to answer the research question and should be based on sound scientific principles. The methodology must be rigorous and must minimize bias and error in data collection and analysis.

3. **Informed Consent**: One of the most critical aspects of GCP compliance is obtaining **informed consent** from all participants. Before enrolling in a clinical trial, participants must be fully informed about the trial's purpose, the procedures involved, the potential risks and benefits, and any alternatives to participation. The consent process must be voluntary, without any coercion, and participants must understand that they can withdraw from the study at any time without penalty.

4. **Monitoring and Reporting**: GCP requires that clinical trials be thoroughly monitored to ensure that they are conducted according to the approved protocol and regulatory standards. Regular monitoring of trial sites helps ensure that any issues or deviations from the protocol are identified and addressed promptly. Additionally, adverse events and serious adverse events must be reported to the regulatory authorities, sponsors, and institutional review boards (IRBs) in a timely manner.

5. **Quality Control and Assurance**: GCP mandates that clinical trials include robust quality control systems to ensure data accuracy and integrity. All aspects of the trial, including recruitment, data collection, and analysis, must adhere to established protocols and guidelines. Data should be carefully documented and verified to ensure it is accurate, complete, and consistent. Any discrepancies in the data must be

investigated and resolved.

6. **Confidentiality**: Maintaining the confidentiality of participant data is a cornerstone of GCP compliance. Participants' personal information, medical history, and trial-related data must be protected from unauthorized access and disclosure. GCP mandates that participant confidentiality be maintained at all times, both during the trial and after it is completed.

7. **Ethical Review**: Clinical trials must be reviewed and approved by an independent ethics committee or institutional review board (IRB) before they can begin. The ethics committee ensures that the trial is ethically sound and that the risks to participants are minimized. This review process helps ensure that the trial is conducted in a way that protects the participants' rights and welfare.

GCP Compliance in Each Phase of Clinical Trials

Compliance with GCP is required at every stage of the clinical trial process. From planning and design to execution and reporting, GCP ensures that clinical trials are conducted with integrity and that participant safety is prioritized.

1. **Phase I – First-in-Human Trials**: In Phase I, GCP ensures that the trial design is scientifically valid, and the drug is tested in a controlled and ethical manner. The trial must be approved by the ethics committee, and participants must give informed consent before participation. Throughout the trial, patient safety is monitored closely, and any adverse events must be reported promptly.

2. **Phase II – Therapeutic Exploratory Trials**: GCP compliance in Phase II ensures that the therapeutic potential of the drug is explored safely. The trial must adhere to the predefined protocol, with a clear description of the therapeutic endpoints and patient eligibility criteria. Participant safety continues to be monitored, and all side effects are carefully documented and analyzed.

3. **Phase III – Confirmatory Trials**: GCP compliance in Phase III ensures that the trial results are scientifically valid and that the drug is tested in a broad patient population. Adherence to the protocol and monitoring of safety are critical in Phase III, as this phase provides the most definitive

data on the drug's efficacy and safety. Any adverse events or safety concerns must be documented and analyzed thoroughly.

4. **Phase IV – Post-Marketing Surveillance**: GCP also applies in Phase IV, where post-marketing studies and surveillance ensure ongoing monitoring of the drug's safety and effectiveness in the general population. Ongoing reporting of adverse events, as well as compliance with regulatory requirements, is essential for continued market approval.

GCP Training and Compliance

For clinical trials to comply with GCP standards, all personnel involved in the trial, including investigators, study coordinators, and data analysts, must be appropriately trained in GCP principles. Training ensures that staff are aware of their responsibilities and the ethical and regulatory requirements involved in conducting clinical trials. It is also important for institutions conducting clinical trials to establish systems that enforce GCP compliance, including regular audits and inspections to ensure that all aspects of the trial adhere to GCP standards.

Furthermore, GCP compliance is not only necessary for clinical trial approval but also for maintaining public trust in the pharmaceutical industry. Adherence to these standards ensures that the data generated in clinical trials are scientifically reliable and ethically collected, and that patient safety is always a priority.

Regulatory Expectations for GCP Compliance

Both the FDA and EMA require that clinical trials conducted within their respective jurisdictions comply with GCP standards. These agencies monitor GCP compliance throughout the entire clinical trial process, from the initial application to conduct the trial to post-marketing surveillance. Non-compliance with GCP can result in the rejection of trial data, regulatory sanctions, and, in some cases, the termination of the drug development program. Regulatory agencies may conduct **inspections** of clinical trial sites to verify that GCP guidelines are being followed. These inspections focus on reviewing documentation, ensuring informed consent procedures are followed, and confirming that the data collected is accurate and reliable.

2.2.3 Post-Marketing Surveillance (Phase IV)

Post-marketing surveillance, also known as **Phase IV** of clinical trials, occurs after a drug has been approved and is available on the market. The goal of Phase IV is to monitor the long-term effects, safety, and efficacy of the drug in a large, diverse population. While Phase I, II, and III trials provide valuable data on the safety and efficacy of a drug in controlled environments, Phase IV allows for the identification of rare adverse effects or long-term safety issues that were not observed during earlier trials. Post-marketing surveillance is a crucial phase because it ensures that the drug continues to be safe and effective for the population that is using it in everyday clinical practice.

2.2.3.1 Adverse Event Reporting

One of the most important aspects of Phase IV surveillance is **adverse event (AE) reporting**, which is essential for identifying and understanding potential risks associated with a drug once it is marketed. Adverse events refer to any unwanted or harmful effects that occur when a patient takes a drug, and they can vary in severity from mild side effects to serious, life-threatening conditions.

Adverse event reporting is a system through which healthcare providers, patients, and manufacturers report any adverse effects that occur after the drug has been approved and is being used in the general population. These reports are collected by regulatory authorities like the **U.S. Food and Drug Administration (FDA)**, **European Medicines Agency (EMA)**, and other national agencies, and they are analyzed to detect patterns, assess the significance of risks, and evaluate whether regulatory actions are needed.

Purpose of Adverse Event Reporting

The purpose of adverse event reporting during Phase IV is to:

1. **Identify and Monitor Rare Adverse Events**: In pre-marketing clinical trials, only a limited number of patients are exposed to the drug, and many rare adverse events may not become apparent. Phase IV surveillance allows for the identification of these rare or delayed adverse events that may only occur once the drug is used by a large and diverse

population over an extended period.

2. **Assess Long-Term Safety**: Some adverse events, particularly those that are long-term or cumulative in nature (such as organ toxicity), might not appear during the clinical trials due to their shorter duration. Post-marketing surveillance helps to monitor these effects over time to ensure that the drug remains safe for long-term use.

3. **Provide Ongoing Safety Monitoring**: Adverse event reporting in Phase IV enables continuous monitoring of the drug's safety profile. It allows regulatory bodies to assess whether the benefit-risk balance remains favorable over time. If significant new risks are identified, regulatory agencies may take action to mitigate these risks, such as updating the drug's labeling, issuing warnings, restricting its use, or even withdrawing it from the market if necessary.

4. **Support Decision-Making for Healthcare Providers**: Continuous adverse event reporting provides healthcare professionals with updated information regarding potential risks associated with the drug. This information is essential for making informed treatment decisions, particularly for patients with special needs or who are at higher risk of adverse events.

Process of Adverse Event Reporting

Adverse event reporting typically follows a structured process that involves healthcare providers, patients, and drug manufacturers. The following steps outline how adverse events are reported:

1. **Reporting by Healthcare Providers**: Healthcare professionals who observe adverse events in patients using the drug are required to report these events to the drug manufacturer or directly to regulatory authorities. In the U.S., healthcare providers can report adverse events through the **FDA's MedWatch program**, while in the European Union, reports can be submitted through the **EMA's EudraVigilance** system. Healthcare providers are typically required to provide detailed information about the event, including the patient's medical history, the dose of the drug, and the nature of the adverse event. Some adverse events are mandatory to report, particularly those that are serious or life-threatening.

2. **Self-Reporting by Patients**: Patients who experience side effects after using a drug can also report adverse events. In many countries, patients can submit reports directly to regulatory agencies or through dedicated patient safety programs. In some cases, manufacturers may have patient hotlines or websites where patients can report adverse events. While patient reports are invaluable, they are often less detailed than those submitted by healthcare providers, and they may require additional follow-up.

3. **Reporting by Drug Manufacturers**: Pharmaceutical companies are legally required to collect and report any adverse events related to their products. Manufacturers must have systems in place to monitor adverse events, collect data, and assess the potential risks associated with their drugs. They are obligated to submit periodic **Periodic Safety Update Reports (PSURs)** to regulatory authorities. These reports provide an overview of the safety profile of the drug and include all adverse events reported during the post-marketing phase.

4. **Regulatory Review and Action**: Once adverse events are reported, regulatory agencies like the FDA or EMA review the data to identify any patterns or trends that may indicate new safety concerns. If a new risk is identified, the regulatory agency may take various actions, including:

    ◦ **Labeling Changes**: Updating the drug's label to include new warnings, contraindications, or safety information.
    ◦ **Risk Management**: Requiring additional risk minimization strategies, such as restricted distribution or additional monitoring programs.
    ◦ **Risk Communication**: Issuing safety alerts to healthcare providers and the public about the risks associated with the drug.
    ◦ **Regulatory Action**: In extreme cases, regulatory agencies may withdraw a drug from the market, restrict its use to certain patient populations, or require additional clinical trials to further assess the drug's safety.

Importance of Reporting Serious Adverse Events

Serious adverse events (SAEs) are defined as any event that results in death, hospitalization, significant disability, or birth defects. SAEs must be reported immediately to the regulatory authorities and manufacturers.

Prompt reporting of SAEs is crucial for detecting severe safety concerns that may have been missed during clinical trials. It allows regulatory agencies to respond quickly to protect public health. For example, if a new drug is found to cause severe liver damage in a small number of patients, immediate reporting of these cases would trigger an investigation into the drug's safety profile.

Additionally, adverse events that are unexpected or not previously documented in the clinical trial data must also be reported to help identify unknown risks associated with the drug. These reports help regulators decide whether additional studies or precautions are necessary to address the emerging risks.

Post-Marketing Risk Management

Adverse event reporting is a key component of a broader **post-marketing risk management plan**. The goal of post-marketing surveillance is to monitor the drug's long-term safety and effectiveness in the real-world population. If new risks are identified through adverse event reporting, the regulatory agencies can implement corrective actions to manage these risks. Some common post-marketing risk management strategies include:

1. **Risk Minimization**: This may involve limiting the use of the drug to certain populations, requiring special monitoring programs for patients who use the drug, or restricting its use to specific settings (such as hospitals or specialized clinics).
2. **Risk Communication**: If a new safety concern arises, regulatory agencies can issue **Safety Communications** or **Dear Healthcare Provider Letters** to inform healthcare providers about the risks and guide them on the appropriate use of the drug.
3. **Additional Studies**: In some cases, regulators may require manufacturers to conduct additional studies or clinical trials to further assess the drug's safety. This might include **post-marketing cohort studies** or **registry studies** to track long-term outcomes and adverse effects in specific patient groups.
4. **Labeling Changes**: Based on adverse event data, drug labels may be updated with new warnings or information regarding potential risks, contraindications, or monitoring requirements.

2.2.3.2 Long-Term Safety Monitoring

Long-term safety monitoring is an essential component of **Phase IV post-marketing surveillance** that ensures the continued safety and effectiveness of a drug once it has been approved and is in widespread use. While pre-marketing clinical trials (Phase I, II, and III) assess the short-term safety and efficacy of drugs, they often cannot capture all potential risks, particularly those that manifest after prolonged use or are extremely rare. Long-term safety monitoring addresses these gaps by tracking the drug's performance over an extended period and across a broader, more diverse population.

This ongoing surveillance is necessary for detecting adverse effects that may take time to develop or that are not seen in smaller, more controlled clinical trial populations. It is also crucial for identifying drug interactions and long-term outcomes that were not anticipated during earlier trial phases. Regulatory authorities, healthcare providers, and pharmaceutical companies work together to collect and analyze long-term data to ensure that drugs remain safe and beneficial for the public.

Purpose of Long-Term Safety Monitoring

The primary objectives of long-term safety monitoring are:

1. **Identification of Long-Term Adverse Effects**: Some adverse effects of drugs may only appear after long-term exposure. These can include cumulative toxicities (such as liver or kidney damage), cancers, or neurological effects. By monitoring patients over extended periods, long-term safety monitoring can identify these risks and ensure that they are addressed appropriately.

2. **Detection of Rare Adverse Events**: Clinical trials, due to their relatively small sample sizes, may not capture all rare adverse events. For example, a side effect that occurs in 1 in 10,000 patients may not appear in a study involving only a few thousand participants. Long-term safety monitoring captures these rare events as the drug is used by millions of people worldwide.

3. **Monitoring Drug Interactions**: Drugs are rarely used in isolation. Patients often take multiple medications for various conditions, and these combinations can sometimes result in adverse drug interactions. Long-term monitoring helps identify these interactions and assess their impact on patient safety.

4. **Confirming Continued Efficacy**: Long-term safety monitoring also includes assessing the drug's continued effectiveness. A drug that is highly effective in the short term may lose efficacy over time, or its benefits may diminish in certain populations. Long-term monitoring helps ensure that the drug continues to provide therapeutic value.

5. **Support for Ongoing Risk Management**: By continuously tracking safety data, long-term monitoring allows regulators and manufacturers to update risk management plans as needed. If new risks are identified, strategies such as restricting the drug's use or modifying the prescribing information can be implemented to minimize harm.

Methods of Long-Term Safety Monitoring

Long-term safety monitoring involves several key methods for collecting and analyzing data:

1. **Adverse Event Reporting Systems**: One of the most crucial methods of long-term safety monitoring is the collection of **adverse event reports** from healthcare providers, patients, and manufacturers. Adverse events are any harmful or unintended effects that patients experience while using the drug. Regulatory agencies, such as the **FDA** and **EMA**, maintain databases for reporting adverse events, such as the **FDA's MedWatch program** and the **EMA's EudraVigilance system**. These systems allow healthcare professionals and patients to report any adverse effects, which are then reviewed by regulatory agencies for potential safety concerns. Through ongoing collection and analysis of these reports, regulatory agencies can track adverse effects and take appropriate action if necessary.

2. **Post-Marketing Cohort Studies**: In some cases, pharmaceutical companies or academic institutions conduct **cohort studies** to monitor the long-term safety of a drug. These studies involve following groups of patients who are taking the drug to track any adverse events or changes in their health over time. These cohort studies may compare the incidence of adverse events in the group using the drug to a control group that is not taking the drug, helping to establish a clearer picture of the drug's safety profile over the long term.

3. **Drug Registries**: **Drug registries** are databases that collect information on patients who are prescribed a particular drug. These registries can be used to monitor the safety of the drug in various patient populations

and track long-term outcomes. For instance, a registry may track patients who have been prescribed a particular medication for a chronic condition and monitor them for any adverse effects over several years. These registries can provide valuable insights into the long-term safety of the drug in real-world settings.

4. **Real-World Data (RWD) and Real-World Evidence (RWE)**: **Real-world data** refers to data collected from sources outside of traditional clinical trials, such as electronic health records (EHRs), insurance claims, patient registries, and patient surveys. **Real-world evidence** is the clinical evidence derived from the analysis of this data. By using RWD and RWE, researchers and regulators can better understand how drugs perform in diverse patient populations, including those with comorbidities or those taking multiple medications. This method provides a comprehensive view of the drug's safety and effectiveness over time, outside the controlled environment of clinical trials.

5. **Phase IV Clinical Trials**: While Phase III trials are designed to confirm the efficacy and safety of a drug before it is approved, **Phase IV clinical trials** continue to monitor the drug's safety once it is on the market. These trials are typically larger and longer in duration than pre-marketing trials and can provide more detailed information about long-term safety. Some Phase IV studies are designed specifically to evaluate rare adverse events or assess the drug's effectiveness in patient subgroups not adequately represented in earlier trials.

6. **Electronic Health Records (EHRs) and Mobile Health Technology**: Advances in **digital health** technologies, such as **mobile health apps**, wearable devices, and **electronic health records (EHRs)**, have significantly improved the ability to monitor long-term safety. EHRs enable the collection of detailed patient data over time, including drug usage, laboratory test results, and clinical outcomes. Additionally, mobile health technologies allow for continuous monitoring of patients and enable the collection of real-time data on drug use and side effects.

7. **Pharmacovigilance**: Pharmacovigilance is the science of detecting, assessing, understanding, and preventing adverse effects or any other drug-related problems. It involves the continuous collection and analysis of safety data, including adverse event reports, to ensure that the benefit-risk balance of a drug remains favorable over time. Regulatory agencies, such as the FDA and EMA, oversee pharmacovigilance activities to ensure that any new risks are promptly identified and

managed.

Actions Based on Long-Term Monitoring

Once data from long-term safety monitoring is collected, several actions may be taken depending on the findings:

1. **Labeling Updates**: If new adverse events or safety concerns are identified, regulatory agencies may require changes to the drug's labeling. This could include adding new warnings, contraindications, or information about specific patient populations that should avoid the drug. For example, if a drug that was previously considered safe for long-term use begins to show evidence of causing organ damage, the labeling may be updated to reflect this risk.
2. **Risk Management Strategies**: Based on the findings from long-term safety monitoring, regulatory agencies may implement additional risk management strategies. These strategies can include restricted use of the drug, special monitoring requirements for certain patient groups, or even limiting the drug's availability through restricted distribution programs.
3. **Market Withdrawal or Restriction**: In extreme cases, if long-term safety monitoring reveals that a drug poses significant risks that outweigh its benefits, regulatory agencies may choose to withdraw the drug from the market or restrict its use to specific patient populations. For example, the drug **thalidomide** was withdrawn in the 1960s due to its association with severe birth defects, a risk that was not identified during earlier clinical trials.
4. **Post-Marketing Studies**: If long-term safety data reveals potential risks, regulatory agencies may require the manufacturer to conduct additional studies, including **Phase IV clinical trials** or **cohort studies**, to further evaluate the drug's safety in larger populations or to investigate specific safety concerns.
5. **Public Health Campaigns**: If new safety issues are identified, regulatory agencies may issue public health advisories or warnings. These advisories provide healthcare professionals and the public with updated information about the drug and its risks.

2.3 Innovator and Generic Drugs

The pharmaceutical market consists of both **innovator drugs** and **generic drugs**, each playing a critical role in drug discovery, development, and accessibility. Innovator drugs are original medications developed by pharmaceutical companies through extensive research and development (R&D). Generic drugs, on the other hand, are essentially copies of innovator drugs, produced once the patent of the original drug expires. Both types of drugs are essential for improving public health, but they differ significantly in terms of development, cost, and regulatory requirements.

2.3.1 Innovator Drugs: Characteristics and Development

Innovator drugs refer to the original drugs developed by pharmaceutical companies after extensive research and development efforts. These drugs are typically the result of a long and costly process of drug discovery and clinical testing, and they are protected by patents that prevent other manufacturers from producing them for a certain period. Innovator drugs play a significant role in addressing unmet medical needs by providing novel therapeutic options and forming the basis for further advancements in medicine.

Characteristics of Innovator Drugs

1. **Novelty and Originality**: Innovator drugs are typically new chemical entities or biologics that provide novel therapeutic options. These drugs are the first of their kind and are developed to address specific diseases or conditions that lack effective treatments. For instance, an innovator drug may be developed to target a specific molecular pathway or receptor involved in a disease process, offering more precise and effective treatment options than existing therapies.

2. **Extensive Research and Development**: The development of innovator drugs involves a rigorous and systematic process that includes the discovery of potential drug candidates, laboratory testing, preclinical studies, and clinical trials. This process often spans several years and requires significant financial investment. Pharmaceutical companies invest millions of dollars into R&D to identify, synthesize, and optimize drug candidates.

3. **Patent Protection**: Innovator drugs are protected by **patents**, which provide the manufacturer exclusive rights to produce and sell the drug

for a defined period (typically 20 years from the date of filing the patent). During this time, no other company can legally produce and market the same drug. The patent protects the drug's chemical formulation, manufacturing processes, and sometimes its therapeutic use, ensuring that the innovator company can recoup its investment in drug development.

4. **Regulatory Approval**: Innovator drugs must go through a detailed approval process by regulatory agencies like the **U.S. Food and Drug Administration (FDA)**, the **European Medicines Agency (EMA)**, or other national authorities. This process involves submitting an **Investigational New Drug (IND)** application, followed by the filing of a **New Drug Application (NDA)**. These applications include data from preclinical studies, clinical trials, and other tests that demonstrate the drug's safety and efficacy.

5. **Market Exclusivity**: The approval of innovator drugs provides **market exclusivity**, meaning that only the innovator company can sell the drug for a period of time, typically 5-7 years, depending on the jurisdiction. This period allows the company to recover its research and development costs and generate profits before generic competition enters the market.

6. **High Development Costs**: The development of innovator drugs is often associated with high costs, including expenses related to discovery, preclinical testing, clinical trials, regulatory submissions, and post-market surveillance. Due to these high costs, innovator drugs are often priced higher than generic alternatives once they are marketed.

The Development Process of Innovator Drugs

The development of an innovator drug is a multi-step process that typically involves the following stages:

1. **Discovery and Preclinical Research**: The process begins with the identification of a target disease or condition that requires treatment. Researchers then explore various molecular pathways involved in the disease and screen for compounds that can effectively interact with these targets. Once a potential compound is identified, preclinical testing is conducted in laboratory and animal studies to assess the compound's **pharmacokinetics** (how the drug is absorbed, distributed, metabolized,

and excreted) and **toxicity.**

2. **Clinical Development (Phase I-III Trials):** After successful preclinical testing, the compound enters clinical trials, which are conducted in human participants. The clinical development phase is divided into three phases:

   - **Phase I:** In this phase, the drug is tested in a small group of healthy volunteers to assess its safety, dosage range, and pharmacokinetics.
   - **Phase II:** The drug is tested in a larger group of patients with the target disease to evaluate its effectiveness, determine the optimal dose, and assess safety.
   - **Phase III:** In this phase, the drug undergoes large-scale trials to confirm its efficacy, monitor side effects, and compare it with existing treatments. If Phase III trials demonstrate the drug's benefits, the company files an **NDA** with regulatory agencies for approval.

3. **Regulatory Approval:** Once clinical trials are completed, the pharmaceutical company submits the **New Drug Application (NDA)** to the regulatory authorities, including detailed data on the drug's safety, efficacy, manufacturing processes, and labeling information. Regulatory bodies review the NDA to assess whether the drug meets the necessary standards for approval.

4. **Post-Marketing Surveillance (Phase IV):** After the drug is approved and marketed, it enters Phase IV, which involves continued monitoring of the drug's safety and effectiveness in the general population. Post-marketing surveillance helps identify any long-term side effects or rare adverse events that were not detected in clinical trials. If safety issues arise, regulatory agencies may take corrective actions, such as issuing warnings, updating the drug's labeling, or withdrawing the drug from the market.

Economic and Strategic Impact of Innovator Drugs

Innovator drugs often represent a significant economic investment for pharmaceutical companies. The high development costs associated with innovator drugs are offset by the exclusivity provided through patent protection and market exclusivity. During this time, the company can set the price of the drug and earn significant profits, which can be reinvested into further R&D. However, once the drug's patent expires, generic versions can enter the market, leading to price reductions and increased competition.

1. **Economic Incentives for Innovation**: The exclusivity period granted to innovator drugs provides pharmaceutical companies with the opportunity to recoup their investment in drug development and earn profits that fund future research and development efforts. This incentivizes innovation and encourages the discovery of new treatments for various diseases. Additionally, the profits from innovator drugs support the broader pharmaceutical industry, including research in related fields and the development of new drug delivery systems, formulations, and technologies.

2. **Pricing and Market Competition**: The pricing of innovator drugs is often high, reflecting the costs associated with their development. Once a drug's patent expires, generic drug manufacturers can produce and sell the same drug at a significantly lower price, leading to increased competition in the market. The introduction of generic drugs drives down the price of the original innovator drug, making it more affordable for patients and healthcare systems.

3. **Impact on Public Health**: Innovator drugs often provide novel and effective treatments for diseases that previously had limited or no therapeutic options. These drugs can improve public health by providing patients with better treatment options, increasing survival rates, and improving quality of life. The development of innovator drugs is essential for advancing medical knowledge and addressing unmet medical needs.

2.3.2 Generic Drug Development Process

The development of generic drugs is an essential part of the pharmaceutical industry. Generic drugs are copies of innovator drugs that are marketed after the patent of the original drug expires. Generic drugs offer significant economic benefits by providing patients with more affordable alternatives to brand-name medications while maintaining the same therapeutic efficacy and safety. The process of developing a generic drug requires careful adherence to regulatory guidelines and rigorous testing to ensure that the generic drug is equivalent to the branded version in terms of quality, performance, and safety. One of the most critical aspects of generic drug development is the **Abbreviated New Drug Application (ANDA)** submission, which is required by regulatory agencies such as the **U.S. Food and Drug Administration (FDA)** for the approval of generic drugs.

2.3.2.1 Requirements for ANDA Submission

The **Abbreviated New Drug Application (ANDA)** is a submission to regulatory authorities for the approval of a generic drug. Unlike the **New Drug Application (NDA)**, which is required for innovator drugs, the ANDA submission for a generic drug is abbreviated because it relies on the clinical data and findings from the innovator's trials rather than requiring the sponsor to conduct new clinical studies. The ANDA submission process is designed to demonstrate that the generic drug is **bioequivalent** to the brand-name drug, meaning that it performs in the same manner in the body and delivers the same therapeutic effects.

In order to obtain approval for a generic drug, the ANDA applicant must fulfill several key requirements set forth by regulatory agencies such as the **FDA**. These requirements are designed to ensure that generic drugs meet the necessary standards for quality, safety, and efficacy. Below are the critical components of the ANDA submission process:

1. Demonstration of Bioequivalence

One of the primary requirements for ANDA submission is the demonstration of **bioequivalence** to the innovator drug. Bioequivalence means that the generic drug delivers the same concentration of the active ingredient into the bloodstream at the same rate and to the same extent as the original brand-name drug. This is typically established through **bioavailability** studies, which measure the rate and extent of drug absorption in the body.

In bioequivalence studies, healthy volunteers are given both the innovator drug and the generic drug in a randomized, crossover design. Blood samples are collected at various time points, and the levels of the drug in the bloodstream are measured. The generic drug is considered bioequivalent if the ratio of the area under the curve (AUC) and the maximum concentration (Cmax) of the generic drug to the innovator drug falls within the acceptable limits set by regulatory authorities (usually 80-125%).

2. Quality and Manufacturing Information

In addition to demonstrating bioequivalence, the ANDA applicant must submit detailed information about the drug's **composition**, **manufacturing process**, and **quality control procedures**. This includes:

- **Drug formulation**: The generic drug's composition must be similar to the innovator drug in terms of the active pharmaceutical ingredient (API), excipients, and dosage form (tablet, capsule, injection, etc.).
- **Manufacturing process**: The applicant must provide details about the process used to manufacture the generic drug, including information about the facilities, equipment, and quality control measures. The FDA will ensure that the manufacturing process meets **Good Manufacturing Practice (GMP)** standards.
- **Stability data**: The ANDA submission must include data on the stability of the drug, which demonstrates that the drug maintains its potency and quality over its shelf life. Stability studies are typically conducted under various environmental conditions, such as temperature and humidity.

3. Labeling Information

The labeling for the generic drug must be consistent with the labeling of the innovator drug, except for certain differences that may occur due to variations in inactive ingredients or the drug's appearance. The ANDA applicant must provide a proposed **drug label** that includes information on:

- **Indications and usage**: The approved uses of the drug, which should match those of the branded drug.
- **Dosage and administration**: The recommended dosage, frequency of administration, and any special considerations (e.g., for specific patient populations such as children, elderly, or those with renal impairment).

- **Warnings and precautions**: The potential side effects, contraindications, and warnings associated with the drug. This must be consistent with the original brand-name drug's label, reflecting any known risks associated with the drug's use.

4. Patent and Exclusivity Information

As part of the ANDA submission, the applicant must provide information about any relevant patents related to the innovator drug. This includes:

- **Patent certification**: The ANDA applicant must certify whether any of the patents related to the innovator drug remain in force and if the generic drug will infringe upon those patents. This certification must follow the requirements outlined in the **Hatch-Waxman Act**, which provides a pathway for generic drug approval while respecting the patent rights of the innovator.

  - If a patent is still active, the ANDA applicant may certify that the patent is invalid or will not be infringed upon by the generic drug.
  - If the patent is set to expire soon, the ANDA applicant may choose to wait until the patent expires before submitting the application.

- **Exclusivity**: Some innovator drugs may be granted market exclusivity by regulatory agencies, preventing generic versions from being approved for a certain period (usually 180 days) after the innovator drug is first marketed. The ANDA applicant must include information about any exclusivity rights that may affect the approval of the generic drug.

5. Preclinical and Clinical Data

Unlike NDAs for innovator drugs, ANDA submissions do not generally require new preclinical or clinical data, as the safety and efficacy of the drug have already been demonstrated by the innovator drug. However, the FDA may request additional studies in some cases, such as when there are concerns about the formulation or bioequivalence of the generic drug. The regulatory agency may also require post-marketing surveillance studies to monitor the long-term safety of the generic drug once it is in use.

6. Environmental Impact Considerations

The ANDA applicant must also include an environmental assessment or a claim of categorical exclusion, as required by the **National Environmental Policy Act (NEPA)**. This ensures that the generic drug's manufacturing and distribution processes do not cause significant environmental harm.

7. FDA Review and Approval Process

Once the ANDA is submitted, the **FDA** reviews the application to ensure that the generic drug meets all regulatory requirements. The review process includes an evaluation of the drug's **bioequivalence, quality, safety**, and **labeling**. The FDA may approve the ANDA if the generic drug is found to be equivalent to the innovator drug in terms of performance and quality. If the FDA identifies any issues with the submission, the applicant will be required to make revisions before approval can be granted.

8. Post-Approval Requirements

After the ANDA is approved, the generic drug can be marketed and sold. However, the generic drug manufacturer is still required to comply with post-approval requirements, including **Good Manufacturing Practice (GMP)** regulations and **pharmacovigilance** obligations to monitor the drug's safety and effectiveness in the general population.

2.3.2.2 Bioequivalence Testing

Bioequivalence testing is a crucial part of the generic drug development process. It is conducted to demonstrate that a generic drug performs in the same way as the original innovator drug. The primary aim of bioequivalence testing is to ensure that the generic drug provides the same therapeutic effect as the brand-name drug, when administered in the same dosage and under similar conditions. This testing ensures that the generic drug is therapeutically equivalent to the innovator drug, meaning it delivers the same amount of active ingredient into the bloodstream, achieving the same rate and extent of absorption. Regulatory agencies like the U.S. Food and

Drug Administration (FDA) and the European Medicines Agency (EMA) require bioequivalence testing to be carried out before a generic drug can be approved for market use.

Objective of Bioequivalence Testing

The core objective of bioequivalence testing is to confirm that the generic drug behaves similarly to the innovator drug in terms of its **pharmacokinetic properties.** Pharmacokinetics refers to how the body absorbs, distributes, metabolizes, and excretes a drug. The parameters that are commonly used to assess bioequivalence include the **area under the concentration-time curve (AUC), maximum concentration (Cmax),** and the **time to reach maximum concentration (Tmax).** By comparing these parameters between the generic and the innovator drug, bioequivalence testing determines if both drugs will produce the same therapeutic outcome in patients.

The goal is to ensure that there is no significant difference in the rate and extent of drug absorption between the generic and innovator drug, so that patients who use the generic version will experience the same clinical benefits as those using the branded version.

Methodology of Bioequivalence Testing

Bioequivalence testing generally involves conducting **clinical studies** that compare the pharmacokinetic parameters of the generic drug to those of the innovator drug. These studies are typically **randomized, crossover** clinical trials involving healthy volunteers. The crossover design means that participants receive both the innovator drug and the generic drug in random order, with a washout period between doses to allow the body to clear the drug before administering the next dose. This design allows for each participant to serve as their own control, reducing variability and increasing the reliability of the results.

Study Design

1. **Selection of Participants:** Healthy adult volunteers are selected for bioequivalence studies to minimize the confounding effects of disease on drug absorption. These volunteers are typically in good general health, with normal laboratory test results. The number of participants required in a bioequivalence study depends on the expected variability of the pharmacokinetic parameters. Typically, 24 to 36 subjects are included, although this number can vary depending on the study's requirements.

2. **Dosing**: In a bioequivalence study, each participant receives a single dose of both the generic and innovator drug, typically with a washout period of several days (usually 7 to 10 days). The dose used in the study is the same as the clinical dose prescribed for the target population. The drugs are usually administered under fasting conditions to minimize the effects of food on drug absorption.

3. **Blood Sampling**: Blood samples are collected at predetermined time points after drug administration, typically at intervals ranging from minutes to hours, depending on the pharmacokinetics of the drug. These samples are analyzed to measure the concentration of the active drug in the bloodstream. The concentration-time data obtained is then used to calculate pharmacokinetic parameters such as Cmax, AUC, and Tmax.

4. **Pharmacokinetic Analysis**: The pharmacokinetic parameters of interest in bioequivalence testing include:

   - **Cmax**: This is the maximum concentration of the drug in the bloodstream. It indicates the peak level that the drug reaches after administration.
   - **AUC (Area Under the Curve)**: This represents the total exposure of the drug over time. It is calculated by plotting the concentration of the drug in the bloodstream against time and measuring the area under the curve. AUC provides an estimate of the total drug absorption.
   - **Tmax**: This is the time it takes for the drug to reach its maximum concentration in the bloodstream.

These parameters are compared between the generic and innovator drug to determine bioequivalence.

Statistical Considerations

To determine whether the generic drug is bioequivalent to the innovator drug, statistical analysis is conducted. The primary statistical method used is the **90% confidence interval (CI)**. The two critical pharmacokinetic parameters, **AUC** and **Cmax**, are compared between the generic and innovator drugs. Bioequivalence is considered acceptable if the 90% CI for the ratio of the **AUC** and **Cmax** falls within the range of **80% to 125%**. This means that the generic drug's pharmacokinetic parameters should be within 80% to 125% of the innovator drug's values, indicating that there is no significant difference in the rate and extent of absorption between the two drugs.

If the 90% CI for either AUC or Cmax falls outside this range, the generic drug is considered to be **not bioequivalent** to the innovator drug. In such cases, the generic drug may need to be reformulated, and further studies may be required to address the issue.

Importance of Bioequivalence Testing

Bioequivalence testing is essential for ensuring that generic drugs meet the same quality, safety, and efficacy standards as the innovator drug. The regulatory requirement for bioequivalence helps protect patients by ensuring that generic drugs perform in the same way as their branded counterparts. Bioequivalence testing also plays a vital role in increasing access to affordable medications. Once a drug's patent expires and generic versions enter the market, patients can benefit from lower-cost alternatives without sacrificing therapeutic efficacy.

In addition to ensuring patient safety, bioequivalence testing promotes market competition, which can lead to significant cost savings for both patients and healthcare systems. The introduction of generic drugs, which are typically priced lower than brand-name drugs, increases the affordability and availability of essential medications, particularly in low-income settings.

Regulatory Requirements for Bioequivalence Testing

Regulatory agencies like the **FDA, EMA**, and other national drug regulatory authorities require bioequivalence testing for the approval of generic drugs. The guidelines set by these agencies outline the methodologies for conducting bioequivalence studies, including the specific criteria for selecting the comparator (usually the innovator drug), the study design, and the statistical analysis required.

For instance, the FDA requires bioequivalence studies to be conducted in accordance with the guidelines provided in the **FDA Bioequivalence Guidance**. These guidelines specify the acceptable ranges for the Cmax and AUC ratios and detail the study design and statistical methods for determining bioequivalence. Similarly, the EMA has its own set of guidelines for bioequivalence testing, which are broadly similar but may include slight variations in terms of study design and acceptance criteria.

Challenges in Bioequivalence Testing

Bioequivalence testing is not without challenges. One of the primary difficulties is ensuring that the generic drug's formulation is truly equivalent to the innovator drug in all aspects, including the **active pharmaceutical ingredient (API), excipients**, and **drug release characteristics**. Variations in formulation can lead to differences in the **rate of absorption** or **bioavailability**, which could affect the drug's efficacy or safety.

Additionally, some drugs may have complex release mechanisms, such as **extended-release formulations**, which can complicate bioequivalence testing. In such cases, specialized testing methods, such as **dissolution testing** and **in vitro-in vivo correlation (IVIVC)** studies, may be required to assess bioequivalence.

Another challenge arises with drugs that have a **narrow therapeutic index (NTI)**, where small differences in drug concentration can result in significant variations in therapeutic effect or toxicity. For such drugs, even small variations in bioavailability between the generic and innovator drug can be clinically significant, and stricter bioequivalence criteria may apply.

2.3.3 *Regulatory Differences Between Innovators and Generics*

The development, approval, and marketing of pharmaceutical products involve distinct regulatory pathways for **innovator drugs** and **generic drugs**. Innovator drugs are original medications developed through extensive research and clinical testing, while generic drugs are copies of these innovator drugs that are produced after the expiration of the innovator drug's patent. The regulatory requirements for innovator and generic drugs differ significantly, particularly in terms of submission procedures and the data required for approval. These differences are crucial to ensure that both types of drugs meet the necessary standards for safety, efficacy, and quality. One of the key areas where the regulatory procedures differ is the submission of **New Drug Applications (NDAs)** for innovator drugs and **Abbreviated New Drug Applications (ANDAs)** for generic drugs.

2.3.3.1 *NDA vs. ANDA Submission Procedures*

The submission procedures for **New Drug Applications (NDA)** and **Abbreviated New Drug Applications (ANDA)** reflect the distinct nature of innovator and generic drugs. Both types of applications are submitted to regulatory authorities such as the **U.S. Food and Drug Administration (FDA)**, but they have different requirements based on the drug's status as an innovator or generic. While NDAs are used for the approval of original drugs, ANDAs are specifically used for the approval of generic drugs. The differences between the NDA and ANDA submission procedures are outlined below.

1. New Drug Application (NDA) Submission

An **NDA** is the formal request for regulatory approval of an **innovator drug**. The NDA submission process is typically much more extensive and involves the submission of a large amount of clinical data, including preclinical studies, human clinical trial data, and detailed information about the drug's formulation, manufacturing processes, and proposed labeling. The NDA application serves as a comprehensive dossier that demonstrates the drug's safety, efficacy, and quality. The key components of an NDA submission include:

- **Preclinical Data**: Before clinical trials can begin, an innovator drug must undergo preclinical testing in laboratories and animal models to assess its toxicity, pharmacokinetics, and pharmacodynamics. The NDA must include detailed data on these preclinical studies.
- **Clinical Trial Data (Phase I, II, and III)**: The NDA must contain results from human clinical trials that demonstrate the drug's safety and efficacy. These trials are typically divided into three phases: Phase I (safety and dosage), Phase II (effectiveness and side effects), and Phase III (confirmatory trials for long-term efficacy and safety). This extensive clinical trial data is crucial for the regulatory body to assess the risk-benefit profile of the drug.
- **Manufacturing Information**: The NDA includes detailed information about the drug's formulation and manufacturing process. This includes the source of raw materials, the production process, quality control measures, and the facilities used for manufacturing. The goal is to ensure that the drug is consistently produced with high quality and meets the required standards for safety.
- **Proposed Labeling**: The NDA submission must include the proposed product labeling, which outlines the drug's indications, dosage instructions, potential side effects, contraindications, and other safety information.

- **Post-Marketing Requirements**: In some cases, the NDA may include post-marketing surveillance plans or studies to assess the drug's long-term safety once it is on the market.

Once an NDA is submitted, it undergoes a comprehensive review process by the regulatory agency, which may involve scientific, clinical, and administrative evaluations. The review process is designed to ensure that the drug meets the necessary criteria for approval and that it provides a therapeutic benefit to patients.

2. *Abbreviated New Drug Application (ANDA) Submission*

In contrast to the NDA process for innovator drugs, the **ANDA** submission procedure is specifically designed for **generic drugs**. The ANDA process is termed "abbreviated" because it does not require the submission of extensive preclinical and clinical trial data that is required for an NDA. This is because the generic drug is intended to be therapeutically equivalent to an already-approved innovator drug. The ANDA submission focuses on demonstrating that the generic drug is **bioequivalent** to the original innovator drug. The key components of an ANDA submission include:

- **Bioequivalence Data**: The most critical requirement for an ANDA submission is the demonstration of **bioequivalence** between the generic drug and the innovator drug. Bioequivalence means that the generic drug must deliver the same amount of the active ingredient into the bloodstream at the same rate and extent as the innovator drug. Bioequivalence is typically established through clinical studies in healthy volunteers that compare the pharmacokinetic parameters (such as **Cmax**, **AUC**, and **Tmax**) of the generic drug to those of the innovator drug.
- **Chemistry, Manufacturing, and Controls (CMC) Information**: Similar to the NDA submission, the ANDA must include detailed information on the generic drug's **composition, manufacturing process**, and **quality control measures**. The applicant must demonstrate that the generic drug is manufactured according to **Good Manufacturing Practice (GMP)** guidelines and that it is consistently produced with high quality.

- **Labeling**: The ANDA must include a proposed labeling that is similar to the innovator drug's labeling. Any differences between the generic drug's labeling and the innovator drug's labeling must be clearly explained. In most cases, the generic drug's labeling should include the same indications, dosages, and safety warnings as the innovator drug.
- **Patent Certification**: The ANDA applicant must also provide certification regarding the status of the innovator drug's patents. The applicant must certify whether any patents for the innovator drug are still in force, and if so, whether the generic drug will infringe on those patents. If a patent is in effect, the generic manufacturer may challenge the patent's validity or claim that the patent will not be infringed upon.
- **Post-Marketing Surveillance**: The FDA may also require post-marketing surveillance for the generic drug, although this is less extensive than the post-marketing requirements for an innovator drug. The generic manufacturer is still obligated to report adverse events associated with the drug and to ensure that the drug maintains safety and efficacy standards.

The ANDA review process is generally faster than the NDA review process, as it primarily involves the evaluation of bioequivalence and manufacturing information. If the regulatory authority determines that the generic drug is bioequivalent to the innovator drug and meets all necessary quality standards, the generic drug is approved for marketing.

Key Differences Between NDA and ANDA Submissions

While both **NDAs** and **ANDAs** are critical to the approval of new pharmaceutical products, the submission procedures differ significantly in terms of the data required:

- **Clinical Data**: An NDA requires comprehensive clinical trial data from Phase I, II, and III studies to demonstrate the drug's safety and efficacy. An ANDA, on the other hand, does not require new clinical trials for safety and efficacy but instead relies on bioequivalence studies to show that the generic drug performs similarly to the innovator drug.
- **Preclinical Data**: NDA submissions include detailed preclinical testing data, while ANDA submissions generally do not require preclinical data because the generic drug is considered equivalent to an already-

approved product.

- **Manufacturing and Labeling**: Both NDA and ANDA submissions require detailed manufacturing and labeling information, although the ANDA labeling must align closely with the innovator drug's labeling.
- **Patent and Exclusivity**: NDA submissions require information about the patents associated with the innovator drug, while ANDA submissions involve patent certifications regarding the innovator drug's patent status. Additionally, the innovator drug may have **market exclusivity** that prevents generic drugs from being approved for a certain period after the innovator drug is marketed.

2.3.3.2 Challenges in Generic Drug Approvals

The approval of generic drugs is a critical process in ensuring the availability of affordable medications. However, despite their potential to provide cost-effective alternatives to branded drugs, the approval process for generic drugs presents several challenges. Regulatory agencies such as the U.S. Food and Drug Administration (FDA) and the European Medicines Agency (EMA) have established rigorous guidelines to ensure that generic drugs are therapeutically equivalent to their branded counterparts. However, navigating these requirements can be complex, particularly when it comes to ensuring bioequivalence, meeting manufacturing standards, and addressing issues related to intellectual property rights.

1. Bioequivalence Issues

Bioequivalence is a key requirement for the approval of generic drugs. For a generic drug to be approved, it must demonstrate that it is bioequivalent to the innovator drug, meaning it delivers the same amount of the active ingredient to the bloodstream at the same rate and extent. Achieving bioequivalence can be particularly challenging in certain cases.

One of the challenges in bioequivalence testing arises with drugs that have a **narrow therapeutic index (NTI)**. NTI drugs are those where small differences in the drug's blood concentration can lead to significant variations in therapeutic effect or toxicity. For such drugs, even minor deviations in bioavailability can have serious clinical consequences, making bioequivalence testing more difficult. Regulatory agencies may impose stricter requirements for bioequivalence studies for NTI drugs to ensure patient safety.

In addition, complex **formulations** such as **extended-release** or **delayed-release** formulations pose challenges in bioequivalence testing. These formulations release the active drug at a controlled rate over time, and achieving the same release profile for the generic drug can be difficult. Generic manufacturers must ensure that the release mechanisms of their product match that of the innovator drug, and this can require specialized testing procedures, such as **in vitro dissolution studies** or **in vivo testing**.

2. Manufacturing and Quality Control Challenges

Generic drug manufacturers must adhere to stringent **Good Manufacturing Practices (GMP)** to ensure the safety, quality, and consistency of their products. However, achieving compliance with GMP standards can be challenging, especially for smaller manufacturers or those entering the market with a new formulation. Any discrepancy in the manufacturing process can result in variations in the quality or performance of the drug, potentially affecting its bioequivalence to the innovator product.

One of the key challenges in manufacturing is ensuring that the active pharmaceutical ingredient (API) and excipients used in the generic drug formulation are of the same quality and performance as those used in the original drug. Even small differences in the quality or source of raw materials can affect the stability, release, and absorption of the drug, leading to issues in bioequivalence. Therefore, maintaining consistent quality control throughout the manufacturing process is crucial to ensure that the generic drug is therapeutically equivalent to the innovator product.

Additionally, the manufacturing process for certain complex drugs, such as biologics or combination therapies, may be more difficult to replicate. Generic versions of biologics, known as **biosimilars**, face additional regulatory hurdles, as the manufacturing processes for biologics are more complex than for traditional small-molecule drugs. Biosimilars require additional studies to demonstrate that they are highly similar to the reference product in terms of structure, biological activity, and clinical performance.

3. Patent and Exclusivity Challenges

Intellectual property issues, particularly those related to patents, present significant challenges in the approval process for generic drugs. The **patent** for a branded drug typically provides the innovator company with exclusive rights to manufacture and sell the drug for a certain period, usually 20 years from the patent filing date. Generic drug manufacturers must navigate these patent restrictions and ensure that they do not infringe on any active patents held by the innovator.

One of the challenges is determining whether the innovator's drug is still under patent protection. Generic manufacturers must carefully analyze the **patent landscape** to assess whether the patent is still in force, whether there are any secondary patents related to formulation, dosing, or delivery methods, and whether the patent is likely to be challenged. In some cases, a generic manufacturer may need to challenge the patent's validity in court, a process that can be time-consuming, costly, and uncertain.

Furthermore, some branded drugs may be granted **market exclusivity** upon approval, which further extends the period during which generics cannot enter the market. Exclusivity can last from six months to several years, depending on the specific circumstances of the drug approval. Generic drug manufacturers must be prepared for these exclusivity periods, which can delay the launch of generic versions and limit competition in the market.

4. Regulatory Approval Delays

Despite meeting the necessary requirements for bioequivalence and manufacturing quality, generic drugs can face delays in regulatory approval. One of the common reasons for such delays is incomplete or incorrect documentation in the **Abbreviated New Drug Application (ANDA)** submission. The FDA or EMA may request additional data, clarification, or changes to the application, which can extend the approval process. Delays in the approval of generic drugs can result in lost market opportunities and increased costs for the manufacturer.

In some cases, **regulatory backlogs** can also delay the review process. Regulatory agencies, especially in high-demand markets, often face an increasing number of generic drug applications, leading to longer waiting times for approval. Such delays may prevent patients from accessing affordable medications in a timely manner.

5. Competition and Market Access

Once generic drugs are approved, they must contend with competition from multiple manufacturers. The entry of multiple generics into the market can drive down the price of the drug, benefiting patients but potentially reducing profit margins for the generic manufacturers. Additionally, the **entry of generics** into the market may face opposition from the originator companies, which can file patent infringement lawsuits, engage in **pay-for-delay agreements**, or use other strategies to delay generic entry.

In some markets, the availability of generics may also be influenced by **market dynamics**, such as pricing regulations or public health policies. In countries with stringent pricing controls, the profitability of generic drugs may be limited, making it harder for generic manufacturers to recover their costs. Similarly, in countries with restrictive regulations on drug approvals, generic manufacturers may encounter obstacles that prevent their drugs from being marketed.

6. Pharmacovigilance and Post-Marketing Surveillance

Generic drug manufacturers are required to monitor the safety and efficacy of their products once they are on the market, just as innovator companies are. **Pharmacovigilance** is critical to identify any adverse effects or long-term safety concerns that may arise with the generic drug after it is widely used. However, many generic manufacturers may not have the same resources as innovator companies to conduct extensive post-marketing surveillance, which can pose challenges in ensuring ongoing drug safety.

Additionally, generic drugs are subject to the same post-marketing reporting requirements as innovator drugs. Regulatory authorities rely on both healthcare professionals and patients to report adverse events, and generic manufacturers must comply with these reporting requirements. Failure to properly monitor and report adverse effects can result in regulatory action, including recalls or market withdrawal of the drug.

Stage	Description	Main Activities	Examples
Target Identification and Validation	Finding a biological molecule that plays a role in the disease	Gene analysis, protein assays, cell-based screening	Gene therapies, antibody targets
Lead Compound Identification	Finding molecules that show desired biological activity	Screening libraries, high-throughput screening	Initial drug candidates
Preclinical Development	Laboratory research and animal testing to assess drug safety	Toxicology studies, pharmacokinetic studies	Animal models of disease
Clinical Trials (Phase I-III)	Testing drug safety and efficacy in humans	Small to large scale testing, safety assessments	Human clinical trials

Table 5: Stages of Drug Discovery

Testing Phase	Purpose	Key Activities	Participants
Preclinical Testing	Testing drug's safety and efficacy in lab and animals	Toxicology studies, pharmacokinetics testing	Animal models, lab-based assays
Phase I Clinical Trials	Evaluate safety, dosage, and pharmacokinetics in humans	Safety tests, drug metabolism study	Healthy volunteers
Phase II Clinical Trials	Assess efficacy and side effects in patients	Efficacy trials, optimal dose finding	Patients with the target condition
Phase III Clinical Trials	Confirm efficacy and monitor safety in large patient group	Randomized controlled trials, safety monitoring	Large group of patients

Table 6. Preclinical Testing vs Clinical Testing

Stage	Activities	Key Players	Outcome
Drug Discovery	Target identification, screening for active compounds	Research scientists, biotech companies	Drug candidates for testing
Preclinical Development	Animal testing, toxicity studies, drug formulation	Pharmaceutical companies, researchers	Lead compounds for clinical trials
Clinical Development	Phase I-III trials, safety and efficacy studies	Contract research organizations (CROs), pharmaceutical companies	Data for NDA submission
Regulatory Approval	Submission of NDA, FDA/EMA review	Regulatory bodies (FDA, EMA)	Approval for marketing
Post-Marketing Surveillance	Monitoring long-term safety and efficacy	Pharmaceutical companies, regulatory agencies	Ongoing safety updates, market surveillance

Table 7: Drug Development Process

Development Phase	Purpose	Testing Stage	Participants
Preclinical	Evaluate safety and biological activity	Laboratory testing, animal studies	Animals, lab models
Clinical	Assess safety, efficacy, and dosing in humans	Phase I-III clinical trials	Human participants

Table 8: Difference Between Preclinical and Clinical

Document	Purpose	Required By
NDA (New Drug Application)	Formal application for approval to market a new drug	FDA, EMA
IND (Investigational New Drug)	Application to begin clinical trials in humans	FDA
ANDA (Abbreviated New Drug Application)	Application for approval of a generic drug	FDA
CTD (Common Technical Document)	Standard format for drug registration	Regulatory Agencies Globally
DMF (Drug Master File)	Confidential information on drug components and manufacturing	FDA, EMA

Table 9: Key Documents in Drug Approval Process

CHAPTER THREE

Regulatory Approval Process

3.1 Drug Approval in the U.S.

The drug approval process in the United States is governed by the **U.S. Food and Drug Administration (FDA)**, which is responsible for ensuring that drugs are safe, effective, and of high quality before they are made available to the public. The FDA follows a structured regulatory pathway that includes several stages, such as **preclinical research**, **clinical trials**, and **post-market surveillance**, to evaluate the safety and efficacy of new drugs. One of the key steps in the regulatory approval process is the submission of the **Investigational New Drug (IND) application**, which marks the beginning of clinical testing in humans.

3.1.1 Investigational New Drug (IND) Application Process

The **IND application** is a request submitted to the FDA by the sponsor (usually the drug manufacturer) to begin clinical trials in humans. Before a new drug can be tested in humans, preclinical data from laboratory and animal studies must be submitted to the FDA to demonstrate that the drug is reasonably safe for human use. The IND application serves as the gateway for progressing from preclinical studies to clinical testing and is an essential part of the drug approval process.

3.1.1.1 Purpose of IND

The **purpose of the IND application** is to ensure that new drugs are tested in a manner that protects the safety and well-being of human participants while generating reliable data on the drug's efficacy and side effects. The IND application serves several important functions in the drug approval process:

1. **Ensure Human Safety**: The primary purpose of the IND is to ensure that a new drug is reasonably safe for use in humans. Before human testing begins, the IND application must provide evidence from preclinical studies (such as in vitro and animal studies) showing that the drug does not pose an unreasonable risk of harm. This is especially important because drugs can have unpredictable effects when used in humans, and the FDA wants to ensure that the initial testing is done in a controlled and safe manner.

2. **Provide Regulatory Oversight**: The IND provides the FDA with the necessary information to review and monitor the progress of clinical trials. The FDA uses the IND to ensure that the clinical trials are scientifically sound and that they follow appropriate ethical guidelines. The IND also ensures that the trials comply with **Good Clinical Practice (GCP)**, a set of internationally recognized standards for conducting clinical trials.

3. **Facilitate Clinical Trial Design**: The IND allows the drug sponsor to describe the **clinical trial protocol**, including the design, objectives, and methodology of the study. The IND helps ensure that the trials are designed to answer the most critical questions about the drug's safety and efficacy. For example, the IND submission will outline the trial's inclusion and exclusion criteria, dosing schedule, and planned endpoints.

4. **Enable Early Human Testing**: Before clinical trials can begin, the sponsor must submit the IND to the FDA. The IND submission is a regulatory requirement that allows the drug to be tested in humans. It provides an essential step toward gathering clinical data that will help determine whether the drug should be approved for widespread use.

5. **Protect Patient Rights and Safety**: Along with providing the necessary information to the FDA, the IND application also outlines how the sponsor plans to protect the rights and safety of the patients participating in the clinical trials. This includes ensuring informed consent from participants, detailing how adverse events will be reported, and ensuring that there are protocols for stopping the trial if safety concerns arise.

6. **Enable Clinical Study of New Drugs**: The IND is required for the clinical investigation of new drugs, including both small-molecule pharmaceuticals and biologics. The IND provides the structure for the FDA to evaluate the safety, efficacy, and potential risks of a drug before it is introduced to the general population. In essence, the IND is a critical document that marks the transition from laboratory and animal testing to human clinical trials.

7. **Regulate Drug Manufacturing and Distribution**: In addition to evaluating safety and efficacy, the IND also serves to ensure that the manufacturing processes for the drug meet appropriate regulatory standards. The IND submission includes information about the manufacturing process, quality control measures, and the consistency of the drug's composition. It ensures that the investigational product will be produced in a way that maintains its quality throughout the clinical trials.

8. **Document Ethical Considerations**: The IND process also documents the ethical considerations involved in the clinical trial. The sponsor must ensure that ethical guidelines are followed, including ensuring participant confidentiality, the right to withdraw from the trial at any time, and a thorough informed consent process. The IND ensures that clinical trials are conducted with respect for the rights and dignity of human participants.

Components of the IND Submission

The IND submission must contain detailed information about the drug being tested and the plans for the clinical trials. It includes the following components:

1. **Preclinical Data**: Information about the results of laboratory and animal studies that demonstrate the drug's safety profile. This includes pharmacology, toxicology, and pharmacokinetics data.

2. **Manufacturing Information**: Details about the drug's composition, manufacturing process, and quality control measures. This section ensures that the drug will be consistently produced with high quality.

3. **Clinical Protocol**: A detailed plan for the clinical trial, including the objectives, design, patient eligibility criteria, dosing schedule, and

endpoints. This section provides a roadmap for how the clinical trials will be conducted.

4. **Investigator Information**: The IND includes information about the qualifications and experience of the principal investigators who will be responsible for conducting the trials. This ensures that the clinical trials will be carried out by qualified professionals who can handle the complexities of human testing.

5. **Informed Consent Process**: Information about how participants will be informed about the trial, including potential risks and benefits. The IND must demonstrate that the drug sponsor has plans in place to obtain **informed consent** from all trial participants.

6. **Risk Assessment**: An evaluation of the risks associated with the investigational drug, including potential side effects, adverse reactions, and toxicity. This risk assessment is critical for determining whether the clinical trials can proceed safely.

Review Process and Timeline

Once the IND application is submitted, the FDA has 30 days to review the application. During this period, the FDA assesses whether the proposed clinical trials are safe and well-designed. If the FDA does not object to the application, the sponsor is allowed to begin clinical testing. If the FDA has concerns about the drug or the trial design, it may place a **clinical hold** on the trials, which means that the sponsor cannot proceed until the issues are addressed. The FDA may also request additional information or modifications to the trial protocol.

Once the IND is approved, clinical trials can proceed in phases:

- **Phase I**: Focuses on safety and pharmacokinetics, typically involving a small group of healthy volunteers.
- **Phase II**: Tests the drug's efficacy and side effects in a larger group of patients with the targeted condition.
- **Phase III**: Involves large-scale trials to confirm the drug's safety and effectiveness in a broader population.

If the trials demonstrate the drug's safety and efficacy, the sponsor can then submit a **New Drug Application (NDA)** for approval, marking the final step in the regulatory process before the drug can be marketed.

3.1.1.2 Preclinical Data Requirements

Preclinical data is a critical component of the **Investigational New Drug (IND)** application process. Before testing a new drug in humans, regulatory agencies like the **U.S. Food and Drug Administration (FDA)** require substantial preclinical evidence to ensure that the drug is reasonably safe for initial human trials. Preclinical studies typically involve laboratory and animal testing, which provide vital information on the drug's **toxicity, pharmacokinetics, pharmacodynamics**, and **pharmacological profile**. The purpose of preclinical data is to assess the potential risks of the drug and determine its suitability for clinical testing.

Preclinical data must be comprehensive, and it is crucial in guiding decisions about the dosing and design of the early-phase clinical trials. The FDA, along with other regulatory bodies, uses this data to evaluate whether the drug should proceed to clinical testing. The preclinical data requirements are structured to ensure that drugs are tested in a safe and controlled manner before they are administered to humans.

Key Components of Preclinical Data

Preclinical data is generally divided into several categories, each of which provides critical information about the drug's characteristics. These include toxicology, pharmacology, pharmacokinetics, and safety assessments. Below are the key components of preclinical data required for an IND submission.

1. Pharmacology Studies

Pharmacology studies examine how the drug works in the body and its **mechanism of action**. These studies are designed to assess the drug's therapeutic effects as well as any potential **side effects**. The key components of pharmacology studies include:

- **Mechanism of Action**: These studies investigate how the drug interacts with its intended biological target (e.g., a receptor or enzyme) to produce its therapeutic effects. Understanding the drug's mechanism of action is crucial for evaluating its potential therapeutic benefits and side effects.

- **Dose-Response Relationship**: Preclinical pharmacology studies include investigations of the dose-response relationship, which helps determine the most effective and safe doses. These studies assess the relationship between the administered dose and the observed pharmacological effect.
- **Toxicology Screening**: Pharmacology studies also involve screening for adverse effects at various doses to identify the **maximum tolerated dose (MTD)** and the **no-observed-adverse-effect level (NOAEL)**.

2. Toxicology Studies

Toxicology studies are designed to assess the **safety** of the drug and identify any **adverse effects** that could pose a risk to humans. These studies are performed in animal models to evaluate the potential toxicity of the drug at various dosages and exposure levels. The key toxicology studies include:

- **Acute Toxicity**: This study evaluates the effects of a single dose of the drug. The primary goal is to identify the immediate toxic effects and determine the **lethal dose** (LD50), or the dose at which 50% of the subjects die. Acute toxicity studies are conducted in multiple species to provide a broad understanding of the drug's safety profile.
- **Subchronic and Chronic Toxicity**: These studies assess the effects of repeated dosing over a period of time, typically ranging from 14 days (subchronic) to several months (chronic). These studies provide information on the long-term safety of the drug, including its effects on organs, tissues, and physiological functions.
- **Carcinogenicity**: Carcinogenicity studies are designed to evaluate whether the drug has the potential to cause cancer. These studies typically involve long-term administration of the drug in animal models and are required for certain types of drugs, particularly those intended for chronic use.
- **Reproductive and Developmental Toxicity**: These studies assess whether the drug has any toxic effects on reproduction or fetal development. They include studies on fertility, embryotoxicity, teratogenicity (birth defects), and postnatal development. Reproductive toxicity studies are essential for drugs intended for use in women of childbearing age.
- **Genotoxicity**: Genotoxicity studies examine whether the drug has the potential to damage the genetic material inside a cell, which could lead to

mutations, cancer, or other genetic abnormalities. Common tests include the **Ames test**, the **micronucleus assay**, and chromosomal aberration tests.

3. Pharmacokinetics Studies

Pharmacokinetics studies are designed to investigate how the drug is absorbed, distributed, metabolized, and excreted (ADME) by the body. These studies provide essential information on the drug's **bioavailability**, **half-life**, and **clearance rate**. The main components of pharmacokinetic studies include:

- **Absorption**: This study measures how the drug is absorbed into the bloodstream after administration. It includes the determination of bioavailability, which indicates the extent to which the drug reaches the systemic circulation.
- **Distribution**: This study investigates how the drug is distributed throughout the body after absorption. It includes studies on the drug's tissue penetration and its ability to reach the intended target site, such as the brain, liver, or kidney.
- **Metabolism**: This study evaluates how the drug is metabolized in the body, primarily in the liver, and the identification of its metabolic products (metabolites). The **cytochrome P450 enzyme system** is often studied to understand how the drug is broken down in the body.
- **Excretion**: This study examines how the drug is eliminated from the body, either through the urine, feces, or exhaled air. It helps determine the **half-life** of the drug, which is critical for understanding the drug's dosing schedule.
- **Drug-Drug Interactions**: Pharmacokinetics studies also investigate the potential for interactions with other drugs, which may affect the drug's absorption, metabolism, or excretion. Identifying potential drug-drug interactions helps in assessing the drug's safety profile when used in combination with other medications.

4. Safety Pharmacology

Safety pharmacology studies are designed to assess any potential **adverse effects** that could affect vital physiological systems, such as the cardiovascular, respiratory, and central nervous systems. These studies are typically conducted in animals and help determine whether the drug could cause harmful effects on critical organ systems.

- **Cardiovascular Safety**: Studies on cardiovascular safety focus on whether the drug causes abnormal heart rates, blood pressure changes, or arrhythmias. They are particularly important for drugs intended for chronic use.
- **Respiratory Safety**: Respiratory safety studies evaluate whether the drug could cause respiratory depression, reduced lung function, or other breathing-related issues.
- **Central Nervous System Safety**: These studies assess whether the drug affects the nervous system in terms of sedative, stimulant, or neurotoxic effects. CNS safety studies are essential for drugs that act on the brain or nervous system, such as sedatives, antidepressants, and pain relievers.

5. Immunotoxicity and Hypersensitivity

Immunotoxicity studies are performed to evaluate whether the drug could cause immune system reactions, such as hypersensitivity or allergic responses. These studies help identify potential risks of **anaphylaxis**, **autoimmune diseases**, or **immune suppression** associated with the drug.

3.1.2 New Drug Application (NDA) Submission and Approval

The **New Drug Application (NDA)** submission is a critical step in the process of bringing a new pharmaceutical product to market. After successful completion of clinical trials and with sufficient evidence of the drug's safety and efficacy, the manufacturer submits the NDA to the regulatory authorities, such as the **U.S. Food and Drug Administration (FDA)**, to request approval for marketing the drug. The NDA process is comprehensive and involves detailed documentation, which demonstrates that the new drug is both safe for human use and effective for its intended purpose. The FDA thoroughly evaluates the submitted application before granting approval, ensuring that all regulatory standards are met.

3.1.2.1 NDA Submission Process

The **NDA submission process** is a multi-step procedure that includes the preparation, submission, and review of a detailed application containing a variety of information regarding the new drug. Below are the key steps involved in the NDA submission process:

1. Preparation of the NDA

Before submitting the NDA to the FDA, the drug sponsor must compile all the necessary data and documentation from preclinical and clinical studies. This includes evidence of the drug's safety, efficacy, and manufacturing quality. The preparation of the NDA typically involves the following components:

- **Preclinical and Clinical Data**: The NDA must include the results of all preclinical and clinical studies conducted on the drug. This includes the **Phase I**, **Phase II**, and **Phase III** clinical trial data that demonstrate the drug's safety, efficacy, and side effects. The clinical trial data should provide a clear understanding of the drug's pharmacokinetics (how the drug is absorbed, distributed, metabolized, and excreted) and pharmacodynamics (how the drug works in the body).
- **Manufacturing Information**: The NDA must provide detailed information on the drug's formulation, manufacturing processes, and the facilities used in production. This section ensures that the drug will be manufactured consistently, adhering to **Good Manufacturing Practice (GMP)** guidelines to ensure product quality. It also includes data on the stability of the drug, demonstrating that it will maintain its potency and quality during its shelf life.
- **Proposed Labeling**: The NDA includes a proposed labeling for the drug, which outlines essential information such as dosage instructions, potential side effects, warnings, contraindications, and other critical information for healthcare providers and patients. The proposed labeling should provide clear guidance on how the drug is to be used safely and effectively.
- **Risk Management Plans**: The NDA must include a risk management plan to identify, evaluate, and manage any potential risks associated with the drug. This may involve additional studies, monitoring, or restrictions to minimize risks to patients.
- **Intellectual Property Information**: If applicable, the NDA must provide details on the patents associated with the drug, as well as any exclusivity rights granted by the regulatory authorities.
- **Post-Marketing Requirements**: The NDA must include a plan for post-marketing surveillance and monitoring, ensuring that the drug's long-term safety and efficacy are tracked once it is released to the market.

2. Submission of the NDA

Once all the required data is compiled, the drug sponsor submits the NDA to the FDA. The submission is typically done electronically, using the **FDA's Electronic Submissions Gateway (ESG)**, although paper submissions are also accepted. The NDA must be filed in accordance with FDA's requirements, which include the **Common Technical Document (CTD)** format, ensuring that the submission is organized and includes all necessary information.

The FDA has specific guidelines for the NDA submission, and sponsors must ensure that the application is complete and that no required information is missing. A complete NDA will include the following:

- **Administrative Information**: This includes details about the drug sponsor, including contact information and the names of the principal investigators involved in clinical trials.
- **Scientific Data**: The bulk of the NDA consists of scientific data, including the results of preclinical and clinical studies.
- **Drug Information**: Detailed information about the drug's chemistry, formulation, and dosage.
- **Labeling**: The proposed labeling must comply with FDA guidelines and be appropriate for the intended drug use.

3. FDA Review of the NDA

Once the NDA is submitted, the FDA conducts a thorough review to assess whether the drug meets the necessary regulatory requirements for safety, efficacy, and quality. The review process typically consists of several steps:

- **Initial Review and Acceptance**: Upon receiving the NDA, the FDA conducts an initial review to ensure that the submission is complete. If the application is missing important information, the FDA may request additional data or clarification. If the NDA is complete and meets basic requirements, the FDA formally accepts the application for review.
- **Scientific and Clinical Review**: The FDA's medical and scientific experts evaluate the clinical data provided in the NDA, focusing on the drug's safety, efficacy, and risk-benefit profile. This involves a detailed examination of the clinical trial results, adverse events, dosing information, and patient populations. The review includes an assessment

of the drug's **clinical pharmacology**, including how it interacts with the body and its intended therapeutic effects.

- **Manufacturing and Quality Review**: The FDA's experts also review the drug's manufacturing data, ensuring that the manufacturing processes meet **Good Manufacturing Practices (GMP)** and that the drug will be produced consistently with high quality. This review also includes an evaluation of the drug's stability and packaging to ensure it will maintain its quality during storage and distribution.

- **Labeling Review**: The FDA reviews the proposed labeling to ensure that it complies with regulatory requirements and provides accurate and clear instructions for healthcare providers and patients. This includes reviewing the indications, dosage instructions, contraindications, and side effects to ensure that the labeling reflects the drug's safety and efficacy profile.

4. Advisory Committee Review

In some cases, the FDA may convene an **Advisory Committee** to review the drug and provide recommendations based on the clinical data. The Advisory Committee is typically made up of independent experts in the field who can provide objective assessments of the drug's safety and efficacy. The committee may also evaluate whether the benefits of the drug outweigh the risks and may offer recommendations on how the drug should be labeled or marketed.

The Advisory Committee's recommendations are not binding, but the FDA typically considers their input when making a final decision.

5. FDA Decision

After completing the review process, the FDA makes a decision regarding the approval of the drug. There are several possible outcomes:

- **Approval**: If the FDA determines that the drug is safe and effective for its intended use, it will approve the NDA, allowing the drug to be marketed and sold in the United States. Once approved, the drug is assigned a **National Drug Code (NDC)**, which is used for identification and billing purposes.

- **Complete Response Letter (CRL)**: If the FDA determines that the drug does not meet the necessary requirements for approval, it will issue a **Complete Response Letter** (CRL), outlining the reasons for rejection. This could be due to issues such as insufficient clinical data, concerns about the drug's safety profile, or manufacturing deficiencies. The sponsor may then address the issues raised in the CRL and resubmit the NDA for further review.

- **Approval with Conditions**: In some cases, the FDA may approve the drug but impose certain conditions. This may include requirements for additional clinical trials, post-marketing surveillance, or risk management measures to ensure the drug's long-term safety and efficacy.

6. Post-Approval Surveillance

Once the NDA is approved and the drug is marketed, the FDA continues to monitor the drug's safety and effectiveness through **post-marketing surveillance**. This includes reviewing reports of adverse events, conducting additional studies, and requiring the manufacturer to provide updates to the labeling as new safety information becomes available.

3.1.2.2 NDA Review and Approval

The **New Drug Application (NDA)** review and approval process is a critical phase in the drug development lifecycle, where the regulatory authorities evaluate all the submitted data to determine whether a new drug can be approved for public use. After the NDA is submitted, the U.S. Food and Drug Administration (FDA) conducts a detailed evaluation of the drug to ensure that it meets the required standards for safety, efficacy, and quality. The review process is thorough and is carried out by experts in various fields, including clinical medicine, pharmacology, toxicology, and chemistry. The goal is to assess whether the drug is appropriate for its intended use and whether the benefits outweigh any potential risks.

Initial Review

Upon receiving the NDA, the FDA initiates an initial review to determine whether the application is complete and includes all the necessary data. The application must follow the FDA's submission guidelines, which include proper formatting and the inclusion of all required sections. If the NDA is incomplete or missing crucial information, the FDA may send a request for additional data or clarification to the sponsor. This could involve asking for more detailed information on the drug's preclinical studies, clinical trial results, manufacturing processes, or proposed labeling.

Once the application is deemed complete, the FDA assigns a review team, which typically includes medical experts, pharmacologists, toxicologists, chemists, and statisticians. The review team is responsible for evaluating the submitted data and making recommendations regarding the approval of the drug.

Review of Clinical Data

The FDA's clinical review is one of the most critical aspects of the NDA review process. This involves a detailed examination of the clinical trial data submitted in the application. The clinical trials included in the NDA must demonstrate that the drug is both **safe** and **effective** for its intended use. The clinical review process focuses on several key factors:

- **Efficacy**: The FDA evaluates the results of the clinical trials to assess the drug's effectiveness in treating the target disease or condition. This involves looking at how well the drug worked in the clinical studies compared to a placebo or existing treatment options. The review team analyzes the statistical significance of the results to ensure that the drug's benefits are not due to chance.
- **Safety**: The FDA reviews the safety data from clinical trials, which includes any adverse events, side effects, or complications that were observed during the studies. The FDA evaluates whether these side effects are acceptable in relation to the potential benefits of the drug. The review team examines the frequency and severity of adverse effects and assesses whether they are manageable or could pose significant risks to patients.
- **Subgroup Analyses**: The FDA also considers whether the drug's effects are consistent across various patient populations, such as children, elderly individuals, or those with specific medical conditions. If the drug is intended for use in certain subgroups (e.g., pregnant women, patients with kidney disease), the clinical data must demonstrate its safety and efficacy in these populations.

Review of Non-Clinical Data

In addition to clinical trial data, the FDA also reviews the **preclinical** (non-clinical) data submitted with the NDA. Preclinical data typically involves laboratory and animal studies that evaluate the drug's pharmacology, toxicology, pharmacokinetics, and pharmacodynamics. The FDA uses this information to assess whether the drug is safe for human use, particularly at the dosages required for therapeutic effectiveness.

- **Toxicity Studies**: The FDA reviews data on the drug's potential toxicity, including its acute and chronic toxic effects, reproductive toxicity, carcinogenicity, and genotoxicity. These studies help the FDA assess whether the drug could cause harm to organs or tissues over time.
- **Pharmacokinetics and Pharmacodynamics**: The FDA evaluates the drug's absorption, distribution, metabolism, and excretion in the body. Understanding the drug's pharmacokinetics is essential for determining the appropriate dosage, dosing schedule, and potential interactions with other medications.

Manufacturing and Quality Review

Another important aspect of the NDA review is the evaluation of the drug's **manufacturing processes** and **quality control procedures**. The FDA assesses whether the drug is produced in accordance with **Good Manufacturing Practices (GMP)**, which are standards designed to ensure that drugs are consistently produced with high quality. The review team examines several factors, including:

- **Manufacturing Facility**: The FDA inspects the facilities where the drug is produced to ensure that they comply with GMP regulations. This includes evaluating the cleanliness of the facility, equipment, and storage conditions, as well as the overall production process.
- **Drug Formulation and Stability**: The FDA reviews data on the drug's formulation, including the ingredients used and their concentrations. Stability studies are conducted to determine the shelf life of the drug and ensure that it remains effective and safe over time. The FDA examines the conditions under which the drug maintains its quality, such as temperature and humidity.
- **Quality Control**: The FDA evaluates the manufacturer's quality control procedures to ensure that the drug is consistently manufactured with the correct composition, strength, and purity. This includes reviewing testing methods for raw materials, in-process materials, and the final product.

Labeling Review

The FDA also reviews the **proposed labeling** for the drug to ensure that it provides accurate, clear, and comprehensive information for both healthcare providers and patients. The labeling must include:

- **Indications and Usage**: The FDA ensures that the labeling accurately reflects the approved uses of the drug and provides appropriate guidance for healthcare providers on how to prescribe the drug for various conditions.
- **Dosage and Administration**: The labeling must clearly indicate the recommended dosages, dosing schedules, and administration routes. It should also provide any special instructions for specific patient populations, such as children, pregnant women, or those with kidney or liver impairment.
- **Warnings and Precautions**: The labeling must include any known risks or side effects associated with the drug. This includes contraindications (conditions under which the drug should not be used), precautions for specific patient populations, and the potential for drug interactions.
- **Adverse Reactions**: The FDA reviews the section of the labeling that lists the adverse effects reported during clinical trials. This section should provide detailed information on the frequency, severity, and management of side effects.

Advisory Committee Review

In some cases, the FDA may convene an **Advisory Committee** to provide additional expert input on the drug's safety and efficacy. The Advisory Committee is typically made up of independent medical and scientific experts who review the data and provide recommendations to the FDA. While the Advisory Committee's recommendations are not binding, they play an important role in helping the FDA make an informed decision about whether to approve the drug.

FDA Decision

After reviewing all the data, the FDA makes a decision regarding the approval of the drug. The possible outcomes include:

- **Approval**: If the FDA determines that the drug is safe and effective for its intended use, it will approve the NDA, and the drug can be marketed to the public. The FDA may require the sponsor to conduct additional studies after the drug is approved to monitor its long-term safety and effectiveness.

- **Complete Response Letter (CRL)**: If the FDA identifies issues with the NDA, it may issue a **Complete Response Letter (CRL)**, outlining the reasons for rejecting the application. The CRL may request additional data, clarification, or changes to the drug's labeling or manufacturing processes. The drug sponsor may address the issues in the CRL and resubmit the NDA for review.
- **Approval with Conditions**: In some cases, the FDA may approve the drug with conditions, such as requiring post-marketing surveillance studies or additional risk management strategies. This ensures that any new safety concerns that arise after approval are addressed promptly.

3.1.3 Abbreviated New Drug Application (ANDA) for Generics

The **Abbreviated New Drug Application (ANDA)** is the regulatory pathway for the approval of **generic drugs** in the United States. Unlike the **New Drug Application (NDA)**, which is required for original or innovator drugs, the ANDA submission process is abbreviated because it does not require the sponsor to conduct new clinical trials to demonstrate safety and efficacy. Instead, the ANDA is designed to show that the generic drug is **bioequivalent** to the innovator drug, meaning that it performs in the same way in the body and delivers the same therapeutic effect. The ANDA process is overseen by the **U.S. Food and Drug Administration (FDA)**, which ensures that generic drugs are safe, effective, and of high quality.

The ANDA submission is a critical step for generic drug manufacturers to gain approval to market their products after the patent and exclusivity rights of the innovator drug expire. By providing an alternative that is therapeutically equivalent to the branded drug, generic drugs can help reduce healthcare costs while maintaining the same level of safety and efficacy.

3.1.3.1 ANDA Requirements

The **Abbreviated New Drug Application (ANDA)** submission involves providing comprehensive information about the generic drug to demonstrate that it is equivalent to the innovator drug. The requirements for ANDA submission are designed to ensure that the generic drug meets the same standards of quality, safety, and efficacy as the original product. The key components of the ANDA submission process are outlined below.

1. Bioequivalence Data

One of the most crucial requirements for ANDA submission is the demonstration of **bioequivalence** between the generic drug and the innovator drug. Bioequivalence means that the generic drug performs in the same way as the original drug when administered at the same dose under the same conditions. The bioequivalence study typically involves clinical trials with healthy volunteers, where the pharmacokinetic parameters of the generic and innovator drugs are compared. The primary pharmacokinetic parameters studied include:

- **Cmax (Maximum Concentration)**: The highest concentration of the drug in the bloodstream after administration.
- **AUC (Area Under the Curve)**: The total exposure of the drug in the bloodstream, representing the drug's bioavailability.
- **Tmax (Time to Reach Maximum Concentration)**: The time it takes for the drug to reach its highest concentration in the bloodstream.

Bioequivalence is typically established if the 90% confidence interval for the ratio of the AUC and Cmax between the generic and innovator drug falls within the range of **80% to 125%**. If the generic drug falls within this range, it is considered bioequivalent to the innovator drug, and the ANDA can be approved.

2. Chemistry, Manufacturing, and Controls (CMC) Information

The ANDA must include detailed information on the **chemistry, manufacturing, and controls** (CMC) for the generic drug. This section ensures that the generic drug is manufactured in compliance with **Good Manufacturing Practice (GMP)** standards and that it meets the required quality standards. The key components of the CMC section include:

- **Drug Composition**: The ANDA must provide detailed information on the **active pharmaceutical ingredient (API)** and any excipients used in the formulation. It must demonstrate that the generic drug uses the same API as the innovator drug and that the excipients do not interfere with the drug's therapeutic effect.

- **Manufacturing Process**: Information about the drug's manufacturing process, including the steps involved in producing the drug, the equipment used, and the facilities where it will be manufactured. The ANDA must ensure that the drug is manufactured consistently and with high quality.
- **Quality Control**: The ANDA must include information about the quality control measures in place to ensure the drug's potency, purity, and stability. This includes information on testing methods for raw materials, in-process materials, and the finished drug product.
- **Stability Data**: The ANDA must provide data demonstrating the stability of the drug over its shelf life. Stability studies ensure that the drug will maintain its quality and potency when stored under recommended conditions.

3. Labeling Information

The labeling for a generic drug must be nearly identical to that of the innovator drug. The ANDA submission must include the proposed labeling, which includes important information for healthcare providers and patients, such as:

- **Indications and Usage**: The proposed labeling must indicate the same therapeutic indications as the innovator drug.
- **Dosage and Administration**: The recommended dosage, administration route, and any special considerations (e.g., dosage adjustments for specific patient populations) should be clearly stated in the labeling.
- **Warnings and Precautions**: The ANDA must include any warnings or precautions that are relevant for the safe use of the drug, consistent with the innovator drug's labeling. This includes information on potential side effects, contraindications, and drug interactions.
- **Adverse Reactions**: The proposed labeling must also include information on adverse effects observed during clinical trials, including the frequency and severity of these effects.

4. Patent and Exclusivity Information

The ANDA must provide a certification regarding the **patents** and **market exclusivity** related to the innovator drug. This is required by the **Hatch-Waxman Act**, which allows generic manufacturers to challenge certain patents or to file an ANDA while respecting the innovator's patent rights. The ANDA must include one of the following certifications:

- **Paragraph I**: The generic manufacturer certifies that no patent for the innovator drug exists, or that the patents have expired.
- **Paragraph II**: The generic manufacturer certifies that the patent for the innovator drug has expired.
- **Paragraph III**: The generic manufacturer certifies that the patent for the innovator drug will expire on a specified date, and that the generic drug will not be marketed before that date.
- **Paragraph IV**: The generic manufacturer challenges the validity or enforceability of the innovator drug's patent. If the FDA agrees with the challenge, the generic drug may be approved earlier, even before the patent expires.

Additionally, the ANDA submission must identify any **exclusivity periods** granted to the innovator drug, which may prevent the generic drug from entering the market for a certain period after the innovator drug's approval.

5. Environmental Impact Assessment

As part of the ANDA submission, the applicant must include an **environmental impact assessment**. This may either be a detailed environmental analysis or a claim of categorical exclusion, which states that the manufacturing and distribution of the generic drug will not result in significant environmental harm. This requirement is part of the **National Environmental Policy Act (NEPA)** and ensures that the approval process considers potential environmental impacts.

6. FDA Review of the ANDA

Once the ANDA is submitted, the FDA evaluates the application to ensure that all the necessary requirements are met. The FDA review process for ANDA is generally faster than that for NDAs because the generic drug is considered to be **bioequivalent** to an already approved innovator drug. The FDA primarily focuses on:

- **Bioequivalence**: Ensuring that the generic drug is pharmacokinetically and pharmacodynamically equivalent to the innovator drug.

- **Manufacturing Quality**: Ensuring that the drug is produced according to GMP standards and that the manufacturing process ensures consistent quality.
- **Labeling Compliance**: Ensuring that the generic drug's labeling is consistent with the innovator drug's labeling.

If the FDA determines that the generic drug meets all the regulatory requirements, the ANDA is approved, and the generic drug can be marketed and sold. If any issues are identified during the review, the FDA may request additional data or clarification from the applicant.

3.1.3.2 Differences Between NDA and ANDA

The **New Drug Application (NDA)** and **Abbreviated New Drug Application (ANDA)** are two regulatory pathways for drug approval in the United States, but they differ significantly in terms of the requirements and the process. The **NDA** is used for the approval of **innovator drugs**—new, original medications that have never been marketed before. The **ANDA**, on the other hand, is used for the approval of **generic drugs**, which are copies of already approved brand-name drugs once the patent for the original drug has expired. While both applications ultimately aim to bring safe and effective drugs to the market, the process for submitting and reviewing each type of application is distinct due to the different nature of the drugs they pertain to.

1. Clinical Data Requirements

One of the most significant differences between an NDA and an ANDA submission is the requirement for clinical data.

- **NDA**: A New Drug Application requires comprehensive clinical trial data from **Phase I, II, and III clinical trials** to demonstrate the drug's **safety** and **efficacy**. These clinical trials are conducted specifically for the drug being developed and are essential for proving that the drug performs as intended in humans.
- **ANDA**: In contrast, an ANDA submission does not require new clinical trial data. Instead, it relies on **bioequivalence studies** to demonstrate that the generic drug performs in the same way as the innovator drug in the body. This means that generic manufacturers do not need to conduct clinical trials on safety and efficacy. The ANDA only requires data that

shows the generic drug is bioequivalent to the innovator drug, which can be achieved by comparing pharmacokinetic parameters such as **Cmax**, **AUC**, and **Tmax** between the generic and the branded drug.

2. Preclinical Data

Another difference lies in the preclinical data requirements:

- **NDA**: An NDA includes extensive **preclinical data**, including **toxicology**, **pharmacokinetics**, and **pharmacodynamics** studies in animal models. These studies provide essential information about the drug's potential safety risks and how it behaves in the body before clinical testing begins.
- **ANDA**: For an ANDA, the generic manufacturer does not need to submit preclinical data. The FDA does not require new toxicology or pharmacokinetic studies because the generic drug is assumed to be equivalent to the innovator drug, and its safety profile has already been established by the original clinical trials.

3. Manufacturing and Quality Control

Both NDA and ANDA submissions require detailed information about the manufacturing process, but the extent and focus of the information differ.

- **NDA**: An NDA requires comprehensive details about the **manufacturing process** for the new drug. This includes information on the **raw materials, formulation, production processes**, and **quality control measures**. The NDA must also include a description of the facilities where the drug will be manufactured to ensure that the drug will be produced according to **Good Manufacturing Practices (GMP)**.
- **ANDA**: The ANDA also requires manufacturing information, but it focuses on ensuring that the **generic drug** is manufactured according to GMP and that the **drug formulation** is equivalent to the innovator drug. This includes detailed data on **active pharmaceutical ingredients (API)** and **excipients** used in the generic product, and the manufacturing process must be shown to consistently produce a product that matches the innovator drug in terms of **strength, dosage form**, and **quality**.

4. Patent and Exclusivity Information

Patent and exclusivity considerations play different roles in the NDA and ANDA submission processes.

- **NDA**: For an NDA submission, the applicant must provide **patent information** regarding the innovator drug, including the relevant patents and their expiration dates. The NDA must also include data on any **exclusivity periods** granted to the innovator drug, which could affect the timing of generic drug entry into the market. If the drug is still under patent or exclusivity, the NDA approval will not grant immediate market access.

- **ANDA**: In contrast, for an ANDA submission, the applicant must certify the status of the innovator drug's patent and exclusivity. The ANDA applicant must provide a certification regarding whether the generic drug will infringe on existing patents, whether the patent is valid, and whether the innovator drug's exclusivity has expired. The ANDA applicant can challenge the validity of the innovator drug's patent through a **Paragraph IV certification**, which may lead to legal disputes if the patent holder disagrees with the certification.

5. Approval Process and Review Time

The approval processes for the NDA and ANDA also differ significantly:

- **NDA**: The approval process for an NDA is usually longer and more complex. Since the NDA is for a new drug, the FDA must conduct a thorough review of the **clinical** and **preclinical** data, manufacturing processes, labeling, and other aspects of the drug. This process typically takes several months to a few years depending on the complexity of the drug, the data provided, and the FDA's evaluation of the drug's benefits and risks.

- **ANDA**: The ANDA review process is generally faster than the NDA review process because it does not require new clinical or preclinical data. The FDA focuses on ensuring that the generic drug is **bioequivalent** to the innovator drug and meets the necessary quality standards. As a result, the approval time for an ANDA is often shorter, typically taking about 6 to 12 months, depending on the completeness of the submission and the FDA's review workload.

6. Cost and Market Entry

The cost and market dynamics for the NDA and ANDA processes differ as well:

- **NDA**: Developing and submitting an NDA can be expensive and time-consuming due to the requirements for clinical trials, preclinical data, and the manufacturing process. However, once approved, the drug may enjoy **market exclusivity** for several years, allowing the innovator company to recoup its investment in research and development. This exclusivity can range from 5 to 7 years depending on the drug and additional exclusivity granted under the **Hatch-Waxman Act**.
- **ANDA**: The ANDA submission process is less costly because the generic manufacturer does not need to conduct new clinical trials. The generic drug enters the market once the **patent** and **exclusivity** of the innovator drug have expired. However, the generic manufacturer will typically face significant competition from other generic producers once the market opens, which can drive down prices and reduce profit margins.

7. Regulatory Agency Involvement
Both NDA and ANDA submissions involve regulatory oversight, but the nature of the oversight differs:

- **NDA**: The FDA conducts a **comprehensive review** of the new drug's safety, efficacy, and manufacturing process. This often includes meetings with the drug sponsor to clarify questions and resolve issues related to the drug's approval. The process may involve the **FDA Advisory Committee**, which provides additional expert recommendations.
- **ANDA**: The FDA's review of an ANDA focuses primarily on **bioequivalence** and ensuring that the generic drug meets the same standards as the innovator drug. Since the ANDA process is abbreviated, there is usually less back-and-forth with the FDA compared to the NDA process. However, the FDA still conducts a thorough evaluation of the submission, particularly regarding the manufacturing process and the accuracy of the labeling.

3.1.4 Changes to Approved NDA/ANDA

Once a drug has received approval through a **New Drug Application (NDA)** or **Abbreviated New Drug Application (ANDA),** the drug sponsor may need to make changes to the drug or its manufacturing process after the product is on the market. These post-approval changes can involve modifications to the drug's formulation, packaging, labeling, manufacturing processes, or other aspects of the product. Any such changes must be evaluated and approved by the U.S. **Food and Drug Administration (FDA)** to ensure that they do not affect the drug's safety, efficacy, or quality.

The FDA has established specific guidelines and requirements for making changes to an approved NDA or ANDA. These changes are classified based on their potential impact on the drug's safety and effectiveness. Depending on the nature of the change, the FDA may require different levels of documentation, testing, and approval before the change can be implemented. The process for submitting these changes is referred to as the **Post-Approval Change Process.**

3.1.4.1 Post-Approval Changes

Post-approval changes refer to modifications made to a drug after it has received approval and is marketed. These changes can occur in various stages of the product's lifecycle and can affect different aspects of the drug, including its formulation, manufacturing process, packaging, labeling, and more. The FDA requires that all post-approval changes be submitted for review and approval to ensure that they do not adversely affect the drug's safety, effectiveness, or quality. The process for submitting post-approval changes is essential for maintaining the integrity of the drug product.

1. Types of Post-Approval Changes

Post-approval changes can be classified into several categories based on their nature and impact on the drug. The FDA has established a framework to categorize these changes as either **minor, moderate,** or **major,** each requiring different levels of regulatory oversight. The three main categories are:

- **Minor Changes:** Minor changes generally involve alterations that are unlikely to affect the drug's safety, efficacy, or quality. These changes may include adjustments to the **manufacturing environment, packaging materials,** or **labeling** (such as minor formatting changes or updated contact information). Minor changes typically do not require extensive data or testing, but the drug sponsor must notify the FDA in a timely manner. In some cases, these changes can be implemented without prior approval, as long as the FDA is informed afterward.

- **Moderate Changes**: Moderate changes involve adjustments that may have a potential effect on the drug's characteristics but do not significantly impact its safety or efficacy. These changes may include modifications to the **formulation** (e.g., slight changes in the concentration of inactive ingredients) or **manufacturing processes** (e.g., changing the supplier of a raw material). For these changes, the sponsor may need to submit a supplemental application to the FDA for approval before implementation. However, extensive clinical data may not be required.

- **Major Changes**: Major changes can have a significant impact on the drug's safety, efficacy, or manufacturing processes. These changes often involve modifications that could alter the drug's **pharmacokinetics**, **stability**, or **bioavailability**. Major changes include changes to the **active pharmaceutical ingredient (API)**, **dosage form**, or **method of synthesis**. For such changes, the sponsor is typically required to submit a **Supplemental New Drug Application (sNDA)** or **Supplemental Abbreviated New Drug Application (sANDA)** to the FDA. Extensive clinical or preclinical data may be required to demonstrate that the change does not affect the drug's performance or safety.

2. Process for Submitting Post-Approval Changes

The process for submitting post-approval changes varies depending on the type of change and its potential impact on the drug's characteristics. The FDA has established specific procedures for submitting these changes, ensuring that all modifications are properly evaluated and approved before they are implemented. The process typically involves the following steps:

- **Identify the Change**: The first step is identifying the specific change that needs to be made to the drug. This could involve an alteration in the drug's formulation, manufacturing process, or labeling, among other factors. The sponsor must assess the potential impact of the change on the drug's safety, efficacy, and quality.

- **Determine the Classification of the Change**: The sponsor must then determine whether the change is **minor**, **moderate**, or **major**. The FDA provides specific guidelines for classifying changes, and the sponsor must evaluate the change based on these criteria. The classification helps determine whether the change can be implemented immediately, requires notification to the FDA, or requires prior approval.

- **Prepare and Submit Documentation**: Once the change is classified, the sponsor must prepare the appropriate documentation and submit it to the FDA. This may include providing information on the **scientific rationale** for the change, **stability data**, **manufacturing details**, or **clinical study data** (if required). The sponsor must also explain how the change will not adversely affect the drug's safety or efficacy.

- **FDA Review**: After the submission, the FDA will review the proposed change to ensure that it does not compromise the drug's safety, efficacy, or quality. For **major changes**, the FDA may conduct a more detailed review, including requesting additional data or studies. For **moderate** or **minor changes**, the review process may be quicker, and in some cases, the sponsor may receive a **notification of acceptance** without the need for further review.

- **Approval or Rejection**: Once the FDA completes its review, it will either approve the change, allow it to proceed, or request additional information. If the change is approved, the sponsor can implement it according to the FDA's recommendations. If the change is rejected or if additional studies are required, the sponsor must address the FDA's concerns before proceeding with the change.

- **Implementation of the Change**: After the FDA approves the post-approval change, the sponsor can implement the change in the drug's production, labeling, or other aspects as necessary. The sponsor must also ensure that the change is reflected in all future batches of the drug and inform relevant stakeholders, including healthcare providers and patients, as appropriate.

3. Types of Post-Approval Changes and Their Impact

Post-approval changes can involve a wide range of modifications to a drug. The impact of these changes depends on the nature of the modification and the stage of the drug's lifecycle. Some common types of post-approval changes include:

- **Formulation Changes**: Changes in the drug's formulation, such as modifying the concentration of excipients or altering the delivery system (e.g., from immediate-release to extended-release), may require submission to the FDA. Depending on the nature of the change, clinical data may be necessary to demonstrate that the drug's safety and efficacy are not affected.

- **Manufacturing Changes**: Modifications to the manufacturing process or the location of production may necessitate post-approval submissions. Changes to the manufacturing process may require additional stability testing or validation studies to ensure that the drug's quality remains consistent.

- **Labeling Changes**: Labeling changes, including updates to the drug's indications, dosage, warnings, or contraindications, may also require FDA approval. These changes are particularly important if new safety concerns are identified or if new data becomes available after the drug is on the market.

- **Packaging Changes**: Changes to the drug's packaging, such as altering the container closure system or labeling, may be required if the changes affect the drug's stability, safety, or ease of use. These changes typically require review by the FDA to ensure that the packaging maintains the drug's integrity and meets regulatory standards.

- **Post-Market Surveillance Studies**: In some cases, the FDA may require the drug sponsor to conduct additional studies after the drug is marketed to gather more data on its long-term safety and effectiveness. These post-marketing surveillance studies may be necessary if new risks are identified once the drug is widely used.

3.1.4.2 *Supplementary NDA and CBE (Changes Being Effected)*

The **Supplementary New Drug Application (sNDA)** and **Changes Being Effected (CBE)** are two important mechanisms in the post-approval regulatory process that allow drug manufacturers to make modifications to an approved drug after it has been brought to market. Both processes are designed to ensure that any changes made to a drug, whether related to its formulation, labeling, manufacturing process, or other factors, are thoroughly reviewed to ensure the drug's continued safety, efficacy, and quality.

These mechanisms are part of the broader process for managing **post-approval changes** to **New Drug Applications (NDAs)** and **Abbreviated**

New Drug Applications (ANDAs). They are used when drug manufacturers need to implement changes but must first receive approval or provide notification to the regulatory authorities.

1. Supplementary New Drug Application (sNDA)

The **Supplementary New Drug Application (sNDA)** is used when a manufacturer wants to make significant changes to a previously approved NDA. The sNDA process is applicable when the change being proposed could affect the drug's safety, efficacy, labeling, or manufacturing process. This is a comprehensive process that typically requires the submission of additional data, including clinical, preclinical, or manufacturing information, to demonstrate that the proposed change does not negatively impact the drug's safety and effectiveness.

1.1 When is an sNDA Required?

An sNDA is required when the manufacturer seeks to modify an existing NDA in ways that are not covered by the original approval. Some common scenarios where an sNDA might be needed include:

- **New Indications or Uses**: If the manufacturer wants to expand the drug's labeling to include additional therapeutic indications or uses not previously approved by the FDA. For example, if a drug is approved for the treatment of **hypertension** and the sponsor later wants to extend its use to treat **heart failure**, they would need to submit an sNDA.
- **Changes in Dosing or Administration**: If the drug's dosing schedule is modified (e.g., moving from once-daily to twice-daily dosing) or if there are changes to the drug's formulation (e.g., changing from oral to intravenous administration), an sNDA is required. This would include any change that could affect how the drug is administered or how it is absorbed in the body.
- **Changes in Manufacturing Process**: If there are significant modifications to the drug's manufacturing process or the facilities used to produce it, an sNDA is necessary. This includes changes to the source of active pharmaceutical ingredients (API) or alterations in the quality control procedures.
- **New Safety Information**: If new safety information emerges from post-marketing surveillance, clinical trials, or other sources that requires changes to the drug's labeling (e.g., adding new warnings or contraindications), an sNDA must be submitted.

1.2 The sNDA Submission Process

The process for submitting an sNDA involves the following steps:

- **Preparation of the sNDA**: The manufacturer must prepare detailed documentation to support the proposed changes, including any new clinical or preclinical data. The submission should include a detailed description of the changes, how they will impact the drug's safety or efficacy, and any relevant evidence that supports the proposed modification.
- **FDA Review**: Once the sNDA is submitted, the FDA reviews the application to determine whether the proposed changes are appropriate and do not compromise the drug's safety or efficacy. Depending on the nature of the changes, the FDA may require additional clinical trials or studies to evaluate the impact of the change.
- **Approval or Rejection**: If the FDA determines that the proposed changes do not compromise the safety or efficacy of the drug, the sNDA is approved. If the FDA finds that the changes are not adequately supported by data or could lead to safety concerns, the sNDA may be rejected, and the manufacturer may need to provide additional data or make revisions to the application.

1.3 Post-Approval Monitoring

Once an sNDA is approved and the changes are implemented, the drug is subject to continued post-marketing surveillance. The manufacturer must monitor the drug's safety and report any new adverse events that may arise due to the changes.

2. Changes Being Effected (CBE)

Changes Being Effected (CBE) is a regulatory process that allows manufacturers to make certain types of changes to an approved drug without waiting for prior approval from the FDA. The CBE process is generally used for less significant changes that do not affect the core safety or efficacy profile of the drug. Instead of submitting a full sNDA, the manufacturer can implement the change immediately and inform the FDA of the change afterward.

2.1 When is CBE Used?

The CBE process can be used for the following types of changes:

- **Labeling Changes**: Changes to the labeling of the drug that do not significantly alter its safety or efficacy profile. This includes adding new safety information, minor revisions to existing labeling, or adjustments to dosage instructions based on new evidence or updated guidelines.
- **Manufacturing Changes**: Minor changes to the manufacturing process, such as adjustments to the equipment or changes in the quality control procedures, that do not impact the drug's safety, efficacy, or overall quality.
- **Post-Marketing Safety Updates**: If new information becomes available that is related to the **safety profile** of the drug, such as the identification of a previously unrecognized adverse event or the inclusion of updated risk information, manufacturers can use the CBE process to implement these updates in the labeling.

2.2 CBE Procedures

The CBE process is designed to allow for timely updates without requiring extensive review periods by the FDA. The steps involved in the CBE process are as follows:

- **Identification of the Change**: The manufacturer identifies the specific change that needs to be made, such as a change to the drug's labeling or minor adjustments to the manufacturing process.
- **Implementation of the Change**: The manufacturer can proceed with implementing the change immediately, without waiting for the FDA's approval. This allows for quicker updates, especially in cases where the change is necessary to address emerging safety concerns.
- **Notification to the FDA**: After implementing the change, the manufacturer is required to submit a **CBE supplement** to the FDA, notifying them of the change and providing all relevant data to support it. This includes information on the nature of the change, any new clinical or preclinical data, and any additional safety information that may impact the drug's labeling.
- **FDA Review**: Once the CBE is submitted, the FDA conducts a review to ensure that the change is appropriate and does not compromise the

drug's safety or effectiveness. If the FDA disagrees with the change, they may request that the manufacturer withdraw or modify the change. However, the manufacturer is generally allowed to implement changes while the FDA review is ongoing.

2.3 CBE Categories

The FDA has categorized changes under the CBE process into two main types:

- **CBE-0**: This category allows for **minor changes** that are considered to have little or no impact on the safety, efficacy, or quality of the drug. Examples include minor revisions to labeling or updates that provide new information related to previously known side effects.
- **CBE-1**: This category allows for **moderate changes** that may require some additional data or evidence but do not have a significant impact on the drug's overall safety or efficacy. For example, minor modifications to the drug's manufacturing process that do not affect the drug's quality or clinical performance would fall under this category.

3. Comparison of sNDA and CBE

While both the **Supplementary New Drug Application (sNDA)** and **Changes Being Effected (CBE)** processes allow for changes to an already approved drug, they differ in terms of the type of changes they address, the review process, and the level of regulatory oversight required:

- **sNDA**: The sNDA process is used for **major changes** that could significantly affect the drug's safety, efficacy, or manufacturing process. It requires detailed documentation, including clinical data, and must be reviewed and approved by the FDA before the change is implemented. The review process for an sNDA is more rigorous and time-consuming.
- **CBE**: The CBE process is used for **minor** or **moderate changes** that do not significantly impact the drug's core characteristics. Manufacturers can implement changes immediately and submit a CBE supplement to notify the FDA. The CBE process is typically faster and allows for timely updates, particularly in response to safety concerns or minor labeling adjustments.

3.2 Approval Process in Other Countries

The approval process for new drugs varies from country to country, with each having its own regulatory framework and requirements. In the **European Union (EU)**, the **Marketing Authorization Application (MAA)** is the primary method for seeking approval for new drugs. The MAA process is governed by the **European Medicines Agency (EMA)**, which is responsible for evaluating and overseeing the approval of medicines within the EU. The MAA process includes different procedures, including the **centralized procedure**, which allows a single application to be evaluated for approval in all EU member states.

3.2.1 European Union: Marketing Authorization Application (MAA)

The **Marketing Authorization Application (MAA)** is the formal application that a drug manufacturer submits to the European Medicines Agency (EMA) to obtain approval for a new drug or therapeutic product. Once the MAA is approved, the drug can be marketed throughout the European Union member states, which includes all 27 EU countries, as well as the **European Economic Area (EEA)** countries, which includes Iceland, Liechtenstein, and Norway.

There are several procedures for submitting the MAA, each tailored to the nature of the drug and the marketing goals of the manufacturer. These procedures include the **centralized procedure, decentralized procedure, and mutual recognition procedure**. Among these, the **centralized procedure** is particularly important because it allows for the simultaneous approval of a drug across all EU countries with a single application.

3.2.1.1 Centralized Procedure

The **centralized procedure** for marketing authorization is a streamlined process that enables a drug to be approved for sale throughout the European Union with a single submission to the **European Medicines Agency (EMA)**. This procedure is mandatory for certain types of drugs, such as **biologic products, orphan drugs**, and drugs that address major public health concerns. The centralized procedure is considered more efficient because it centralizes the evaluation and approval process, eliminating the need for multiple submissions to different national regulatory authorities within the EU.

The centralized procedure is governed by the **EU Regulation No 726/ 2004**, which established the EMA and outlined the requirements for marketing authorization of medicinal products in the EU. The procedure aims to harmonize the approval process, ensuring that drugs that meet the necessary safety, efficacy, and quality standards are accessible across the EU in a timely manner.

1. Eligibility for the Centralized Procedure

The centralized procedure is not mandatory for all drugs. However, certain categories of drugs are required to undergo the centralized procedure for approval:

- **Biologic Medicines**: Drugs derived from living organisms, such as monoclonal antibodies, recombinant proteins, and gene therapies, must go through the centralized procedure. These products often involve more complex manufacturing processes and pose unique regulatory challenges, making centralized approval necessary to ensure safety and efficacy across all EU member states.
- **Orphan Drugs**: Drugs intended to treat rare diseases affecting fewer than 5 in 10,000 people in the EU are considered **orphan drugs**. The centralized procedure ensures that these drugs, which may not be financially viable in some markets, are still available across the EU. Orphan drug status provides certain benefits, including financial incentives and longer market exclusivity.
- **Advanced Therapy Medicinal Products (ATMPs)**: These include **gene therapy**, **somatic-cell therapy**, and **tissue-engineered products**. The complexity of these treatments requires a comprehensive evaluation to ensure they are safe and effective. The centralized procedure facilitates approval for these innovative therapies.
- **Pandemic and Public Health Crisis Drugs**: In situations of public health emergencies, such as pandemics, the European Commission may mandate the use of the centralized procedure to expedite the approval of medicines addressing urgent public health needs, such as vaccines and antiviral treatments.

2. Steps in the Centralized Procedure

The **centralized procedure** follows a set sequence of steps, ensuring that the drug undergoes a thorough evaluation by regulatory experts across the EU. The process includes the following stages:

- **Pre-Submission**: Before submitting the MAA, the drug sponsor is encouraged to engage in **scientific advice** meetings with the EMA to discuss the regulatory requirements and data needed for approval. These meetings are particularly useful for addressing complex issues related to clinical trials, quality control, and manufacturing processes.
- **Application Submission**: The sponsor submits the MAA to the **EMA**, which includes comprehensive data on the drug's **clinical trials**, **preclinical data**, **manufacturing processes**, and **risk management plans**. The application must also include proposed **labeling** and **risk-benefit assessments** based on the drug's safety and efficacy profiles.
- **EMA Evaluation**: Once the application is received, the EMA's **Committee for Medicinal Products for Human Use (CHMP)** evaluates the drug. The CHMP is a group of scientific experts who review all aspects of the drug, including its clinical data, manufacturing details, and proposed use. The evaluation process typically lasts about **210 days**, although the timeline can be extended if additional information is required.
- **CHMP Opinion**: After reviewing the data, the CHMP issues an **opinion** on whether the drug should be approved for use within the EU. This opinion is based on the drug's **safety, efficacy**, and **quality** as well as its **risk-benefit profile**. If the CHMP recommends approval, the opinion is sent to the **European Commission** for a final decision.
- **European Commission Decision**: The European Commission, based on the CHMP's opinion, issues a final **marketing authorization** decision. This decision allows the sponsor to market the drug in all EU member states and EEA countries. The authorization is typically valid for **five years**, after which it can be renewed.
- **Post-Authorization Requirements**: Once a drug is approved through the centralized procedure, the sponsor must continue to monitor the drug's safety and efficacy through **post-marketing surveillance**. This may include conducting **Phase IV trials, adverse event reporting**, and fulfilling **risk management obligations**. The EMA and national regulatory authorities will continue to oversee the drug's use and ensure that it remains safe and effective over time.

3. Advantages of the Centralized Procedure

The **centralized procedure** offers several advantages for both the manufacturer and patients:

- **Single Approval Process**: A major advantage of the centralized procedure is that it allows the drug manufacturer to submit a single application to the EMA, which is then reviewed for approval across all EU member states. This eliminates the need for multiple national applications and provides a faster and more efficient route to market for certain types of drugs.
- **Harmonized Approval Across the EU**: Once approved through the centralized procedure, the drug is granted marketing authorization in all EU member states and the EEA countries. This ensures that patients in these countries have access to the same drug without delays or variations in approval.
- **Access to Large Market**: The EU represents a significant market for pharmaceutical products, and approval through the centralized procedure provides access to a population of over 500 million people. For manufacturers, this means a wider market for their products, which can enhance their financial returns.
- **Incentives for Orphan Drugs**: The centralized procedure offers several incentives for orphan drug development, including market exclusivity for **10 years**, which is longer than the typical exclusivity period for non-orphan drugs. This encourages the development of treatments for rare diseases, which may not otherwise be commercially viable.

4. Limitations of the Centralized Procedure

While the centralized procedure offers many benefits, there are also some limitations and challenges:

- **Mandatory for Certain Drugs**: The centralized procedure is required for certain types of drugs, such as biologics, orphan drugs, and ATMPs. However, it is **not available for all types of drugs**, and some drugs may need to go through other procedures, such as the **decentralized procedure** or **mutual recognition procedure**, depending on the market needs and the drug's characteristics.
- **Cost and Complexity**: The submission and evaluation process for the centralized procedure can be more complex and costly for manufacturers, especially for smaller companies or those introducing novel drugs. The data requirements for approval can be significant, and sponsors must ensure that they meet the EMA's regulatory standards.

- **Risk of Rejection**: Although the centralized procedure allows for broader access to the market, the drug is subject to rigorous scrutiny by the EMA. If the drug is not deemed safe or effective, it may be rejected or delayed, which can have financial implications for the manufacturer.

3.2.1.2 Mutual Recognition Procedure

The **Mutual Recognition Procedure (MRP)** is one of the regulatory pathways available for drug approval in the **European Union (EU)**. Unlike the **Centralized Procedure**, which involves a single application evaluated by the **European Medicines Agency (EMA)** for approval across all EU member states, the Mutual Recognition Procedure allows a drug to be approved by multiple EU countries based on the approval of one member state. This procedure is typically used for drugs that are not subject to the mandatory **centralized procedure**, such as **generic drugs** or those that are already marketed in one EU country and are seeking approval in others.

Overview of the Mutual Recognition Procedure

The Mutual Recognition Procedure is based on the principle of **mutual recognition** between EU member states. When a drug is approved by one member state (the **Reference Member State**, RMS), other member states (the **Concerned Member States**, CMS) are expected to recognize the approval decision made by the RMS. This means that the concerned countries rely on the scientific evaluation conducted by the RMS, without needing to conduct their own full evaluation. Instead, they assess whether the drug complies with their national regulatory requirements and standards. If the CMS agrees with the RMS's evaluation, the drug is granted marketing authorization in those countries.

When is the Mutual Recognition Procedure Used?

The MRP is often used in situations where:

- **A Drug Has Already Been Approved in One Member State**: If a drug has already received marketing authorization in one EU member state, the manufacturer can apply for approval in other member states using the MRP. This process is faster and more efficient than submitting a full application in each individual country.
- **For Generic Drugs**: Generic drugs that are identical to an innovator drug in terms of active ingredients, strength, dosage form, and route

of administration can also use the MRP for approval in multiple EU member states after receiving approval in one country. The generic drug must be shown to be bioequivalent to the original innovator drug.

- **For Well-Established Medicinal Products**: If a drug has been on the market for a long time and there are no new safety concerns, the MRP may be used to expand its market access to other EU member states.

Steps in the Mutual Recognition Procedure

The Mutual Recognition Procedure follows a well-defined series of steps:

1. Initial Application Submission

The process begins when the manufacturer submits a **Marketing Authorization Application (MAA)** to the **Reference Member State (RMS)**. The RMS is typically the country where the drug was first approved, and it takes on the responsibility of evaluating the application and providing the scientific review.

The submission must include comprehensive data on the drug, such as **clinical trial data, preclinical studies**, **manufacturing information**, and **proposed labeling**. If the drug is a generic, bioequivalence studies must also be included to demonstrate that the generic drug is equivalent to the innovator product.

2. Scientific Evaluation by the RMS

The RMS conducts a detailed scientific evaluation of the drug, assessing its **safety, efficacy**, and **quality**. The evaluation is similar to the process followed in the **Centralized Procedure**, but it is conducted solely by the RMS. If the RMS is satisfied with the drug's data and meets its regulatory requirements, it issues a **positive opinion** and grants marketing authorization for the drug.

3. Notification to the Concerned Member States (CMS)

Once the RMS grants marketing authorization, the manufacturer notifies the **Concerned Member States (CMS)**, which are the countries in which the manufacturer seeks to market the drug. The CMS countries are then required to assess whether they accept the RMS's evaluation. The CMS may request further clarifications, but they are expected to recognize the RMS's decision as long as the drug meets their local regulatory standards.

4. Assessment by the Concerned Member States (CMS)

The CMS countries review the application and the RMS's evaluation to ensure that the drug complies with their national laws. They may also request additional data or clarification if necessary, but they are not expected to conduct a full scientific evaluation of the drug. The CMS countries should complete their evaluation within a specific timeframe, typically **90 days** after receiving the RMS's approval.

During this evaluation period, the CMS can raise concerns if they believe there are issues related to safety, efficacy, or quality. If the CMS agrees with the RMS, they issue a **positive opinion** and grant marketing authorization.

5. Possible Disagreements Between RMS and CMS

In some cases, disagreements may arise between the RMS and one or more CMS. If a CMS does not agree with the RMS's decision, a **mutual recognition dispute** can be initiated. In such cases, the **Coordination Group** of the EU regulatory bodies may intervene to help resolve the issue. If the disagreement cannot be resolved, the matter may be referred to the **European Medicines Agency (EMA)** for further review and arbitration.

If the dispute is not resolved and the CMS still refuses to grant marketing authorization, the applicant may need to pursue other procedures, such as the **Centralized Procedure** or the **Decentralized Procedure**.

6. Granting Marketing Authorization

Once all CMS agree with the RMS's evaluation, marketing authorization is granted for the drug in all participating countries. The manufacturer is then free to market the drug across the **EU** and **European Economic Area (EEA)** countries. The marketing authorization typically lasts for **five years**, after which it can be renewed based on ongoing safety monitoring and post-marketing data.

Advantages of the Mutual Recognition Procedure

The MRP offers several key advantages:

- **Efficiency:** The MRP reduces the regulatory burden on manufacturers by allowing a drug to be approved in multiple EU member states based on the evaluation of a single reference country. This process saves time and resources compared to submitting individual applications to each member state.
- **Faster Market Access:** Since the RMS has already conducted the full evaluation of the drug, the approval process in the CMS is often quicker, allowing the drug to reach more markets more rapidly.
- **Cost-Effectiveness:** The MRP helps reduce costs for drug manufacturers by simplifying the approval process and eliminating the need for multiple applications and evaluations in each country.

- **Flexibility**: The MRP allows manufacturers to extend their market reach to multiple EU countries without going through the lengthy **Centralized Procedure**. This can be particularly advantageous for smaller manufacturers or for drugs that do not require centralized approval.

Limitations of the Mutual Recognition Procedure
While the MRP offers many advantages, there are also some limitations:

- **Not Applicable to All Drugs**: The MRP is not available for all types of drugs. For certain drugs, such as biologics and innovative medicines, the **Centralized Procedure** may be required instead of the MRP.
- **Disagreements Between Member States**: While the MRP is designed to simplify the approval process, disagreements between the RMS and CMS can slow down or complicate the process. These disputes can lead to delays and potential legal challenges.
- **Limited to European Economic Area**: The MRP is only applicable to EU member states and EEA countries. For countries outside this region, manufacturers must submit separate applications to their respective regulatory agencies.

3.2.2 Japan: New Drug Application (NDA) Process

Japan has a well-defined regulatory framework for the approval of new drugs, overseen by the **Pharmaceuticals and Medical Devices Agency (PMDA)**. The **New Drug Application (NDA)** process in Japan is designed to ensure that drugs introduced to the market are safe, effective, and of high quality. The **PMDA** plays a critical role in evaluating the safety and efficacy of new pharmaceutical products before they are allowed for sale in Japan. The application requirements for an NDA in Japan are rigorous and comprehensive, reflecting the country's commitment to public health and patient safety.

3.2.2.1 Application Requirements for Japan

The application requirements for a **New Drug Application (NDA)** in Japan involve several stages, each of which ensures that the drug meets Japan's strict regulatory standards for safety, efficacy, and quality. The **PMDA** requires detailed documentation, including clinical trial data, preclinical studies, and manufacturing information, to assess the drug's overall performance and its suitability for the Japanese market.

1. Pre-Application Stage

Before submitting the formal NDA, it is recommended that drug sponsors engage in consultations with the **PMDA** through the **pre-NDA consultation** process. This consultation allows sponsors to discuss the scientific, regulatory, and clinical requirements for their drug, providing guidance on the data needed to support the application.

- **Preclinical Data**: As part of the NDA submission, the manufacturer must provide **preclinical data**, which includes toxicological studies, pharmacological data, and information on how the drug behaves in animal models. This data is essential to assess the drug's safety before it is tested in humans.
- **Clinical Trial Design**: In the pre-application stage, sponsors may also seek the PMDA's guidance on clinical trial design. The **PMDA** provides feedback on clinical trial protocols to ensure that the studies will be sufficient to demonstrate the drug's safety and efficacy in the Japanese population.

2. NDA Submission

Once the drug sponsor has completed the necessary clinical trials and preclinical studies, they can proceed to submit the formal **NDA** to the **PMDA**. The submission must include the following key components:

- **Clinical Data**: The NDA must include the results of **clinical trials** conducted on the drug, including **Phase I**, **Phase II**, and **Phase III** trials. The clinical data should demonstrate that the drug is both **safe** and **effective** for its intended use. This includes information on dosing, pharmacokinetics, pharmacodynamics, and any observed adverse effects during the trials. The data must show that the benefits of the drug outweigh any potential risks.
- **Preclinical Data**: The submission must also include the **preclinical data** generated in animal studies. This includes **toxicology studies**, **pharmacokinetics**, **pharmacodynamics**, and other essential data that support the safety of the drug.
- **Manufacturing Information**: Detailed information about the drug's **manufacturing process** is required. This includes information on the raw materials used, the production process, the **Good Manufacturing**

Practice (GMP) compliance of the manufacturing facilities, and the quality control measures in place to ensure consistent product quality.

- **Stability Data**: Stability data is essential to demonstrate that the drug will remain effective and safe throughout its shelf life. The stability studies provide information on the drug's **shelf life**, storage conditions, and the impact of environmental factors on its stability.
- **Risk Management Plan**: The sponsor must provide a **risk management plan**, which outlines the potential risks associated with the drug and the steps that will be taken to mitigate those risks. This may include **post-marketing surveillance** to monitor the drug's safety once it is on the market.
- **Proposed Labeling**: The NDA must also include proposed **labeling** for the drug. This includes the drug's **indications**, **dosing information**, **warnings**, **side effects**, **contraindications**, and **drug interactions**. The proposed labeling must be clear and accurate, ensuring that healthcare providers can prescribe the drug appropriately and safely.

3. Review Process by PMDA

Once the NDA is submitted, the **PMDA** begins its detailed review process, which typically involves the following stages:

- **Initial Review**: The PMDA conducts an initial review to ensure that the application is complete and that all required data and documentation are included. If the application is missing critical information, the PMDA may request additional data from the sponsor.
- **Scientific Evaluation**: The **PMDA** conducts a comprehensive evaluation of the clinical and preclinical data provided in the NDA. This involves a detailed review of the drug's **safety** and **efficacy** based on the clinical trial results. The PMDA will assess the drug's **risk-benefit profile** and determine whether it meets Japan's stringent regulatory standards.
- **Manufacturing and Quality Review**: The PMDA also reviews the drug's **manufacturing processes** and quality control systems to ensure that the drug can be consistently produced to high standards. This includes evaluating the facilities where the drug is produced to ensure **GMP** compliance.
- **Advisory Committees**: In some cases, the PMDA may consult with independent **advisory committees** to seek expert opinions on the drug's safety and efficacy. These committees provide additional insights,

especially for drugs that involve complex or novel mechanisms of action.

4. Approval Decision

Once the PMDA has completed its review of the NDA, it issues an approval decision. There are several possible outcomes:

- **Approval**: If the PMDA determines that the drug is safe and effective, the NDA will be approved, and the drug will be granted marketing authorization in Japan. The approval allows the drug to be sold in Japan, with the drug's labeling, manufacturing processes, and risk management plans subject to ongoing monitoring.
- **Conditional Approval**: In some cases, the PMDA may grant **conditional approval**, allowing the drug to be marketed in Japan with specific conditions. These conditions may include the requirement for additional **post-marketing studies**, such as Phase IV trials, to further monitor the drug's safety and efficacy in the broader population.
- **Rejection**: If the PMDA determines that the drug does not meet the necessary standards for safety or efficacy, the NDA may be rejected. In such cases, the sponsor may be asked to submit additional data, modify the drug's formulation or labeling, or conduct further clinical trials to address the PMDA's concerns.

5. Post-Approval Requirements

Once a drug is approved, the sponsor must fulfill various **post-approval obligations** to ensure the drug remains safe and effective in the market:

- **Post-Marketing Surveillance**: The manufacturer must monitor the drug's performance in the market and report any adverse events or new safety concerns to the PMDA. This includes regular safety reports and updates to the **labeling** based on new information.
- **Risk Management**: The drug sponsor is required to implement any **risk management strategies** outlined in the NDA and continue to monitor the drug's safety profile after approval. This may involve conducting additional **Phase IV clinical trials** or surveillance studies.
- **Renewal of Approval**: In Japan, the drug's marketing authorization is typically valid for **five years**. After this period, the manufacturer must apply for **renewal** of the approval, providing updated safety data, efficacy information, and any new clinical or manufacturing

developments.

3.2.2.2 *Pharmaceutical and Medical Device Agency (PMDA) Process*

The **Pharmaceutical and Medical Device Agency (PMDA)** is the primary regulatory body in Japan responsible for ensuring the safety, efficacy, and quality of pharmaceutical products, medical devices, and regenerative medicines. The PMDA operates under the jurisdiction of the **Ministry of Health, Labour, and Welfare (MHLW)** and plays a central role in Japan's drug approval process. It is tasked with evaluating **New Drug Applications (NDAs)**, overseeing **clinical trials**, ensuring compliance with **Good Manufacturing Practices (GMP)**, and conducting **post-marketing surveillance**.

The PMDA process is comprehensive, designed to ensure that only drugs meeting the highest standards of safety and efficacy are approved for use in Japan. It includes rigorous assessments of clinical, preclinical, and manufacturing data, and the agency often works closely with other national and international regulatory bodies to maintain a global standard of drug evaluation.

1. Role and Functions of the PMDA

The **PMDA** is responsible for a broad range of activities throughout the lifecycle of a drug product, from the early stages of drug development to post-marketing surveillance. The primary functions of the PMDA include:

- **Evaluation of New Drugs**: The PMDA is responsible for reviewing New Drug Applications (NDAs), assessing the clinical and preclinical data, and determining whether the drug is safe, effective, and of high quality.
- **Monitoring Clinical Trials**: The PMDA oversees clinical trials in Japan, ensuring that they adhere to **Good Clinical Practice (GCP)** guidelines and that the rights and safety of participants are protected.
- **Manufacturing and Quality Control**: The PMDA conducts inspections of manufacturing facilities and evaluates the quality control processes used to ensure that drugs are consistently produced with the required standards of quality.
- **Post-Marketing Surveillance**: After a drug is approved, the PMDA monitors its safety and effectiveness in the general population through

post-marketing surveillance activities, including **adverse event reporting** and **risk management**.

- **Regulation of Medical Devices**: In addition to pharmaceutical products, the PMDA also regulates medical devices and regenerative medicines, ensuring they meet safety and quality standards.

2. The PMDA Review Process for New Drugs

The PMDA's review process for new drugs involves several steps to assess the drug's safety, efficacy, and quality. The process is designed to be thorough but efficient, ensuring that only drugs that meet Japan's high regulatory standards are approved. The review process includes the following stages:

2.1 Pre-Application Consultation

Before submitting a formal New Drug Application (NDA), sponsors are encouraged to engage in **pre-application consultations** with the PMDA. These consultations allow manufacturers to discuss the regulatory requirements, clinical trial design, and data expectations with the PMDA, ensuring that their submission meets the agency's standards.

- **Scientific Advice**: During these consultations, the PMDA provides guidance on the type of data required for approval. This may include recommendations on **clinical trial design**, **endpoints**, and **statistical methodologies**.
- **Guidance on GCP Compliance**: The PMDA also provides advice on **Good Clinical Practice (GCP)** compliance, helping sponsors design clinical trials that meet the agency's regulatory requirements.

2.2 Submission of the New Drug Application (NDA)

Once the clinical trials and preclinical studies are completed, the drug sponsor submits a **New Drug Application (NDA)** to the PMDA. The NDA must include comprehensive data, including:

- **Clinical Trial Data**: Results from Phase I, II, and III clinical trials demonstrating the drug's safety and efficacy for its intended use. The clinical trial data should show that the drug is effective in treating the condition for which it is intended and that its benefits outweigh the risks.

- **Preclinical Data**: Data from laboratory and animal studies assessing the drug's toxicity, pharmacokinetics, pharmacodynamics, and other key safety parameters.
- **Manufacturing Information**: Detailed information on the drug's manufacturing process, including the source of **active pharmaceutical ingredients (API)**, formulation, **quality control** measures, and compliance with **Good Manufacturing Practice (GMP)**.
- **Risk Management Plan**: A detailed plan outlining the steps that will be taken to manage any risks associated with the drug, including post-marketing surveillance activities.
- **Proposed Labeling**: The proposed labeling for the drug, which includes **indications**, **dosage instructions**, **warnings**, and **precautions**. The labeling must provide clear and accurate information to healthcare providers and patients.

2.3 Evaluation of the NDA

Once the NDA is submitted, the PMDA conducts a detailed evaluation of the drug. The evaluation process typically involves the following steps:

- **Initial Review**: The PMDA conducts an initial review of the submission to ensure that all necessary documents and data are included. If any information is missing or unclear, the PMDA may request additional data from the sponsor.
- **Scientific Review**: The PMDA's **Committee on New Drugs** conducts a thorough review of the clinical, preclinical, and manufacturing data to assess the drug's safety and efficacy. This review includes a detailed analysis of the clinical trial data to determine whether the drug provides a significant benefit over existing treatments.
- **GMP Inspection**: The PMDA inspects the manufacturing facilities to ensure that the drug is produced according to **Good Manufacturing Practice (GMP)**. This includes evaluating the drug's production process, quality control systems, and testing procedures to ensure that the drug meets the required quality standards.
- **Consultation with Advisory Committees**: In some cases, the PMDA may consult with independent advisory committees composed of scientific experts. These committees provide advice on complex issues, such as the drug's risk-benefit profile, therapeutic indications, or adverse

event profile.

2.4 Decision Making

After completing the review, the PMDA issues a decision regarding the approval of the drug. The possible outcomes include:

- **Approval**: If the PMDA determines that the drug is safe, effective, and of high quality, it grants **marketing authorization** for the drug. This allows the drug to be sold in Japan and enables the manufacturer to begin marketing the drug to healthcare providers and patients.
- **Conditional Approval**: In certain cases, the PMDA may grant **conditional approval**, allowing the drug to be marketed in Japan while the manufacturer conducts additional post-marketing studies or surveillance to further assess the drug's safety and efficacy.
- **Rejection**: If the PMDA determines that the drug does not meet the required safety and efficacy standards, it may reject the NDA. In this case, the manufacturer can appeal the decision or submit additional data to address the PMDA's concerns.

2.5 Post-Approval Monitoring and Surveillance

After a drug is approved, the PMDA continues to monitor its safety and efficacy in the general population. This is done through **post-marketing surveillance**, which includes:

- **Adverse Event Reporting**: The manufacturer is required to report any adverse events or side effects associated with the drug. This allows the PMDA to monitor the drug's safety profile over time and take action if necessary.
- **Risk Management**: The PMDA may require the manufacturer to implement additional risk management strategies if new safety concerns arise after the drug is marketed. This could include revising the drug's labeling, conducting additional clinical trials, or restricting the drug's use in certain patient populations.
- **Renewal of Marketing Authorization**: The marketing authorization for a drug is typically valid for **five years**. After this period, the manufacturer must submit an application for renewal, which includes updated data on the drug's safety and efficacy, as well as any new information from post-marketing surveillance.

3. Benefits of the PMDA Process

The PMDA process offers several benefits for both drug manufacturers and patients:

- **Efficient Review Process**: The PMDA is known for its efficient and transparent review process, which allows drugs to reach the Japanese market in a timely manner while ensuring that they meet high safety and efficacy standards.
- **High Regulatory Standards**: The PMDA ensures that all drugs approved in Japan meet rigorous regulatory standards for safety, efficacy, and quality. This provides confidence to healthcare providers and patients that the drugs they use are both effective and safe.
- **Support for Innovation**: The PMDA provides support for innovative drugs, including **orphan drugs** and **regenerative medicines,** by offering expedited review procedures and financial incentives to encourage the development of treatments for rare diseases.

3.2.3 Australia and Canada: Regulatory Pathways

Both **Australia** and **Canada** have well-established regulatory frameworks for the approval and monitoring of pharmaceutical products. These regulatory agencies ensure that drugs and medical devices available in these countries are safe, effective, and of high quality. In Australia, the **Therapeutic Goods Administration (TGA)** is responsible for regulating pharmaceutical products, while in Canada, the **Health Canada** plays a similar role. The regulatory pathways in both countries are designed to provide access to innovative medicines while ensuring patient safety and public health.

3.2.3.1 *Therapeutic Goods Administration (TGA), Australia*

The **Therapeutic Goods Administration (TGA)** is Australia's national regulatory authority for **therapeutic goods**, which include pharmaceuticals, medical devices, biological products, and related products. The TGA operates under the **Department of Health** and is responsible for evaluating, approving, and monitoring the safety and efficacy of therapeutic products in Australia. The TGA ensures that drugs and medical devices are available to the Australian population while minimizing risks to health.

The regulatory pathway for drugs in Australia involves a comprehensive evaluation process that includes submission of clinical data, manufacturing information, and post-marketing surveillance. The TGA's role is to ensure that all medicines meet high standards of safety and efficacy before they are marketed in Australia.

1. Overview of the TGA's Role in Drug Regulation

The TGA's mission is to protect public health by ensuring that medicines and medical devices are safe, effective, and of high quality. The TGA evaluates products from the **pre-market** stage to ensure safety and efficacy, and it also plays a vital role in **post-market surveillance** to monitor the continued safety of products once they are in use.

The TGA's responsibilities include:

- **Regulation of Medicines**: This includes the approval of pharmaceutical products, herbal medicines, and biologics. The TGA evaluates new drug applications, monitors the use of existing medicines, and ensures compliance with regulatory standards.
- **Regulation of Medical Devices**: The TGA also regulates medical devices, including diagnostics, surgical instruments, and implants, ensuring that these products are safe for use.
- **Post-Market Monitoring**: The TGA conducts ongoing monitoring of medicines and medical devices once they are available on the market. This includes monitoring adverse events, conducting audits of manufacturing facilities, and assessing post-marketing data.

2. The TGA Approval Process for Pharmaceuticals

The TGA approval process for pharmaceuticals is a structured and multi-step process designed to ensure that drugs entering the Australian market are safe, effective, and of high quality. The main stages in the approval process include:

2.1 Pre-Market Assessment

Before a drug can be marketed in Australia, the manufacturer must submit an application to the TGA for evaluation. The application must include a comprehensive range of data, including:

- **Clinical Data**: The TGA requires clinical trial data that demonstrates the drug's safety and efficacy. This data is typically derived from Phase I, II, and III clinical trials. The clinical trials should show that the drug is effective for its intended use and that its benefits outweigh any potential risks.

- **Preclinical Data**: The TGA also requires preclinical data, including toxicology studies and pharmacokinetic data, to assess the drug's safety profile in animal models before human trials begin.
- **Manufacturing Information**: The TGA evaluates the manufacturing processes used to produce the drug, ensuring that the drug is manufactured in compliance with **Good Manufacturing Practice (GMP)** standards. This includes a review of the facilities, raw materials, quality control measures, and production processes.
- **Proposed Labeling**: The manufacturer must submit proposed labeling for the drug, including the indications for use, dosage information, warnings, and contraindications. The TGA ensures that the labeling is clear, accurate, and provides sufficient information for healthcare providers and patients.

2.2 Evaluation Process

Once the application is submitted, the TGA conducts a detailed evaluation. This involves the following steps:

- **Scientific Review**: The TGA's **Expert Committees** conduct a scientific review of the clinical, preclinical, and manufacturing data to evaluate the drug's safety and efficacy. This includes reviewing the results of clinical trials and determining whether the drug's benefits outweigh the risks.
- **GMP Inspection**: The TGA conducts inspections of the manufacturing facilities to ensure that the drug is produced in compliance with GMP standards. This includes assessing the production process, quality control systems, and testing procedures to ensure that the drug is consistently produced to high standards.
- **Advisory Committees**: For complex or novel drugs, the TGA may consult with independent advisory committees that provide expert opinions on the drug's safety, efficacy, and quality. These committees may include specialists in clinical medicine, pharmacology, toxicology, and other relevant fields.

2.3 Approval or Rejection

After the evaluation process, the TGA makes a decision on the application. There are three potential outcomes:

- **Approval**: If the TGA determines that the drug is safe, effective, and of high quality, it grants marketing authorization, and the drug can be sold in Australia. The approval is generally granted for a period of **five years**, after which it must be renewed.
- **Conditional Approval**: In some cases, the TGA may grant **conditional approval** if additional data or post-marketing studies are needed to further assess the drug's safety or efficacy. This may involve additional clinical trials or post-marketing surveillance.
- **Rejection**: If the TGA determines that the drug does not meet the required standards for safety, efficacy, or quality, the application is rejected. In such cases, the manufacturer may appeal the decision or submit additional data to address the TGA's concerns.

3. Post-Market Surveillance and Monitoring

Once a drug is approved and marketed in Australia, the TGA continues to monitor the drug's safety and effectiveness through **post-market surveillance**. This involves:

- **Adverse Event Reporting**: Healthcare providers, patients, and manufacturers are required to report any adverse events or side effects associated with the drug. The TGA monitors these reports to identify any potential safety concerns that may arise after the drug is on the market.
- **Periodic Safety Update Reports (PSURs)**: Manufacturers are required to submit **Periodic Safety Update Reports** to the TGA, providing updated information on the drug's safety profile. This allows the TGA to track the drug's performance over time and take action if new risks are identified.
- **Risk Management**: The TGA may require manufacturers to implement **risk management strategies** if new safety issues are identified. This may include revising the drug's labeling, conducting additional clinical studies, or restricting the drug's use in certain populations.

4. The TGA's Role in Medical Device Regulation

In addition to pharmaceuticals, the TGA also regulates **medical devices** in Australia. The process for approving medical devices is similar to that for pharmaceuticals, with the TGA ensuring that devices meet safety and performance standards before they are marketed. Medical devices are classified based on their risk level, with higher-risk devices requiring more extensive evaluation and clinical data.

5. Advantages of the TGA Process

The TGA approval process offers several advantages for drug manufacturers and patients:

- **Efficiency**: The TGA's regulatory process is streamlined, allowing for the timely approval of drugs and medical devices while maintaining high safety and quality standards.
- **Rigorous Safety and Efficacy Standards**: The TGA ensures that all drugs and medical devices approved in Australia meet stringent safety, efficacy, and quality standards. This provides confidence to healthcare providers and patients that the products are safe and effective.
- **Global Recognition**: The TGA's approval process is internationally recognized, and drugs approved by the TGA are often accepted by regulatory bodies in other countries, facilitating global market access.

3.2.3.2 Health Canada: Drug Submission Process

Health Canada is the regulatory authority responsible for approving and overseeing pharmaceuticals, biologics, and medical devices in **Canada**. Through the **Health Products and Food Branch (HPFB)**, Health Canada ensures that drugs available in Canada meet stringent standards for **safety**, **efficacy**, and **quality**. The **drug submission process** in Canada is designed to protect public health while ensuring that patients have access to effective treatments. This process includes detailed steps from initial submission to post-market surveillance, allowing Health Canada to evaluate and monitor drugs throughout their lifecycle.

1. Overview of Health Canada's Role in Drug Regulation

Health Canada's role in drug regulation is critical to ensuring that pharmaceutical products in Canada are safe, effective, and of high quality. Health Canada evaluates drugs through a **comprehensive drug submission process**, which is governed by the **Food and Drugs Act** and its associated regulations. The approval process includes the assessment of clinical trial data, preclinical studies, and manufacturing practices, among other factors.

Health Canada's responsibilities include:

- **Evaluating New Drugs**: Health Canada is responsible for reviewing new drug submissions, ensuring that drugs are thoroughly evaluated before reaching the market.
- **Post-Market Surveillance**: After a drug is approved, Health Canada monitors its safety through **adverse event reporting** and other surveillance mechanisms.
- **Regulating Clinical Trials**: Health Canada ensures that clinical trials conducted in Canada adhere to ethical and scientific standards to protect the safety of participants.
- **Regulating Medical Devices and Biologics**: Health Canada also oversees the regulation of medical devices, biologics, and natural health products to ensure they meet safety and efficacy standards.

2. The Drug Submission Process in Canada

The drug submission process in Canada is a multi-step process that involves the submission of detailed data, review by Health Canada, and approval before a drug can be marketed in Canada. The primary pathway for drug approval in Canada is through the **New Drug Submission (NDS)**, which requires manufacturers to submit comprehensive documentation regarding the drug's safety, efficacy, and quality.

2.1 Pre-Submission Consultation

Before submitting a formal application, manufacturers are encouraged to consult with Health Canada through the **pre-submission consultation** process. This consultation allows sponsors to clarify the regulatory requirements for their drug submission, ensuring that they provide the necessary data and documentation to support their application.

- **Scientific Advice**: In the pre-submission stage, Health Canada provides guidance on **clinical trial designs, data requirements**, and **regulatory expectations**. This step helps manufacturers understand how to meet Health Canada's requirements and streamline the submission process.
- **Regulatory Strategy**: Manufacturers can discuss the **regulatory strategy** with Health Canada, including the appropriate pathway for approval, whether through the **New Drug Submission (NDS)** or the **Abbreviated New Drug Submission (ANDS)** for generics.

2.2 Submission of the New Drug Submission (NDS)

Once clinical trials and preclinical studies are completed, the manufacturer can submit the **New Drug Submission (NDS)** to Health Canada. The NDS includes a comprehensive set of documents that provide evidence of the drug's **safety, efficacy,** and **quality**. The submission generally includes:

- **Clinical Data**: The NDS must include the results from **clinical trials** that demonstrate the drug's safety and efficacy for its intended use. This data is collected from Phase I, II, and III clinical trials and must show that the drug is both safe and effective for its intended use in humans.
- **Preclinical Data**: Preclinical studies, including **toxicology** and **pharmacokinetics**, must be submitted to show how the drug behaves in animal models and to identify potential risks before human trials.
- **Manufacturing Information**: The NDS must also include detailed information about the **manufacturing process**, including the **raw materials** used, the **formulation** of the drug, and the quality control measures in place to ensure consistent production of the drug. The manufacturer must ensure that their production facilities comply with **Good Manufacturing Practices (GMP)**.
- **Stability Data**: Stability studies must be included to demonstrate that the drug will maintain its effectiveness and safety over time under various environmental conditions. This data helps establish the **shelf life** of the drug.
- **Risk Management Plan**: A **risk management plan** is required to identify and address any potential risks associated with the drug. This plan outlines how adverse events will be monitored and managed once the drug is marketed.
- **Proposed Labeling**: The manufacturer must submit the proposed labeling for the drug, including dosage instructions, potential side effects, warnings, and contraindications. Health Canada ensures that the labeling is clear, accurate, and informative for healthcare providers and patients.

2.3 Health Canada's Evaluation Process

Once the **New Drug Submission (NDS)** is submitted, Health Canada begins a detailed review process to evaluate the drug's safety, efficacy, and quality. The evaluation is conducted by **Health Canada's Therapeutic Products Directorate (TPD)**, which oversees the review of pharmaceuticals. The review process typically involves the following steps:

- **Initial Review**: Health Canada first conducts an initial review to ensure that the submission is complete and contains all the required data and documentation. If any essential information is missing, the manufacturer will be asked to provide additional data.
- **Scientific Evaluation**: The TPD assesses the scientific data included in the NDS. This evaluation includes a detailed review of clinical trial results to determine the **risk-benefit profile** of the drug. Health Canada ensures that the clinical data supports the drug's safety and efficacy for its intended indications.
- **GMP Inspection**: Health Canada conducts inspections of the manufacturing facilities to ensure compliance with **Good Manufacturing Practices (GMP)**. This step ensures that the drug is produced in facilities that meet the required standards for quality, consistency, and safety.
- **Expert Review**: In some cases, Health Canada may seek input from independent **advisory committees** of external experts. These committees provide advice on complex regulatory issues and help guide the decision-making process.

2.4 Approval or Rejection

After the review, Health Canada makes a decision on whether to approve or reject the drug. The possible outcomes are:

- **Approval**: If Health Canada determines that the drug meets the necessary standards for safety, efficacy, and quality, it grants **marketing authorization** for the drug. The drug is then allowed to be sold in Canada.
- **Conditional Approval**: In some cases, Health Canada may grant **conditional approval**. This is typically granted if additional post-market studies or risk management measures are required to confirm the drug's

safety or efficacy. The drug may be approved with conditions such as restricted use or mandatory post-marketing studies.

- **Rejection**: If Health Canada finds that the drug does not meet the required safety, efficacy, or quality standards, the submission may be rejected. In such cases, the manufacturer can appeal the decision or provide additional data to address Health Canada's concerns.

2.5 Post-Approval Requirements

Once a drug is approved in Canada, the manufacturer is required to fulfill ongoing obligations to monitor the drug's safety and efficacy:

- **Post-Marketing Surveillance**: The manufacturer must report any adverse events or new safety concerns associated with the drug. Health Canada monitors these reports and may take regulatory actions, such as modifying the drug's labeling or restricting its use if new risks are identified.
- **Periodic Safety Update Reports (PSURs)**: Manufacturers must submit **Periodic Safety Update Reports (PSURs)**, which include updated data on the drug's safety profile. These reports are used to assess whether new risks or concerns have emerged during the drug's use in the broader population.
- **Risk Management**: If new safety issues arise, Health Canada may require the manufacturer to implement additional **risk management strategies**, such as issuing safety warnings or restricting the drug's use in certain patient populations.
- **Renewal of Marketing Authorization**: Marketing authorization for most drugs is granted for **five years**, after which it must be renewed. Renewal requires the submission of updated safety data and evidence that the drug continues to meet Health Canada's standards.

3. Advantages of Health Canada's Drug Submission Process
Health Canada's drug submission process provides several benefits:

- **Thorough Evaluation**: The process ensures that only drugs that are proven to be safe, effective, and of high quality are approved for sale in Canada. This protects public health and ensures that patients have access to safe treatments.

- **Clear Guidelines**: Health Canada provides clear guidelines on the data required for drug approval, helping manufacturers prepare complete and compliant submissions.
- **Post-Marketing Monitoring**: Health Canada's robust post-marketing surveillance system ensures that any new safety concerns are identified and addressed promptly, ensuring that drugs remain safe for consumers once they are on the market.

3.3.1 Timeframes for IND, NDA, and ANDA Approvals

The approval of new drugs is a detailed and lengthy process that involves several stages, from the early **Investigational New Drug (IND)** application to the final marketing authorization. The regulatory agencies, such as the **U.S. Food and Drug Administration (FDA)**, set specific timeframes for reviewing and approving drug applications, including INDs, New Drug Applications (NDAs), and Abbreviated New Drug Applications (ANDAs). These timelines are critical for pharmaceutical companies to plan and manage the development and launch of new drugs in the market. Each type of application follows its own set of regulatory timelines, which depend on the nature of the drug, the data submitted, and the regulatory process involved.

1. Investigational New Drug (IND) Approval Process

The **Investigational New Drug (IND)** application is the first step in the regulatory process for a new drug. Before a new drug can be tested in human clinical trials, the manufacturer must submit an IND to the **U.S. Food and Drug Administration (FDA)** for review and approval. The IND provides the FDA with all the preclinical data required to assess the safety and biological activity of the drug.

1.1 Timeline for IND Approval

- **FDA Review Timeframe**: The FDA is required to review the IND within **30 days** of receiving the application. During this time, the FDA assesses the preclinical data, including the results of toxicology studies and other safety-related information, to ensure that the drug can be safely tested in humans. If the FDA does not raise any objections within 30 days, the IND is automatically allowed to proceed, and the manufacturer can begin

Phase I clinical trials.

- **Objections and Delays**: If the FDA identifies safety concerns or missing data in the IND, it may place a **clinical hold** on the trial, which halts the development of the drug until the issues are resolved. This hold can result in delays, and the manufacturer must address the FDA's concerns before proceeding with human trials.
- **Effect of Expedited Pathways**: For drugs that meet certain criteria, such as those addressing **unmet medical needs** or **rare diseases**, the FDA may offer **expedited review** pathways, such as **Fast Track, Breakthrough Therapy Designation**, or **Priority Review**. These programs may expedite the review and approval of the IND, allowing for earlier initiation of clinical trials.

2. New Drug Application (NDA) Approval Process

Once the clinical trials are completed, a manufacturer submits a **New Drug Application (NDA)** to the FDA to seek approval for the drug's marketing. The NDA includes all clinical trial data, preclinical studies, manufacturing information, and labeling for the drug. The FDA reviews the NDA to determine whether the drug is safe and effective for its intended use.

2.1 Timeline for NDA Approval

- **FDA Review Timeframe**: The standard review time for an NDA is **10 months** from the date the application is received. This period is known as the **Prescription Drug User Fee Act (PDUFA) goal date**, which is a timeline set under the PDUFA to ensure timely review of new drug applications.
- **Priority Review**: For drugs that offer significant improvements over existing treatments, such as those addressing serious conditions with no current treatments, the FDA may grant **Priority Review** status. This status shortens the review period to **6 months** instead of the standard 10 months. Priority Review is designed to expedite the availability of important new therapies to the public.
- **Standard vs. Priority Review**: Standard review timelines can take up to 10 months, but drugs with significant advantages or addressing serious health conditions may qualify for Priority Review. The FDA may also grant **Accelerated Approval** if the drug meets specific criteria related to unmet needs, which can further expedite the approval process.

- **Complete Response Letter (CRL):** If the FDA finds issues with the NDA that cannot be addressed quickly, it may issue a **Complete Response Letter (CRL),** which may delay approval. The CRL may request additional studies, manufacturing information, or changes to the proposed labeling.

3. Abbreviated New Drug Application (ANDA) Approval Process

An **Abbreviated New Drug Application (ANDA)** is submitted for **generic drugs,** which are copies of branded drugs that are already approved by the FDA. The ANDA includes evidence that the generic drug is **bioequivalent** to the reference drug, meaning it performs in the same way in the body. The goal of the ANDA process is to provide an expedited approval pathway for generic drugs once the patent for the original drug has expired.

3.1 Timeline for ANDA Approval

- **FDA Review Timeframe:** The standard review time for an ANDA is typically around **10 months,** similar to the NDA process. However, the review time may vary depending on the complexity of the drug and whether the submission includes any issues that require additional information or clarification.
- **Priority Review for Generics:** In some cases, the FDA may offer **Priority Review** for generic drugs, especially when the reference product is in high demand or there is an urgent need for a generic alternative. Priority Review for generic drugs can expedite the review process and shorten the approval time.
- **GDUFA and User Fees:** The **Generic Drug User Fee Amendments (GDUFA)** program requires generic drug manufacturers to pay user fees when submitting an ANDA. The timeline for ANDA review can be impacted by the efficiency of the **FDA's Generic Drug Program,** which has streamlined review processes to accelerate the availability of generic drugs.
- **Challenges in Generic Drug Approvals:** Generic drugs are often subject to more extensive scrutiny than brand-name drugs, particularly if there are concerns about bioequivalence, manufacturing processes, or intellectual property disputes. The review process may be delayed if the FDA finds issues with the application or if the manufacturer faces legal challenges regarding patent disputes.

4. Factors That Can Impact Approval Timelines

The timelines for IND, NDA, and ANDA approvals are influenced by several factors, including:

- **Completeness of the Application**: Incomplete or inaccurate applications can delay the approval process. Manufacturers must ensure that all necessary data and documentation are submitted to avoid delays caused by requests for additional information from regulatory agencies.
- **Complexity of the Drug**: Drugs that involve new technologies, complex formulations, or novel mechanisms of action may require longer review times due to the need for detailed scientific analysis. Similarly, generic drugs with complex formulations or those involving new delivery methods may also face longer approval timelines.
- **Regulatory Backlog**: Regulatory agencies like the FDA may experience backlogs of applications, especially during periods of high submission volumes. This can lead to delays in review and approval.
- **Priority Designations**: Drugs that qualify for **Fast Track, Breakthrough Therapy, Priority Review,** or **Accelerated Approval** pathways are subject to shorter review timelines, allowing for quicker approval in certain circumstances.
- **Clinical Trial Data**: The quality and completeness of clinical trial data are central to the review process. If the clinical trials do not meet regulatory expectations, additional studies may be required, leading to delays.
- **Post-Approval Commitments**: Regulatory agencies may require additional post-marketing studies or data to monitor the drug's long-term safety and efficacy, especially for drugs approved under **Accelerated Approval** or **Priority Review**.

3.3.2 Critical Pathways and Steps for Drug Approval

The process of drug approval is a complex and rigorous journey, often requiring multiple stages of review and evaluation to ensure the safety, efficacy, and quality of a new drug. During this process, regulatory agencies such as the **FDA** offer certain **critical pathways** and programs to expedite the approval of drugs that address urgent medical needs, provide significant therapeutic advantages, or offer alternative treatments for serious diseases.

Fast Track and **Priority Review** are two such programs that accelerate the approval process, ensuring quicker access to critical treatments for patients. These pathways aim to shorten the overall time it takes for drugs to move from development to the market, helping to address urgent healthcare needs more swiftly.

3.3.2.1 Fast Track and Priority Review Programs

The **Fast Track** and **Priority Review** programs, offered by the **U.S. Food and Drug Administration (FDA)**, are essential tools that aim to expedite the approval process for drugs that show significant potential in treating serious conditions. These programs are designed to facilitate quicker access to innovative therapies, particularly those that address unmet medical needs or serious diseases for which there are limited treatment options available. While both programs are intended to speed up the drug approval process, they operate under different conditions and with distinct criteria.

1. Fast Track Program

The **Fast Track Program** is a regulatory pathway designed to expedite the development and review of drugs that address unmet medical needs for serious conditions. The program is specifically intended for **drugs** that treat **serious** or **life-threatening** diseases or conditions where there are no adequate treatments available or where the drug may offer an advantage over existing treatments.

1.1 Eligibility for Fast Track

For a drug to qualify for the **Fast Track** designation, the drug must meet the following criteria:

- **Serious Condition**: The drug must be intended to treat a **serious** or **life-threatening** condition. These conditions can range from cancer, HIV/AIDS, and neurological disorders to rare diseases or other conditions with limited treatment options.
- **Unmet Medical Need**: The drug must address an **unmet medical need**. This means the drug must provide an alternative to existing treatments or offer a significant improvement in the treatment of the condition.
- **Potential for Improved Outcomes**: The drug should have the potential to offer better outcomes than existing treatments. This could be through improved efficacy, fewer side effects, or a more convenient method of administration.

1.2 Benefits of Fast Track Designation

The **Fast Track** designation offers several benefits to drug manufacturers, which ultimately expedite the drug development and approval process:

- **Frequent Communication with FDA**: Drugs with Fast Track status receive **frequent interactions** and meetings with the FDA during the development process. This provides an opportunity to discuss study designs, data collection methods, and other regulatory issues to ensure that the development path aligns with FDA expectations.
- **Rolling Review**: The Fast Track program allows for **rolling reviews**, where the drug manufacturer can submit sections of the New Drug Application (NDA) for review before the entire application is complete. This can speed up the overall review process, as the FDA begins its evaluation of the data as it becomes available.
- **Accelerated Approval**: If the drug shows promising results in clinical trials and demonstrates the potential to meet an unmet medical need, the FDA may grant **Accelerated Approval**, allowing the drug to reach the market more quickly. This approval is typically based on surrogate endpoints or early clinical evidence that suggests the drug will benefit patients.
- **Eligibility for Priority Review**: Drugs that receive Fast Track status are often eligible for **Priority Review**, which further shortens the FDA review time from the standard 10 months to 6 months.

1.3 Example of Fast Track Drugs

Drugs that have received **Fast Track** designation include treatments for serious conditions like **HIV, cancer,** and **Alzheimer's disease.** For instance, the **HIV** medication **Isentress** received Fast Track designation due to its potential to improve the treatment options available for people with HIV, a disease with high unmet medical needs.

2. Priority Review Program

The **Priority Review** program is another mechanism used by the FDA to expedite the approval process, but it is focused on drugs that offer significant improvements over existing therapies. The program is specifically aimed at **drugs** that **treat serious diseases** or conditions and represent a **breakthrough** in treatment options.

2.1 Eligibility for Priority Review

Drugs that are eligible for **Priority Review** typically meet the following criteria:

- **Significant Improvement in Treatment**: The drug must offer a significant improvement over existing treatments. This could be in terms of **efficacy**, **safety**, or **convenience**. For example, a drug that demonstrates a major advance in treating cancer could qualify for Priority Review if it provides significant survival benefits over current options.
- **Serious or Life-Threatening Disease**: Similar to the Fast Track program, Priority Review is intended for drugs that treat serious or life-threatening diseases. This can include diseases such as cancer, neurological disorders, cardiovascular conditions, and other high-impact health issues.

2.2 Benefits of Priority Review Designation

The **Priority Review** program offers several advantages to sponsors:

- **Faster Review Time**: The primary benefit of the Priority Review designation is that the FDA shortens the review timeline from the standard **10 months** to **6 months**. This allows new treatments to reach the market more quickly, which is particularly important for drugs addressing serious health conditions.
- **Expedited Access to Market**: Priority Review can significantly shorten the time it takes for a drug to be available to patients. This is particularly crucial for drugs that address urgent medical needs or provide new treatment options for diseases with no adequate therapies.
- **More Efficient FDA Review**: With Priority Review, the FDA commits to completing its review process in a more expedited manner. This includes providing a higher level of resources to review the drug and prioritizing the application in the regulatory queue.

2.3 Example of Priority Review Drugs

An example of a drug that has been granted **Priority Review** is **Keytruda**, a **cancer immunotherapy** developed by **Merck**. Keytruda, which showed significant improvements in overall survival rates for various cancers, was granted Priority Review because it represented a breakthrough in the treatment of cancer, offering hope for patients with limited options.

3. Comparison of Fast Track and Priority Review Programs

While both **Fast Track** and **Priority Review** are designed to expedite the drug approval process, they differ in their specific focus and eligibility criteria:

- **Fast Track** is designed for drugs that address **unmet medical needs** and treat **serious conditions**. The program facilitates **early communication with the FDA, rolling reviews**, and the possibility of **Accelerated Approval**. Fast Track drugs may also be eligible for **Priority Review** if they meet the necessary criteria.
- **Priority Review**, on the other hand, is granted to drugs that offer a **significant improvement** over existing treatments. While the **Priority Review** designation speeds up the review time to 6 months, it does not include all of the additional benefits of the Fast Track program, such as **rolling reviews** or **Accelerated Approval**.

4. Regulatory Impact

Both **Fast Track** and **Priority Review** are important tools that help regulatory agencies like the FDA provide quicker access to promising therapies for patients with serious or life-threatening diseases. These programs can reduce the time it takes for life-saving drugs to be available to the public, which is particularly important in cases where existing treatments are inadequate or where new innovations are urgently needed.

By expediting the approval process, the FDA can facilitate access to critical therapies and ensure that patients benefit from the most advanced treatment options as soon as they are deemed safe and effective. These programs are part of the broader effort to meet the needs of patients and healthcare providers in addressing serious diseases in a timely manner.

3.3.2.2 Accelerated Approval Process

The **Accelerated Approval Process** is a regulatory pathway designed by the **U.S. Food and Drug Administration (FDA)** to expedite the approval of drugs that address serious or life-threatening conditions, particularly those where there is an unmet medical need. The process allows for faster access to potentially life-saving therapies, especially when existing treatment options are limited or unavailable. This pathway is vital for speeding up the availability of drugs that show significant promise, allowing them to reach patients more quickly while still maintaining high safety and efficacy standards.

1. Overview of the Accelerated Approval Process

The **Accelerated Approval** program was established under the **FDA Modernization Act of 1997** to expedite the approval of drugs for serious or life-threatening diseases and conditions. The primary goal of this program is to allow earlier access to drugs that demonstrate meaningful benefits to patients, even when the full data required for traditional approval is not yet available.

Accelerated approval is typically granted for drugs that:

- **Treat Serious or Life-Threatening Diseases**: The drug must be intended for the treatment of serious conditions, such as cancer, Alzheimer's disease, HIV/AIDS, or rare diseases, where there are limited treatment options or no adequate therapies currently available.
- **Address Unmet Medical Needs**: The drug must provide a treatment option for diseases or conditions where there is an unmet medical need, such as offering a new mechanism of action or showing promising efficacy in a patient population that has not responded to current therapies.
- **Show Promise Based on Surrogate Endpoints**: Unlike traditional drug approval, which requires clinical evidence of direct benefit, the FDA may grant accelerated approval based on **surrogate endpoints** or **early clinical evidence**. Surrogate endpoints are indirect measures of a drug's effect that can predict clinical benefits, such as tumor shrinkage in cancer patients or improvement in biomarkers related to disease progression.

2. Eligibility for Accelerated Approval

To be eligible for **Accelerated Approval**, the drug must meet specific criteria. The primary factors considered include:

- **Serious Disease**: The drug must be for a **serious** or **life-threatening condition**. Conditions like cancer, heart disease, and neurological disorders, among others, are examples of diseases that qualify for accelerated approval.
- **Unmet Medical Need**: The drug must provide a therapeutic advantage over existing treatment options, particularly in cases where there are

limited or no other treatments available. Drugs that offer novel mechanisms of action, better efficacy, or improved safety profiles compared to current treatments are often prioritized for accelerated approval.

- **Surrogate Endpoints or Early Evidence**: Accelerated approval can be granted based on **surrogate endpoints**, which are indirect measures that predict clinical benefits. For example, a drug for cancer may be approved based on evidence that it causes a significant reduction in tumor size, even if it has not yet been demonstrated to extend survival rates. Similarly, biomarkers, such as changes in blood pressure or cholesterol levels, may be used to predict clinical benefit for drugs targeting cardiovascular diseases.

- **Evidence from Clinical Trials**: The drug must show sufficient evidence from early-phase clinical trials, demonstrating promising results that suggest it will improve patient outcomes. This evidence must be robust enough to justify earlier access to the drug, even if long-term data is not yet available.

3. Process of Accelerated Approval

The **Accelerated Approval** process involves several steps, which, while faster than the traditional approval process, still ensure rigorous evaluation of the drug's safety and efficacy. These steps are designed to provide early access to promising treatments without compromising patient safety.

3.1 Application for Accelerated Approval

To begin the accelerated approval process, the manufacturer submits a **New Drug Application (NDA)** or a **Biologics License Application (BLA)** to the FDA. The application must include data from clinical trials showing that the drug has demonstrated efficacy through **surrogate endpoints** or early clinical evidence, along with supporting data on the drug's safety profile.

- **Clinical Data**: The application must include data from Phase I, II, and sometimes Phase III trials, demonstrating that the drug has shown **preliminary evidence of efficacy**. The data should focus on **surrogate endpoints** that suggest the drug will have a meaningful impact on patient health.

- **Manufacturing Information**: As with all drug applications, the NDA or BLA must include detailed information about the drug's manufacturing process, ensuring that it can be consistently produced with high quality.

3.2 FDA Review and Decision

Once the application is submitted, the **FDA** conducts a review of the clinical data, including the surrogate endpoints or early clinical evidence supporting the drug's efficacy. The FDA will evaluate whether the data justifies granting **Accelerated Approval** for the drug, based on the following factors:

- **Risk-Benefit Assessment**: The FDA conducts a **risk-benefit analysis** to assess whether the drug's potential benefits outweigh any known risks, especially for serious or life-threatening conditions. This includes evaluating the drug's safety profile, the severity of potential side effects, and the expected benefits for patients.
- **Scientific Review**: The FDA's **Center for Drug Evaluation and Research (CDER)** reviews the submitted clinical trial data and considers whether the drug meets the necessary criteria for approval. For drugs based on surrogate endpoints, the FDA evaluates whether the surrogate markers are valid predictors of clinical benefits.
- **Consultation with Advisory Committees**: In some cases, the FDA may consult with independent **advisory committees** of external experts, who provide additional insights and guidance on whether the drug should receive Accelerated Approval.

If the FDA grants **Accelerated Approval**, the drug can be marketed in the U.S., even if additional clinical trials are required to confirm its clinical benefit in the long term.

3.3 Post-Approval Requirements

Once the drug is approved, there are several post-approval commitments required to confirm the drug's efficacy and safety in the broader patient population:

- **Confirmatory Trials**: The manufacturer is required to conduct **Phase IV confirmatory trials** to further evaluate the drug's long-term benefits and risks. These trials must confirm that the drug provides the anticipated clinical benefit that was predicted based on the surrogate endpoints used in the initial approval.
- **Post-Market Surveillance**: The FDA monitors the drug's performance in the market through **post-marketing surveillance**. This includes collecting data on any adverse events, side effects, or long-term effects, which can inform the FDA's decision to continue, modify, or revoke the drug's approval.
- **Labeling Updates**: Based on post-market data, the manufacturer may be required to update the drug's labeling, including any newly discovered side effects or updated safety information.

3.4 Withdrawal of Accelerated Approval

In some cases, if the confirmatory trials fail to show the expected clinical benefit or if new safety concerns arise, the FDA may withdraw the **Accelerated Approval** for the drug. This may happen if the drug's risk outweighs its benefits or if it is shown not to provide the anticipated therapeutic advantages.

4. Benefits of Accelerated Approval

The **Accelerated Approval** process provides several benefits, including:

- **Faster Access to Life-Saving Drugs**: The primary advantage of the Accelerated Approval process is that it allows patients to access drugs much sooner than the traditional approval process would permit. This is particularly important for drugs treating serious or life-threatening conditions where there are no existing effective therapies.
- **Support for Innovative Treatments**: Accelerated approval encourages the development of innovative drugs that may otherwise face long delays in the approval process. By allowing drugs based on surrogate endpoints to be approved, the FDA fosters the development of cutting-edge therapies.
- **Ongoing Monitoring**: While the approval is expedited, the FDA continues to monitor the drug's safety and effectiveness once it is available in the market, ensuring that any emerging risks are addressed

promptly.

5. Challenges of Accelerated Approval

While the **Accelerated Approval** process speeds up access to critical drugs, it also faces challenges:

- **Uncertainty in Long-Term Outcomes**: Since accelerated approval is based on surrogate endpoints, there is uncertainty about the long-term clinical benefit of the drug. Confirmatory trials are essential, and delays in these trials can pose risks.
- **Post-Marketing Surveillance**: Ongoing monitoring is essential to ensure that the drug remains safe and effective once it reaches the market. However, there can be delays in identifying potential long-term side effects, which can raise concerns about patient safety.
- **Regulatory Complexity**: The process requires significant coordination between drug manufacturers, the FDA, and other regulatory bodies to ensure that drugs are continuously evaluated and monitored post-approval.

Step	Description	Responsible Party	Documents/Actions Involved
Preclinical Testing	Laboratory and animal testing to assess drug safety and efficacy	Pharmaceutical Company	Preclinical data, toxicology studies
Clinical Trials (Phase I-III)	Human testing to evaluate drug safety and efficacy	Clinical Research Organization	Clinical trial protocols, informed consent
NDA Submission	Submitting clinical trial data for approval to market the drug	Pharmaceutical Company	NDA application, clinical trial data, drug composition
Regulatory Review	Reviewing NDA submission to ensure safety, efficacy, and quality	Regulatory Agencies (FDA, EMA)	Review of clinical trial data, manufacturing data
Post-Marketing Surveillance	Monitoring drug safety after approval	Pharmaceutical Company, Regulatory Agencies	Adverse event reporting, post-marketing studies

Table 10: Regulatory Approval Process Overview

Step	Purpose	Documents/Actions Involved
IND Application Submission	Request permission to begin human clinical trials	Preclinical data, trial protocols, drug formulation
FDA Review	Evaluate the safety and protocol for clinical trials	Review of IND application and preclinical studies
Clinical Trial Start	Begin Phase I clinical trials in humans	Informed consent, monitoring for adverse events
Progress Reports	Provide updates on the trial's progress to the FDA	Data on adverse events, efficacy
Approval or Denial	FDA approval or denial based on trial results	Approval for clinical trials or additional data requests

Table 11: Investigational New Drug (IND) Process

Step	Purpose	Documents/Actions Involved	Responsible Party
Pre-NDA Meeting	Meet with regulatory authorities to discuss submission	Preclinical and clinical trial data, manufacturing process	Pharmaceutical Company, FDA/EMA
NDA Submission	Submit all required documents for regulatory review	Clinical trial results, proposed labeling, manufacturing data	Pharmaceutical Company
FDA/EMA Review	Regulatory authorities review the application for approval	Review of safety, efficacy, and manufacturing data	FDA/EMA
Approval or Rejection	Regulatory authorities grant approval or request more data	Approval letter or additional study requests	FDA/EMA
Post-Marketing Requirements	Monitor safety and efficacy after approval	Ongoing adverse event reporting, post-marketing studies	Pharmaceutical Company

Table 12: New Drug Application (NDA) Process

Document	Purpose	Required By
NDA (New Drug Application)	Request approval to market a new drug	FDA, EMA
IND (Investigational New Drug)	Request permission to start clinical trials	FDA
ANDA (Abbreviated New Drug Application)	Approval for generic drugs	FDA
CTD (Common Technical Document)	Standard format for drug registration	Global regulatory agencies
DMF (Drug Master File)	Detailed information about drug manufacturing	FDA, EMA

Table 13: Regulatory Documents in Drug Approval

Change Type	Description	Documents/Actions Involved	Approval Process
Post-Approval Supplement	Change to manufacturing or labeling after approval	Supplementary NDA or CBE submission	FDA/EMA review
Changes Being Effected (CBE)	Minor changes to approved NDA/ANDA	CBE submission with data supporting change	FDA/EMA review
New Drug Labeling	Modification of drug's labeling based on new data	Updated labeling submission	FDA/EMA approval
Manufacturing Change	Change in manufacturing process or location	Manufacturing change documentation	FDA/EMA approval

Table 14: Post-Approval Changes to NDA/ANDA

Registration of Indian Drug Products in Overseas Markets

4.1 Export Procedures for Pharmaceutical Products

The export of pharmaceutical products from India to overseas markets involves a multi-step process that requires compliance with international regulatory standards. The pharmaceutical industry in India is one of the largest and most dynamic in the world, and India is a significant supplier of generic medicines globally. To ensure the quality, safety, and efficacy of these medicines, Indian drug manufacturers must adhere to strict export procedures and regulatory requirements. The export process is not only governed by the rules and regulations in India but also by the specific regulatory standards of the destination country or region. These regulatory requirements ensure that Indian pharmaceutical products meet the standards set by the importing country and that they are suitable for sale in foreign markets.

4.1.1 Regulatory Requirements for Drug Exports

For a pharmaceutical product to be exported from India, it must meet the regulatory requirements set by both **Indian authorities** and the regulatory agencies in the importing country. These requirements typically include compliance with **Good Manufacturing Practices (GMP)**, approval from the **Central Drugs Standard Control Organization (CDSCO)**, and adherence to specific documentation requirements.

India's **Drugs and Cosmetics Act, 1940** and the **Drugs and Cosmetics Rules, 1945** govern the export of pharmaceutical products, ensuring that all drugs exported from India meet international quality standards. Additionally, the **Directorate General of Foreign Trade (DGFT)** plays a critical role in facilitating and regulating pharmaceutical exports. Exporters must also be aware of the **World Trade Organization (WTO)** regulations, especially the **Trade-Related Aspects of Intellectual Property Rights (TRIPS)** agreement, which governs the patenting and export of pharmaceutical products.

The export of pharmaceutical products involves several key regulatory requirements:

- **Registration with the CDSCO:** Manufacturers must be registered with the **Central Drugs Standard Control Organization (CDSCO)**, which is the national regulatory authority in India. The CDSCO ensures that drugs manufactured and exported from India comply with the required standards of quality, safety, and efficacy.
- **Compliance with International Standards**: Pharmaceutical exports from India must comply with the regulatory standards of the destination country. These may include compliance with **Good Manufacturing Practices (GMP)**, **Good Clinical Practices (GCP)**, and other international standards.
- **Licensing and Certification**: Indian pharmaceutical manufacturers must obtain the required licenses and certifications for exporting their products. These may include the **Manufacturing License** for the company, the **Export License**, and certifications from the regulatory authority confirming compliance with local regulations.
- **Labeling and Packaging Compliance:** The labeling and packaging of pharmaceutical products must meet the specific requirements of the importing country. This may include translating labels into the official language(s) of the destination country, providing specific dosage information, and listing all ingredients, side effects, and contraindications.

4.1.1.1 Documentation for Exporting Pharmaceutical Products

The documentation required for exporting pharmaceutical products is critical for ensuring smooth processing at customs, regulatory bodies, and destination countries. Proper and comprehensive documentation helps prevent delays, regulatory issues, and potential rejections at the importing country's borders. Below are the key documents required for the export of pharmaceutical products:

1. Commercial Invoice

A **commercial invoice** is a key document required for the export of pharmaceutical products. It provides detailed information about the transaction, including:

- **Seller and buyer details**
- **Description of the pharmaceutical product(s)**
- **Quantity** and **unit price**
- **Total value** of the shipment
- **Payment terms**
- **Shipping terms** (Incoterms)
- **Export license number** (if applicable)

This document serves as a legal record of the transaction and is required for customs clearance at both the **Indian customs office** and the **destination country's customs office.**

2. Export License

An **export license** is required for pharmaceutical manufacturers and exporters to legally export medicines from India. The **Directorate General of Foreign Trade (DGFT)** issues the export license, ensuring that the pharmaceutical products meet the standards for export. In some cases, certain medicines may be subject to export restrictions or require additional approvals from the **Ministry of Health and Family Welfare (MHFW)** or CDSCO.

3. Certificate of Pharmaceutical Product (CPP)

A **Certificate of Pharmaceutical Product (CPP)** is issued by the **Central Drugs Standard Control Organization (CDSCO)** and is required for exporting pharmaceutical products to most countries. The CPP certifies that the pharmaceutical product conforms to the quality standards specified by the Indian authorities and complies with the regulations of the importing country.

- The **WHO Certificate of Pharmaceutical Product (WHO CPP)** is widely recognized and accepted by many countries and is used to ensure the safety and efficacy of the product.
- The **CPP** includes details such as the product name, manufacturing license, GMP compliance, and export license number.

4. GMP Certificate

A **Good Manufacturing Practice (GMP) certificate** is required to confirm that the manufacturing facility where the pharmaceutical product is produced complies with the GMP standards. **GMP compliance** ensures that the product is consistently produced and controlled according to the required standards of quality, safety, and efficacy.

- The **GMP certificate** is typically issued by the CDSCO or the relevant regulatory authority in the country where the product is manufactured.
- The certificate may also be required by the importing country's regulatory authorities to ensure that the drug has been manufactured in facilities that meet international standards.

5. Free Sale Certificate

A **Free Sale Certificate (FSC)** is an important document that certifies that a pharmaceutical product is **approved** and legally marketed in India. The FSC is required for the **registration of the product** in the importing country and assures the authorities that the product is already in free sale in India.

The **Free Sale Certificate** is issued by the **CDSCO** and provides information about the product's **market approval status** in India. It is typically required for countries that require evidence of the drug's market approval in the country of origin before it can be imported.

6. Certificate of Origin

The **Certificate of Origin** is required to verify that the pharmaceutical product was **manufactured** in India. This certificate is typically issued by the **Chamber of Commerce** in India or other recognized authorities. The **Certificate of Origin** is important for determining the **origin of goods** for trade agreements, tariffs, and import duties in the destination country.

7. Bill of Lading (B/L) or Airway Bill (AWB)

The **Bill of Lading (B/L)** or **Airway Bill (AWB)** serves as the transport document for shipping pharmaceutical products overseas. This document contains the details of the shipment, including the names of the shipper and consignee, the destination, the nature of the goods, and the shipping terms. It is issued by the shipping company or air carrier and acts as a receipt for the goods in transit.

8. Customs Declaration Form

The **Customs Declaration Form** is a mandatory document that is submitted to **Indian customs** during the export process. It includes details about the product being exported, the value of the goods, the consignee, and other relevant information required for customs clearance.

This form is critical to ensure that the pharmaceutical products are cleared through Indian customs and that all export duties or taxes are paid.

9. Other Documentation (as per Importing Country)

In addition to the documents mentioned above, each importing country may require specific additional documentation for the registration and clearance of pharmaceutical products. These may include:

- **Clinical trial data** for new drugs
- **Product samples** for inspection or laboratory analysis
- **Import licenses** and **registration certificates** from the importing country's regulatory authorities
- **Environmental health and safety compliance** certifications, depending on the country's regulations

3. Compliance with International Standards

In addition to the required documentation, pharmaceutical exporters must ensure that their products meet the relevant international standards for quality and safety. This includes compliance with **Good Manufacturing Practices (GMP)**, **International Council for Harmonisation (ICH)** guidelines, and any other regulations set forth by the importing country or region.

Many countries, especially those in the **European Union (EU)**, the **United States**, and **Australia**, require strict adherence to international standards to ensure that drugs are safe and effective for patients.

4.1.1.2 Export Licensing and Approvals

Export licensing and approvals are critical steps in the process of exporting pharmaceutical products from India to international markets. These regulatory steps ensure that the products being exported comply with both Indian regulations and the regulatory requirements of the destination country. Pharmaceutical products must meet stringent standards to ensure that they are safe, effective, and of high quality before they can be marketed abroad. The export licensing and approval process helps to maintain these standards, protect public health, and ensure compliance with international trade agreements.

1. Export Licensing in India

In India, the export of pharmaceutical products is regulated by various government agencies to ensure that these products meet national and international standards. Export licensing involves obtaining permission from Indian authorities to export drugs and medicines legally.

1.1 Directorate General of Foreign Trade (DGFT)

The **Directorate General of Foreign Trade (DGFT)** is the primary agency responsible for regulating and promoting India's international trade, including the export of pharmaceutical products. The DGFT issues the **Export License**, which allows pharmaceutical companies to legally export their products abroad. The **Export License** is essential for ensuring that the drugs meet the necessary compliance requirements, including adherence to India's export laws and regulations.

- **Registration with DGFT**: Indian pharmaceutical manufacturers must be registered with the DGFT to be eligible for export. They need to apply for an **Importer Exporter Code (IEC)**, which is a mandatory requirement for all exporters in India.
- **Export Promotion**: The DGFT also facilitates the export process by providing guidelines and ensuring that exporters adhere to the provisions of India's trade agreements. Pharmaceutical companies are encouraged to follow these guidelines to ensure smooth export operations.

1.2 Central Drugs Standard Control Organization (CDSCO)

The **Central Drugs Standard Control Organization (CDSCO)** is the national regulatory body responsible for overseeing the manufacturing, approval, and quality control of pharmaceutical products in India. CDSCO plays a significant role in regulating the export of pharmaceutical products, ensuring they meet the necessary safety, efficacy, and quality standards before being shipped internationally.

- **Manufacturing License**: Indian pharmaceutical companies must obtain a **Manufacturing License** from CDSCO to ensure that the drugs being produced meet **Good Manufacturing Practices (GMP)**. This license is crucial for the export of drugs to foreign markets, as most countries require that imported drugs come from GMP-compliant facilities.
- **Certificate of Pharmaceutical Product (CPP)**: The CDSCO issues a **Certificate of Pharmaceutical Product (CPP)**, which is essential for the export of pharmaceutical products. The CPP certifies that the pharmaceutical product has been manufactured in compliance with Indian regulations and is suitable for export. Many foreign regulatory authorities require the CPP to ensure that the product meets the necessary safety and quality standards for importation.

1.3 Drug Export License

To obtain a **drug export license**, pharmaceutical companies must submit an application to the **Drug Controller General of India (DCGI)**, a division of CDSCO. The export license ensures that the company complies with both Indian and international pharmaceutical standards. The license allows the manufacturer to export specific pharmaceutical products, including prescription drugs, over-the-counter medicines, and other health-related products.

- **Inspection of Manufacturing Facility**: The **CDSCO** or **State Drug Control Authorities** may inspect the manufacturing facility before granting the export license. This inspection is to verify that the manufacturer is following GMP guidelines and other quality control measures to ensure the safety and quality of the products being exported.
- **Approval for Specific Drugs**: The export license is typically granted for specific drugs. Pharmaceutical manufacturers must apply for approval for each individual drug they wish to export. This ensures that all products meet the required regulatory standards before being shipped internationally.

2. Export Approvals from Importing Countries

In addition to Indian regulatory requirements, pharmaceutical products must meet the approval requirements set by the regulatory authorities in the destination country. Each country has its own regulations and licensing requirements for importing drugs, and pharmaceutical companies must ensure that they comply with these regulations before shipping products abroad.

2.1 Regulatory Authorities in Importing Countries

Each importing country has a designated **regulatory body** responsible for approving pharmaceutical products. These authorities may require manufacturers to submit various documents, including product samples, clinical trial data, and compliance certifications, before approving the import of pharmaceutical products. Some of the key regulatory authorities include:

- **U.S. Food and Drug Administration (FDA)**: The FDA regulates the import of pharmaceutical products into the United States. Indian exporters must ensure that their products comply with **FDA guidelines**, including **GMP** standards and **FDA labeling** requirements.
- **European Medicines Agency (EMA)**: For exporting to European countries, Indian pharmaceutical manufacturers must meet the standards set by the **EMA**, which regulates pharmaceutical products within the European Union. This includes obtaining **European market authorization** for the drugs.
- **Therapeutic Goods Administration (TGA), Australia**: In Australia, the TGA regulates pharmaceutical imports. Indian exporters must ensure that their products meet the TGA's standards for **quality control**, **safety**, and **efficacy**.
- **Health Canada**: Indian pharmaceutical products must meet the requirements set by **Health Canada** for approval in Canada. This includes submitting the appropriate **certifications** and **documentation** to ensure that the products meet Canadian standards.

2.2 Import License from Destination Countries

Many countries require pharmaceutical manufacturers to obtain an **import license** before allowing products into their market. An import license ensures that the products comply with local health and safety regulations. To obtain this license, manufacturers must submit the following documents:

- **Certificate of Free Sale**: This document certifies that the pharmaceutical product is legally sold in India and is available in the market. It is often required by regulatory authorities in importing countries.
- **Certificate of Origin**: This document verifies the country of origin of the pharmaceutical product, which is important for tariff and trade agreements.
- **Product Registration**: In some cases, pharmaceutical products must be **registered** with the regulatory authority in the importing country before they can be marketed. This involves submitting detailed data on the product's composition, manufacturing process, and clinical trial results.
- **Good Manufacturing Practices (GMP) Certificate**: Many countries require a **GMP certificate** to confirm that the pharmaceutical products are manufactured according to international quality standards.

2.3 Documentation for Export Approvals

To ensure compliance with both Indian and international regulations, the following documents are required for obtaining export approvals:

- **Export License**: Issued by the Indian authorities to allow the legal export of pharmaceutical products.
- **Manufacturing License**: Certifies that the pharmaceutical manufacturer complies with **Good Manufacturing Practices (GMP)**.
- **Certificate of Pharmaceutical Product (CPP)**: Issued by CDSCO to certify that the product complies with Indian regulations and is suitable for export.
- **Free Sale Certificate (FSC)**: Certifies that the pharmaceutical product is available for sale in the domestic market and meets the standards required by the exporting country.
- **GMP Certificate**: Validates that the manufacturing facility follows **Good Manufacturing Practices** and meets international standards.

3. Compliance with International Standards

Indian pharmaceutical exporters must ensure that their products comply with **international standards** for quality, safety, and efficacy. This includes adherence to:

- **International Council for Harmonisation (ICH) Guidelines**: These guidelines provide a set of standards for drug approval that ensure consistency and quality in the pharmaceutical industry.
- **World Health Organization (WHO) Guidelines**: WHO's **Good Manufacturing Practice (GMP)** guidelines are globally recognized and ensure that pharmaceutical products meet international standards for quality.
- **Trade-Related Aspects of Intellectual Property Rights (TRIPS)**: TRIPS governs the protection of intellectual property rights in international trade, which is particularly important for the export of patented pharmaceutical products.

4.2 Technical Documentation for Registration

When it comes to exporting pharmaceutical products, having the right technical documentation is crucial for ensuring that the products meet the required regulatory standards of both the exporting country and the importing countries. One of the key elements of technical documentation for pharmaceutical registration is the **Drug Master File (DMF)**. The DMF plays a significant role in facilitating the registration process for pharmaceutical products, providing detailed information about the quality, manufacturing, and safety of the product. Regulatory agencies around the world rely on the DMF to assess the safety, efficacy, and quality of drugs before they are approved for market entry.

4.2.1 Drug Master File (DMF) and Its Role in Registration

A **Drug Master File (DMF)** is a confidential document submitted to regulatory authorities, providing detailed information about the manufacturing, quality control, and composition of a drug product. The DMF is primarily submitted to regulatory agencies like the **U.S. Food and Drug Administration (FDA), European Medicines Agency (EMA)**, and others, and serves as a comprehensive source of information for evaluating the safety and quality of pharmaceutical products.

The **DMF** is not a product registration application, but rather a supporting document that provides essential data for drug approval and registration processes. Manufacturers typically submit a DMF for the **Active Pharmaceutical Ingredients (APIs)** or the **drug substance** used in the formulation of a pharmaceutical product, but it may also include information on **drug formulations**, **excipients**, and **packaging materials**. A DMF ensures that regulatory agencies can assess the drug's quality and manufacturing processes without having to review proprietary information, thus protecting the intellectual property of the manufacturer.

1. Components of a Drug Master File (DMF)

The **DMF** contains comprehensive technical details about the drug product or API, including but not limited to:

- **Manufacturer Information**: Details about the manufacturer's name, address, and the manufacturing site(s). The DMF also includes the name of the **contact person** for the regulatory authority, ensuring that all communication can be directed efficiently.

- **Drug Substance Information**: Detailed information about the **Active Pharmaceutical Ingredient (API)**, including its **chemical structure**, **physical characteristics**, and **stability data**. This section often includes details about the **synthesis** or **extraction methods**, including **raw materials**, **reaction pathways**, and **purification processes**.

- **Manufacturing Process**: Comprehensive information on the **manufacturing processes** used for the drug substance or product. This includes information on the **production environment**, **equipment used**, and **control measures** in place to ensure the consistent production of high-quality products.

- **Quality Control**: A detailed description of the **quality control procedures** in place, including **testing protocols** for **raw materials, in-process materials**, and **final drug products**. This section may include information about **analytical methods** used to test the drug for potency, purity, and safety.

- **Stability Data**: Information about the **stability studies** conducted on the drug product or API. This data helps determine the **expiration date**, **storage conditions**, and the **shelf life** of the drug. Stability studies are essential to ensure that the drug maintains its quality and efficacy throughout its shelf life.

- **Packaging and Labeling**: Information about the **packaging materials** used for the drug and the **labeling** required by regulatory agencies. The packaging must be suitable for protecting the drug from degradation, contamination, and damage, and the labeling must meet the legal and regulatory requirements of the destination country.

- **Excipients Information**: Details of the **inactive ingredients** (excipients) used in the drug formulation, such as stabilizers, binders, fillers, and preservatives. Regulatory agencies require this information to ensure that excipients do not adversely affect the drug's quality or safety.
- **Toxicological Data**: Any available **toxicological data** related to the drug product or its ingredients. This section may include information on **acute toxicity**, **chronic toxicity**, and **mutagenicity** studies conducted on the API or finished drug product to assess safety.
- **Environmental Impact Data**: Some regulatory authorities may require **environmental impact assessments** related to the drug manufacturing process, especially for drugs that involve the use of hazardous substances or chemicals.

2. Types of Drug Master Files (DMFs)

There are several types of **DMFs**, each focusing on different aspects of drug product development and registration. The specific type of DMF that a manufacturer submits depends on the nature of the drug and its role in the pharmaceutical product. The primary types of DMFs are:

- **Type I: Drug Master File for Drug Substance (API)**: This type of DMF contains information related to the **Active Pharmaceutical Ingredient (API)**, including the chemical composition, manufacturing process, stability data, and quality control tests. Type I DMFs are essential for ensuring that the API meets regulatory standards for safety, efficacy, and quality.
- **Type II: Drug Master File for Drug Products (Formulation)**: This type of DMF contains information related to the **formulation** of the finished pharmaceutical product. It includes data on the drug product's composition, manufacturing process, packaging, labeling, and quality control procedures. Type II DMFs are submitted by manufacturers of finished drug products.
- **Type III: Drug Master File for Packaging Materials**: This DMF includes information on the **packaging materials** used to protect the drug product, including **plastic containers, blister packs, vials**, and other packaging components. Type III DMFs ensure that packaging meets regulatory requirements for safety, compatibility, and stability.
- **Type IV: Drug Master File for Excipients**: Excipients are inactive ingredients used in drug formulations, such as binders, fillers,

preservatives, and stabilizers. Type IV DMFs provide detailed information on excipients to ensure they meet regulatory standards for safety and compatibility with the active pharmaceutical ingredient.

- **Type V: Drug Master File for Combination Products**: This DMF type is for drugs that combine multiple components, such as a drug combined with a device (e.g., a **drug-eluting stent**). Type V DMFs include information on the combination product's components, including the drug, the device, and their interactions.

3. Role of DMF in Drug Registration

The **DMF** plays an essential role in the **drug registration process** with regulatory agencies. Its key functions include:

- **Supporting Drug Applications**: A DMF provides regulatory agencies with the essential information needed to assess the safety, efficacy, and quality of a drug product. It serves as a critical part of the **New Drug Application (NDA)** or **Abbreviated New Drug Application (ANDA)** process, as it allows the regulatory authorities to evaluate the drug's manufacturing process, quality control, and stability without disclosing proprietary or confidential information.

- **Ensuring Compliance with International Standards**: DMFs ensure that the pharmaceutical product meets **international regulatory standards**, including those set by the **U.S. FDA, EMA, World Health Organization (WHO)**, and other global regulatory bodies. They provide a structured framework for demonstrating **Good Manufacturing Practices (GMP)** and other quality standards.

- **Facilitating International Market Access**: A well-prepared and compliant DMF facilitates the **global registration** of a drug product. Once a DMF is submitted to regulatory authorities, it can be used to support registration in multiple countries, ensuring consistency in the quality and safety standards across international markets.

- **Confidentiality**: The DMF is a **confidential** document, which protects the intellectual property of the manufacturer. It enables the manufacturer to submit detailed manufacturing processes, raw material sources, and other sensitive data to regulatory authorities without making these details public. This confidentiality is crucial for protecting proprietary manufacturing techniques and formulations.

4.2.2 Common Technical Document (CTD)

The **Common Technical Document (CTD)** is an internationally recognized format for submitting regulatory information about pharmaceutical products to regulatory authorities. Developed by the **International Conference on Harmonisation of Technical Requirements for Pharmaceuticals for Human Use (ICH)**, the CTD is designed to streamline the submission process for drug approvals and harmonize the format across different regions, including the **U.S.**, **Europe**, and **Japan**. The CTD structure is intended to provide a consistent, organized format for submitting the required technical documentation, ensuring that regulatory agencies have the necessary information to evaluate the safety, efficacy, and quality of a drug product.

4.2.2.1 Structure and Requirements of CTD

The **CTD** is divided into five modules, with each module containing specific types of information required for drug registration. These modules include the administrative, clinical, and non-clinical data that regulators need to assess the drug's safety, efficacy, and quality. The modular structure is designed to facilitate the submission process and provide regulatory agencies with the detailed information necessary to make informed decisions about the approval of a drug product.

1. Module 1: Administrative and Prescribing Information

Module 1 of the CTD contains country-specific administrative information and requirements related to the drug submission. This module is not standardized across regions and will vary depending on the regulatory authority (e.g., **FDA, EMA, PMDA, TGA**, or **Health Canada**). However, it typically includes the following documents:

- **Application Forms**: These forms include the administrative details of the application, such as the drug name, applicant's details, and the proposed indication(s).
- **Cover Letter**: A formal cover letter introducing the application, providing a brief overview of the drug, and indicating the submission type (e.g., **New Drug Application (NDA), Abbreviated New Drug Application (ANDA)**).

- **Labeling and Package Inserts**: Detailed information about the drug's labeling, including instructions for use, dosage, contraindications, and warnings. The label is required to meet the regulatory standards of the country where the drug is being marketed.
- **Drug Master File (DMF)**: If applicable, a **Drug Master File (DMF)** may be referenced in this module, especially if the drug contains **active pharmaceutical ingredients (APIs)** or **excipients** that are sourced from different manufacturers.
- **Clinical Trial Certificates**: If the product has undergone clinical trials, details about the trial certificates and study reports may be included.
- **Fee and Payment Information**: The regulatory fee required for the submission may also be included in this module.

2. Module 2: Summaries

Module 2 contains summaries of the clinical, non-clinical, and quality data provided in the subsequent modules. This module provides a high-level overview of the key findings and results, making it easier for regulatory authorities to assess the drug's overall risk-benefit profile. Key documents in **Module 2** include:

- **Summary of Quality (SQA)**: A summary of the chemistry, manufacturing, and controls (CMC) data provided in **Module 3**. This summary highlights key aspects of the drug's formulation, stability, and manufacturing processes.
- **Summary of Non-Clinical Data**: A brief summary of the **toxicological studies, pharmacokinetic data**, and **pharmacodynamic data** provided in **Module 4**. This summary outlines the safety and efficacy of the drug in animal models.
- **Summary of Clinical Data**: A summary of the **clinical trials** and **clinical pharmacology studies** provided in **Module 5**. This includes a discussion of the drug's efficacy, safety, dosing, and potential risks, as demonstrated in human clinical trials.
- **Integrated Summary of Safety and Efficacy**: This section provides an overview of the overall safety and efficacy profile of the drug, including an analysis of adverse events, therapeutic outcomes, and the risk-benefit ratio.

3. Module 3: Quality

Module 3 focuses on the **quality** of the drug product and includes detailed information on the chemistry, manufacturing, and controls (CMC). It provides the regulatory authority with a comprehensive understanding of the manufacturing process, drug substance, drug product, and related quality control measures. The main components of **Module 3** include:

- **Drug Substance (API)**: Detailed information on the **active pharmaceutical ingredient (API)**, including its **chemical composition**, **physical properties**, **manufacturing process**, **characterization**, and **quality control tests**. This section also includes data on the **stability** of the API.
- **Drug Product (Finished Formulation)**: Information about the finished drug product, including its **formulation**, **dosage form**, **strength**, **route of administration**, and **packaging**. This section includes detailed manufacturing processes, quality control tests, and packaging information to ensure that the drug product is safe, effective, and of high quality.
- **Manufacturing Process**: Detailed description of the **manufacturing process** used to produce the drug substance and drug product. This includes the source of raw materials, the steps involved in the manufacturing process, and the quality control measures employed during production to ensure consistent product quality.
- **Control of Excipients**: Information on the **inactive ingredients (excipients)** used in the drug formulation, including their quality, safety, and compatibility with the active ingredient.
- **Stability Studies**: Data on the **stability** of the drug substance and drug product, including storage conditions, shelf life, and packaging materials used to maintain product quality over time.

4. Module 4: Non-Clinical Study Reports

Module 4 includes the results of **non-clinical studies** (also known as preclinical studies) that assess the safety and pharmacological properties of the drug. This module contains data from **animal studies**, toxicological tests, and other non-clinical investigations that support the clinical development of the drug. Key components of **Module 4** include:

- **Pharmacology Studies**: Data on the drug's **pharmacological effects**, including its mechanism of action, therapeutic target, and biological effects in animal models.

- **Toxicology Studies**: Information on the **toxicity** of the drug, including **acute, sub-chronic**, and **chronic toxicity** studies, as well as **genotoxicity** and **carcinogenicity** studies. This data helps assess the drug's safety profile and potential risks.
- **Pharmacokinetics**: Data on the **absorption, distribution, metabolism, and excretion (ADME)** of the drug in animal models. This helps understand how the drug behaves in the body and its potential effectiveness in humans.
- **Reproductive Toxicity**: Studies that assess the potential risks of the drug for reproductive health, including effects on fertility, pregnancy, and offspring development.
- **Environmental Risk Assessment**: Information on the potential environmental impact of the drug, especially if it is excreted into water systems or has other ecological concerns.

5. Module 5: Clinical Study Reports

Module 5 contains detailed reports of **clinical studies** conducted in humans to assess the drug's safety, efficacy, and dosage. This module is the core of the clinical evidence submitted to regulatory authorities for approval. The components of **Module 5** include:

- **Clinical Study Protocols**: Detailed descriptions of the **study design**, including the objectives, methodology, patient population, and statistical analysis methods used in clinical trials.
- **Clinical Trial Results**: Data on the **efficacy** and **safety** of the drug, including the **clinical endpoints, adverse events**, and **patient outcomes** observed during the trial.
- **Clinical Pharmacology**: Information on the **pharmacodynamics** and **pharmacokinetics** of the drug in human subjects, including how the drug behaves in the body, its dose-response relationship, and its therapeutic effects.
- **Post-Marketing Data**: If applicable, any data from **post-marketing studies** or **long-term surveillance** conducted after the drug was approved for use.

4.2.2.2 Benefits and Use of eCTD

The **electronic Common Technical Document (eCTD)** is an advanced, digital version of the Common Technical Document (CTD) used in regulatory submissions for pharmaceutical products. As the global pharmaceutical industry moves towards greater digitization, the eCTD has become the preferred format for submitting drug applications to regulatory authorities worldwide. The transition from paper-based submissions to electronic submissions has significantly improved the efficiency, accuracy, and speed of regulatory processes. The eCTD format is endorsed by many regulatory agencies, including the U.S. **Food and Drug Administration (FDA)**, the **European Medicines Agency (EMA)**, and the **Japan Pharmaceuticals and Medical Devices Agency (PMDA)**.

1. What is eCTD?

The eCTD is a **structured electronic format** used to submit regulatory information in the form of a digital file. It serves the same purpose as the traditional paper-based CTD but offers several advantages, including easier navigation, faster processing, and the ability to include more comprehensive data. The eCTD enables regulatory authorities to receive and review submissions efficiently, improving communication between pharmaceutical companies and regulatory agencies.

The **eCTD format** organizes all documents in a modular structure, just like the CTD. These modules include administrative information, quality data, non-clinical and clinical study data, and any other supporting documents required for drug approval. This structured approach ensures that the data is presented in a clear, organized manner that can be easily reviewed and assessed by regulatory authorities.

2. Benefits of eCTD

The eCTD offers numerous benefits over the traditional paper-based submission method, not only for regulatory authorities but also for pharmaceutical companies and stakeholders involved in the drug development and approval process.

2.1 Improved Efficiency and Speed

One of the most significant advantages of eCTD is the **improved efficiency** and **speed** of the submission process. Electronic submissions allow for **faster preparation** and **delivery** of regulatory documents, which reduces the time required to prepare a submission. With eCTD, documents are automatically formatted and indexed, eliminating the need for physical handling, which traditionally slowed down the process.

Regulatory authorities also benefit from faster processing times, as the eCTD format allows for quick access to the relevant sections of a submission, facilitating quicker reviews and approvals. This leads to **shorter approval timelines**, which can accelerate the introduction of new drugs to the market, benefiting patients in need of timely treatments.

2.2 Enhanced Accuracy and Quality Control

With paper-based submissions, there is a higher risk of **human error**, such as missing or incorrectly formatted documents. In contrast, eCTD submissions are **automated** and **structured**, reducing the likelihood of errors. Electronic submissions also allow for **real-time validation** of the documents, ensuring that they meet the technical and regulatory requirements set by the regulatory agencies.

Additionally, the eCTD format allows for **version control** and **audit trails**, meaning that any updates made to a submission are tracked and documented. This ensures that all parties involved can review the history of the submission and access the most up-to-date documents.

2.3 Global Harmonization

The eCTD format supports **global harmonization** by providing a standardized method for submitting regulatory documents. The format is widely accepted by regulatory agencies across the world, making it easier for pharmaceutical companies to submit their drug applications to multiple authorities without needing to adapt their submissions to different formats for each country. This reduces the complexity and cost of regulatory submissions and ensures that the submission process is consistent across different regions.

For example, the **U.S. FDA**, **EMA**, and **PMDA** all accept eCTD submissions, and many other countries are adopting the format as well. By aligning with international standards, the eCTD facilitates smoother global drug approvals and the easier introduction of drugs into global markets.

2.4 Better Communication and Tracking

eCTD submissions enhance **communication** between pharmaceutical companies and regulatory agencies. Submissions are transmitted electronically, and both the company and the regulatory authority can track the submission in real-time. This enables quicker responses to requests for additional information, updates, or clarifications.

Regulatory agencies can easily provide feedback to the pharmaceutical company through the eCTD system, and the company can submit responses or revised documents without delay. This streamlined communication fosters a more collaborative relationship between the company and the regulatory authority.

Furthermore, the eCTD allows for **centralized tracking** of all submissions, making it easier for both companies and regulators to monitor the progress of an application, see any outstanding issues, and manage approvals efficiently.

2.5 Cost Savings

While the initial setup and conversion to an eCTD system may involve some investment, the long-term benefits of **cost savings** are substantial. By eliminating the need for paper-based submissions, companies save on printing, packaging, shipping, and storage costs. Additionally, the eCTD format allows for **faster submissions**, which can reduce regulatory fees associated with delayed approval.

For regulatory agencies, the adoption of the eCTD format reduces administrative overheads, such as managing and storing large volumes of paper documents. It also reduces the cost of physical infrastructure, allowing authorities to streamline their operations and focus resources on reviewing and processing submissions.

2.6 Regulatory Flexibility and Ease of Updates

The eCTD format makes it easier to submit **supplements** or **amendments** to an existing submission. When new information becomes available, such as updated clinical trial results or changes to the drug's labeling, these updates can be submitted electronically and integrated into the existing submission. This eliminates the need to submit an entirely new application and ensures that the regulatory agency has the most current information on the drug.

Additionally, the eCTD system supports **rolling submissions**, where data can be submitted incrementally as it becomes available. This can expedite the approval process, as certain sections of the application, such as preclinical or early-phase clinical data, can be reviewed while other data is still being finalized.

2.7 Environmental Impact

The transition to **electronic submissions** has a positive environmental impact. By reducing the need for paper, ink, and other materials used in traditional submissions, the eCTD contributes to **environmental sustainability**. Companies and regulatory agencies alike benefit from a more eco-friendly submission process that helps reduce the overall carbon footprint of the pharmaceutical industry.

3. Use of eCTD in Regulatory Submissions

The eCTD is used in regulatory submissions at various stages of drug development and approval. These include:

- **New Drug Applications (NDAs):** The eCTD format is used for submitting comprehensive regulatory information when a new drug is being introduced to the market. This submission includes preclinical, clinical, and manufacturing data, as well as labeling information.
- **Abbreviated New Drug Applications (ANDAs):** For generic drug submissions, the eCTD format simplifies the process of demonstrating **bioequivalence** to the reference drug, ensuring that the generic drug meets the same safety and efficacy standards.
- **Supplemental Applications:** The eCTD is used for submitting **supplements** to existing drug applications, including changes to the formulation, labeling, or manufacturing process.
- **Annual Reports:** Pharmaceutical companies submit **annual reports** using the eCTD format, providing updates on the drug's performance in the market, including safety data and post-marketing surveillance information.

4.3 ASEAN Common Technical Document (ACTD)

The **ASEAN Common Technical Document (ACTD)** is a harmonized format for regulatory submissions in the **Association of Southeast Asian Nations (ASEAN)** region. This region consists of **10 member countries**, each with its own regulatory body for approving pharmaceutical products. The ACTD was developed to streamline the regulatory submission process and reduce duplication of efforts in ASEAN countries, ensuring consistency, efficiency, and compliance with international standards. The ACTD is modeled after the **Common Technical Document (CTD)** used in other regions, such as the **European Union (EU)**, **United States (US)**, and **Japan**, with adaptations to suit the regulatory requirements of ASEAN member states.

The **ACTD** facilitates the submission of drug applications for approval by regulatory authorities within the ASEAN region, ensuring that all necessary data on the **safety, efficacy,** and **quality** of the pharmaceutical product are included. This standardized approach helps regulatory authorities evaluate applications more efficiently and consistently.

4.3.1 Structure and Guidelines of ACTD

The **ACTD** is divided into several modules, similar to the **CTD**, which organize the regulatory data into logical sections. Each module contains specific types of information required by the regulatory authorities in the ASEAN region. The structure of the ACTD includes **administrative documents**, **quality information**, **non-clinical data**, **clinical data**, and **additional documentation** related to the drug's safety, efficacy, and manufacturing processes.

The main components of the ACTD are as follows:

1. Module 1: Administrative Information and Prescribing Information
Module 1 of the **ACTD** provides all the essential administrative and prescribing information required for drug registration in ASEAN countries. This module is specific to each member state and may vary slightly depending on the country's regulatory requirements. Common elements in Module 1 include:

- **Application Form**: The **regulatory application form** includes the administrative details of the drug product, including the name of the applicant, the drug's name, proposed indication(s), and the regulatory submission type (e.g., new drug application, supplementary application).
- **Cover Letter**: A formal cover letter introducing the application, providing a summary of the drug, and specifying the submission type.
- **Drug Product Information**: Information regarding the drug product, including **dosage form**, **strength**, **route of administration**, and **packaging**.
- **Labeling and Package Inserts**: Information about the labeling and packaging for the drug, including its proposed uses, dosing instructions, contraindications, warnings, and adverse effects. This information must comply with the regulatory requirements of the specific ASEAN country.
- **Certificate of Pharmaceutical Product (CPP)**: The **Certificate of Pharmaceutical Product** is a key document that certifies that the drug has been approved and is legally marketed in the country of origin (usually the manufacturer's country).

- **Manufacturing Licenses**: A copy of the **manufacturing license** issued by the regulatory authority in the country of manufacture. This ensures that the drug is produced in a GMP-compliant facility.

2. Module 2: Common Technical and Clinical Summaries

Module 2 provides an overview of the **drug product** and its clinical and non-clinical data. This module contains summaries of the information provided in Modules 3 and 4 and serves as a high-level overview of the application. It typically includes:

- **Quality Overview**: A summary of the quality-related information provided in **Module 3**, which covers the **manufacturing process, quality control tests, stability data**, and **composition of the drug product**.
- **Non-Clinical Overview**: A summary of the **non-clinical data** provided in **Module 4**, including pharmacology, toxicology, and pharmacokinetics studies. This section highlights the drug's safety profile based on animal studies.
- **Clinical Overview**: A summary of the **clinical data** provided in **Module 5**, which includes data from human clinical trials, focusing on the drug's **efficacy, safety, dosage**, and **clinical pharmacology**.
- **Benefit-Risk Assessment**: A summary of the **risk-benefit analysis** based on the clinical and non-clinical data. This assessment weighs the potential therapeutic benefits of the drug against its known risks and adverse effects.

3. Module 3: Quality (CMC)

Module 3 contains all the detailed **chemistry, manufacturing, and control (CMC)** data required to demonstrate the drug's **quality** and **consistency**. This module is essential for ensuring that the drug meets the required standards for **manufacturing** and **quality control**. Key components of **Module 3** include:

- **Drug Substance (API)**: Detailed information on the **Active Pharmaceutical Ingredient (API)**, including its **chemical structure, physical properties, synthesis** process, and **quality control tests**. This section also includes stability data for the API, which helps determine the **shelf life** of the drug.

- **Drug Product (Finished Formulation)**: Detailed information about the **formulation** of the drug product, including its **composition, dosage form, strength,** and **route of administration**. It also includes information on **manufacturing processes, quality control measures,** and packaging.
- **Manufacturing Process and Facilities**: Information on the **manufacturing process**, including the production steps, equipment used, and quality control measures employed to ensure the consistent production of high-quality products. This section also provides details on the **manufacturing facility** where the drug is produced and whether it meets **Good Manufacturing Practice (GMP)** standards.
- **Stability Data**: Data from stability studies that assess how the drug product performs over time under various storage conditions. This data helps determine the **expiration date** and storage conditions required for the product.
- **Excipients Information**: Information about the **inactive ingredients (excipients)** used in the drug product, such as binders, fillers, preservatives, and stabilizers. The excipients must meet quality standards to ensure compatibility with the drug's active ingredient.

4. Module 4: Non-Clinical Study Reports

Module 4 contains the results of **non-clinical studies**, also known as **preclinical studies**, which provide essential data on the safety and pharmacological properties of the drug. These studies are usually conducted in animals before the drug is tested in humans. Key components of **Module 4** include:

- **Pharmacology**: Data on the **pharmacological effects** of the drug, including its **mechanism of action, therapeutic target,** and biological effects in animal models.
- **Toxicology**: Data from **toxicology studies**, including **acute, sub-chronic,** and **chronic toxicity** studies, as well as **genotoxicity** and **carcinogenicity** studies.
- **Pharmacokinetics**: Information on the **absorption, distribution, metabolism,** and **excretion (ADME)** of the drug in animal models.
- **Reproductive Toxicity**: Studies to assess the potential effects of the drug on **reproduction**, including effects on fertility, pregnancy, and offspring development.

- **Environmental Risk Assessment**: An assessment of the **environmental impact** of the drug, particularly if it is excreted in the environment or has potential ecological effects.

5. Module 5: Clinical Study Reports

Module 5 contains the results of **clinical trials** in humans, providing data on the drug's **efficacy**, **safety**, and **dosage**. This is the most important module for evaluating the drug's potential benefit-risk profile. Key components of **Module 5** include:

- **Clinical Study Protocols**: Detailed descriptions of the **clinical trial designs**, including the objectives, methodology, patient population, and statistical analysis methods.
- **Clinical Trial Results**: Data on the **efficacy** and **safety** of the drug, including adverse events, therapeutic outcomes, and other relevant findings.
- **Clinical Pharmacology**: Information on the **pharmacodynamics** and **pharmacokinetics** of the drug in human subjects.

4.3.2 Exporting to ASEAN Countries: Documentation and Approvals

Exporting pharmaceutical products to **ASEAN (Association of Southeast Asian Nations)** countries involves a comprehensive regulatory process, with specific documentation and approvals required by the regulatory authorities in each member state. The ASEAN region comprises ten countries, and while there is an increasing push for harmonization across these nations, each country still has its own regulatory requirements. However, the **ASEAN Common Technical Document (ACTD)** has been established to provide a unified framework for submitting pharmaceutical applications in the region, which helps streamline the export process and ensures compliance with the standards for drug approval across member states.

Pharmaceutical manufacturers wishing to export drugs to ASEAN countries must ensure that they meet both the **ASEAN-wide** and **country-specific** regulatory requirements. This includes obtaining the necessary **licenses**, **certificates**, and completing **documentation** to gain approval for market entry. The following outlines the key documentation and approval processes required for exporting pharmaceutical products to ASEAN countries.

1. Regulatory Authorities in ASEAN Countries

Each ASEAN country has its own regulatory authority that governs the importation and marketing of pharmaceutical products. The most common regulatory agencies include:

- **Indonesia**: The **National Agency of Drug and Food Control (BPOM)** regulates the pharmaceutical market and ensures the safety and efficacy of drug products in Indonesia.
- **Malaysia**: The **National Pharmaceutical Regulatory Agency (NPRA)** under the Ministry of Health is responsible for the registration and control of pharmaceutical products in Malaysia.
- **Singapore**: The **Health Sciences Authority (HSA)** oversees pharmaceutical product approvals, ensuring safety, efficacy, and quality standards.
- **Thailand**: The **Food and Drug Administration (FDA)** in Thailand regulates pharmaceutical products, ensuring they meet the required quality standards for importation and sale.
- **Philippines**: The **Food and Drug Administration (FDA)** regulates pharmaceuticals in the Philippines, ensuring compliance with both domestic and international standards.
- **Vietnam**: The **Drug Administration of Vietnam (DAV)** handles the regulatory process for drug products in Vietnam.

Although these countries have their own regulatory authorities, they all recognize the **ACTD** for submitting technical documentation, streamlining the process for manufacturers seeking approval across multiple ASEAN countries.

2. Key Documentation Required for Export

To export pharmaceutical products to ASEAN countries, manufacturers must ensure they have the required documentation in place. The **ACTD** serves as the primary guideline for submitting drug registration applications, but additional country-specific documentation may also be required. Some of the essential documents include:

2.1 Drug Master File (DMF)

A **Drug Master File (DMF)** is a crucial document required for the export of pharmaceutical products to ASEAN countries. The DMF provides detailed information about the **drug substance** (API) or the **finished pharmaceutical product**. It includes:

- Information on the **chemical composition** and **manufacturing process** of the active pharmaceutical ingredient (API).
- **Quality control** procedures, including **stability data**, and **analytical methods** for ensuring the product meets international standards.
- **Packaging and labeling** details, demonstrating compliance with the importing country's requirements.

A **DMF** ensures that the drug meets the necessary **quality** and **safety** standards for importation and sale. This is an important step for regulatory approval and is often required by multiple ASEAN countries.

2.2 Certificate of Pharmaceutical Product (CPP)

The **Certificate of Pharmaceutical Product (CPP)** is issued by the **regulatory authority** in the exporting country, such as the **Central Drugs Standard Control Organization (CDSCO)** in India, and serves as proof that the drug is legally sold and authorized for use in the domestic market. The **CPP** is an essential document for gaining approval in ASEAN countries, as it provides evidence that the product has been **marketed** and **approved** in the country of origin. The CPP includes the following information:

- **Drug registration details** in the country of origin.
- Confirmation that the drug complies with **Good Manufacturing Practices (GMP)**.
- Details of **clinical trials** and **efficacy** data, as applicable.

2.3 Free Sale Certificate (FSC)

A **Free Sale Certificate (FSC)** is a document issued by the regulatory authority in the country of origin that certifies the drug product is sold in the local market and meets national regulatory standards. The FSC assures ASEAN authorities that the pharmaceutical product is of sufficient quality to be traded internationally. This certificate often accompanies the **CPP** and helps speed up the **registration process** in ASEAN countries.

2.4 Good Manufacturing Practice (GMP) Certificate

A **GMP Certificate** is necessary to ensure that the **manufacturing facility** complies with **Good Manufacturing Practices**. The GMP certification verifies that the drugs are produced in an environment that meets high standards of **quality control** and **manufacturing consistency**. Many ASEAN countries require this certification before importing pharmaceutical products to ensure the drugs are manufactured in facilities that meet international safety and quality standards.

2.5 Clinical Trial Data and Approval

For new drugs, or if there is a change to an existing formulation, **clinical trial data** may be required as part of the submission process. This includes data from clinical studies that show the drug's **efficacy** and **safety** in humans. Some ASEAN countries may require the results of **clinical trials** conducted in accordance with **Good Clinical Practices (GCP)** to assess whether the drug is safe and effective for its intended use.

The clinical trial data is essential for proving the drug's **therapeutic benefits** and to demonstrate that it does not present unacceptable **risks** to patients.

2.6 Certificate of Origin

The **Certificate of Origin** certifies that the pharmaceutical product was **manufactured** in the exporting country, which is necessary for determining the country of origin for customs and import duty purposes. It is an important document required by **ASEAN customs authorities** for **tariff and trade purposes**.

2.7 Labeling and Packaging Information

Each ASEAN country has specific requirements for **labeling** and **packaging** pharmaceutical products. This may include the **language** of the labeling, specific **health warnings**, dosage instructions, and **expiration dates**. Manufacturers must ensure that their packaging and labeling comply with the local laws of the importing country. Labeling typically includes the following details:

- Product name and dosage form.
- **Batch number, manufacturing date**, and **expiration date**.
- **Storage conditions** and **handling instructions**.
- **Warnings, contraindications**, and **precautions**.

2.8 Import License and Registration Certificate

Some ASEAN countries require an **import license** or a **registration certificate** from local authorities before drugs can be marketed. The **import license** verifies that the importer has the necessary approvals to bring pharmaceutical products into the country. Once the drug is registered, a **registration certificate** is issued by the regulatory authority, allowing the drug to be legally sold within the country.

3. Approval Process for Exporting to ASEAN Countries

The approval process for exporting pharmaceutical products to ASEAN countries typically involves several key steps:

1. **Submission of Application**: The manufacturer submits the relevant documents to the **national regulatory authority** in the destination country, in line with the **ACTD** format. This may include the DMF, CPP, FSC, GMP certificate, clinical trial data, and other supporting documentation.

2. **Regulatory Review**: The regulatory authority in the importing country reviews the submission to ensure that the drug meets local safety, efficacy, and quality standards. This may involve additional inspections of manufacturing facilities or additional requests for data.

3. **Approval and Registration**: Once the regulatory authority is satisfied with the submission, the drug is **approved** and **registered** for sale in the country. The manufacturer receives the **import license** and **registration certificate**, allowing the drug to enter the market.

4. **Post-Marketing Surveillance**: After approval, the drug is subject to post-marketing surveillance, including monitoring for **adverse events** and other safety concerns. The manufacturer is required to submit regular reports to the regulatory authorities regarding the drug's performance in the market.

Step	Description	Responsible Party	Documents/Actions Involved
Regulatory Requirements for Export	Ensure compliance with destination country's regulatory standards	Pharmaceutical Company, Regulatory Authorities	Certificate of Pharmaceutical Product (CPP), DMF, CTD
Application for Drug Export	Submit necessary application to export drugs	Pharmaceutical Company	Export license, required documentation
Regulatory Authority Review	Review application and documents	Regulatory Authorities	Approval/rejection of the application
Approval for Export	Authorization to export drugs	Regulatory Authorities	Approval letter, license for export
Post-Export Monitoring	Monitor the safety and quality of exported products	Pharmaceutical Company, Regulatory Authorities	Adverse event reports, safety monitoring

Table 15: Export Procedures for Pharmaceutical Products

Step	Purpose	Documents/Actions Involved	Responsible Party
Preparation of DMF	Document detailed information about drug's composition and manufacturing process	DMF document including manufacturing process, quality control data	Pharmaceutical Company
Submission to Regulatory Authorities	Submit DMF to relevant authorities for review	DMF submission, required regulatory forms	Pharmaceutical Company
Review of DMF	Evaluate the content of the DMF to ensure regulatory compliance	Regulatory authority reviews DMF	Regulatory Authorities
Approval of DMF	Grant approval for the manufacturing and marketing of the drug	Approval letter or additional data request	Regulatory Authorities
Post-Approval Monitoring	Monitor continued compliance with regulatory standards	Ongoing adverse event reporting, product inspections	Pharmaceutical Company

Table 15: Drug Master File (DMF) and Its Role in Registration

Section	Content	Purpose	Required By	Examples
Module 1	Administrative and prescribing information	Provide general information required for regulatory approval	Regulatory Authorities	FDA, EMA
Module 2	Overview of the drug's clinical and nonclinical data	Summarize the drug's safety and efficacy	Regulatory Authorities	Clinical trial reports, pharmacokinetics data
Module 3	Drug quality, manufacturing, and controls	Provide details on the drug's composition, manufacturing process	Regulatory Authorities	Drug master file, GMP compliance documentation
Module 4	Nonclinical study reports	Provide preclinical safety data	Regulatory Authorities	Toxicology studies, animal testing data
Module 5	Clinical study reports	Provide data from clinical trials to support drug safety and efficacy	Regulatory Authorities	Phase I-III clinical trial results

Table 16: Common Technical Document (CTD)

Section	Content	Purpose	Examples
Module 1	Administrative information	Provide basic administrative and submission details	Regulatory Authorities, ASEAN member states
Module 2	Summary of the drug's clinical and nonclinical data	Provide an overview of clinical trials, safety, and efficacy	Regulatory Authorities, ASEAN member states
Module 3	Drug quality and manufacturing data	Provide information on drug composition and GMP compliance	Regulatory Authorities, ASEAN member states
Module 4	Nonclinical study reports	Summarize animal testing and safety data	Regulatory Authorities, ASEAN member states
Module 5	Clinical study reports	Detailed results from clinical trials	Regulatory Authorities, ASEAN member states

Table 17: ASEAN Common Technical Document (ACTD)

Step	Action Required	Responsible Party	Documents Involved
Prepare Export Documentation	Assemble necessary documents including CTD, DMF, stability data	Pharmaceutical Company	CTD, DMF, stability data
Submit to ASEAN Regulatory Authority	Submit all documents and application to the relevant ASEAN authority	Pharmaceutical Company	Application form, clinical trial data
Regulatory Review	Review the submitted documents for regulatory compliance	ASEAN Regulatory Authority	CTD, clinical study reports
Obtain Approval	Receive authorization for export	ASEAN Regulatory Authority	Approval letter, license for export
Post-Export Monitoring	Monitor and report any adverse events post-export	Pharmaceutical Company	Post-marketing surveillance data, adverse event reports

Table 18: Exporting to ASEAN Countries - Documentation and Approvals

CHAPTER FIVE

Clinical Trials and Ethics

5.1 Clinical Trial Protocol Development

The development of a **clinical trial protocol** is a critical step in the clinical research process. It serves as a roadmap for the study, outlining the plan, methodology, and procedures for conducting a clinical trial. A well-designed protocol is essential to ensure that the study is scientifically valid, ethically sound, and compliant with regulatory requirements. It also serves as a guide for all stakeholders involved, including investigators, participants, regulatory bodies, and sponsors, ensuring that the trial is conducted in a standardized and reproducible manner.

5.1.1 Writing a Clinical Trial Protocol: Key Elements

A **clinical trial protocol** is a detailed document that provides the framework for the clinical trial. It includes several key elements that guide the trial from its initiation to its completion. These elements ensure that the trial is conducted with rigor, consistency, and ethical standards. The key elements of a clinical trial protocol include the following:

1. Title and Identification of the Study

The title of the clinical trial should be clear, concise, and reflective of the study's purpose. It typically includes information about the intervention being tested and the condition or disease being treated. The title should provide enough detail for the study to be easily identified and differentiated from other trials. This section also includes **identification numbers** and **study references** for tracking purposes.

2. Study Objectives

The **objectives** of the clinical trial define the primary and secondary goals of the study. These objectives specify what the study aims to achieve and how the success of the intervention will be measured. Objectives typically include:

- **Primary Objective**: This is the main goal of the trial, such as demonstrating the efficacy of a drug in treating a specific condition. It is usually measured by the primary endpoint, such as the change in the severity of symptoms or survival rates.
- **Secondary Objectives**: These are additional goals of the study that may explore other aspects of the drug's effects, such as safety, quality of life, or pharmacokinetics. Secondary objectives help to provide a more comprehensive understanding of the drug's potential benefits.

3. Study Design

The **study design** describes the overall structure of the clinical trial. It includes the methodology used to address the study objectives and the type of trial being conducted. Key elements of the study design include:

- **Type of Study**: The study design can be a **randomized controlled trial (RCT)**, **observational study**, **open-label trial**, or **blinded trial**. The design should be chosen based on the research question, the condition being studied, and the type of intervention.
- **Control Group**: If applicable, the study should include a **control group**, which serves as a comparison to the experimental group receiving the intervention. The control group may receive a placebo, standard treatment, or no treatment at all.
- **Randomization**: If the study is randomized, this section describes the randomization process used to assign participants to different treatment groups. Randomization helps minimize bias and ensures that each participant has an equal chance of being assigned to any group.
- **Blinding**: If the study is blinded, the protocol should describe whether it is **single-blinded** (where the participants do not know which treatment they are receiving) or **double-blinded** (where both the participants and the researchers do not know which treatment is being administered).

4. Study Population and Eligibility Criteria

The **study population** refers to the group of individuals who will be eligible to participate in the clinical trial. The protocol should clearly define the **inclusion and exclusion criteria** for participants. Inclusion criteria specify the characteristics that participants must have to be eligible for the study, while exclusion criteria define the conditions or factors that disqualify individuals from participation.

- **Inclusion Criteria**: These might include factors such as age range, gender, specific medical conditions, or certain test results that align with the study's objectives.
- **Exclusion Criteria**: These might include conditions that could interfere with the study's outcomes, such as other serious health conditions, ongoing treatment with conflicting medications, or pregnancy.

The protocol should also define the **sample size** and explain how the number of participants was determined. The sample size should be large enough to provide statistically significant results but also feasible in terms of resources and time.

5. Intervention and Treatment Regimen

The **intervention** refers to the treatment or drug being tested in the study. The protocol should provide detailed information about the intervention, including:

- **Dosage and Administration**: This includes the specific **dose** of the drug, the **route of administration** (e.g., oral, intravenous), the **schedule** for administering the treatment, and the **duration** of the treatment period.
- **Control Treatments**: If a **placebo** or **standard treatment** is being used as a control, this should be clearly described, including the **dosage** and **administration schedule** for the control group.

The protocol should also include details about the **handling** and **storage** of the intervention, ensuring that the treatment is administered consistently and according to regulatory requirements.

6. Outcome Measures and Endpoints

The **outcome measures** or **endpoints** are the variables that the study will measure to assess the effectiveness of the intervention. These endpoints are directly related to the study's objectives and should be defined clearly in the protocol. Common types of endpoints include:

- **Primary Endpoint**: This is the main measure of the study's success. For example, in a cancer trial, the primary endpoint might be **overall survival** or **tumor size reduction**.
- **Secondary Endpoints**: These are additional measures of effectiveness or safety, such as improvements in **symptom severity**, **quality of life**, or **biomarker levels**.

Each endpoint should be measured using **validated instruments** or **scales** and should be clearly defined in terms of how and when data will be collected. For example, if the endpoint is a change in symptom severity, the protocol should specify the exact rating scale or test used to assess the severity.

7. Safety Monitoring and Adverse Event Reporting

The protocol should outline the procedures for **monitoring the safety** of the participants throughout the clinical trial. This includes details about the **adverse events (AEs)** and **serious adverse events (SAEs)** that will be monitored, as well as how they will be reported. Key components include:

- **Adverse Event Monitoring**: Participants must be closely monitored for any side effects or adverse reactions to the treatment. The protocol should specify how AEs will be recorded, categorized, and assessed for severity.
- **Safety Committees**: The protocol may include the formation of a **Data Safety Monitoring Board (DSMB)** or **Independent Ethics Committee (IEC)** that oversees the safety of participants and ensures that the trial is conducted ethically.
- **Reporting Procedures**: The protocol should define the timelines and procedures for reporting adverse events to regulatory authorities and stakeholders.

8. Statistical Methods and Data Analysis

The protocol should include a **statistical analysis plan** that describes how the study data will be analyzed to determine the efficacy and safety of the intervention. This section should define:

- **Statistical Methods**: The statistical techniques and tests that will be used to analyze the primary and secondary endpoints (e.g., t-tests, ANOVA, survival analysis).

- **Data Handling**: Procedures for handling missing data, ensuring data integrity, and dealing with outliers.
- **Interim Analysis**: If applicable, the protocol should outline when and how **interim analyses** will be conducted, particularly if there is a need to modify the study design or discontinue the trial early due to safety concerns or significant findings.

9. Ethical Considerations

The protocol must address ethical considerations, ensuring that the study is conducted in compliance with **ethical guidelines** and **regulations**. This includes obtaining informed consent from all participants, protecting their privacy, and ensuring that they are fully aware of the risks and benefits of participation.

- **Informed Consent**: The protocol must specify the process for obtaining **informed consent** from participants. This includes informing them of the study's purpose, procedures, potential risks, and their right to withdraw at any time.
- **Ethics Approval**: The protocol should also detail how the study will be reviewed and approved by an **Independent Ethics Committee (IEC)** or **Institutional Review Board (IRB)**, which ensures that the study adheres to ethical standards.

5.1.2 Designing Clinical Trials: Randomized, Controlled, and Blinded Studies

Designing clinical trials is a critical aspect of clinical research as it directly influences the reliability, validity, and applicability of the study findings. One of the most robust and reliable methods for evaluating the safety and efficacy of a drug or treatment is through **randomized controlled trials (RCTs)**, which are often designed to be **blinded**. These designs help eliminate bias, ensure rigorous comparison, and provide high-quality data that can inform regulatory decisions and clinical practice.

1. Randomized Clinical Trials (RCTs)

A **randomized clinical trial (RCT)** is considered the gold standard for clinical research. It is a type of experimental study where participants are **randomly assigned** to different groups to receive either the treatment under investigation or a placebo or standard treatment. The randomization process ensures that the groups are comparable at the start of the trial, helping to reduce potential confounding factors and biases that could affect the study's outcomes.

1.1 Purpose of Randomization

The primary purpose of randomization is to minimize **selection bias**, ensuring that the groups are comparable in terms of both known and unknown factors. By assigning participants randomly to different groups, researchers can control for **confounding variables**, which are factors that could influence the results independently of the treatment being tested. Randomization allows for the assumption that any differences between the groups can be attributed to the treatment itself and not to underlying differences between participants.

For example, in a trial comparing a new cancer drug to a placebo, randomization ensures that the participants in both groups are balanced in terms of age, gender, baseline health status, and other variables that might affect cancer outcomes.

1.2 Types of Randomization

There are several methods of randomization, including:

- **Simple Randomization**: Involves randomly assigning participants to groups using a random number generator or a similar method. This approach is easy to implement but can lead to imbalances in group characteristics by chance, especially in small sample sizes.
- **Stratified Randomization**: This method ensures that certain characteristics (e.g., age, gender, disease severity) are equally distributed between the groups by dividing participants into strata based on these characteristics before random assignment. It is particularly useful when variables are known to affect the outcome.
- **Block Randomization**: Used to ensure that groups remain balanced throughout the trial. Participants are assigned to treatment groups in "blocks" of a fixed size, ensuring that each group has a roughly equal number of participants at any given point during the study.

1.3 Importance of Randomization in Clinical Trials

The benefits of randomization include:

- **Control of Confounding Factors**: By randomly assigning participants, the treatment groups are likely to be similar in terms of both known and unknown factors, reducing the potential for confounding effects.
- **Validity of Results**: Randomized trials provide robust evidence that the observed effects are due to the treatment rather than other factors.
- **Minimizing Bias**: Randomization helps eliminate bias in treatment assignment, ensuring that neither the researcher nor the participants have control over the allocation of treatments.

2. Controlled Clinical Trials

A **controlled clinical trial** is a study where one group of participants receives the treatment or intervention being tested, while another group receives a **control** treatment. This control group can be given a placebo (an inactive substance) or the current standard of care, depending on the trial's objectives. The use of a control group provides a benchmark for evaluating the effect of the intervention.

2.1 Purpose of a Control Group

The control group serves as a comparison to the experimental group to determine whether the treatment has any effect beyond what might occur naturally. For example, if a drug is being tested for lowering blood pressure, the control group might receive a placebo or an existing blood pressure medication. By comparing the results from both groups, researchers can assess whether the new drug provides additional benefits over the current treatment or a placebo.

2.2 Types of Control Groups

- **Placebo-Controlled Trials**: Participants in the control group receive a placebo, which is a substance with no therapeutic effect. This is useful in evaluating the **true efficacy** of the intervention by comparing it with a baseline where no active treatment is given.
- **Active-Controlled Trials**: In this type of trial, the control group receives a known, effective treatment rather than a placebo. This design is used when withholding an active treatment might not be ethical, especially for serious conditions where effective treatments already exist.
- **Historical Control**: In some studies, a **historical control** is used, where the outcomes of the experimental group are compared to outcomes from previous studies rather than a contemporaneous control group. This design can be useful when it is not feasible to have a control group within

the same trial.

3. Blinded Clinical Trials

Blinding in clinical trials refers to the practice of keeping either the participants, researchers, or both unaware of which treatment each participant is receiving. The goal of blinding is to prevent bias in the results by ensuring that expectations or knowledge of treatment assignment do not influence the outcome.

3.1 Types of Blinding

- **Single-Blind Study**: In a **single-blind study**, participants are unaware of which treatment they are receiving, but the researchers know. This prevents **participant bias**, as participants' expectations regarding the treatment may influence their perception of the drug's effectiveness or side effects.
- **Double-Blind Study**: In a **double-blind study**, both the participants and the researchers are unaware of which treatment the participants are receiving. This prevents both **participant bias** and **investigator bias**, ensuring that neither group's expectations can influence the trial's outcome. Double-blind studies are considered the gold standard in clinical trial design, as they minimize both types of bias and provide the most reliable results.
- **Triple-Blind Study**: In a **triple-blind study**, not only the participants and researchers are blinded, but also the **statisticians** who analyze the data. This design is used to further eliminate any potential bias that might arise during the data analysis process.

3.2 Importance of Blinding in Clinical Trials

Blinding plays a crucial role in ensuring the **validity** of the trial results by reducing the influence of bias. Without blinding, both participants and researchers may unknowingly influence the results due to their expectations or preconceived notions about the treatment. Blinding ensures that:

- **Participants' expectations** do not influence how they report symptoms or respond to treatment.
- **Researchers' expectations** do not influence how they administer the treatment, collect data, or interpret results.

- The **investigational treatment's effects** can be objectively assessed without being skewed by the subjective views of participants or researchers.

4. Ethical Considerations in Randomized, Controlled, and Blinded Trials

While randomized, controlled, and blinded trials are the most rigorous methods for testing new treatments, they must also be conducted in an **ethically responsible** manner. Ethical considerations include:

- **Informed Consent**: Participants must be fully informed about the trial's nature, including the potential risks and benefits, and must voluntarily consent to participate. This is especially important in blinded trials, where participants may not know which treatment they are receiving.
- **Minimizing Harm**: The potential benefits of the trial must outweigh the risks. If there are any concerns about participant safety, the trial should be stopped or modified.
- **Equity in Participation**: Participants should be selected fairly, without discrimination, and should be treated with respect throughout the trial.
- **Post-Trial Access to Treatment**: If the investigational treatment proves effective, participants should have access to the treatment after the trial ends, especially if it provides significant therapeutic benefit.

5.2 Ethical Considerations in Clinical Trials

Ethical considerations are a cornerstone of clinical trials, ensuring the safety, well-being, and rights of participants while maintaining the integrity of the research process. Clinical trials involve human subjects, and it is crucial that they are conducted ethically to avoid harm and ensure scientific validity. The **Institutional Review Board (IRB)** and **Independent Ethics Committee (IEC)** play critical roles in overseeing the ethical conduct of clinical trials. These committees are responsible for ensuring that clinical trials adhere to established ethical guidelines and regulatory standards, protecting the participants from unnecessary risks and ensuring that the trial's objectives are met without compromising ethical principles.

5.2.1 Institutional Review Board (IRB) and Independent Ethics Committee (IEC)

The **Institutional Review Board (IRB)** and **Independent Ethics Committee (IEC)** are responsible for reviewing and approving clinical trial protocols to ensure that they meet ethical, legal, and regulatory standards. While the terms "IRB" and "IEC" are used in different regions, their functions are essentially the same: to ensure the ethical conduct of clinical trials and protect the rights and safety of the trial participants.

5.2.1.1 Roles and Functions of IRBs/IECs

Both the IRB and the IEC are tasked with reviewing clinical trial protocols before they begin, monitoring the trials during their execution, and ensuring that the ethical guidelines are adhered to throughout the research process. The functions of IRBs and IECs are similar but may vary slightly depending on the country or region in which they operate. These committees perform several essential roles in the conduct of clinical trials:

1. Reviewing and Approving Study Protocols

One of the primary functions of the IRB/IEC is to review the **study protocol** submitted by the sponsor or investigator before the clinical trial begins. The protocol outlines the trial's objectives, design, methodology, inclusion and exclusion criteria, and how the safety and efficacy of the intervention will be evaluated.

- The IRB/IEC ensures that the **study design** aligns with ethical standards, ensuring that the risks to participants are minimized and that the trial is scientifically sound.
- The committee evaluates whether the potential benefits of the study outweigh the risks to the participants and ensures that the study's objectives are clear, justified, and feasible.

2. Ensuring Informed Consent

The **informed consent process** is one of the most important ethical considerations in clinical trials. It is the responsibility of the IRB/IEC to ensure that the **informed consent** process is adequate, transparent, and respectful of participants' autonomy.

- **Informed Consent:** The IRB/IEC ensures that the consent form provides clear, understandable, and complete information about the study, including the purpose of the trial, procedures involved, potential risks and benefits, confidentiality measures, and the participant's right to withdraw from the study at any time without penalty.

- The committee ensures that **vulnerable populations** (such as children, pregnant women, and individuals with cognitive impairments) are adequately protected during the consent process, with additional safeguards in place where necessary.

3. Monitoring Safety and Well-being of Participants

The IRB/IEC is responsible for overseeing the safety and well-being of the participants throughout the trial. This includes evaluating the **risk-to-benefit ratio** and ensuring that the trial does not expose participants to unnecessary risks.

- The committee reviews any adverse events (AEs) or serious adverse events (SAEs) that occur during the trial to determine whether they are related to the intervention and whether the study should be modified or halted for safety reasons.
- The IRB/IEC ensures that **appropriate medical care** and emergency procedures are in place to manage any adverse reactions or complications during the study.

4. Reviewing and Approving the Participant Recruitment Process

The IRB/IEC reviews the **participant recruitment process** to ensure that the methods used to enroll participants are ethical. This includes:

- Ensuring that recruitment materials and advertisements are **clear, truthful,** and **non-coercive**.
- Making sure that **undue influence** or **coercion** is not used to enroll participants, and that individuals are freely participating based on a clear understanding of the trial.

The IRB/IEC ensures that participant recruitment reflects **diversity,** preventing any discrimination or exclusion of certain populations based on gender, ethnicity, or socio-economic status unless there is a scientifically justified reason.

5. Ensuring Confidentiality and Data Protection

In clinical trials, the confidentiality of participant information is critical. The IRB/IEC is responsible for reviewing procedures to ensure that **confidentiality** is maintained at all stages of the trial. This includes:

- Ensuring that **personal data** is kept confidential and is only accessible to authorized personnel.
- Reviewing the procedures for handling **data storage**, ensuring that it complies with privacy laws and regulations such as the **General Data Protection Regulation (GDPR)** in the European Union or **Health Insurance Portability and Accountability Act (HIPAA)** in the U.S.

The IRB/IEC ensures that personal identifiers are removed or anonymized in study data to protect the participants' privacy.

6. Ensuring Ethical Conduct of the Trial

The IRB/IEC oversees the **ethical conduct** of the trial, ensuring that all participants are treated with dignity and respect. This includes:

- **Ethical oversight**: Ensuring that the trial is conducted according to **Good Clinical Practice (GCP)** guidelines, which are internationally recognized standards for conducting clinical trials.
- Reviewing the **scientific integrity** of the study, ensuring that the trial design is sound and the data generated will be meaningful and reliable.

The IRB/IEC is also responsible for ensuring that any conflicts of interest are disclosed, and they help identify and address any potential ethical concerns that could arise during the trial.

7. Reviewing Amendments to the Study

Clinical trials may evolve over time, and new information or concerns may arise that necessitate changes to the study protocol. The IRB/IEC plays a role in **reviewing amendments** to the study protocol, informed consent forms, or any other relevant documents.

- If significant changes are made to the study, such as adding new treatments, altering the participant population, or extending the study duration, the IRB/IEC must review and approve these changes to ensure they are ethically sound and that participants are still adequately protected.

8. Ensuring Compliance with Ethical Guidelines and Regulations

The IRB/IEC ensures that the study complies with **national and international ethical guidelines** and **regulatory standards**. These include:

- **International Guidelines**: Such as the **Declaration of Helsinki**, which provides ethical principles for medical research involving human subjects, and **Good Clinical Practice (GCP)** guidelines, which ensure the quality and integrity of clinical trial data.
- **National Guidelines**: Depending on the country, the IRB/IEC ensures compliance with local regulatory requirements, such as those set forth by national health authorities like the **FDA, EMA**, or local counterparts.

5.2.1.2 Ethics Review and Approval Process

The **ethics review and approval process** is a critical step in the clinical trial process that ensures the safety, rights, and well-being of participants are protected. This process is carried out by the **Institutional Review Board (IRB)** or **Independent Ethics Committee (IEC)**, which reviews all aspects of a clinical trial to ensure that it complies with ethical standards, regulatory guidelines, and legal requirements. The ethics review process is designed to assess the risk-to-benefit ratio of the trial, ensuring that the trial provides scientifically valuable information while minimizing potential harm to participants.

The **ethics review and approval process** typically involves several stages, beginning with the submission of the clinical trial protocol and concluding with the ongoing monitoring of the trial to ensure that it remains ethically sound throughout its duration.

1. Initial Submission of Clinical Trial Protocol

The process begins with the **sponsor** or **investigator** submitting the **clinical trial protocol** to the **IRB/IEC** for review. The protocol includes details about the study's design, objectives, methodology, participant recruitment criteria, informed consent procedures, and any potential risks to participants. In addition to the protocol, the sponsor also submits the following documents:

- **Informed consent form (ICF)**: This document outlines the information that will be provided to participants regarding the trial, including the purpose, procedures, risks, and benefits of participation.

- **Investigator's Brochure (IB)**: A document that provides the IRB/IEC with detailed information about the investigational product, including preclinical and clinical data, potential risks, and known side effects.
- **Case report forms (CRFs)**: Forms used to collect data from the participants during the study.
- **Recruitment materials**: Documents that will be used to inform potential participants about the study, including advertisements and informational brochures.
- **Safety monitoring plan**: A plan outlining how adverse events (AEs) and serious adverse events (SAEs) will be monitored and reported during the trial.

2. Ethical Review by the IRB/IEC

Once the clinical trial protocol and supporting documents are submitted, the **IRB/IEC** conducts a thorough **ethical review**. The committee's primary task is to ensure that the trial is ethically justified and that the rights, safety, and well-being of participants are adequately protected. The review process includes several key aspects:

2.1 Risk-Benefit Assessment

The IRB/IEC evaluates whether the **potential benefits** of the study outweigh the **risks** to participants. In assessing the risks, the committee considers factors such as:

- The nature of the **disease or condition** being studied.
- The **severity** and **probability** of potential **adverse events** or **side effects** associated with the treatment being tested.
- The **availability** of other treatment options and the **potential therapeutic benefit** of the investigational drug or intervention.

The committee must ensure that the **risks** are **minimized** and that participants are exposed to no greater risk than is necessary to achieve the study's objectives.

2.2 Informed Consent Review

A major component of the ethical review is ensuring that the **informed consent process** is thorough, transparent, and clearly explained. The IRB/IEC reviews the **informed consent form (ICF)** to ensure that it includes:

- Clear, simple language that participants can easily understand.
- A description of the study's **purpose, procedures**, and **duration**.
- A summary of **potential risks** and **benefits** to the participants.
- An explanation of the **right to withdraw** from the study at any time without consequences.
- Information about the **confidentiality** of participant data.
- Contact information for the study team and ethics committee for any queries or concerns.

The committee ensures that participants will be adequately informed about what their participation entails and that they are not coerced into joining the study.

2.3 Ethical Soundness of the Study Design

The IRB/IEC reviews the **study design** to ensure that it is scientifically valid and ethically sound. The committee evaluates the following:

- Whether the study's **scientific objectives** justify the participation of humans and if the design is appropriate for achieving the study goals.
- Whether the **methodology** is appropriate to minimize harm and maximize the benefits of the trial. For example, is a placebo-controlled group ethically justifiable if an existing treatment is available?
- Whether the **participant selection criteria** (inclusion and exclusion criteria) are fair and non-discriminatory.

2.4 Protection of Vulnerable Populations

The IRB/IEC ensures that additional protections are in place for **vulnerable populations** that may be at greater risk during clinical trials. Vulnerable groups include children, pregnant women, prisoners, and individuals with cognitive impairments. The committee checks that the trial design includes safeguards to protect these groups, such as additional informed consent procedures, and ensures that participation is voluntary and based on full understanding.

2.5 Confidentiality and Data Protection

The committee reviews the **confidentiality** and **data protection** measures in place to safeguard participants' personal and medical information. The trial must comply with **local and international data protection laws**, such as the **General Data Protection Regulation (GDPR)** or **HIPAA** in the United States. The committee ensures that participant information will be stored securely and that only authorized individuals will have access to sensitive data.

3. Approval or Rejection of the Study

After the review is completed, the **IRB/IEC** will make a decision about the clinical trial protocol. The committee may:

- **Approve** the protocol as submitted if it meets all ethical and regulatory requirements.
- **Approve with modifications** if the protocol can be ethically sound with certain changes or clarifications (e.g., revisions to the informed consent form or additional risk mitigation strategies).
- **Reject** the protocol if it is found to be ethically flawed, if the risks to participants are deemed too high, or if the study design is not scientifically valid.

The approval or rejection decision is typically provided in writing, and if modifications are requested, the protocol must be resubmitted for further review.

4. Ongoing Monitoring and Review

The IRB/IEC's role does not end with initial approval. They are also responsible for overseeing the study throughout its duration to ensure ongoing ethical compliance. This includes:

- **Reviewing amendments**: Any changes to the study protocol, informed consent form, or recruitment process must be submitted to the IRB/IEC for approval before implementation.
- **Monitoring adverse events**: The IRB/IEC regularly reviews reports of adverse events and serious adverse events during the trial to ensure that any issues are appropriately addressed.
- **Reviewing progress reports**: The sponsor or investigator is usually required to submit regular progress reports to the IRB/IEC, detailing the number of participants enrolled, safety issues, and overall progress.
- **Final study report**: Upon completion of the trial, the IRB/IEC reviews the final study report to ensure that the trial was conducted ethically and that the results are reported transparently and accurately.

5.2.2 Informed Consent Process

The **informed consent process** is a fundamental ethical requirement in clinical trials. It ensures that participants are fully aware of the nature of the trial, including its risks, benefits, and procedures, and that they voluntarily agree to participate. The process is designed to protect participants' autonomy and rights, ensuring that they make an informed decision about their involvement in the trial. It also provides legal and ethical safeguards for both the participants and the researchers, ensuring that the trial is conducted in compliance with regulatory standards and ethical principles.

5.2.2.1 Legal and Ethical Implications

The **informed consent process** carries significant **legal and ethical implications** for clinical trials. Both the participants' rights and the responsibilities of the researchers are shaped by these considerations, and failure to adhere to the proper informed consent procedures can have serious consequences. These implications can affect the credibility of the research, the protection of participants, and the legal standing of the study.

1. Ethical Implications

Ethically, the informed consent process is rooted in the **principles of autonomy, beneficence**, and **justice**. These principles ensure that participants are treated with respect and fairness, their rights are protected, and they are not subjected to unnecessary harm during the trial.

1.1 Autonomy

The principle of **autonomy** means that individuals have the right to make their own decisions about their involvement in a clinical trial, free from coercion or undue influence. Informed consent ensures that participants have sufficient understanding of the trial's purpose, procedures, risks, and potential benefits, allowing them to make an informed, voluntary decision to participate. This principle emphasizes the need for clear communication and transparency, as participants should fully understand what they are consenting to.

1.2 Beneficence

The principle of **beneficence** requires researchers to act in the best interest of participants, ensuring that the trial is designed to maximize potential benefits and minimize harm. This principle ensures that participants are not exposed to unnecessary risks, and that any risks they do face are justified by the potential benefits of the research. The informed consent process helps safeguard this principle by requiring participants to be fully informed about the nature of the risks involved in the study and how these risks are being mitigated.

1.3 Justice

The principle of **justice** involves ensuring fairness in the distribution of the benefits and burdens of clinical research. It requires that participants are selected fairly, without discrimination, and that the research does not exploit vulnerable populations. The informed consent process is vital in ensuring that vulnerable individuals, such as those with cognitive impairments or those from marginalized communities, are not coerced or taken advantage of during the trial.

2. Legal Implications

In addition to its ethical importance, the informed consent process has significant **legal implications** for both participants and researchers. Legal requirements surrounding informed consent are designed to ensure that participants' rights are protected, and that the trial is conducted within the framework of national and international law.

2.1 Regulatory Compliance

Legal standards for informed consent are set by regulatory authorities such as the **U.S. Food and Drug Administration (FDA)**, **European Medicines Agency (EMA)**, and other national health authorities. These regulatory bodies require that researchers adhere to strict guidelines for obtaining and documenting informed consent. These guidelines ensure that the consent process is thorough, transparent, and compliant with local laws and ethical standards.

In the U.S., for example, the **Common Rule (45 CFR 46)** sets out the requirements for informed consent in research involving human subjects. Similarly, the **Declaration of Helsinki** provides international ethical standards for clinical trials involving human participants. Both of these guidelines mandate that participants must voluntarily consent to participate in research after being fully informed about the risks and benefits.

2.2 Protection of Participant Rights

The legal implications of the informed consent process primarily revolve around the **protection of participant rights**. If a participant's consent is not obtained in a legally compliant manner, it may render the clinical trial invalid or unethical. Failure to properly inform participants about the risks, benefits, and procedures of the trial can result in legal consequences for the researchers, including potential lawsuits for damages caused by negligence or failure to obtain proper consent.

The **right to withdraw** from the study at any time without facing consequences is a key legal element of informed consent. Participants must be informed of their right to discontinue participation at any point during the trial without any adverse effects on their future treatment or care. Legal protections ensure that participants are not penalized or discriminated against if they decide to withdraw from the study.

2.3 Accountability of Researchers

Researchers have a **legal responsibility** to ensure that informed consent is obtained properly and documented in accordance with the law. This includes providing participants with an **informed consent form (ICF)** that outlines the details of the study and ensuring that participants understand the contents before agreeing to participate.

Researchers must also ensure that informed consent is **documented** properly, typically through signed consent forms, and that participants' consent is obtained **prior to** the initiation of any study procedures. If any changes are made to the study protocol that affect participant safety or the risk/benefit ratio, participants must be re-consented before continuing in the study.

2.4 Legal Consequences of Non-Compliance

If the informed consent process is not carried out properly, it can have serious legal implications. Failure to obtain valid consent could result in:

- **Lawsuits**: Participants or their families may sue for damages if it is found that they were not properly informed of the risks or were coerced into participating in the trial.
- **Regulatory Action**: Regulatory bodies such as the **FDA, EMA,** or local health authorities can take action against researchers, including halting the study, issuing fines, or even pursuing criminal charges if the informed consent process is not properly adhered to.
- **Loss of Research Integrity**: A trial conducted without proper informed consent may be considered ethically compromised, leading to **rejection of results or disqualification** from publication in peer-reviewed journals.

3. Components of the Informed Consent Process

For the informed consent process to be legally and ethically sound, it must include certain key components:

3.1 Disclosure of Information

Participants must be fully informed about the **nature of the trial**, including its purpose, duration, and procedures. The informed consent form should describe the expected **risks** and **benefits**, as well as any alternative treatments that might be available. Importantly, participants must be informed of their **right to withdraw** at any time, with no consequences to their future medical care.

3.2 Comprehension

Participants must have the opportunity to ask questions and ensure that they understand the information provided. Researchers should check for **comprehension** to ensure that the participant fully understands the information before consenting. This may involve explaining complex medical terminology in layman's terms or providing additional clarifications as needed.

3.3 Voluntariness

The decision to participate must be made voluntarily, without coercion or undue influence. Participants should feel free to decline or withdraw from the study at any time without fear of retribution.

5.3 Good Clinical Practice (GCP)

Good Clinical Practice (GCP) is a set of international ethical and scientific quality standards that must be followed when conducting clinical trials involving human participants. GCP guidelines are designed to ensure that clinical trials are conducted ethically, that participant safety is a priority, and that the data generated from the trials are credible and reliable. GCP outlines the roles and responsibilities of key stakeholders in the clinical trial process, including **investigators**, **sponsors**, and **monitors**. It also provides a framework for ensuring that the trial is conducted according to regulatory requirements and in compliance with international standards.

5.3.1 Guidelines for Investigators, Sponsors, and Monitors

The guidelines provided by GCP focus on the ethical and scientific principles that investigators, sponsors, and monitors must adhere to during the design, conduct, and reporting of clinical trials. These guidelines are essential to ensure the safety, rights, and well-being of participants while maintaining the integrity of the research process. Below are the key responsibilities of each of these stakeholders:

1. Role of Investigators

The **investigator** is the person responsible for conducting the clinical trial at the study site. The principal investigator (PI) is responsible for the overall conduct of the trial, and may have one or more sub-investigators who assist with various aspects of the trial. The key responsibilities of the investigator according to GCP include:

1.1 Study Design and Execution

- **Protocol Adherence**: The investigator must ensure that the clinical trial is conducted in accordance with the approved study protocol. The protocol outlines the objectives, methodology, and ethical considerations for the trial.
- **Informed Consent**: The investigator is responsible for obtaining **informed consent** from each participant, ensuring that they understand the study's purpose, procedures, risks, and benefits. The investigator must ensure that informed consent is obtained before any trial procedures are performed.
- **Participant Safety**: The investigator must ensure that the **safety and well-being** of participants are prioritized throughout the trial. This includes monitoring for adverse events (AEs) or serious adverse events (SAEs) and taking appropriate action when necessary.
- **Confidentiality**: The investigator must ensure the confidentiality of participant data and personal information throughout the trial. This includes proper handling, storage, and sharing of sensitive information in compliance with local privacy laws.
- **Adverse Event Reporting**: The investigator must report any **adverse events** or **serious adverse events** that occur during the trial to the relevant regulatory authorities and the sponsor as per regulatory guidelines.
- **Ethical Conduct**: The investigator must follow **ethical principles** throughout the study, ensuring that the trial adheres to the principles of **Good Clinical Practice (GCP)**, as well as other relevant ethical and legal guidelines such as the **Declaration of Helsinki.**

2. Role of Sponsors

The **sponsor** is the entity responsible for initiating, managing, and financing the clinical trial. The sponsor may be a pharmaceutical company, a government agency, or an academic institution. The sponsor plays a critical role in ensuring that the clinical trial is conducted in compliance with GCP and regulatory requirements. The key responsibilities of the sponsor include:

2.1 Study Design and Protocol Development

- **Protocol Development**: The sponsor is responsible for developing the study protocol, which is a key document that outlines the trial's objectives, design, methodology, and ethical considerations.
- **Regulatory Submissions**: The sponsor ensures that the trial protocol is submitted for approval to the relevant regulatory authorities and ethics committees, and that any required permits or approvals are obtained before the trial begins.

2.2 Participant Recruitment and Site Selection

- **Site Selection**: The sponsor is responsible for selecting qualified investigators and study sites that are equipped to conduct the trial. The sponsor ensures that sites have the necessary infrastructure, resources, and experience to safely and effectively conduct the trial.
- **Recruitment Plans**: The sponsor ensures that participant recruitment procedures comply with ethical guidelines, and that recruitment materials and advertisements are clear, truthful, and non-coercive.

2.3 Monitoring and Oversight

- **Monitoring and Auditing**: The sponsor is responsible for ensuring that the trial is conducted according to the protocol and that data is accurately recorded. Sponsors often set up **monitoring teams** that periodically visit study sites to review trial progress, verify data, and ensure compliance with ethical and regulatory requirements.
- **Data Management**: The sponsor ensures that **data management systems** are in place to collect, store, and analyze trial data in a way that protects the integrity of the study and participants' confidentiality.

2.4 Safety Monitoring

- **Safety Reporting**: The sponsor is responsible for ensuring that all **adverse events** and **serious adverse events** are reported promptly to regulatory authorities and to the ethics committee. Sponsors are also responsible for implementing **corrective actions** if any safety concerns arise during the trial.

3. Role of Monitors

Monitors play a crucial role in ensuring that clinical trials are conducted according to the protocol, GCP guidelines, and regulatory requirements. **Clinical trial monitors** are typically employed by the sponsor and are responsible for ensuring that the trial is being carried out correctly at the study sites. The key responsibilities of monitors include:

3.1 Study Oversight and Compliance

- **Protocol Compliance**: Monitors are responsible for ensuring that the investigator and study site staff adhere to the study protocol. This includes verifying that participant recruitment, informed consent, and data collection are done in accordance with the protocol.
- **Regulatory Compliance**: Monitors ensure that the trial is conducted in compliance with relevant regulatory guidelines, including GCP, as well as any local regulatory requirements.

3.2 Site Visits and Data Verification

- **Site Visits:** Monitors regularly visit study sites to review trial progress, assess compliance with the protocol, and verify that data is being accurately recorded and reported. They ensure that any deviations from the protocol are identified and addressed.
- **Data Verification**: Monitors verify that the data collected at the site is consistent with the source documents (e.g., medical records) and that data entry is accurate. This includes checking for discrepancies and ensuring that all required documentation is complete.

3.3 Training and Support

- **Training**: Monitors provide ongoing training and guidance to study site staff, ensuring that they are familiar with the protocol, GCP guidelines, and regulatory requirements.

- **Troubleshooting**: Monitors provide support to investigators and study sites in addressing any issues or challenges that arise during the trial, ensuring that these issues are resolved promptly and in compliance with the protocol.

3.4 Reporting and Documentation

- **Monitoring Reports**: Monitors are responsible for generating **monitoring reports** that summarize their findings during site visits. These reports detail any deviations from the protocol, issues related to participant safety, and recommendations for corrective actions.
- **Escalating Issues**: If significant issues are identified during monitoring, such as safety concerns or violations of the protocol, monitors are responsible for escalating these issues to the sponsor and regulatory authorities as appropriate.

4. GCP Compliance and Ethical Considerations

Ensuring compliance with **Good Clinical Practice (GCP)** is essential for maintaining the ethical standards of clinical trials. GCP guidelines require that all parties involved in the trial, including investigators, sponsors, and monitors, work collaboratively to ensure that the rights, safety, and well-being of participants are prioritized at all times. Key ethical considerations in GCP compliance include:

- **Informed Consent**: Ensuring that participants are fully informed about the trial and voluntarily consent to participate.
- **Participant Safety**: Taking appropriate measures to minimize risks to participants and providing them with medical care in case of adverse events.
- **Data Integrity**: Ensuring that trial data is accurate, reliable, and transparently reported.
- **Ethical Oversight**: Ensuring that the study is conducted according to ethical principles, including respect for participants' autonomy, beneficence, and justice.

5.3.2 GCP Compliance in Drug Development

Good Clinical Practice (**GCP**) compliance in drug development is essential to ensure that clinical trials are conducted ethically, safely, and scientifically. Adhering to GCP guidelines ensures that data generated in clinical trials are credible, reliable, and accurate, and that the rights, safety, and well-being of participants are protected. GCP compliance is not only a regulatory requirement but also a critical factor in the successful approval of new drug therapies.

In the context of drug development, **GCP compliance** applies to the design, conduct, monitoring, and reporting of clinical trials. It ensures that trials are conducted according to the highest ethical standards, that all participants provide informed consent, and that the trial's outcomes are valid and reproducible.

1. Key Aspects of GCP Compliance in Drug Development

There are several key aspects of GCP compliance that play a significant role throughout the clinical trial process, from **trial planning** to **study completion**. These include **protocol design, informed consent, participant safety, data integrity**, and **monitoring**.

1.1 Protocol Design and Compliance

The trial protocol is a foundational document in clinical trials and must be developed in compliance with GCP. The protocol outlines the trial's objectives, design, methodology, and the criteria for selecting participants. For GCP compliance, the protocol must:

- **Define clear objectives**: The primary and secondary endpoints should be scientifically sound and relevant to the research question.
- **Ensure ethical study design**: The study should minimize risks to participants while maximizing potential benefits, ensuring that the risk-benefit ratio is acceptable.
- **Specify appropriate methodology**: The protocol should describe how data will be collected, analyzed, and interpreted, and should outline the statistical methods to be used.
- **Include adequate monitoring**: The protocol should include provisions for regular monitoring of data and participant safety throughout the trial.

The investigator and sponsor must ensure that the study is conducted exactly as outlined in the protocol, with any amendments needing prior approval from the **Institutional Review Board (IRB)** or **Independent Ethics Committee (IEC)**.

1.2 Informed Consent

Informed consent is a critical element of GCP compliance. Before participating in a clinical trial, all participants must be fully informed about the trial, including its risks, benefits, procedures, and any alternative treatments. The informed consent process must be:

- **Voluntary**: Participation must be entirely voluntary, with no coercion or undue influence.
- **Comprehensive**: Participants must be provided with sufficient information about the study to make an informed decision, including the potential risks and benefits, the duration of the study, and the possible alternatives.
- **Written consent**: After receiving adequate information, participants must sign an informed consent form (ICF) acknowledging their understanding and voluntary participation.
- **Ongoing process**: The informed consent process is continuous. Participants should be updated on any new information that may affect their decision to continue in the trial.

The **IRB/IEC** ensures that the informed consent form is clear, comprehensive, and ethically appropriate, and that the participants are fully capable of understanding the information provided.

1.3 Participant Safety and Monitoring

Ensuring the **safety and well-being** of participants is a central component of GCP compliance. Throughout the trial, researchers must actively monitor participants for adverse events (AEs) and serious adverse events (SAEs), and take immediate action when necessary. Key aspects of participant safety include:

- **Safety monitoring**: Regular checks for AEs and SAEs should be performed to assess participant health and detect any adverse effects of the investigational product.
- **Adverse event reporting**: All AEs, regardless of severity, should be reported according to regulatory requirements, with serious AEs requiring immediate notification to regulatory authorities, the sponsor, and the ethics committee.
- **Risk minimization**: Researchers must implement risk management strategies, including discontinuation of treatment if necessary, to protect

participant safety. For example, if any participant is at significant risk, the trial may need to be paused or terminated.

The **Data Safety Monitoring Board (DSMB)** or **monitoring committee** is often involved in overseeing the safety of participants and providing guidance on whether the trial should continue, be modified, or be halted based on safety concerns.

1.4 Data Integrity and Confidentiality

The integrity of the data collected in a clinical trial is paramount to GCP compliance. All data should be accurately recorded, maintained, and analyzed, and must reflect the true outcomes of the trial without alteration or manipulation. Ensuring data integrity involves:

- **Accurate documentation**: All participant information, clinical observations, and test results must be recorded accurately and in a timely manner. This ensures that the data collected is reliable and can be used to draw valid conclusions.
- **Data confidentiality**: The privacy of participants must be protected at all stages of the trial. Personal identifiers should be removed or anonymized when collecting and storing data. Researchers must comply with **data protection regulations**, such as the **General Data Protection Regulation (GDPR)** or **Health Insurance Portability and Accountability Act (HIPAA)**, to ensure that participants' data is securely stored and shared only with authorized personnel.
- **Electronic records**: In modern trials, electronic data capture (EDC) systems are commonly used to manage and store clinical trial data. These systems must be validated to ensure that they are secure, accurate, and compliant with regulatory requirements.

1.5 Monitoring and Auditing

Regular monitoring and auditing are essential components of GCP compliance. Monitoring ensures that the clinical trial is conducted according to the protocol and that data is collected accurately. The key roles of monitoring in GCP compliance include:

- **Site visits**: Clinical trial monitors perform regular site visits to ensure that the study is being conducted according to the protocol and that investigators are following GCP guidelines. During site visits, monitors verify that informed consent is being obtained, data is being accurately recorded, and adverse events are reported promptly.

- **Data verification**: Monitors compare trial data against source documents (e.g., medical records) to ensure the accuracy of the information. This is crucial for ensuring that the data generated from the trial is reliable and trustworthy.
- **Audit trails**: Maintaining audit trails of changes made to the trial protocol, data, and documentation is a critical part of ensuring compliance. This allows for tracking of any modifications and provides transparency in the trial process.

1.6 Training and Qualifications

All personnel involved in the clinical trial, including investigators, study staff, and monitors, must receive appropriate training and have the necessary qualifications to perform their roles. This includes:

- **Training in GCP**: All individuals involved in the trial must be trained in **Good Clinical Practice (GCP)** to ensure they understand the ethical and regulatory requirements of clinical trials and can perform their duties correctly.
- **Continuous education**: As GCP guidelines and regulatory requirements evolve, ongoing training is necessary to keep all staff updated on the latest best practices and legal requirements.

2. Regulatory Compliance and Ethical Review

GCP compliance is critical for obtaining regulatory approval for a new drug. Regulatory authorities, such as the **U.S. FDA, European Medicines Agency (EMA),** and other national health agencies, require that clinical trials follow GCP guidelines to ensure the safety, rights, and well-being of participants are protected and that the trial results are credible. The ethics review process, typically conducted by an **Institutional Review Board (IRB)** or **Independent Ethics Committee (IEC)**, ensures that the trial meets all ethical standards and that participants are not exposed to undue risk.

The ethical review process also assesses whether the **study design** is scientifically valid, whether **informed consent** procedures are adequate, and whether the **risks** of the trial are acceptable in light of the potential **benefits**.

5.4 Pharmacovigilance

Pharmacovigilance is the science and activities related to the detection, assessment, understanding, and prevention of adverse effects or any other drug-related problems. Ensuring the **safety** and **efficacy** of pharmaceutical products is critical throughout their lifecycle, and it becomes particularly important during the clinical trial phase. During this phase, safety monitoring is an integral part of pharmacovigilance, where any **adverse events (AEs)** or **serious adverse events (SAEs)** that occur are systematically reported, analyzed, and acted upon to protect participants and ensure the validity of the trial.

5.4.1 Safety Monitoring During Clinical Trials

The safety of participants in clinical trials is paramount, and continuous monitoring is essential to identify and manage any adverse events (AEs) or serious adverse events (SAEs) that may arise. **Pharmacovigilance** during clinical trials helps to assess the **risk-benefit ratio** of an investigational drug, identify potential safety signals, and take timely corrective actions if necessary. Safety monitoring is critical to ensuring that participants' well-being is protected, that the trial's integrity is maintained, and that the findings are credible and reliable.

1. Adverse Event (AE) Reporting

An **adverse event (AE)** is any undesirable experience associated with the use of a medicinal product, whether or not it is related to the product. **Adverse events** may include side effects, complications, or unexpected reactions to a drug. These events are categorized by their **severity** and **relationship to the treatment**. Key aspects of AE reporting during clinical trials include:

1.1 Definition and Types of AEs

- **Mild AEs:** These may cause discomfort but do not require medical intervention or change in the treatment regimen.
- **Moderate AEs:** These may require some intervention or treatment, though they are not life-threatening.
- **Severe AEs:** These are serious and may cause permanent damage, hospitalization, or even death.

The investigator is responsible for identifying and documenting any AE that occurs during the trial, regardless of whether it is related to the investigational drug. These events should be recorded in the **Case Report Form (CRF)** and reported to the sponsor, **regulatory authorities**, and the **Ethics Committee**.

1.2 Serious Adverse Events (SAEs)

A **serious adverse event (SAE)** is an adverse event that results in death, is life-threatening, requires hospitalization, causes a persistent or significant disability or incapacity, or results in a congenital anomaly or birth defect. SAEs must be reported immediately to the sponsor and the relevant regulatory authorities.

- **Immediate reporting**: As soon as a SAE is identified, it must be reported to the sponsor within **24 hours**. The sponsor then informs the regulatory authorities and the Ethics Committee.
- **Investigator's responsibility**: The investigator must assess whether the SAE is related to the investigational product and provide appropriate medical care to the participant.
- **Follow-up**: Continuous monitoring and documentation of SAEs are necessary to determine if they are **expected** or **unexpected**. Follow-up visits and additional tests may be required to assess the ongoing impact of the SAE.

2. Risk-Benefit Assessment

A core principle of safety monitoring in clinical trials is the ongoing **risk-benefit assessment**. The **risk** refers to the potential harm associated with the investigational product, while the **benefit** refers to the therapeutic effect. A drug may provide significant therapeutic benefits, but if its risks outweigh these benefits, it may be deemed unsuitable for market approval.

2.1 Ongoing Safety Monitoring

Throughout the trial, the safety profile of the investigational drug should be continuously assessed. The data collected on adverse events is analyzed to determine whether the risks associated with the drug are acceptable in relation to the benefits. This ongoing safety monitoring helps to:

- **Identify safety signals**: A safety signal is an indication that an adverse event may be related to the investigational product. Early detection of safety signals can prompt further investigation, modifications to the study design, or even termination of the trial if necessary.

- **Modify treatment protocols**: If new safety concerns arise during the trial, the sponsor and investigators may need to modify the treatment protocol, such as reducing the dose or implementing additional safety precautions.
- **Stop or continue the trial**: If the risks are deemed unacceptable, the trial may be halted. On the other hand, if the benefits outweigh the risks, the trial may continue, possibly with adjustments to the safety monitoring procedures.

2.2 Data Safety Monitoring Board (DSMB)

The **Data Safety Monitoring Board (DSMB)** is an independent group of experts that oversees the safety of participants during a clinical trial. The DSMB is responsible for:

- **Reviewing interim data**: The DSMB periodically reviews interim data to assess the safety and efficacy of the investigational product.
- **Recommending actions**: Based on the safety data, the DSMB may recommend that the trial be stopped, modified, or continued as planned. They ensure that the study is conducted ethically and that participants' safety is prioritized.
- **Ensuring transparency**: The DSMB provides an additional layer of accountability by ensuring that safety data is reviewed independently, without bias from the study sponsor or investigators.

3. Regulatory Reporting and Compliance

Pharmacovigilance activities are regulated by national and international agencies, such as the **U.S. Food and Drug Administration (FDA)**, **European Medicines Agency (EMA)**, and **World Health Organization (WHO)**, to ensure that clinical trials meet safety standards. Investigators, sponsors, and monitors must comply with reporting requirements and timelines to ensure that any risks to participants are promptly addressed.

3.1 Periodic Reporting

- **Clinical Trial Safety Reports (CTSRs)**: Sponsors are required to submit periodic reports on the safety data from the trial to regulatory authorities. These reports may include summaries of adverse events, SAEs, and any modifications to the trial protocol due to safety concerns.

- **Annual safety reports**: In addition to ongoing SAE reporting, annual safety reports must be submitted to provide an updated overview of the trial's safety profile.

3.2 Post-Marketing Surveillance

Once a drug is approved for marketing, **post-marketing surveillance** becomes crucial in identifying long-term or rare adverse events that may not have been detected during clinical trials. Pharmacovigilance continues in the post-marketing phase through:

- **Spontaneous reporting**: Patients, healthcare providers, and pharmaceutical companies report any adverse events that occur during the use of the drug.
- **Risk management plans**: Companies must create plans to minimize risks associated with the drug, which may include providing updated warnings or restricting the use of the drug to certain populations.
- **Periodic safety update reports (PSURs)**: These reports provide an ongoing assessment of the safety data gathered after the drug is on the market, ensuring that the benefit-risk profile remains favorable.

5.4.2 Reporting Adverse Events and Reactions

Reporting adverse events (AEs) and **adverse reactions (ADRs)** is a crucial aspect of **pharmacovigilance** during clinical trials. The primary purpose of reporting AEs and ADRs is to ensure that any **potential risks** associated with the investigational drug are identified early and managed appropriately. This process is not only essential for participant safety but also helps to build a comprehensive safety profile of the drug, which is critical for the **regulatory approval process** and ongoing post-marketing surveillance.

1. Definition of Adverse Events and Adverse Reactions

Before delving into the reporting procedures, it is important to distinguish between **adverse events** and **adverse reactions**, as these terms are often used interchangeably but have distinct meanings in pharmacovigilance.

1.1 Adverse Event (AE)

An **adverse event** is any undesirable experience associated with the use of a medicinal product, whether or not it is directly related to the product. AEs can occur during the course of the clinical trial and may be caused by the investigational drug, the underlying disease, or other factors unrelated to the drug. The key characteristics of an AE include:

- **Any negative outcome** experienced by a participant during the trial, such as illness, injury, or any other unwanted medical condition.
- **Not necessarily related** to the investigational drug. AEs could occur in participants receiving the investigational product, a placebo, or standard treatment.

1.2 Adverse Reaction (ADR)

An **adverse reaction** is a harmful and unintended response to a drug that occurs at doses normally used in humans for prophylaxis, diagnosis, or treatment. An ADR is always related to the investigational drug and is caused by the pharmacological properties of the drug. ADRs are critical for evaluating the safety profile of a drug, and they typically involve:

- **Harmful effects directly related** to the investigational drug's properties.
- A **causal relationship** between the drug and the adverse event.

2. Reporting Requirements and Timelines

Reporting AEs and ADRs is mandated by **regulatory authorities**, such as the **U.S. FDA, EMA, Health Canada**, and **other national health agencies**, to ensure participant safety and facilitate early detection of potential safety issues. The specific requirements for reporting, including **timing, format, and responsibility**, vary by jurisdiction but generally include the following:

2.1 Immediate Reporting of Serious Adverse Events (SAEs)

SAEs must be reported **immediately** to the trial sponsor and regulatory authorities. An SAE is any adverse event that results in death, is life-threatening, requires hospitalization, causes a persistent disability, or results in a congenital anomaly or birth defect. Timely reporting is critical for:

- **Safety monitoring**: Regulators and ethics committees need to assess the severity and potential risk of the investigational drug.
- **Modifying study protocols**: Immediate reporting allows sponsors and investigators to make necessary adjustments to the study, such as altering dosages or halting the study.

- **Protecting participant health**: Early identification of serious issues enables prompt medical intervention to protect participants.

2.2 Reporting of Non-Serious Adverse Events

While **serious adverse events (SAEs)** are prioritized, all AEs, whether serious or non-serious, must also be recorded and reported. Non-serious AEs are typically reported within a specified timeframe, which is often **15 days** for non-serious adverse events in clinical trials. These reports help monitor the safety profile of the investigational drug and contribute to overall data integrity.

2.3 Follow-up Reporting

After the initial report of an AE or ADR, follow-up information must be provided to regulatory authorities, ethics committees, and other relevant parties. This follow-up can include additional medical details, lab results, or changes in the participant's condition, particularly in cases of SAEs or significant AEs. Follow-up reporting is vital to provide a complete picture of the participant's health status and the potential relationship between the drug and the adverse event.

3. Methods of Reporting Adverse Events and Reactions

The **method of reporting** adverse events and reactions is highly structured to ensure accurate and consistent data. Most regulatory authorities require the use of **standardized forms** and electronic systems to collect, process, and report AE and ADR information. These systems include:

3.1 Case Report Forms (CRFs)

Case Report Forms (CRFs) are used to collect detailed information on adverse events and reactions from each participant. CRFs should be filled out immediately following the occurrence of an AE or ADR and include:

- **Detailed description** of the event, including the onset, severity, and duration.
- **Causal relationship** with the investigational drug, based on clinical judgment and data.
- **Medical interventions** required, if any, to address the AE or ADR.
- **Outcome of the event** (recovery, resolution, permanent disability, etc.).

The CRFs are submitted to the trial sponsor, and the data is reviewed to determine whether any changes are needed in the trial protocol or the drug's safety profile.

3.2 Electronic Reporting Systems

Regulatory authorities often require the use of **electronic reporting systems** to streamline and expedite AE and ADR reporting. Some common systems include:

- **EudraVigilance** (European Medicines Agency) for reporting to European regulatory authorities.
- **FDA's Adverse Event Reporting System (FAERS)** in the United States.
- **MedDRA (Medical Dictionary for Regulatory Activities)** is a standardized medical terminology used for coding and reporting adverse events consistently across different clinical trials and regulatory agencies.

Electronic reporting systems improve the speed and accuracy of AE reporting, allowing for quick analysis and decision-making by regulatory bodies.

4. Data Management and Analysis of Adverse Events

Once reported, the adverse event data must be carefully managed, analyzed, and reviewed to identify potential safety signals and ensure appropriate follow-up actions. Key activities in the data management and analysis process include:

4.1 Data Collection and Organization

Adverse events and reactions should be consistently documented across all clinical trial sites. Standardization of data collection, including accurate recording of event types, severity, timing, and outcomes, is essential for ensuring the credibility of the data.

4.2 Causality Assessment

In many clinical trials, it is important to assess whether the adverse event or reaction is related to the investigational product. This is done through a **causality assessment**, which evaluates the strength of the relationship between the drug and the adverse event. There are several methods used for causality assessment, including:

- **WHO-UMC scale**: A widely used system for assessing the probability of a causal relationship between a drug and an adverse event.
- **Naranjo Algorithm**: A method to determine whether an adverse event is likely related to the drug based on several questions regarding the

timing, previous occurrences, and other factors.

4.3 Safety Signal Detection

As data accumulates, the monitoring of adverse events can help detect **safety signals**—unanticipated patterns of adverse events that could indicate a previously unknown risk. A **safety signal** is defined as information that suggests a new and potentially significant drug-related risk. If a safety signal is detected, additional investigations are conducted to confirm the risk, and regulatory actions, such as labeling changes or additional studies, may be required.

5. Reporting Adverse Events After Trial Completion

Once the clinical trial is completed, **post-marketing surveillance** continues to monitor the safety of the drug. Post-marketing surveillance involves ongoing reporting of adverse events through systems such as **MedWatch** (FDA) or **EudraVigilance** (EMA). These systems allow healthcare providers, patients, and manufacturers to report adverse events associated with a drug once it has been marketed.

- **Spontaneous reporting**: Healthcare providers and patients are encouraged to report adverse events that occur once the drug is available in the market.
- **Long-term safety monitoring**: Long-term studies or registries may be required to track any delayed or rare adverse effects that were not identified during the clinical trial phase.

Element	Description	Purpose	Examples
Study Objectives	Clear and concise statement of the goals of the clinical trial	Defines the trial's primary and secondary endpoints	Assess the drug's efficacy in treating a disease
Study Design	Description of the type of trial (randomized, open-label, etc.)	Guides trial execution, ensuring scientific validity	Randomized controlled trial, cross-over design
Inclusion/Exclusion Criteria	Criteria to select eligible participants	Ensures participant safety and suitability	Age, health status, comorbidities
Endpoints	Primary and secondary outcomes to be measured	Measures the trial's success or failure	Reduction in tumor size, improvement in symptoms
Data Collection Methods	Procedures for collecting data during the trial	Standardizes how data will be gathered	Clinical assessments, laboratory tests

Table 19: Key Elements of Clinical Trial Protocol

Study Type	Purpose	Examples	Benefits
Randomized Controlled Trials (RCT)	Minimize bias by randomly assigning participants to groups	Testing new drug vs placebo	High reliability and validity of results
Cohort Studies	Follow a group of people over time to see outcomes	Observing the impact of a treatment	Longitudinal data on treatment effects
Case-Control Studies	Compare patients with a disease to those without	Comparing drug exposure in patients with cancer vs non-cancer	Effective for rare diseases
Cross-Sectional Studies	Collect data at one point in time	Survey of health behaviors in a population	Quick and cost-effective
Open-Label Studies	Participants and researchers know the treatment	Testing drugs with known side effects	Useful for initial testing or when blinding is not feasible

Table 20: Types of Clinical Trial Studies

Ethical Issue	Description	Purpose	Regulatory Guidance
Informed Consent	Ensuring participants understand the trial and its risks	Protects participant autonomy	Declaration of Helsinki, GCP guidelines
Participant Safety	Ensuring that participants are not exposed to unnecessary harm	Protects health and wellbeing	GCP, FDA regulations
Confidentiality	Protecting participants' private information	Ensures privacy and trust in the trial	HIPAA, GCP guidelines
Fair Participant Selection	Ensuring equitable recruitment without discrimination	Ensures justice in the trial	GCP, IRB guidelines
Post-Trial Access to Treatment	Providing access to effective treatments after the trial ends	Ensures participants benefit from the trial	GCP, ethical considerations in clinical trials

Table21: Ethical Considerations in Clinical Trials

Role	Function	Purpose
Review and Approve Protocols	Ensure the study follows ethical and scientific standards	Protect participants' rights and safety
Monitor Ongoing Trials	Review ongoing studies for compliance	Ensure safety and protocol adherence
Evaluate Risk vs. Benefit	Assess the risks of the trial versus potential benefits	Ensure that benefits outweigh risks for participants
Ensure Informed Consent	Review the informed consent process	Guarantee that participants understand their participation

Table 22: Roles of Institutional Review Board (IRB) and Ethics Committees (EC)

Event Type	Description	Reporting Requirements	Regulatory Body
Serious Adverse Event (SAE)	Any event that results in death, hospitalization, or disability	Must be reported immediately to regulatory bodies	FDA, EMA
Non-Serious Adverse Event	Any event that does not meet SAE criteria	Reported in periodic safety updates	FDA, EMA
Unexpected Adverse Event	Adverse event not listed in the drug's labeling	Must be reported immediately	FDA, EMA
Serious and Unexpected Event	Event that is both serious and unexpected	Must be reported within 24 hours	FDA, EMA

Table 23: Adverse Event Reporting in Clinical Trials

CHAPTER SIX

Regulatory Concepts and Terminologies

6.1 Basic Regulatory Terminologies

In the realm of **pharmaceutical regulatory science**, several key terms are frequently used to describe the various frameworks, standards, and procedures that govern the development, approval, and monitoring of pharmaceutical products. Understanding these terms is crucial for navigating the complex landscape of pharmaceutical regulation. In this section, we will define and distinguish between essential regulatory terms such as **regulations**, **guidelines**, **laws**, and **acts**. These terms form the foundation of pharmaceutical regulations and are often used interchangeably, although they have distinct meanings and implications.

6.1.1 Definitions: Regulations, Guidelines, Laws, Acts

1. Regulations

Regulations are detailed and legally binding rules established by regulatory bodies or authorities to implement specific laws and ensure compliance with legal requirements. In the context of pharmaceutical regulation, regulations govern various aspects of drug development, testing, manufacturing, and marketing. These regulations provide a framework for how the industry must operate and set out the **mandatory** requirements that companies must follow.

- **Legal Binding**: Regulations are enforceable by law, and non-compliance can lead to penalties, fines, or legal action.
- **Detailed Requirements**: Regulations often provide detailed instructions on how specific aspects of pharmaceutical processes must be conducted.

For example, regulations may dictate the procedures for **Good Manufacturing Practice (GMP)**, **clinical trial conduct**, or **adverse event reporting**.

- **Examples:**

    ◦ The **FDA regulations** under the **Code of Federal Regulations (CFR)**, specifically **21 CFR** for drug products.
    ◦ **EMA regulations** that govern the approval of medicines within the European Union.

Regulations are more specific than laws and are designed to ensure that the broader legal framework is adhered to in practical terms.

2. Guidelines

Guidelines are recommendations or instructions provided by regulatory bodies or organizations to help industry stakeholders comply with regulations, laws, or best practices. Unlike regulations, guidelines are not legally binding. However, they are widely respected and followed within the industry as they provide **best practice** standards for specific processes, including clinical trial design, drug testing, or safety monitoring.

- **Advisory in Nature**: While guidelines carry significant weight and are often followed closely, failure to adhere to them does not result in legal penalties. Instead, companies must justify why they did not follow the guidelines if questioned.
- **Flexibility**: Guidelines offer some flexibility compared to regulations. They provide a framework but may allow for some degree of interpretation or adaptation depending on the circumstances.
- **Examples:**

    ◦ **ICH (International Council for Harmonisation)** guidelines, which provide global standards for pharmaceutical development, particularly in clinical trials.
    ◦ **FDA guidelines** for the design and conduct of clinical trials.

Guidelines help align industry practices with regulatory expectations but provide enough leeway for innovation and adjustments.

3. Laws

Laws are broad legal frameworks enacted by legislative bodies (such as **parliaments** or **congresses**) that establish the foundational rules for society, including the **pharmaceutical industry**. Laws are the primary source of authority in a legal system and are enforceable by the judiciary. In the context of pharmaceutical regulation, laws define the overall legal framework for drug development, approval, marketing, and monitoring.

- **Enforceability**: Laws are legally binding, and non-compliance can result in criminal prosecution, civil penalties, or other legal actions.
- **Broad Scope**: Laws provide a broad set of rules and principles, often with more general applicability. They set the boundaries within which regulations and guidelines can be established.
- **Examples**:

  - The **Federal Food, Drug, and Cosmetic Act (FDCA)** in the U.S., which provides the legal basis for regulating food, drugs, and cosmetics.
  - The **Medicines Act** in the U.K., which regulates the approval and sale of medicinal products.

Laws serve as the foundation for the regulatory environment, establishing overarching principles and authority that guide the development of regulations and guidelines.

4. Acts

An **act** is a specific type of law that is passed by a legislative body to establish a new law or to amend an existing one. Acts are typically more specific than laws, detailing the precise legal rules that govern a particular issue or subject matter. In the context of pharmaceuticals, **acts** are often used to define the regulatory framework for drug approval, safety, labeling, and post-marketing surveillance.

- **Specific in Nature**: Acts are often focused on specific areas of regulation. For example, an act might regulate the **approval process for new drugs, clinical trials**, or the **post-market surveillance** of pharmaceuticals.
- **Implementation of Broad Laws**: Acts are usually the result of broader **laws** passed by the legislature. They provide more detailed rules for the **implementation** of these laws.
- **Examples**:

- ◦ The **Drug Approval Act** (e.g., **Food, Drug, and Cosmetic Act (FDCA)**) in the U.S., which governs the approval of new drugs by the **FDA.**
- ◦ The **Pharmaceuticals and Cosmetics Act** in India, which regulates the manufacture, sale, and distribution of drugs in the country.

Acts are legally binding documents that lay down specific regulations governing various facets of the pharmaceutical industry. They often serve as the foundation for creating regulatory frameworks and guidelines for pharmaceutical practices.

5. Summary of Key Differences

Term	Definition	Legally Binding?	Scope	Examples
Regulations	Detailed rules created to implement laws and ensure compliance with legal requirements.	Yes	Specific requirements for conducting pharmaceutical activities.	21 CFR (FDA regulations), EMA regulations
Guidelines	Non-binding recommendatio ns to support compliance with regulations or best practices.	No	Advisory, flexible recommendatio ns for best practices.	ICH guidelines, FDA clinical trial guidelines
Laws	Broad legal frameworks that establish foundational rules for the entire legal system.	Yes	General legal rules, foundation of the regulatory framework.	Federal Food, Drug, and Cosmetic Act (FDCA)
Acts	Specific laws passed by a legislative body to regulate particular areas or activities.	Yes	Detailed legal rules for specific areas within the regulatory framework.	Drug Approval Act, Pharmaceutical and Cosmetics Act (India)

Summary of Key Differences between Regulations, Guidelines, Laws, and Acts

6.1.2 *Key Regulatory Terms in Pharmaceutical Development*

In the field of **pharmaceutical development**, numerous **regulatory terms** are used to define and guide the processes involved in the creation, approval, and monitoring of pharmaceutical products. These terms provide the foundational language for regulatory bodies, sponsors, investigators, and other stakeholders to communicate clearly and ensure that drugs are developed, tested, and distributed in compliance with legal and ethical standards. In this section, we will explore some of the key regulatory terms that are fundamental to the pharmaceutical development process.

1. Investigational New Drug (IND)

An **Investigational New Drug (IND)** refers to a drug that has been approved by the regulatory authority (such as the **FDA** in the U.S.) to be tested in clinical trials. The **IND application** is a submission made to the regulatory authorities to obtain approval to begin human clinical trials for a new drug or biological product.

- **Purpose**: To demonstrate the safety and efficacy of a new drug or biologic before it can be marketed.
- **Requirements**: The IND application must include preclinical data, manufacturing information, proposed clinical trial protocols, and information about the drug's chemical structure and mechanism of action.
- **Example**: An IND is required before conducting Phase I clinical trials on a new drug that has not been previously tested in humans.

2. New Drug Application (NDA)

A **New Drug Application (NDA)** is the formal submission made to regulatory authorities (such as the **FDA** in the U.S.) to request approval for marketing a new drug product. The NDA includes comprehensive data from all stages of drug development, including preclinical and clinical trial data, and information on the drug's safety, efficacy, manufacturing, and labeling.

- **Purpose**: To evaluate whether the new drug can be safely marketed to the public.
- **Requirements**: The NDA must include clinical trial data demonstrating the drug's safety and efficacy, as well as manufacturing practices, labeling, and proposed drug indications.
- **Example**: A pharmaceutical company submits an NDA to the FDA after completing clinical trials and gathering enough evidence to prove that the new drug is safe and effective.

3. Abbreviated New Drug Application (ANDA)

An **Abbreviated New Drug Application (ANDA)** is a submission made to regulatory authorities for the approval of a generic drug. Unlike the **NDA**, which is for new drugs, the **ANDA** is used for drugs that are identical to already approved reference drugs but typically come in a different brand name or a generic version.

- **Purpose**: To obtain approval for the generic version of an already approved drug, ensuring that the generic product has the same **active ingredient**, **dosage form**, and **strength** as the reference drug.
- **Requirements**: The ANDA application includes data demonstrating **bioequivalence** to the reference drug, meaning the generic drug has the same rate and extent of absorption in the bloodstream.
- **Example**: A generic version of a branded drug like **atorvastatin** (Lipitor) is submitted as an ANDA for approval to the regulatory authorities.

4. Good Manufacturing Practice (GMP)

Good Manufacturing Practice (GMP) refers to a system of regulations and guidelines that ensure the consistent production and control of pharmaceutical products. GMP sets the standards for the production process, from the sourcing of raw materials to the packaging and labeling of finished products, to ensure that they meet safety, quality, and efficacy standards.

- **Purpose**: To ensure that drugs are consistently produced and controlled according to quality standards.
- **Requirements**: GMP requires strict adherence to proper facilities, equipment, quality control, personnel training, and documentation to prevent contamination, errors, or defects in the final product.

- **Example**: Pharmaceutical manufacturers must implement GMP to ensure that their products are of consistent quality, free from contamination, and meet all regulatory standards.

5. Clinical Trial Authorization (CTA)

Clinical Trial Authorization (CTA) is the approval granted by regulatory authorities to begin clinical trials on a new drug or biologic. Before any clinical trial can begin, the sponsor must submit a CTA application that includes detailed information about the trial design, participant recruitment criteria, informed consent processes, and safety monitoring protocols.

- **Purpose**: To obtain permission to start testing a new drug or biologic in human subjects.
- **Requirements**: The CTA must include preclinical data, trial protocols, and safety information to demonstrate that the trial will be conducted ethically and that participants will be protected from harm.
- **Example**: A pharmaceutical company applies for a CTA before starting Phase I clinical trials for a new drug.

6. Post-Marketing Surveillance

Post-marketing surveillance refers to the activities conducted after a drug is approved and marketed to monitor its safety, effectiveness, and any adverse events or long-term effects that may not have been identified during clinical trials. Post-marketing surveillance is essential for detecting rare side effects or issues that only become apparent once a drug is used by a larger population.

- **Purpose**: To monitor the safety and efficacy of a drug once it is available to the public.
- **Requirements**: Includes ongoing collection of **adverse event reports**, long-term health outcomes, and population-based studies to assess the drug's real-world effectiveness and safety.
- **Example**: After a vaccine is approved and marketed, post-marketing surveillance is conducted to monitor any potential side effects or adverse reactions reported by the general population.

7. Risk Management Plan (RMP)

A **Risk Management Plan (RMP)** is a strategic document required by regulatory authorities for the safe use of a drug once it is marketed. The RMP outlines strategies to identify, assess, and minimize the risks associated with a drug. This plan includes risk communication strategies, risk minimization measures, and post-marketing safety monitoring.

- **Purpose**: To minimize potential risks associated with the drug's use after it enters the market.
- **Requirements**: The RMP must include data on known or potential risks, details on how these risks will be monitored, and strategies for minimizing adverse outcomes.
- **Example**: A risk management plan may require the implementation of additional safety monitoring or restricted use of a drug in certain patient populations to mitigate risks.

8. Bioequivalence

Bioequivalence refers to the comparison of the **bioavailability** of two drug products, typically a generic drug and its reference brand-name counterpart, to ensure they perform similarly in the body. Bioequivalence testing is a requirement for the approval of generic drugs to ensure they are therapeutically equivalent to the original product.

- **Purpose**: To demonstrate that the generic version of a drug produces the same effect as the brand-name version when administered in the same dosage.
- **Requirements**: Bioequivalence studies compare the rate and extent of absorption of the generic drug versus the reference drug. This is usually done through clinical trials measuring plasma drug concentrations over time.
- **Example**: A generic drug manufacturer must conduct bioequivalence studies to prove that its version of a drug like **ibuprofen** is absorbed in the same way as the original, ensuring similar therapeutic effects.

9. Fast Track Designation

Fast Track Designation is a regulatory pathway that expedites the development and approval process for drugs that address unmet medical needs, particularly for serious conditions or diseases where no effective treatment exists. Drugs that receive **Fast Track Designation** may be eligible for **accelerated approval** processes and **priority review**.

- **Purpose**: To speed up the availability of drugs that have the potential to treat serious conditions.
- **Requirements**: The drug must demonstrate the potential to address a **serious condition** and show preliminary clinical evidence suggesting it could provide a significant benefit over existing therapies.
- **Example**: A **cancer drug** showing early signs of efficacy in clinical trials may be granted **Fast Track Designation** to accelerate its approval and bring it to market faster.

10. Orphan Drug Designation

The **Orphan Drug Designation** is granted to drugs that are intended to treat rare diseases, typically those affecting fewer than 200,000 people in the U.S. Orphan drugs are eligible for various incentives, including market exclusivity, tax credits, and assistance with clinical trial costs.

- **Purpose**: To encourage the development of drugs for rare or neglected diseases by providing regulatory incentives.
- **Requirements**: The drug must be for the treatment of a disease that affects a small patient population and must demonstrate a significant benefit over existing treatments.
- **Example**: A drug developed for **cystic fibrosis**, a rare genetic disorder, could receive **Orphan Drug Designation** to help bring it to market.

11. Good Laboratory Practice (GLP)

Good Laboratory Practice (GLP) refers to a set of principles and guidelines that ensure the quality, integrity, and reliability of laboratory studies, particularly preclinical studies, that support regulatory submissions. GLP is crucial for maintaining the **scientific credibility** of data used to support drug development.

- **Purpose**: To ensure that laboratory studies, such as toxicology studies, are conducted systematically and that results are reproducible and reliable.
- **Requirements**: GLP includes standards for laboratory facilities, equipment, personnel training, and the documentation of studies.

- **Example**: Before a drug can proceed to human trials, preclinical **toxicology studies** conducted under GLP standards are necessary to evaluate the drug's safety.

6.2 Major Regulatory Guidelines and Books

In the field of **pharmaceutical development**, various regulatory guidelines and books serve as authoritative references for manufacturers, researchers, and regulatory bodies. These documents provide essential standards, instructions, and criteria that guide the development, approval, and marketing of pharmaceutical products. Among these references, **The Orange Book** holds significant importance in regulating and ensuring the safety, efficacy, and bioequivalence of drugs. This section focuses on **The Orange Book** and its role in bioequivalence studies.

6.2.1 The Orange Book: Role in Bioequivalence Studies

The Orange Book, formally known as the **Approved Drug Products with Therapeutic Equivalence Evaluations**, is a comprehensive resource published by the **U.S. Food and Drug Administration (FDA)**. It provides a list of FDA-approved drug products, including both brand-name and generic drugs, and contains valuable information on their **therapeutic equivalence**. The **Orange Book** plays a critical role in ensuring that generic drugs meet the same safety and efficacy standards as their branded counterparts, particularly in the context of **bioequivalence** studies.

1. Purpose and Importance of The Orange Book

The primary purpose of **The Orange Book** is to guide healthcare providers, pharmaceutical companies, and regulatory authorities by offering a reliable and up-to-date reference for **FDA-approved drugs**. It supports the **generic drug approval process** by identifying drugs that have been proven to be **therapeutically equivalent** to brand-name drugs.

- **Therapeutic Equivalence**: The Orange Book categorizes drugs based on their **therapeutic equivalence**. This means that the generic drug must be bioequivalent to the brand-name drug in terms of **pharmacokinetic properties** (i.e., how the drug is absorbed, distributed, metabolized, and excreted in the body).
- **Regulatory Reference**: The Orange Book serves as a reference for regulatory authorities to assess whether a generic drug can be

substituted for a brand-name drug without compromising safety or effectiveness.

- **Market Access**: The information in the Orange Book helps facilitate the **market entry of generic drugs** by providing evidence of equivalence, which is required for **Abbreviated New Drug Application (ANDA)** approval.

2. Role in Bioequivalence Studies

Bioequivalence is a key concept in the **approval of generic drugs**, ensuring that a generic drug performs similarly to the brand-name drug it is intended to replace. **Bioequivalence studies** are critical for determining whether a generic product can be safely substituted for the brand-name drug.

The **Orange Book** plays a pivotal role in **bioequivalence studies** by:

- **Identifying Reference Drugs**: The Orange Book provides a list of **reference drugs** (brand-name drugs) that have been FDA-approved. These reference drugs serve as the standard for comparison in bioequivalence studies for generic drugs.
- **Incorporating Bioequivalence Data**: The Orange Book includes data on **therapeutic equivalence** for drugs that have been approved by the FDA, which encompasses the results of bioequivalence studies. It categorizes generic drugs based on their equivalence to brand-name drugs, providing clear guidelines on which generic drugs can be substituted for their branded counterparts.

3. Categories of Therapeutic Equivalence in The Orange Book

The **Orange Book** classifies drugs based on their **therapeutic equivalence** evaluations, using specific codes to indicate whether a generic drug is equivalent to the brand-name drug. These categories are based on the findings from bioequivalence studies, which assess the pharmacokinetic similarity between the two drugs.

- **Code "A"**: This indicates that the generic drug is **therapeutically equivalent** to the reference drug. It has been shown through bioequivalence studies that the generic drug is equivalent to the brand-name drug in terms of its pharmacokinetic properties and efficacy. An "A" rating means that the generic product can be safely substituted for the branded product.

- ◦ **Example**: A generic drug with an "A" rating is considered **bioequivalent** to its brand-name counterpart and can be marketed as a substitute.

- **Code "B"**: This indicates that the generic drug is **not therapeutically equivalent** to the reference drug. This may be due to differences in the formulation, manufacturing processes, or lack of bioequivalence data. Drugs classified under "B" should not be substituted for the brand-name drug without further studies or approval.

  - ◦ **Example**: A drug with a "B" rating does not meet the requirements for bioequivalence and may require additional clinical studies before it can be considered equivalent.

- **"AB" Rating**: A subcategory of "A" rating that signifies that the drug is **bioequivalent** but requires additional clinical studies to confirm this equivalence, such as tests under different conditions (e.g., fasting versus fed states).

4. Bioequivalence and Clinical Considerations

Bioequivalence studies are typically conducted to compare the **pharmacokinetic profiles** of the generic and reference drugs. These studies evaluate:

- **Rate of Absorption**: The time it takes for the drug to reach peak blood concentration (Cmax).
- **Extent of Absorption**: The area under the curve (AUC), which represents the total drug exposure over time.
- **Time to Peak Concentration (Tmax)**: How long it takes for the drug to reach its peak concentration in the bloodstream.

The **Orange Book** includes information on the **bioequivalence studies** conducted for both the reference drug and the generic product, ensuring that the generic drug meets the same **therapeutic** and **pharmacokinetic** standards as the original product.

5. Regulatory Implications for Generic Drug Approval

The **Orange Book** serves as a regulatory guide for the approval of **generic drugs**. The **FDA** uses the information in the Orange Book to determine whether a generic drug can be substituted for a brand-name drug without compromising safety or efficacy. Key implications of the Orange Book for generic drug approval include:

- **ANDA Submission**: Generic drug manufacturers must submit an **Abbreviated New Drug Application (ANDA)** to the FDA, demonstrating that their drug is **bioequivalent** to the reference drug. The **Orange Book** is used to support the ANDA submission by providing a record of approved reference drugs.
- **FDA Reviews**: The FDA evaluates the **bioequivalence data** provided by the applicant to determine if the generic drug can be substituted for the reference drug. This includes evaluating the results of clinical studies that measure **pharmacokinetic similarity** between the two products.

6.2.2 The Federal Register and Its Importance

The **Federal Register** is a key publication in the United States that plays a central role in the **regulatory process** for drugs, medical devices, and other products. Published by the **U.S. Government Publishing Office**, it serves as the official journal for public notices and updates from federal agencies, including the **FDA, EPA, OSHA,** and other agencies involved in regulating public health and safety. It is a vital tool for ensuring transparency in government actions, and it directly impacts the development and approval of pharmaceutical products. This section explores the role and importance of the Federal Register in the context of pharmaceutical regulations.

1. **What is the Federal Register?**

The **Federal Register** is the daily publication that provides **official notices** of the actions taken by federal agencies. It includes a wide range of materials, including proposed rules, final rules, notices, and public announcements. It is an essential resource for anyone working within the **regulatory framework** in the U.S., as it informs the public and stakeholders about regulatory updates, policy changes, public hearings, and much more.

- **Publication Frequency**: The Federal Register is published every **weekday** (except federal holidays).

- **Official Government Record**: It serves as the **official government record** for administrative actions and notices from various agencies, making it the primary source for **public access** to information on government policies, proposals, and decisions.

2. Structure and Contents of the Federal Register

The Federal Register is divided into several key sections, each serving a distinct purpose:

2.1 Proposed Rules

The **Proposed Rules** section includes notices from agencies like the **FDA** about new regulations or modifications to existing regulations. These proposed rules are often open for public comment, allowing stakeholders (including pharmaceutical companies, healthcare professionals, and the general public) to provide feedback before a rule is finalized.

- **Public Input**: Regulatory agencies are required by law to seek public comments on certain proposed rules. This ensures that the regulatory process is transparent and considers the views of relevant stakeholders before final decisions are made.
- **Impact on Pharmaceutical Industry**: Proposed rules related to drug development, marketing, and post-market surveillance are often published in this section, providing the pharmaceutical industry with an opportunity to engage with regulatory bodies early in the decision-making process.

2.2 Final Rules

The **Final Rules** section includes regulations that have been finalized after the public comment period. Once finalized, these rules have the force of law, and stakeholders must comply with them.

- **Regulatory Enforcement**: For pharmaceutical companies, this section is critical as it provides the final legal text of the regulations that govern drug approval, clinical trials, labeling, advertising, and post-market surveillance.
- **FDA Regulatory Updates**: The FDA uses this section to announce the finalization of regulatory guidance, such as those related to **Good Manufacturing Practices (GMP)**, **clinical trial conduct**, and **new drug application (NDA)** procedures.

2.3 Notices

The **Notices** section includes **administrative announcements** from federal agencies. These notices may include updates about **meetings**, **public hearings**, or **grant opportunities**.

- **Public Meetings and Hearings**: The Federal Register frequently publishes notices about public meetings or workshops held by regulatory agencies. These gatherings are important opportunities for pharmaceutical industry stakeholders to participate in discussions about new regulatory frameworks, guidelines, or public health concerns.
- **Drug Recalls**: Notices also contain information about the recall of drugs, medical devices, or other products, offering transparency about actions taken by the FDA or other agencies to protect public health.

2.4 Requests for Comments

This section invites public comments on regulatory issues, allowing stakeholders to engage in the decision-making process. Agencies, such as the FDA, may request feedback on new draft regulations, policies, or guidance documents.

- **Engagement with Stakeholders**: Pharmaceutical companies and other stakeholders can submit comments to express their views on proposed changes in drug regulations, clinical trial requirements, or safety monitoring protocols.
- **Transparency and Inclusivity**: This system ensures that regulatory decisions are not made in isolation, allowing for input from experts in various fields, including science, healthcare, and patient advocacy groups.

2.5 Executive Orders and Presidential Documents

This section publishes **executive orders** and **presidential proclamations** that impact regulatory practices. These may include directives that guide the actions of regulatory agencies, including the FDA.

- **Executive Oversight**: Executive orders can direct changes in regulations or set the agenda for federal agencies, influencing how the FDA or other regulatory bodies enforce drug safety and efficacy standards.

3. Importance of the Federal Register in Pharmaceutical Regulation

The **Federal Register** plays an essential role in the pharmaceutical industry by ensuring that there is a transparent and well-documented process for the development, approval, and monitoring of drugs and medical devices. Its importance can be highlighted in several key areas:

3.1 Regulatory Transparency and Public Access

The Federal Register ensures that all regulatory changes are publicly available, which enhances **transparency** in the decision-making process. Pharmaceutical companies, healthcare professionals, researchers, and the general public can easily access the latest information on drug approvals, regulatory guidelines, and new legislative changes that may affect drug development.

- **Public Engagement**: By publishing proposed rules and requests for comments, the Federal Register allows stakeholders to engage with the regulatory process and influence decisions that impact drug safety, approval, and marketing.
- **Up-to-date Information**: The publication of proposed and final rules, along with public comments, helps keep stakeholders informed of changes in regulations and policies that could affect the development and sale of pharmaceutical products.

3.2 Compliance with FDA Regulations

For pharmaceutical companies, compliance with FDA regulations is crucial for ensuring that drugs are brought to market safely and efficiently. The Federal Register serves as the official source of updates on **FDA regulations**, ensuring that companies are aware of the latest changes that may affect their compliance efforts.

- **Regulatory Updates**: Pharmaceutical companies rely on the Federal Register to stay up-to-date on the FDA's **new drug application (NDA)** procedures, **clinical trial requirements, post-marketing surveillance protocols**, and **guidelines for manufacturing and labeling**.
- **Record of Drug Approvals**: The Federal Register also publishes notices of **new drug approvals** and changes to existing drug applications, offering a record of regulatory actions taken by the FDA.

3.3 Enabling Public Health and Safety

By publishing notices about **drug recalls**, **safety alerts**, and **adverse event reports**, the Federal Register plays a critical role in maintaining public health and safety. It ensures that health professionals and the public are aware of any potential issues with drug products, such as those related to **drug efficacy**, **adverse reactions**, or **manufacturing defects**.

- **Recall Notices**: Pharmaceutical companies must respond quickly to any **drug recalls** published in the Federal Register, ensuring that products are removed from the market or re-labeled as needed to protect consumers.

3.4 Facilitating International Collaboration

The Federal Register also plays a role in **global pharmaceutical regulation** by publishing regulations and guidelines that may influence international standards. For example, **international regulatory bodies**, such as the **European Medicines Agency (EMA)** and the **World Health Organization (WHO)**, often align their standards with those set by the FDA.

- **Global Regulatory Harmonization**: The Federal Register's publication of new regulations and guidelines can impact drug development standards worldwide, encouraging alignment and cooperation between regulatory agencies.

6.2.3 *Code of Federal Regulations (CFR)*

The **Code of Federal Regulations (CFR)** is a critical legal resource in the United States that contains the full text of regulations enacted by federal agencies. It serves as the official source for the regulations that govern the operation of various industries, including pharmaceuticals, and is instrumental in ensuring compliance with federal law. The CFR is organized into **titles** and **sections**, each covering specific regulatory areas. In the context of pharmaceutical development, the CFR provides detailed rules for drug approval, manufacturing, labeling, clinical trials, and post-marketing surveillance. This section explores the importance and role of the CFR in pharmaceutical regulations.

1. What is the Code of Federal Regulations (CFR)?

The **Code of Federal Regulations (CFR)** is an annually updated compilation of all federal regulations in the United States. It is published by the **U.S. Government Publishing Office (GPO)** and is designed to provide public access to the regulatory rules established by federal agencies. The CFR is organized into **50 titles**, each focusing on a specific area of U.S. federal regulation. For the pharmaceutical industry, relevant sections of the CFR provide detailed instructions and requirements for the approval, manufacture, testing, and marketing of drugs and medical devices.

- **Official Legal Resource**: The CFR serves as the official legal text for all federal regulations, making it a vital tool for anyone involved in regulatory affairs, compliance, and policy-making.
- **Updating Process**: The CFR is updated annually, with amendments made throughout the year as new regulations are implemented or existing regulations are revised.

2. Organization of the Code of Federal Regulations (CFR)

The CFR is divided into **50 titles**, with each title covering a broad subject area. Each title is further subdivided into **chapters** and **parts** that focus on specific aspects of the subject. The most relevant titles for the pharmaceutical industry include:

- **Title 21**: Food and Drugs
- **Title 40**: Protection of Environment (for environmental regulations related to pharmaceutical waste)
- **Title 42**: Public Health (covering health regulations, including public health policies related to drug safety and testing)

The **FDA** regulations, which directly impact drug development, approval, and monitoring, are found in **Title 21** of the CFR. This title includes a comprehensive set of rules regarding **drug manufacturing, clinical trials, drug labeling**, and **good manufacturing practices (GMP)**.

3. Key Parts of Title 21 of the CFR Relevant to Pharmaceuticals

Title 21 of the CFR is the most relevant to pharmaceutical companies and regulatory professionals, as it outlines the standards and requirements for pharmaceutical development, from drug approval to post-marketing surveillance. Some of the key parts of Title 21 include:

3.1 Part 310 - New Drug Applications (NDA)

Part 310 provides detailed information about the **new drug application (NDA)** process, including the requirements for submitting a drug for FDA approval. It specifies the necessary documentation, safety and efficacy data, and clinical trial requirements for approval.

- **NDA Process**: This part outlines the process by which a pharmaceutical company can apply for approval to market a new drug in the U.S. The application must include comprehensive preclinical and clinical data, manufacturing processes, labeling information, and other relevant details.
- **FDA Review**: The FDA reviews the NDA submission to ensure that the drug meets **safety** and **efficacy** standards. The approval is based on the evidence provided, including **clinical trial data.**

3.2 Part 314 - Applications for FDA Approval to Market a New Drug

Part 314 covers the detailed process for submitting drug applications, including both the **new drug application (NDA)** and **abbreviated new drug application (ANDA)** for generic drugs. It includes instructions on the submission format, clinical data requirements, labeling guidelines, and post-approval conditions.

- **NDA and ANDA**: It details the submission process for both original new drugs (NDA) and generic drugs (ANDA). For generic drugs, the **bioequivalence** requirement is a critical part of the application.
- **Post-Marketing Requirements**: This section also includes information on **post-marketing surveillance**, including mandatory reporting of adverse events and maintaining updated labeling for the drug.

3.3 Part 211 - Current Good Manufacturing Practice for Finished Pharmaceuticals

Part 211 of the CFR outlines the **Good Manufacturing Practices (GMP)** required for the manufacturing of pharmaceutical products. GMP ensures that drugs are consistently produced and controlled to quality standards.

- **Manufacturing Standards**: This section covers **facility conditions**, equipment, documentation, and personnel requirements for drug manufacturing.

- **Quality Control**: GMP also includes requirements for ensuring product quality, such as regular **quality control tests, batch release procedures**, and maintaining clean and controlled environments.

3.4 Part 312 - Investigational New Drug Applications (IND)

Part 312 of the CFR outlines the regulatory requirements for **Investigational New Drug (IND) applications**, which are necessary for beginning clinical trials in humans. The IND application is critical in the early stages of drug development and serves as the foundation for later NDA submissions.

- **Clinical Trials**: This section specifies the requirements for conducting clinical trials, including **informed consent**, trial design, and data reporting.
- **Preclinical Data**: The IND application must include preclinical data on the drug's safety and efficacy in laboratory and animal studies, as well as the proposed clinical trial protocols.

3.5 Part 320 - Bioavailability and Bioequivalence Requirements

Part 320 specifies the criteria for evaluating the **bioavailability** and **bioequivalence** of drug products. This is particularly relevant for generic drug approval, where the generic must be shown to be **bioequivalent** to the branded drug.

- **Bioequivalence Studies**: This section provides guidelines on how to design and conduct **bioequivalence studies** for generic drugs. These studies typically assess the **pharmacokinetic profiles** of both the generic and the reference drug to ensure they perform similarly in the body.

4. Importance of the Code of Federal Regulations (CFR) in Pharmaceutical Development

The **CFR** is essential for the pharmaceutical industry as it ensures that all drugs marketed in the U.S. meet the highest standards of safety, efficacy, and quality. The importance of the CFR can be highlighted in several key areas:

4.1 Regulatory Compliance

The CFR provides the specific guidelines that pharmaceutical companies must follow to comply with federal regulations. It includes detailed instructions on how to conduct clinical trials, manufacture drugs, label products, and report adverse events. For companies to remain compliant and avoid penalties, they must adhere strictly to the rules set out in the CFR.

- **Drug Approval**: The regulatory pathway for obtaining **FDA approval** for new drugs is clearly defined in the CFR. It is the primary guide for ensuring that drug products meet all **scientific** and **ethical standards**.
- **Post-Marketing Surveillance**: The CFR also establishes the requirements for ongoing monitoring and reporting after a drug has been approved and marketed. This ensures that any long-term safety issues are addressed in a timely manner.

4.2 Safety and Efficacy Standards

The CFR ensures that pharmaceutical products are not only safe for human use but also effective in treating the conditions they are intended to address. By outlining the clinical and preclinical requirements for drug testing, the CFR establishes a clear framework for the **evaluation of safety** and **efficacy**.

- **Clinical Trials**: The CFR establishes the necessary guidelines for conducting **clinical trials**, ensuring that they are designed to protect participants and generate reliable data that will demonstrate the drug's safety and efficacy.
- **Manufacturing Standards**: By enforcing **Good Manufacturing Practices (GMP)**, the CFR ensures that drugs are consistently produced under controlled conditions, minimizing the risk of contamination, errors, or defects.

4.3 Public Health Protection

The CFR plays a critical role in protecting **public health** by regulating the approval and monitoring of drugs. It ensures that pharmaceutical products available in the market do not pose an unacceptable risk to consumers. The **FDA** uses the regulations in the CFR to assess the safety and quality of drugs, and to take corrective actions such as **product recalls** or **labeling updates** when safety issues are identified.

6.3 Special Regulatory Concepts

In the pharmaceutical industry, **special regulatory concepts** address the unique regulatory pathways for specific types of drugs or drug products. One of the most significant advancements in biotechnology has been the development of **biosimilars**—drugs that are similar to already approved biologic products but not identical. As these drugs have distinct regulatory requirements, the **Purple Book** has become a critical resource for understanding the approval process for **biosimilars**. This section explores **The Purple Book** and its role in the regulatory pathway for biosimilars.

6.3.1 The Purple Book: Biosimilars and Their Regulatory Pathways

The **Purple Book** is an essential resource published by the **U.S. Food and Drug Administration (FDA)** that specifically addresses the approval process and regulatory status of **biosimilars** and **biological products**. It is an official guide for identifying approved biosimilars and their reference biologic drugs, and it plays a crucial role in the regulatory oversight of biologic and biosimilar drug products in the United States.

1. What is the Purple Book?

The **Purple Book** is the official FDA publication that lists **licensed biological products** including biosimilars and reference products. It serves as a resource for understanding the **approval status**, **licensing history**, and **therapeutic equivalence** of biologics and biosimilars under the **Public Health Service Act (PHSA)**. The Purple Book is updated regularly to reflect the latest FDA approvals and status changes in the biologics industry.

- **Biologics**: A biologic is a large, complex molecule produced by living organisms. These can include **monoclonal antibodies, vaccines, recombinant proteins**, and **gene therapies**.
- **Biosimilars**: A biosimilar is a biological product that is highly similar to an already-approved reference biologic. The biosimilar must demonstrate no clinically meaningful differences in terms of safety, purity, and potency compared to the reference product.

The Purple Book provides key information about each licensed biosimilar, helping stakeholders navigate the complexities of the biologic drug market. Unlike traditional small-molecule drugs, biosimilars have more complex regulatory pathways due to their larger, more variable structures.

2. Role of the Purple Book in Biosimilar Approval

The **Purple Book** is vital in ensuring that biosimilars meet the necessary regulatory standards for approval and market entry. It provides detailed information on biosimilar products, helping pharmaceutical companies, healthcare providers, and regulatory authorities navigate the biosimilar approval process. Key aspects of the Purple Book's role in biosimilar regulation include:

2.1 Listing of Biosimilars and Reference Products

The **Purple Book** lists all **FDA-approved biosimilars** along with their **reference biologic products**. This information is crucial for healthcare providers, as it allows them to identify the reference product and its corresponding biosimilar, ensuring the right drug is prescribed for patients.

- **Biosimilar Products**: The Purple Book provides a list of biosimilars that have been approved by the FDA, along with the **reference biologic** each biosimilar is compared to.
- **Therapeutic Equivalence**: While biosimilars are not considered identical to their reference biologic, they must demonstrate **therapeutic equivalence** in terms of safety and efficacy. The Purple Book is used to identify the equivalence of biosimilars to their reference drugs.

2.2 Exclusivity and Interchangeability

The **Purple Book** also provides information about the **exclusivity** and **interchangeability** of biosimilars:

- **Exclusivity**: Biologics, particularly reference biologics, are granted **exclusivity** to prevent the approval of similar products for a period of time. This exclusivity protects the innovator's investment in the biologic and prevents the entry of biosimilars into the market until the exclusivity period expires.
- **Interchangeability**: The **FDA** can approve a biosimilar as an **interchangeable biosimilar**, meaning it can be substituted for the reference biologic without the intervention of the prescribing healthcare provider. The Purple Book indicates whether a biosimilar has been designated as **interchangeable**, which has important implications for drug substitution and reimbursement policies.

2.3 Approval Pathway for Biosimilars

The FDA regulates biosimilars under the **Biologics Control Act (BLA)**, which is part of the **Public Health Service Act (PHSA)**. The **Purple Book** outlines the pathway for approval, which involves a series of steps that must be completed to demonstrate the **biosimilarity** of a new product to an already approved reference biologic.

- **Clinical Trial Requirements**: To gain approval, biosimilars must undergo a rigorous process that includes **preclinical** and **clinical testing** to demonstrate they are highly similar to the reference biologic in terms of structure, biological activity, and clinical efficacy. This often involves **comparative clinical studies**.
- **Manufacturing Requirements**: The manufacturing processes for biosimilars must closely mirror the process used for the reference biologic. The **FDA** requires that the biosimilar manufacturer demonstrate that their process is capable of producing a product that is consistent in terms of quality, safety, and efficacy.
- **No Clinically Meaningful Differences**: The key criteria for biosimilar approval is that the biosimilar must show no clinically meaningful differences from the reference biologic, in terms of **safety**, **purity**, and **potency**.

2.4 Regulatory Pathway for Biosimilars in Other Countries

While the **Purple Book** focuses on biosimilars in the United States, the regulatory pathway for biosimilars in other countries is also influenced by similar principles. For example, the **European Medicines Agency (EMA)** has its own procedures for biosimilars, and countries such as **Japan** and **Canada** also have specific regulations governing the approval of biosimilars.

The **Purple Book** serves as a reference for the **global biosimilars market** by aligning the **FDA's approval standards** with international norms, ensuring a consistent approach to biosimilar regulation and providing a framework for the global approval process.

3. Importance of the Purple Book in Biosimilar Regulation

The **Purple Book** plays an important role in the regulation of **biosimilars** by providing essential information on approved products and guiding manufacturers and stakeholders through the approval process. Its significance can be understood in the following ways:

3.1 Promoting Market Access for Biosimilars

The **Purple Book** helps promote access to safe and effective biosimilars by providing clear guidelines for the approval process and ensuring that these drugs meet high standards of safety and efficacy. Biosimilars provide a more affordable option for patients and healthcare systems, particularly for biologic treatments that are **high-cost** and essential for managing chronic diseases, such as **cancer** and **autoimmune disorders**.

- **Increased Competition**: By listing biosimilars alongside reference biologics, the Purple Book helps foster competition in the biologic drug market, leading to more affordable treatment options for patients.

3.2 Ensuring Safe Substitution Practices

For a biosimilar to be substituted for a reference biologic, it must meet the **FDA's stringent standards** for bioequivalence. The **Purple Book** provides transparency about which biosimilars are interchangeable with their reference biologics, facilitating the safe substitution of drugs in clinical practice.

- **Healthcare Provider Guidance**: The Purple Book serves as a reliable resource for healthcare providers to ensure that they are prescribing appropriate biosimilars for their patients, ensuring both safety and efficacy.

3.3 Global Regulatory Consistency

The **Purple Book** aligns the **FDA's approach** to biosimilar regulation with international standards, helping to create a globally recognized framework for the approval and regulation of biosimilars. This consistency benefits **pharmaceutical companies**, allowing them to navigate the approval process more easily across multiple jurisdictions.

- **Global Market Access**: By understanding the requirements laid out in the Purple Book, biosimilar manufacturers can better prepare for regulatory submissions in different countries, increasing the potential for global market access.

6.3.2 Regulatory Terms in Drug Development

In the field of pharmaceutical regulation, understanding specific **regulatory terms** is essential for professionals involved in the **development**, **approval**, and **monitoring** of drugs. These terms help ensure that all stakeholders, including pharmaceutical companies, regulatory bodies, healthcare providers, and researchers, are aligned in their understanding of the processes and standards that govern drug development. This section defines and explains several key regulatory terms commonly used in the context of drug development.

1. Clinical Trial

A **clinical trial** is a research study designed to assess the **safety**, **efficacy**, and **pharmacokinetics** of a drug or biologic in human participants. Clinical trials are the backbone of **drug development**, as they provide the essential data needed to support regulatory approvals.

- **Phases of Clinical Trials**: Clinical trials are divided into several phases:

  - **Phase I**: Focuses on the safety and dosage of a drug, typically involving a small group of healthy volunteers.
  - **Phase II**: Investigates the drug's efficacy and side effects in a larger group of participants who have the condition the drug is intended to treat.
  - **Phase III**: Confirms the drug's efficacy and monitors its side effects in a large group of participants.
  - **Phase IV**: Post-marketing studies that track the drug's long-term effects and identify rare side effects in a broader population.

Clinical trials must be approved by **regulatory authorities** such as the **FDA** or **EMA**, and ethical oversight is typically provided by an **Institutional Review Board (IRB)** or **Independent Ethics Committee (IEC)**.

2. Good Clinical Practice (GCP)

Good Clinical Practice (GCP) refers to a set of international ethical and scientific quality standards for designing, conducting, recording, and reporting clinical trials. GCP ensures that the **rights**, **safety**, and **well-being** of participants are protected and that the clinical trial data is credible and accurate.

- **Compliance**: Compliance with GCP is mandatory for regulatory approval and is closely monitored by regulatory agencies.

- **Key Principles**: GCP includes principles such as **informed consent**, **confidentiality**, and ensuring that clinical trials are conducted with scientific integrity.

3. Investigational New Drug (IND)

An **Investigational New Drug (IND)** application is submitted to the **FDA** to request authorization to begin clinical trials in humans. The IND application includes preclinical data on the drug's safety and pharmacological profile, along with the proposed clinical trial protocol.

- **Purpose**: The IND allows sponsors to test the safety and efficacy of a new drug in humans before seeking full market approval.
- **Approval**: If the IND is approved by the FDA, the clinical trial can begin under the guidelines outlined in the application.

4. New Drug Application (NDA)

A **New Drug Application (NDA)** is the formal request submitted to the **FDA** (or other regulatory bodies) to seek approval to market a new drug. The NDA must contain all data from preclinical and clinical studies, manufacturing processes, labeling, and other relevant information.

- **Approval Process**: The FDA reviews the NDA to ensure the drug is safe and effective for the proposed indication. If the NDA is approved, the drug can be marketed to the public.
- **Data Required**: NDA submissions require data on **clinical trials**, **pharmacology, toxicology**, and **drug interactions**.

5. Abbreviated New Drug Application (ANDA)

An **Abbreviated New Drug Application (ANDA)** is submitted by a manufacturer to obtain approval for a generic version of an already approved drug. The ANDA process is "abbreviated" because it does not require the submission of extensive clinical trial data—rather, the applicant must demonstrate that the generic drug is **bioequivalent** to the reference product.

- **Bioequivalence**: To be approved through the ANDA process, the generic drug must show that it has the same **rate** and **extent** of absorption as the reference drug.

- **Regulatory Benefits**: The ANDA pathway allows for faster approval of generics, thus providing more affordable alternatives to patients.

6. Bioequivalence

Bioequivalence refers to the comparison of two drug products to determine whether they are equivalent in terms of their **bioavailability** (how the drug is absorbed into the bloodstream). Bioequivalence is essential in the approval of generic drugs, where the generic must show that it delivers the same therapeutic effect as the brand-name product.

- **Testing Method**: Bioequivalence is usually tested through **pharmacokinetic studies** that measure the rate and extent of the drug's absorption in the body.
- **Relevance for Generics**: A generic drug is considered bioequivalent to its reference product if it has the same **pharmacokinetic profile**, ensuring the same clinical outcomes.

7. Pharmacovigilance

Pharmacovigilance is the process of monitoring and assessing the safety of drugs after they have been approved and marketed. The goal of pharmacovigilance is to detect and evaluate **adverse drug reactions (ADRs)** and ensure that drugs remain safe for long-term use.

- **Post-Market Surveillance**: Pharmacovigilance continues after a drug's approval through **post-marketing surveillance**, where adverse events are reported and evaluated.
- **Reporting**: Both healthcare professionals and patients can report adverse events to regulatory agencies, such as the **FDA's MedWatch program**.

8. Good Manufacturing Practice (GMP)

Good Manufacturing Practice (GMP) refers to a set of regulations enforced by regulatory authorities to ensure that pharmaceutical products are consistently produced and controlled according to quality standards. GMP covers all aspects of manufacturing, including **facilities, equipment, personnel**, and **documentation**.

- **Quality Control**: GMP ensures that every batch of pharmaceutical products is produced with the same high level of quality and free from contamination.
- **Regulatory Requirement**: Compliance with GMP is mandatory for all pharmaceutical manufacturers, and failure to comply can result in regulatory sanctions or product recalls.

9. Risk Management Plan (RMP)

A **Risk Management Plan (RMP)** is a strategic document that outlines the strategies and actions that a pharmaceutical company will take to minimize the risks associated with a drug after it has been marketed. The RMP includes **risk minimization** strategies, post-marketing surveillance, and reporting of adverse events.

- **Post-Marketing Risk Monitoring**: The RMP is part of a broader risk management framework that continues throughout the lifecycle of the drug, ensuring its ongoing safety.
- **Regulatory Requirement**: Regulatory authorities may require a RMP for certain drugs, particularly those with known risks or side effects.

10. Orphan Drug Designation

Orphan Drug Designation is granted by regulatory authorities to drugs developed for the treatment of rare diseases, typically those affecting fewer than 200,000 people in the United States. Drugs with orphan designation are eligible for **regulatory incentives**, including **market exclusivity, tax credits**, and **assistance with clinical trial costs**.

- **Market Exclusivity**: Orphan drugs may receive up to **seven years** of market exclusivity in the U.S., meaning that no other similar drugs can be approved during this period.
- **Incentives**: The designation helps stimulate the development of drugs for rare diseases by offering financial and regulatory incentives to manufacturers.

11. Fast Track Designation

Fast Track Designation is a regulatory process that speeds up the development and approval of drugs that address unmet medical needs for serious conditions. Drugs with Fast Track status can benefit from

accelerated approval and **priority review** processes.

- **Regulatory Benefit**: Fast Track designation allows for more frequent meetings with the FDA, earlier drug development assistance, and a quicker time to market.
- **Eligibility**: The drug must show **preliminary clinical evidence** that it can provide a significant benefit over existing treatments for serious conditions.

12. Interchangeability

Interchangeability refers to a regulatory designation that allows a biosimilar to be substituted for its reference biologic without the intervention of the prescribing healthcare provider. To be designated as interchangeable, a biosimilar must demonstrate not only **biosimilarity** but also **no clinically meaningful differences** in terms of safety and efficacy when substituted for the reference product.

- **FDA Approval**: The FDA grants interchangeable status to biosimilars after reviewing clinical trial data that proves the biosimilar can be safely substituted for the reference biologic.
- **Impact**: Interchangeable biosimilars can be substituted at the pharmacy level, improving patient access to lower-cost treatments.

Review Questions And Answers

Chapter 1: Introduction to Pharmaceutical Regulatory Science

1. What is Pharmaceutical Regulatory Science?

Answer: Pharmaceutical Regulatory Science is the study of the processes, rules, and guidelines used by regulatory bodies to ensure the safety, efficacy, and quality of pharmaceutical products. It involves understanding how drugs are developed, tested, approved, and monitored for public use.

2. Why is Regulatory Science important in drug development?

Answer: Regulatory science ensures that drugs are safe, effective, and of high quality before reaching the market. It plays a key role in protecting public health by setting standards for clinical trials, drug approvals, and post-market surveillance.

3. What are the primary objectives of pharmaceutical regulations?

Answer: The primary objectives are to ensure the safety, efficacy, and quality of drugs, protect public health, maintain transparency in drug approval processes, and foster innovation in pharmaceutical science while preventing fraud and abuse.

4. What is the role of regulatory bodies in pharmaceutical science?

Answer: Regulatory bodies, such as the FDA, EMA, and other national health authorities, establish and enforce regulations for drug approval, clinical trials, and post-marketing surveillance. They ensure that drugs meet safety and efficacy standards and monitor their effects on public health.

5. Name the major regulatory authorities in pharmaceutical sciences.

Answer: Some major regulatory authorities include the U.S. **Food and Drug Administration (FDA), European Medicines Agency (EMA), Pharmaceutical and Medical Devices Agency (PMDA)** in Japan, **Therapeutic Goods Administration (TGA)** in Australia, and **Health Canada.**

6. What is the purpose of the FDA's role in drug regulation?

Answer: The **FDA** ensures that drugs are **safe, effective,** and **properly labeled.** It oversees the approval process of new drugs, clinical trials, and post-marketing surveillance, and enforces good manufacturing practices.

7. What is the role of the European Medicines Agency (EMA)?

Answer: The **EMA** coordinates the evaluation and supervision of medicinal products in the European Union. It ensures that drugs are safe and effective for human use across EU member states.

8. What is an Investigational New Drug (IND)?

Answer: An **IND** is an application submitted to regulatory authorities, like the FDA, requesting permission to begin clinical trials of a new drug in humans. It includes preclinical data and clinical trial protocols.

9. What is the New Drug Application (NDA)?

Answer: The **NDA** is a formal request submitted to regulatory authorities to market a new drug after completing clinical trials. It includes evidence of safety, efficacy, and proposed labeling.

10. What is an Abbreviated New Drug Application (ANDA)?

Answer: An **ANDA** is an application for the approval of a generic drug. It must demonstrate bioequivalence to a reference brand-name drug without requiring the extensive clinical trial data that an NDA would need.

11. What is bioequivalence?

Answer: Bioequivalence means that a generic drug is absorbed into the body at the same rate and to the same extent as the reference brand-name drug. It must show no significant difference in efficacy or safety.

12. What are Good Manufacturing Practices (GMP)?

Answer: GMP refers to regulations that ensure that drugs are consistently produced and controlled according to quality standards. It involves requirements for equipment, personnel, manufacturing processes, and documentation to ensure safety and product quality.

13. What is the significance of clinical trials in regulatory science?

Answer: Clinical trials provide the data needed to evaluate the safety, efficacy, and pharmacokinetics of a drug. Regulatory bodies review these data to determine whether a drug can be approved for use in the general population.

14. What is the difference between a generic drug and a brand-name drug?

Answer: A **brand-name drug** is the original product developed and patented by a pharmaceutical company. A **generic drug** is a copy of a brand-name drug that is bioequivalent but sold at a lower cost once the patent expires.

15. What is the importance of post-marketing surveillance?

Answer: Post-marketing surveillance monitors the long-term safety and effectiveness of a drug after it has been approved. It helps identify rare or delayed adverse effects and ensures continued compliance with regulatory standards.

16. What are orphan drugs?

Answer: **Orphan drugs** are developed to treat rare diseases, typically those affecting fewer than 200,000 people. These drugs receive special regulatory incentives, such as market exclusivity and tax credits.

17. What is a Risk Management Plan (RMP)?

Answer: An **RMP** outlines strategies to minimize and monitor the risks associated with a drug after it has been approved. It includes post-marketing surveillance and safety monitoring measures.

18. What is the role of the World Health Organization (WHO) in pharmaceutical regulation?

Answer: **WHO** provides global guidelines and standards for pharmaceutical development, including quality assurance, drug safety, and regulatory harmonization, especially in resource-limited countries.

19. What is the role of regulatory harmonization across countries?

Answer: Regulatory harmonization seeks to align the rules and procedures of different countries to make drug approval processes more efficient, reduce duplication, and foster global access to safe and effective medications.

20. How does the FDA ensure drug safety post-approval?

Answer: The FDA monitors drugs through adverse event reporting systems, inspections, and regulatory actions such as drug recalls. It works with healthcare providers and manufacturers to address safety issues after a drug is marketed.

21. What are the key phases of drug development?

Answer: The key phases include **Preclinical Development**, **Clinical Development** (Phases I-III), and **Post-Marketing Surveillance** (Phase IV). Each phase focuses on different aspects of safety, efficacy, and public health.

22. What is the purpose of the FDA's Orange Book?

Answer: The **Orange Book** lists all FDA-approved drug products, including their therapeutic equivalence. It is an important resource for healthcare providers, pharmacists, and regulators.

23. What is an Institutional Review Board (IRB)?

Answer: An **IRB** is a committee that reviews and approves clinical trial protocols to ensure that they meet ethical standards and protect the rights and welfare of human participants.

24. What is Good Clinical Practice (GCP)?

Answer: **GCP** refers to the ethical and scientific quality standards for conducting, recording, and reporting clinical trials. GCP ensures that clinical trials are designed to protect participants and produce reliable results.

25. What are therapeutic equivalence and its importance?

Answer: **Therapeutic equivalence** means that two drugs (typically a brand-name and a generic) are expected to have the same clinical effect and safety profile when administered to patients under similar conditions.

26. What is an Investigational New Drug (IND) application used for?

Answer: The **IND** application is submitted to the FDA to seek approval to begin clinical trials for a new drug. It includes preclinical data and clinical trial protocols.

27. How are adverse events reported during clinical trials?

Answer: Adverse events are reported through the **FDA's MedWatch program** or other national reporting systems. Healthcare providers, patients, and pharmaceutical companies report adverse events that may arise during trials.

28. What is the purpose of clinical trial randomization?

Answer: **Randomization** is used to eliminate bias in clinical trials by randomly assigning participants to different treatment groups. This ensures that results are scientifically valid and reliable.

29. What are the requirements for a drug to be approved for market in the U.S.?

Answer: A drug must demonstrate its safety, efficacy, and quality through clinical trials, meet manufacturing standards, and comply with labeling and post-marketing surveillance requirements as per FDA regulations.

30. What is bioequivalence, and why is it important for generic drugs?

Answer: **Bioequivalence** refers to the similarity between the generic drug and its reference product in terms of absorption, distribution, and elimination. It is critical for ensuring that a generic drug performs the same as the brand-name product.

31. What is the role of the European Medicines Agency (EMA) in drug regulation?

Answer: The **EMA** evaluates and supervises medicinal products for human and veterinary use in the European Union. It ensures that drugs are safe and effective before they are marketed within the EU.

32. What is a fast track designation, and how does it affect drug approval?

Answer: A **fast track designation** allows for expedited development and review of drugs that address unmet medical needs for serious conditions. It shortens the time to market and can include benefits like priority review and accelerated approval.

33. What is a clinical trial protocol?

Answer: A clinical trial protocol is a detailed plan that outlines the study design, objectives, methodologies, and ethical considerations for a clinical trial. It is reviewed and approved by regulatory authorities and an IRB.

34. What is the role of the FDA's Purple Book in drug approval?

Answer: The **Purple Book** lists approved biologics, including biosimilars, and provides information on their equivalence and interchangeability. It is an essential resource for understanding the regulatory status of biologics.

35. How does the FDA regulate biosimilars?

Answer: The FDA regulates biosimilars under the **Biologics Control Act** and ensures that biosimilars are **highly similar** to their reference biologics in terms of safety, efficacy, and manufacturing processes before approval.

36. What is an orphan drug designation?

Answer: **Orphan drug designation** is granted to drugs developed to treat rare diseases affecting fewer than 200,000 people. It provides regulatory incentives such as market exclusivity, tax credits, and grant funding.

37. What is the significance of the Drug Master File (DMF)?

Answer: The **DMF** is a confidential document submitted to regulatory authorities that provides detailed information about the drug's composition, manufacturing process, and quality control. It is used in the approval process for new drugs and generics.

38. What is the role of pharmacovigilance in drug development?

Answer: **Pharmacovigilance** monitors and evaluates the safety of drugs after they have been approved and marketed. It aims to identify, assess, and prevent adverse drug reactions and improve patient safety.

39. What is a Risk Management Plan (RMP)?

Answer: An **RMP** is a document outlining strategies to identify and minimize risks associated with a drug. It includes monitoring safety data and ensuring compliance with safety protocols.

40. What is an FDA clinical trial protocol review?

Answer: The FDA reviews clinical trial protocols to ensure that the study is scientifically sound, ethically conducted, and designed to meet the regulatory requirements for drug approval.

41. What is the role of an Institutional Review Board (IRB)?

Answer: An **IRB** reviews and approves clinical trial protocols to ensure that they meet ethical standards and protect the rights and welfare of participants.

42. What are good laboratory practices (GLP)?

Answer: **Good Laboratory Practices (GLP)** are regulatory guidelines that ensure the quality and integrity of laboratory studies, especially preclinical safety studies, by setting standards for laboratory environments, equipment, and procedures.

43. What is the purpose of the FDA's Orange Book?

Answer: The **Orange Book** lists FDA-approved drugs, including generics, and provides information on their therapeutic equivalence, helping ensure safe and effective drug substitutions.

44. How does the FDA approve clinical trials for a new drug?

Answer: The FDA reviews the **IND application**, which includes preclinical data, clinical trial protocols, and safety information, to ensure that the trial can be conducted ethically and safely.

45. What is a regulatory submission?

Answer: A **regulatory submission** is the formal process of providing regulatory authorities with the data and documentation required for drug approval. This includes clinical trial data, manufacturing information, and labeling proposals.

46. What is the regulatory approval process for biologics?

Answer: The approval process for biologics involves submitting a **Biologics License Application (BLA)** to the FDA, which includes clinical trial data, manufacturing information, and other documentation to demonstrate the drug's safety, efficacy, and quality.

47. What is the role of the FDA in post-market surveillance?

Answer: The FDA monitors the safety of drugs after they are approved and marketed by collecting **adverse event** reports, conducting inspections, and taking regulatory actions, such as recalls if necessary.

48. What is a clinical endpoint?

Answer: A **clinical endpoint** is a characteristic or outcome that is measured in a clinical trial to determine the effectiveness of a drug. Examples include **reduction in symptoms, improvement in disease progression**, or **survival rates.**

49. What are the regulatory standards for drug labeling?

Answer: Drug labeling must comply with regulatory guidelines that include clear instructions on **dosage, side effects, indications,** and **contraindications** to ensure proper use and safety for consumers.

50. What is the significance of post-marketing surveillance?

Answer: Post-marketing surveillance helps track long-term safety and identify rare adverse effects. It is essential for ensuring that drugs continue to be safe for consumers once they are widely available.

Chapter 2: New Drug Discovery and Development

1. What are the main stages of drug discovery?

Answer: The main stages of drug discovery are **target identification, lead compound identification, preclinical studies, clinical trials (Phase I, II, III),** and **regulatory approval.**

2. What is target identification in drug discovery?

Answer: Target identification involves finding a **biological molecule** (usually a protein) that plays a role in a disease process. This target is then studied to determine if modulating it can lead to therapeutic effects.

3. What is lead compound identification?

Answer: Lead compound identification involves finding molecules that have the desired biological activity and can be optimized into a potential drug candidate.

4. What is the role of preclinical studies in drug development?

Answer: Preclinical studies involve testing a drug in laboratory and animal models to evaluate its safety, toxicity, pharmacokinetics, and potential efficacy before it can be tested in humans.

5. What is the difference between preclinical and clinical trials?

Answer: Preclinical trials involve laboratory and animal testing to assess a drug's safety and efficacy, while **clinical trials** involve testing the drug in human volunteers to confirm safety, efficacy, and appropriate dosages.

6. What is a clinical trial protocol?

Answer: A clinical trial protocol is a detailed plan that outlines the study's objectives, design, methodology, and ethical considerations, ensuring the trial is conducted consistently and ethically.

7. What are the key phases of clinical trials?

Answer: Clinical trials are typically divided into **Phase I** (safety testing in healthy volunteers), **Phase II** (efficacy and dosing in patients), **Phase III** (confirmation of efficacy and safety in larger patient populations), and **Phase IV** (post-marketing surveillance).

8. What is the role of Phase I clinical trials?

Answer: Phase I clinical trials focus on determining the **safety, dosage,** and

pharmacokinetics of a drug in healthy volunteers, typically with a small number of participants.

9. What is the goal of Phase II clinical trials?

Answer: The goal of Phase II trials is to evaluate the **efficacy** of the drug in patients, as well as to gather data on side effects and the optimal dose.

10. What happens in Phase III clinical trials?

Answer: Phase III trials involve testing the drug in a larger patient population to confirm its efficacy and safety, often comparing it with existing treatments. This phase is critical for regulatory approval.

11. What is the role of regulatory authorities in clinical trials?

Answer: Regulatory authorities like the **FDA** or **EMA** oversee and approve clinical trial designs, ensure ethical standards are met, and review trial results for drug approval.

12. What is Good Clinical Practice (GCP)?

Answer: Good Clinical Practice (GCP) refers to a set of international standards for conducting clinical trials that ensure participant safety, data integrity, and compliance with ethical guidelines.

13. What is a biologic drug?

Answer: A **biologic drug** is a product derived from living organisms, such as monoclonal antibodies, vaccines, and gene therapies, used to treat a variety of diseases.

14. What are biosimilars?

Answer: Biosimilars are biologic products that are highly similar to already approved reference biologics, with no clinically meaningful differences in terms of safety and efficacy.

15. How is a new drug candidate selected?

Answer: New drug candidates are selected based on their ability to target specific disease mechanisms, their safety profile in preclinical studies, and their potential efficacy in treating a given disease.

16. What is the importance of animal testing in drug development?

Answer: Animal testing provides early safety and efficacy data, helping to identify potential risks and determine safe dosages for initial human trials.

17. What are pharmacokinetics and why are they important in drug development?

Answer: Pharmacokinetics refers to the study of the drug's **absorption, distribution, metabolism,** and **excretion** (ADME). It helps determine the appropriate dosage and frequency of administration for the drug.

18. What are pharmacodynamics in drug development?

Answer: **Pharmacodynamics** is the study of the **biological effects** of a drug on the body and the mechanisms by which the drug exerts its effects. It helps understand the relationship between drug concentration and therapeutic response.

19. How are drug formulations developed?

Answer: Drug formulations are developed by selecting the appropriate **drug delivery system**, such as **tablets, injectables**, or **topicals**, and optimizing the formulation for stability, bioavailability, and ease of use.

20. What is the role of regulatory agencies in drug approval?

Answer: Regulatory agencies like the **FDA** and **EMA** review clinical trial data, evaluate drug safety and efficacy, and ensure that drugs meet the required standards before they are approved for marketing.

21. What is the significance of clinical trial phase designation?

Answer: The clinical trial phase designation helps categorize the **stage** of drug development and determines the type of data required for approval. It ensures that each phase addresses specific research objectives.

22. What are adverse effects in clinical trials?

Answer: **Adverse effects** are unwanted or harmful reactions to a drug. These are closely monitored during clinical trials to ensure patient safety and assess the overall benefit-risk ratio of the drug.

23. What is dose-response relationship in clinical trials?

Answer: The **dose-response relationship** refers to the correlation between the **dose** of a drug and the **response** it produces. It is essential for determining the optimal therapeutic dose.

24. What is the purpose of randomization in clinical trials?

Answer: **Randomization** ensures that participants are assigned to treatment groups randomly, reducing bias and ensuring the reliability of trial results.

25. What are the ethical considerations in drug development?

Answer: Ethical considerations include ensuring **informed consent**, maintaining **confidentiality**, protecting participants' **rights and well-being**, and ensuring the integrity of clinical trial data.

26. What is informed consent in clinical trials?

Answer: **Informed consent** is the process by which participants are provided with all relevant information about the trial, including risks, benefits, and alternatives, and voluntarily agree to participate.

27. What is blinding in clinical trials?

Answer: **Blinding** refers to the practice of keeping participants and/or investigators unaware of which treatment group a participant is in to reduce bias and ensure the integrity of trial results.

28. What is the significance of post-marketing surveillance in drug development?

Answer: Post-marketing surveillance monitors the long-term safety and effectiveness of a drug after it has been approved and marketed to the general population, detecting rare or delayed adverse effects.

29. What is the Abbreviated New Drug Application (ANDA) used for?

Answer: An **ANDA** is used by generic drug manufacturers to seek approval for a generic version of a brand-name drug. The application must demonstrate that the generic drug is **bioequivalent** to the reference drug.

30. What is bioequivalence in drug development?

Answer: **Bioequivalence** refers to the similarity between the bioavailability of a generic drug and its reference brand-name drug. It ensures that the generic drug performs in the same manner as the original.

31. How does clinical trial randomization reduce bias?

Answer: **Randomization** ensures that each participant has an equal chance of being assigned to any treatment group, minimizing selection bias and providing more reliable results.

32. What is the role of the Institutional Review Board (IRB) in drug development?

Answer: An **IRB** reviews and approves clinical trial protocols to ensure the safety, ethical standards, and rights of participants are upheld during the study.

33. What is clinical trial registration?

Answer: **Clinical trial registration** involves entering trial details into a public database, such as **ClinicalTrials.gov**, to ensure transparency and allow for public access to information about ongoing or completed trials.

34. What are the risks and benefits of drug development?

Answer: The **risks** include adverse effects, toxicity, and failure to achieve efficacy, while the **benefits** include successful treatment, marketability, and patient health improvements.

35. What is the role of animal models in preclinical testing?

Answer: Animal models are used in preclinical testing to evaluate the safety and efficacy of a drug before it is tested in humans, helping identify potential toxicity and dosing issues.

36. What is drug repurposing?

Answer: **Drug repurposing** involves using existing drugs to treat new diseases. This strategy can save time and cost in drug development since the safety profile of the drug is already known.

37. What is regulatory submission in drug development?

Answer: **Regulatory submission** is the process of submitting all necessary data, including clinical trial results and manufacturing information, to regulatory authorities to obtain approval to market a drug.

38. What is the role of pharmacokinetics in drug development?

Answer: **Pharmacokinetics** studies how the body absorbs, distributes, metabolizes, and excretes a drug. It is essential in determining appropriate dosages, dosing intervals, and the safety of a drug.

39. What is pharmacodynamics and its relevance in drug development?

Answer: **Pharmacodynamics** is the study of a drug's effects on the body, including its mechanism of action. It helps to understand the **therapeutic effects** and **side effects** of a drug.

40. How do preclinical studies support clinical trials?

Answer: Preclinical studies provide the safety and efficacy data required to justify testing the drug in humans. They help identify any potential risks that could be harmful in clinical trials.

41. What is the significance of regulatory agencies in drug approval?

Answer: Regulatory agencies, such as the **FDA** and **EMA**, ensure that drugs meet stringent safety and efficacy standards before they are allowed to be marketed, protecting public health.

42. What is a clinical trial endpoint?

Answer: A **clinical trial endpoint** is a specific outcome used to measure the effectiveness of a drug in a clinical trial, such as a reduction in symptoms or an improvement in disease markers.

43. How does phase IV of clinical trials differ from other phases?

Answer: Phase IV trials, or **post-marketing surveillance**, monitor the long-term effects and safety of a drug after it is marketed, addressing rare adverse effects and assessing its real-world effectiveness.

44. What is the role of clinical trial monitoring?

Answer: **Clinical trial monitoring** ensures that clinical trials are conducted according to the protocol, regulatory requirements, and GCP standards. It involves regular audits to track progress, ensure participant safety, and ensure data integrity.

45. What are clinical trial ethics?

Answer: **Clinical trial ethics** involves ensuring that clinical trials are conducted in a way that respects participants' rights, provides informed consent, and follows ethical standards to protect participant well-being.

46. What are the challenges in generic drug development?

Answer: Challenges in generic drug development include proving **bioequivalence** to the reference drug, ensuring manufacturing quality, and dealing with **patent issues**.

47. What is preclinical toxicity testing?

Answer: Preclinical toxicity testing evaluates the safety of a drug in animal models to identify any harmful effects before the drug is tested in humans.

48. What are pharmacovigilance systems?

Answer: Pharmacovigilance systems track and monitor the safety of drugs after they are marketed, collecting and analyzing data on adverse drug reactions.

49. What is accelerated approval for drugs?

Answer: Accelerated approval allows drugs that treat serious conditions with unmet medical needs to be approved based on early evidence, speeding up the approval process to make drugs available faster.

50. How do regulatory guidelines impact drug development?

Answer: Regulatory guidelines ensure that drug development is conducted according to scientific and ethical standards, providing a clear framework for testing, approval, and post-marketing monitoring. These guidelines ensure that drugs are safe and effective for consumers.

Chapter 3: Regulatory Approval Process

1. What is the regulatory approval process for drugs?

Answer: The regulatory approval process involves a series of steps where a drug is tested for safety, efficacy, and quality. The process includes **preclinical testing, clinical trials (Phases I, II, III),** submission of an **NDA** (New Drug Application) or **ANDA** (Abbreviated New Drug Application), and finally approval by regulatory agencies like the **FDA** or **EMA**.

2. What is an Investigational New Drug (IND) application?

Answer: An **IND application** is a request submitted to the FDA to begin human clinical trials of a new drug. It includes preclinical study data, proposed clinical trial protocols, and details on the drug's composition and manufacturing process.

3. Why is the IND process important?

Answer: The IND process ensures that a drug is safe to test in humans by evaluating the results of preclinical studies and clinical trial protocols. It provides regulatory agencies with the necessary information to safeguard human participants.

4. What is the purpose of Phase I clinical trials?

Answer: Phase I clinical trials are designed to evaluate the safety, **dosage**, and **pharmacokinetics** of a drug in a small group of healthy volunteers. The focus is on identifying any potential adverse effects and establishing safe dosage ranges.

5. What is the role of Phase II clinical trials?

Answer: Phase II clinical trials assess the drug's **efficacy** and further evaluate its safety in a larger group of patients who have the condition the drug aims to treat. The results help identify optimal dosing and the drug's therapeutic effects.

6. What are Phase III clinical trials?

Answer: Phase III clinical trials involve large-scale testing in diverse patient populations to confirm the drug's **efficacy** and **safety**. These trials often compare the new drug with existing treatments to demonstrate its benefit.

7. What happens during Phase IV clinical trials?

Answer: Phase IV trials, or **post-marketing surveillance**, track the long-term safety and effectiveness of a drug once it has been approved and is available on the market. These trials monitor rare or delayed adverse effects.

8. What is the New Drug Application (NDA) process?

Answer: The **NDA** is a formal application submitted to regulatory agencies (e.g., FDA) to request approval to market a new drug. It includes clinical trial data, preclinical safety data, manufacturing processes, and labeling information.

9. What is the Abbreviated New Drug Application (ANDA)?

Answer: The **ANDA** is an application submitted by manufacturers to obtain approval for generic drugs. It demonstrates that the generic drug is **bioequivalent** to the brand-name drug, with the same rate and extent of absorption.

10. What is the difference between NDA and ANDA?

Answer: The **NDA** is used for original drugs and includes extensive clinical trial data, while the **ANDA** is used for generics and relies on demonstrating **bioequivalence** to an already approved brand-name drug without the need for clinical trials.

11. What are the key requirements for an NDA submission?

Answer: An NDA requires data from clinical trials showing **safety** and **efficacy**, **manufacturing information**, proposed **labeling**, and **pharmacovigilance** plans. It also includes detailed data on the **drug's**

composition and formulation.

12. How do regulatory agencies review NDA submissions?

Answer: Regulatory agencies, such as the FDA, review the NDA submission to assess the drug's **safety, efficacy**, and **quality**. This review includes an evaluation of clinical trial data, proposed labeling, and manufacturing processes.

13. What is the Orange Book and how is it related to drug approval?

Answer: The **Orange Book** is a publication by the FDA that lists all **approved drug products** in the U.S., including their **therapeutic equivalence**. It helps healthcare providers, regulators, and consumers identify whether a generic drug is interchangeable with a reference product.

14. What is bioequivalence?

Answer: **Bioequivalence** refers to the comparison of the bioavailability (rate and extent of absorption) of two drug products, showing that a generic drug performs in the same manner as the reference product.

15. What is a Post-Approval Supplement?

Answer: A **Post-Approval Supplement** is a submission made after a drug's approval to request changes in the **labeling, manufacturing process**, or **formulation**. It must be reviewed and approved by the regulatory agency before the changes can be implemented.

16. What are the requirements for submitting a Post-Approval Change?

Answer: Post-approval changes require a **supplementary NDA** or a **CBE (Changes Being Effected)** submission, which includes detailed information about the change and the results of any studies or tests conducted to support it.

17. What is the Code of Federal Regulations (CFR)?

Answer: The **CFR** is a collection of the **regulations** promulgated by federal agencies, including the FDA. It provides the legal framework for drug development, approval, manufacturing, and marketing in the U.S.

18. What is the Federal Register and its role in the approval process?

Answer: The **Federal Register** publishes official notices, including proposed and final rules, **FDA approvals**, and **drug recalls**. It is an important resource for anyone involved in the drug development and approval process.

19. What is the FDA's role in post-marketing surveillance?

Answer: The FDA monitors the safety of approved drugs through **adverse event reporting systems** and **drug recalls**. It ensures that drugs continue to meet safety and efficacy standards after they reach the market.

20. What is the significance of risk management in drug development?

Answer: Risk management involves identifying, assessing, and minimizing the risks associated with a drug. It includes **post-marketing surveillance,** adverse event reporting, and the implementation of safety protocols.

21. What is the role of clinical trial monitoring in regulatory approval?

Answer: Clinical trial monitoring ensures compliance with the trial protocol, GCP standards, and regulatory requirements. It helps ensure data accuracy, participant safety, and the integrity of the trial.

22. How do regulatory bodies ensure drug safety?

Answer: Regulatory bodies ensure safety by requiring comprehensive clinical trial data before approval, monitoring adverse events, conducting inspections, and implementing recall procedures when necessary.

23. What is the role of an Institutional Review Board (IRB)?

Answer: An **IRB** reviews and approves clinical trial protocols to ensure the protection of participants' rights and safety, ensuring that the trial complies with ethical standards.

24. What is the role of the European Medicines Agency (EMA)?

Answer: The **EMA** evaluates and supervises medicines in the European Union, ensuring that drugs meet safety and efficacy standards before they are marketed in member states.

25. What is the role of Health Canada in drug approval?

Answer: Health Canada is responsible for assessing the safety, efficacy, and quality of drugs before they can be marketed in Canada. It works closely with other regulatory bodies like the FDA and EMA.

26. What are the key components of a New Drug Application (NDA)?

Answer: Key components of an NDA include **clinical trial data, preclinical data, drug composition, manufacturing processes,** and **proposed labeling.**

27. What is the purpose of a clinical trial protocol review?

Answer: A clinical trial protocol review ensures that the trial is scientifically valid, ethically sound, and compliant with regulatory requirements. It protects participant safety and ensures the integrity of the trial data.

28. What are the regulatory requirements for drug labeling?

Answer: Drug labeling must include information on **dosage, side effects, contraindications, warnings,** and other essential data to guide proper use and ensure patient safety.

29. What is the role of the FDA's Drug Approval Process?

Answer: The FDA's **drug approval process** ensures that drugs are thoroughly tested for safety and efficacy before they are marketed. It includes reviewing clinical trial data, conducting inspections, and approving drug labeling.

30. What is the significance of therapeutic equivalence in drug approval?

Answer: **Therapeutic equivalence** means that two drugs (often a brand-name and a generic) have the same **clinical effect** and **safety profile** when administered to patients under the same conditions.

31. What are the steps involved in regulatory approval for biosimilars?

Answer: Biosimilars must demonstrate **biosimilarity** to their reference biologic, including data from **clinical trials** to prove that the biosimilar has the same **safety** and **efficacy** profiles. Regulatory bodies like the **FDA** review the data before approval.

32. What is the role of the FDA's Purple Book in drug approval?

Answer: The **Purple Book** provides information on FDA-approved biosimilars and reference biologics. It helps ensure the safe substitution of biosimilars for their reference biologics.

33. How does the FDA expedite drug approval?

Answer: The FDA can expedite drug approval through programs like **Fast Track**, **Priority Review**, and **Accelerated Approval** for drugs that treat serious conditions with unmet medical needs.

34. What are the requirements for drug manufacturing in regulatory approval?

Answer: Drug manufacturing must meet strict **Good Manufacturing Practices (GMP)**, which include guidelines for equipment, facilities, personnel, and documentation to ensure the consistent quality and safety of drugs.

35. How are post-approval changes regulated?

Answer: Post-approval changes, such as changes to manufacturing or labeling, require a **supplementary NDA** or **CBE** submission. These changes must be reviewed and approved by regulatory authorities before they are implemented.

36. What is the role of pharmacovigilance in regulatory science?

Answer: **Pharmacovigilance** involves the detection, assessment, and prevention of adverse effects related to drugs after they are marketed, ensuring the ongoing safety of pharmaceutical products.

37. What is the difference between generic drugs and brand-name drugs in terms of regulatory approval?

Answer: Generic drugs are approved through an **ANDA**, showing **bioequivalence** to the brand-name drug. Brand-name drugs undergo the **NDA** process, which includes extensive clinical trial data.

38. What is post-marketing surveillance?

Answer: Post-marketing surveillance tracks the safety and effectiveness of drugs once they are available on the market, monitoring long-term effects and rare adverse events.

39. How do regulatory agencies ensure drug efficacy?

Answer: Regulatory agencies ensure **drug efficacy** by reviewing data from **clinical trials** that demonstrate the drug's ability to achieve the desired therapeutic effect in patients.

40. What is the FDA's review process for drug approval?

Answer: The FDA's review process involves reviewing clinical trial data, manufacturing information, and labeling proposals. The agency ensures that the drug is safe, effective, and of high quality before approval.

41. What is fast track designation in drug approval?

Answer: Fast track designation expedites the development and review of drugs that treat serious conditions with unmet medical needs. It allows for more frequent meetings with the FDA and faster approval timelines.

42. What is the role of the FDA's Accelerated Approval process?

Answer: The **Accelerated Approval process** allows for drugs to be approved based on early evidence of efficacy, particularly for serious conditions where no effective treatments exist, thus speeding up market access.

43. What is the importance of clinical trial registration?

Answer: Clinical trial registration ensures transparency in the research process, allowing the public to access information about ongoing or completed trials and their outcomes.

44. What are the steps involved in obtaining approval for a biosimilar?

Answer: Obtaining approval for a **biosimilar** involves demonstrating **biosimilarity** to an already approved biologic through preclinical studies and clinical trials, ensuring the drug has the same **safety** and **efficacy** profiles.

45. What is the role of ethics committees in drug approval?

Answer: **Ethics committees**, such as **IRBs** or **IECs**, review clinical trial protocols to ensure that they meet ethical standards and protect participants' rights and safety.

46. How do regulatory authorities monitor drug manufacturing?

Answer: Regulatory authorities ensure compliance with **Good Manufacturing Practices (GMP)** by inspecting manufacturing facilities and reviewing production records to ensure that drugs are consistently produced to the required standards.

47. What is the importance of informed consent in clinical trials?

Answer: **Informed consent** ensures that clinical trial participants understand the potential risks, benefits, and objectives of the trial before agreeing to participate.

48. What are adverse drug reactions?

Answer: **Adverse drug reactions (ADRs)** are unwanted or harmful effects that occur when a drug is administered. They are closely monitored during clinical trials and post-marketing surveillance.

49. How are drug recalls handled by regulatory authorities?

Answer: When a drug is found to be unsafe or defective, regulatory authorities issue a **drug recall**, instructing manufacturers to remove the drug from the market and notify healthcare providers and patients.

50. What is the significance of clinical trial reporting in drug approval?

Answer: **Clinical trial reporting** ensures transparency in the research process. It allows regulatory agencies, healthcare providers, and patients to access accurate information about a drug's safety, efficacy, and potential risks.

Chapter 4: Registration of Indian Drug Products in Overseas Markets

1. What is the process for registering Indian drug products in overseas markets?

Answer: The process for registering Indian drug products in overseas markets involves **preparation** of **technical documentation**, including **drug master files (DMF)** and **common technical documents (CTD)**, submission to the relevant **regulatory authorities** in the target market, and obtaining approvals for export.

2. What is the role of regulatory bodies in the registration of drug products?

Answer: Regulatory bodies like the **FDA** in the U.S., the **EMA** in Europe, and others globally evaluate the safety, efficacy, and quality of drugs before they are approved for marketing in their respective regions. These bodies also monitor post-market drug safety and compliance with local regulations.

3. What are the key documents required for drug product registration in foreign markets?

Answer: Key documents include the **Drug Master File (DMF)**, **Common Technical Document (CTD)**, **Certificate of Pharmaceutical Product (CPP)**, **stability data**, **clinical trial reports**, **manufacturing data**, and **labeling information.**

4. What is a Drug Master File (DMF)?

Answer: A **DMF** is a confidential document submitted to regulatory authorities that provides detailed information about the drug's composition, manufacturing process, and quality control. It supports the registration process and is required in many countries for drug product approvals.

5. What is the Common Technical Document (CTD)?

Answer: The **CTD** is a standard format for drug registration submissions that includes information on **quality**, **safety**, and **efficacy**. It is used to facilitate drug approval in multiple countries and is recognized by regulatory bodies like the **FDA, EMA,** and **PMDA.**

6. What is the purpose of the Certificate of Pharmaceutical Product (CPP)?

Answer: The **CPP** is an official document issued by the regulatory authority in the home country that certifies that the drug complies with local regulatory requirements and is authorized for sale in the domestic market.

7. What is the ASEAN Common Technical Document (ACTD)?

Answer: The **ACTD** is a regulatory framework used by **ASEAN** countries for drug product registration. It is designed to harmonize the registration process across member countries by standardizing the format for submission documents.

8. How does the regulatory approval process differ between the U.S., EU, and India?

Answer: Regulatory approval processes differ in terms of required documentation, timelines, and submission procedures. For example, the **FDA** requires an **NDA** or **ANDA** for new and generic drugs, while the **EMA** uses the **MAA** (Marketing Authorization Application) process. In India, the **CDSCO** (Central Drugs Standard Control Organization) evaluates drug registration submissions before granting approval.

9. What is the role of the FDA in registering foreign drug products?

Answer: The **FDA** evaluates the safety, efficacy, and quality of foreign drug products through submissions such as **NDAs** or **ANDAs**. The agency ensures that foreign drugs meet U.S. standards before they can be marketed in the U.S.

10. What are the regulatory requirements for exporting pharmaceutical products from India?

Answer: The requirements for exporting pharmaceutical products from India include obtaining a **Certificate of Pharmaceutical Product (CPP)**, preparing **DMF** and **CTD**, ensuring compliance with **GMP (Good Manufacturing Practices)**, and meeting the regulatory requirements of the target market.

11. What is the significance of Good Manufacturing Practices (GMP) in drug registration?

Answer: **GMP** ensures that drugs are consistently produced and controlled to quality standards. Compliance with **GMP** is essential for obtaining regulatory approvals in both domestic and international markets.

12. How does the EMA regulate drug registration in Europe?

Answer: The **EMA** evaluates drug registration applications through procedures like the **Centralized Procedure** for products intended for EU-wide marketing and the **Mutual Recognition Procedure** for drugs approved in one EU member state seeking approval in others.

13. What is the Centralized Procedure used by the EMA?

Answer: The **Centralized Procedure** allows companies to apply for a single marketing authorization that is valid in all EU member states. It is used for innovative medicines or products for rare diseases and certain biologics.

14. What is the Mutual Recognition Procedure (MRP) in Europe?

Answer: The **MRP** is a procedure where a drug approved in one EU member state can be recognized and approved by other EU countries. It is used when the drug has already been authorized in one member state, and the manufacturer seeks approval in other states.

15. How is the registration process for Indian drug products in Canada handled?

Answer: In Canada, Indian drug products must comply with the **Health Canada** regulations. Manufacturers must submit an **NDA** or **New Drug Submission (NDS)**, including data on clinical trials, manufacturing processes, and labeling.

16. What are the requirements for drug registration in Japan?

Answer: In Japan, drug registration requires submission to the **Pharmaceutical and Medical Device Agency (PMDA)**, including clinical trial data, manufacturing information, and a **New Drug Application (NDA)**. The PMDA evaluates the drug's safety and efficacy before granting approval.

17. What is the role of the Pharmaceutical and Medical Device Agency (PMDA) in Japan?

Answer: The **PMDA** is responsible for the regulatory approval of drugs in Japan. It evaluates clinical trial data, manufacturing practices, and the safety and efficacy of drug products before they can be marketed in Japan.

18. What are the export requirements for pharmaceutical products to Australia?

Answer: In Australia, pharmaceutical products must meet the regulatory standards set by the **Therapeutic Goods Administration (TGA)**. The export process requires submission of a **marketing authorization application**, including clinical and manufacturing data, and compliance with **GMP**.

19. What is the role of the Therapeutic Goods Administration (TGA) in Australia?

Answer: The **TGA** regulates the supply of therapeutic goods, including drugs and medical devices, in Australia. It ensures that products are safe, effective, and of high quality by evaluating clinical data, manufacturing processes, and labeling.

20. What is the process for drug registration in ASEAN countries?

Answer: Drug registration in ASEAN countries follows the **ASEAN Common Technical Document (ACTD)** guidelines. The ACTD harmonizes the regulatory process across ASEAN member states, streamlining the approval process for drugs by using a common format for submission.

21. How do regulatory agencies ensure the safety of drugs in overseas markets?

Answer: Regulatory agencies ensure drug safety through **clinical trials**, **post-marketing surveillance**, **adverse event reporting**, and periodic inspections of manufacturing facilities to ensure ongoing compliance with **Good Manufacturing Practices (GMP)**.

22. What is the significance of stability data in drug registration?

Answer: Stability data is crucial for determining a drug's shelf life and ensuring its **efficacy** and **safety** throughout its shelf life. It is required as part of the drug registration process to meet regulatory requirements.

23. How does Health Canada regulate drug registration in Canada?

Answer: Health Canada evaluates drug products through the **New Drug Submission (NDS)** process. This involves reviewing clinical trial data, manufacturing processes, and labeling to ensure the drug meets safety, efficacy, and quality standards.

24. What is a certificate of pharmaceutical product (CPP) and why is it necessary for export?

Answer: The **CPP** is a document issued by the drug regulatory authority in the home country (India) that certifies that the drug product is licensed for use in India and meets the necessary regulatory standards. It is required for the export of pharmaceutical products to foreign markets.

25. What are the main regulatory challenges when registering Indian drugs in overseas markets?

Answer: Regulatory challenges include meeting different **regulatory requirements** in each country, **ensuring GMP compliance**, navigating complex **documentation processes**, and **adhering to local labeling and testing standards.**

26. How does the FDA regulate imported drugs from India?

Answer: The **FDA** regulates imported drugs by ensuring that they meet U.S. safety, efficacy, and quality standards. Drugs must comply with **Good Manufacturing Practices (GMP)**, undergo thorough testing, and be appropriately labeled before approval for marketing.

27. What is the pharmaceutical export license and how is it obtained in India?

Answer: A **pharmaceutical export license** is issued by India's **Central Drugs Standard Control Organization (CDSCO)**. It authorizes the export of pharmaceutical products to other countries and is issued after ensuring compliance with Indian drug regulations.

28. What is the difference between a drug master file (DMF) and a new drug application (NDA)?

Answer: A **DMF** provides detailed information about the drug's **manufacturing process, composition,** and **quality control** to regulatory bodies. An **NDA** is a comprehensive application for approval to market a new drug, including clinical trial data, preclinical data, and manufacturing details.

29. How do regulatory agencies ensure compliance with GMP for drug manufacturers?

Answer: Regulatory agencies ensure **GMP** compliance by conducting **inspections** of manufacturing facilities, reviewing **quality control data**, and requiring manufacturers to adhere to stringent quality assurance procedures.

30. What is the role of the EMA's centralized procedure in global drug registration?

Answer: The **EMA's centralized procedure** allows drug manufacturers to submit a single application for approval, which is valid across all EU member states. This procedure helps streamline the drug approval process for certain drugs, including biologics and orphan drugs.

31. What is the FDA's role in foreign drug registration?

Answer: The **FDA** evaluates the safety, efficacy, and quality of foreign drug products through submissions like **NDAs** or **ANDAs**. It ensures that imported drugs meet U.S. standards before they can be marketed in the U.S.

32. How does the FDA handle the importation of generic drugs?

Answer: The **FDA** evaluates generic drugs through the **ANDA** process, which requires proof of **bioequivalence** to the reference product. It ensures that generics are safe, effective, and of the same quality as the brand-name drug.

33. What is Regulatory Harmonization and how does it benefit drug manufacturers?

Answer: **Regulatory harmonization** involves aligning the drug approval processes across countries to make it easier for manufacturers to submit a single application and gain approval in multiple markets, reducing costs and time to market.

34. What is the role of clinical trial data in the drug registration process?

Answer: Clinical trial data provides evidence of a drug's **safety** and **efficacy**. It is critical in the drug registration process as it forms the basis for regulatory decisions regarding approval.

35. What are the key elements in drug labeling during the registration process?

Answer: Key elements in drug labeling include **dosage instructions, side effects, precautions, contraindications, warnings,** and **storage instructions**, which must be in compliance with local regulations.

36. What role does stability testing play in drug product registration?

Answer: **Stability testing** determines the shelf life of a drug and ensures that the drug maintains its **efficacy** and **safety** throughout its shelf life. It is a crucial part of the regulatory submission process.

37. What is the impact of regulatory delays on the drug development process?

Answer: **Regulatory delays** can impact the timely availability of new drugs, potentially affecting public health, increasing development costs, and delaying the return on investment for manufacturers.

38. How are drug products from India regulated in African markets?

Answer: Drug products from India are regulated by national health authorities in African countries, which often follow **WHO** standards for quality, safety, and efficacy. Indian manufacturers must submit required documents such as **CTD, DMF,** and **GMP certificates.**

39. What is the significance of pharmaceutical exports for India?

Answer: Pharmaceutical exports are crucial for India's economy, as India is one of the largest producers of generic drugs globally. Exporting helps meet the growing demand for affordable medications worldwide.

40. How does India's regulatory system align with international standards?

Answer: India's regulatory system is aligned with international standards set by **WHO, ICH,** and **GMP.** This alignment helps Indian manufacturers meet global quality requirements and gain market access in international markets.

****41. What is the regulatory role of the FDA in approving foreign-made drugs for the U.S. market?**

Answer: The **FDA** ensures that foreign-made drugs meet the same standards as U.S.-made drugs. It evaluates the safety, efficacy, and manufacturing processes of imported drugs before they can be marketed in the U.S.

42. What are the challenges faced by Indian pharmaceutical companies in global markets?

Answer: Challenges include navigating **complex regulatory requirements, adhering to different standards** for **manufacturing** and **labeling,** and managing the **cost** and **time** involved in meeting regulatory demands across multiple countries.

43. How does post-marketing surveillance work for drugs exported from India?

Answer: Post-marketing surveillance involves monitoring the safety and efficacy of drugs after they are approved and marketed. Regulatory agencies collect adverse event reports, conduct inspections, and may implement regulatory actions if issues arise.

44. How does the FDA handle foreign inspections?

Answer: The **FDA** conducts foreign inspections to ensure that manufacturing facilities comply with **Good Manufacturing Practices (GMP)**. Inspections are critical for ensuring that foreign drugs meet U.S. safety and quality standards.

45. What is the ASEAN regulatory framework for pharmaceutical products?

Answer: The **ASEAN regulatory framework** is based on harmonized standards and procedures for drug registration, including the **ACTD**, which simplifies the process for exporting pharmaceutical products to member states.

46. How does India's CDSCO regulate pharmaceutical exports?

Answer: The **CDSCO** is responsible for ensuring the quality, safety, and efficacy of drugs exported from India. It provides the necessary certifications and monitors the compliance of Indian drug manufacturers with international regulatory standards.

****47. What is the role of international trade agreements in drug product registration?**

Answer: International trade agreements help standardize regulatory requirements, streamline drug approval processes, and promote the free flow of pharmaceutical products between countries while maintaining safety and efficacy standards.

48. What is drug export licensing, and why is it important?

Answer: Drug export licensing ensures that pharmaceutical companies meet regulatory standards before their products can be exported to other countries. It helps maintain product quality and compliance with international regulations.

49. How do regulatory inspections impact drug exports?

Answer: Regulatory inspections ensure that drug products meet the required standards for safety, efficacy, and quality. These inspections can lead to approvals or rejections of export applications based on compliance with regulatory guidelines.

50. What are the future trends in global pharmaceutical regulation?

Answer: Future trends include increased **regulatory harmonization, accelerated approval processes, greater focus on pharmacovigilance,** and the adoption of **digital technologies** in regulatory submissions and monitoring.

Chapter 5: Clinical Trials and Ethics

1. What are clinical trials?

Answer: Clinical trials are research studies that test new drugs, devices, or treatment methods in humans to assess their **safety, efficacy,** and **side effects**. They are essential for evaluating how well a new treatment works in patients and ensuring that it is safe for public use.

2. What is the purpose of clinical trial phases?

Answer: Clinical trial phases (I, II, III, IV) serve to evaluate a drug's **safety** and **efficacy** at different stages of development, from initial testing in healthy volunteers (Phase I) to monitoring long-term safety in the general population (Phase IV).

3. What is the significance of Phase I clinical trials?

Answer: Phase I clinical trials are the first stage of testing a new drug in humans. Their main focus is to assess the drug's **safety, dosage,** and **pharmacokinetics** (how the drug is absorbed, distributed, metabolized, and excreted).

4. What are the goals of Phase II clinical trials?

Answer: Phase II trials aim to evaluate the drug's **efficacy** in patients with the condition the drug is intended to treat. They also provide further safety data and help determine the optimal **dose**.

5. What happens in Phase III clinical trials?

Answer: Phase III trials involve large groups of patients and are designed to confirm the drug's **efficacy**, monitor its **side effects**, and compare it with existing treatments. These trials provide the data necessary for regulatory approval.

6. What is the role of Phase IV clinical trials?

Answer: Phase IV trials, or **post-marketing surveillance,** occur after a drug has been approved and is available on the market. They are designed to monitor the drug's long-term safety and effectiveness and identify any **rare** or **delayed** adverse effects.

7. What is the Institutional Review Board (IRB)?

Answer: An **Institutional Review Board (IRB)** is a committee that reviews and approves clinical trial protocols to ensure that the study meets ethical standards and that the rights, safety, and well-being of participants are protected.

8. What are the responsibilities of an IRB?

Answer: The IRB ensures that the clinical trial is ethically sound, that participants provide **informed consent**, and that the study complies with relevant **regulations** and **guidelines** such as **Good Clinical Practice (GCP)**.

9. What is the informed consent process in clinical trials?

Answer: The **informed consent** process ensures that participants are fully aware of the study's goals, potential risks, and benefits before agreeing to participate. It requires clear communication and voluntary participation without coercion.

10. What are the key components of informed consent?

Answer: Key components include **information about the trial, potential risks and benefits, alternatives**, and the participant's right to **withdraw** at any time without consequence.

11. What is the importance of ethics in clinical trials?

Answer: Ethics ensure that clinical trials are conducted in a manner that respects the rights, dignity, and safety of participants. Ethical guidelines help prevent exploitation and ensure that trials contribute to scientific and medical progress while maintaining public trust.

12. What are Good Clinical Practices (GCP)?

Answer: **Good Clinical Practices (GCP)** are international ethical and scientific standards for designing, conducting, recording, and reporting clinical trials. They are aimed at ensuring participant safety and the reliability of clinical trial data.

13. How does GCP ensure patient safety in clinical trials?

Answer: GCP ensures that clinical trials are designed and conducted to prioritize patient safety, including ensuring **informed consent, risk minimization**, and **regular monitoring** of adverse events during the trial.

14. What are the roles of investigators, sponsors, and monitors in clinical trials?

Answer: Investigators conduct the trial and ensure patient safety; sponsors provide financial support and oversee the trial; monitors ensure compliance with protocol and regulatory standards.

15. What is a clinical trial protocol?

Answer: A **clinical trial protocol** is a detailed plan that outlines the trial's **objectives, design, methods, and statistical analysis**, ensuring that the study is conducted consistently and ethically.

16. What are the ethical issues in clinical trials?

Answer: Ethical issues include **informed consent, participant selection, vulnerable populations, balancing risks and benefits**, and ensuring **confidentiality** of participant data.

17. What are vulnerable populations in clinical trials?

Answer: **Vulnerable populations** are groups that may have limited ability to provide informed consent, such as children, pregnant women, prisoners, or people with cognitive impairments. Special ethical protections are required when involving these groups in trials.

18. What is the significance of randomization in clinical trials?

Answer: **Randomization** helps ensure that participants are assigned to treatment groups without bias, reducing the influence of confounding factors and increasing the reliability of trial results.

19. What are blinded studies in clinical trials?

Answer: In **blinded studies**, participants and/or researchers are unaware of which treatment the participant is receiving (active drug or placebo) to prevent bias in assessing outcomes.

20. What are placebo-controlled trials?

Answer: In **placebo-controlled trials**, one group receives the experimental drug, while another group receives a placebo. This comparison helps determine whether the observed effects are due to the drug or other factors.

21. What is randomized controlled trial (RCT)?

Answer: An **RCT** is a clinical trial in which participants are randomly assigned to treatment or control groups. It is considered the gold standard in clinical research due to its ability to minimize bias and confounding variables.

22. What are adverse events in clinical trials?

Answer: **Adverse events** are any undesirable experiences or side effects reported by participants during a clinical trial. They are closely monitored and documented to assess the drug's safety.

23. What is the role of pharmacovigilance in clinical trials?

Answer: **Pharmacovigilance** involves monitoring and assessing the safety of drugs during clinical trials and after they are marketed. It includes the collection and evaluation of **adverse event** reports to ensure ongoing safety.

24. What is the importance of data monitoring committees (DMC) in clinical trials?

Answer: **Data monitoring committees** are independent groups that regularly review clinical trial data to ensure participant safety, determine if the trial should continue, or if the treatment is proven to be ineffective.

25. What is the process of adverse event reporting during clinical trials?

Answer: Adverse event reporting involves documenting any negative health effects that occur during the trial and reporting them to the regulatory authorities. These events are then investigated to determine their relationship to the drug.

26. How do regulatory agencies monitor clinical trials?

Answer: Regulatory agencies monitor clinical trials by reviewing trial protocols, inspecting trial sites for compliance with GCP, and evaluating adverse event reports to ensure participant safety and data integrity.

27. What is the role of informed consent in protecting participants' rights?

Answer: Informed consent protects participants' rights by ensuring they understand the risks, benefits, and purpose of the trial. It allows participants to make an informed decision about whether to participate.

28. What is the Declaration of Helsinki?

Answer: The **Declaration of Helsinki** is a set of ethical principles for conducting medical research involving human participants. It emphasizes the importance of **informed consent, participant safety**, and **scientific integrity**.

29. How does the Belmont Report guide clinical trials?

Answer: The **Belmont Report** outlines ethical principles for research involving human subjects, focusing on **respect for persons, beneficence,** and **justice**. It provides guidelines for obtaining informed consent, minimizing harm, and ensuring fair participant selection.

30. What is ethical review in clinical trials?

Answer: Ethical review involves assessing a clinical trial's protocol, informed consent process, and overall study design to ensure it meets ethical standards for participant protection.

31. What are double-blind trials?

Answer: In **double-blind trials**, neither the participants nor the investigators know who is receiving the active treatment or placebo. This helps minimize bias and ensures the reliability of trial results.

32. What are the challenges in clinical trial ethics?

Answer: Challenges include obtaining truly **informed consent**, ensuring **vulnerable populations** are protected, **balancing risk vs. benefit**, and ensuring **confidentiality** of participant data.

33. What is the Helsinki Declaration's impact on clinical research?

Answer: The **Helsinki Declaration** has set international ethical standards for human medical research. It emphasizes the protection of human rights, the safety of trial participants, and the importance of scientific integrity in research.

34. What is the Ethics Committee's role in a clinical trial?

Answer: The **Ethics Committee** reviews clinical trial protocols to ensure that the study respects the participants' rights and follows ethical standards. It ensures that the trial does not expose participants to unnecessary risks.

35. What is the importance of clinical trial monitoring?

Answer: **Clinical trial monitoring** ensures that the trial is conducted according to the protocol, **regulatory standards**, and **GCP guidelines**, maintaining data integrity and participant safety.

36. How does the research sponsor ensure ethical conduct in clinical trials?

Answer: The **sponsor** ensures ethical conduct by overseeing the clinical trial, ensuring that it adheres to regulatory and ethical guidelines, funding ethical review processes, and ensuring participants' rights are protected.

37. What are the confidentiality requirements in clinical trials?

Answer: Clinical trials require strict **confidentiality** of participant data to protect personal information. Participants' identities must be protected, and their data must only be used for the purpose of the trial.

38. How do clinical trial protocols ensure scientific integrity?

Answer: Clinical trial protocols ensure **scientific integrity** by detailing the trial design, including the **research methodology**, **data collection**, and **analysis techniques** to ensure accurate, unbiased results.

39. What is clinical trial transparency and why is it important?

Answer: **Clinical trial transparency** ensures that the trial's methods, results, and potential conflicts of interest are openly communicated to the public, regulatory agencies, and participants, promoting trust and accountability.

40. How are adverse drug reactions handled during clinical trials?

Answer: **Adverse drug reactions (ADRs)** are closely monitored during clinical trials. If an ADR occurs, it must be documented, reported to regulatory authorities, and analyzed to determine if the drug should continue to be tested or modified.

41. What is the difference between pharmacovigilance and clinical trial monitoring?

Answer: **Pharmacovigilance** is focused on **monitoring the safety** of drugs after they have been marketed, while **clinical trial monitoring** occurs during the study phase and ensures compliance with the protocol and safety guidelines.

42. How does randomization help minimize bias in clinical trials?

Answer: **Randomization** ensures that participants are randomly assigned to treatment or control groups, reducing selection bias and providing a more reliable comparison of the treatment's effect.

43. What is the importance of ethical research in drug development?

Answer: Ethical research ensures that drugs are developed and tested safely, that participant rights are upheld, and that the results are scientifically valid and trustworthy.

44. How are placebos used in clinical trials?

Answer: **Placebos** are inactive substances used in control groups to compare the effects of the active drug. They help determine whether the observed effects are due to the drug or other factors like **expectations**.

45. What is the role of institutional review boards (IRBs) in protecting clinical trial participants?

Answer: IRBs ensure that clinical trials are ethically sound by reviewing protocols, ensuring informed consent is obtained, and monitoring trials to prevent harm to participants.

46. How are clinical trial protocols monitored for compliance?

Answer: **Clinical trial protocols** are monitored through periodic inspections, reviews of trial records, and audits to ensure that the study is conducted according to regulatory guidelines and ethical standards.

47. What is informed consent documentation in clinical trials?

Answer: **Informed consent documentation** is the signed agreement by participants acknowledging their understanding of the risks, benefits, and purposes of the trial before participating.

48. How are ethical dilemmas handled in clinical trials?

Answer: **Ethical dilemmas** are addressed by adhering to **ethical guidelines**, obtaining informed consent, and ensuring that participants are not exposed to unnecessary risks.

49. What is the role of clinical research associates (CRAs)?

Answer: **Clinical research associates (CRAs)** monitor and manage clinical trials, ensuring adherence to protocols, regulatory requirements, and ethical standards, and ensuring that participant data is collected and reported accurately.

50. What are the consequences of ethical violations in clinical trials?

Answer: **Ethical violations** can lead to legal action, regulatory sanctions, the termination of trials, loss of public trust, and potential harm to participants. Ensuring ethical standards helps maintain the credibility of clinical research.

Chapter 6: Regulatory Concepts and Terminologies

1. What is the meaning of regulatory science?

Answer: Regulatory science is the field that applies scientific principles and methods to develop policies and regulations for the approval, regulation, and monitoring of drugs, devices, biologics, and other healthcare products to ensure public safety and efficacy.

2. What is the difference between regulations and guidelines in the regulatory context?

Answer: **Regulations** are legally binding requirements set by government agencies, while **guidelines** are non-mandatory recommendations designed to assist manufacturers and researchers in meeting regulatory standards.

3. What is the role of laws and acts in the regulatory framework?

Answer: Laws and acts, such as the **Food, Drug, and Cosmetic Act (FDCA)**, establish the legal framework for the regulation of drugs, ensuring their safety, efficacy, and proper manufacturing. They are enforced by regulatory bodies like the **FDA** and **EMA**.

4. What is the Orange Book and what is its significance?

Answer: The **Orange Book** is a publication by the **FDA** that lists all approved drug products in the U.S., including their **therapeutic equivalence**. It is used to assess the equivalence of generic drugs to their brand-name counterparts.

5. How does the FDA use the Purple Book in regulatory decisions?

Answer: The **Purple Book** is used by the **FDA** to provide information on **biosimilars** and **reference biologics**. It helps determine whether a biosimilar can be safely substituted for a reference biologic in clinical practice.

6. What is the significance of the Federal Register in drug approval?

Answer: The **Federal Register** publishes official notices from the **FDA** and other regulatory agencies, including **new drug approvals, drug recalls**, and **regulatory updates**. It is a key resource for tracking regulatory changes.

7. What does the Code of Federal Regulations (CFR) cover?

Answer: The **CFR** is a collection of rules and regulations issued by federal agencies in the U.S., including the **FDA**, related to the manufacturing, labeling, testing, and marketing of drugs and other medical products.

8. What is the role of regulatory agencies in ensuring drug safety?

Answer: Regulatory agencies ensure drug safety by reviewing clinical trial data, conducting inspections of manufacturing facilities, monitoring adverse drug reactions, and enforcing regulations that govern drug production and marketing.

9. What is biosimilarity in the context of drug regulation?

Answer: **Biosimilarity** refers to the close similarity between a **biosimilar** and its **reference biologic** in terms of safety, efficacy, and quality. Biosimilars must demonstrate **no clinically meaningful differences** from the original biologic in their mechanisms of action and side effects.

10. What is the difference between an NDA and an ANDA?

Answer: An **NDA (New Drug Application)** is submitted for approval of a new drug, including clinical trial data and preclinical studies. An **ANDA (Abbreviated New Drug Application)** is submitted for approval of a **generic drug**, demonstrating **bioequivalence** to the original brand-name drug without the need for extensive clinical trials.

11. What does GxP stand for in the regulatory context?

Answer: GxP stands for **Good Practices** and includes guidelines such as **Good Manufacturing Practices (GMP)**, **Good Clinical Practices (GCP)**, and **Good Laboratory Practices (GLP)**. These standards ensure that products are consistently produced and controlled to quality standards.

12. What is a Drug Master File (DMF)?

Answer: A **DMF** is a confidential document submitted to regulatory agencies that contains detailed information about the **drug's composition**, **manufacturing processes**, and **quality control** procedures.

13. What are clinical trial phases?

Answer: **Clinical trial phases** are stages of drug testing in humans. **Phase I** tests the safety and dosage in healthy volunteers, **Phase II** evaluates efficacy and safety in patients, **Phase III** confirms efficacy and safety in a larger population, and **Phase IV** monitors long-term effects after approval.

14. What is the Orange Book used for in generic drug development?

Answer: The **Orange Book** provides information on whether a generic drug is therapeutically equivalent to the brand-name drug, which is essential for **substitution** and **interchangeability** in clinical settings.

15. What are adverse drug reactions (ADR)?

Answer: **Adverse drug reactions (ADRs)** are unwanted or harmful effects caused by a drug. These can range from mild symptoms to serious life-threatening conditions and are closely monitored during clinical trials and after market approval.

16. What does fast track approval mean in drug regulation?

Answer: **Fast track approval** is a regulatory process that expedites the review and approval of drugs intended to treat serious conditions with unmet medical needs. This process allows for **early access** to promising therapies.

17. What is the priority review designation in drug approval?

Answer: A **priority review** designation accelerates the review process for drugs that provide significant improvements in the treatment of serious conditions, ensuring quicker approval and market availability.

18. What is an abbreviated new drug application (ANDA)?

Answer: An **ANDA** is a regulatory submission for generic drugs, demonstrating that the generic product is **bioequivalent** to an approved reference product. This process does not require the clinical trial data necessary for an **NDA**.

19. What is a biologic license application (BLA)?

Answer: A **Biologic License Application (BLA)** is submitted to the **FDA** for the approval of biologic products, such as vaccines, **monoclonal antibodies**, and **gene therapies**, demonstrating their safety, efficacy, and manufacturing processes.

20. How does the EMA's centralized procedure benefit drug manufacturers?

Answer: The **centralized procedure** allows drug manufacturers to submit a single application for approval to the **European Medicines Agency (EMA)**, which is valid across all EU member states. This simplifies the registration process and provides quicker access to the European market.

21. What is informed consent in clinical trials?

Answer: **Informed consent** is the process by which participants are fully informed about the trial's risks, benefits, objectives, and their rights before agreeing to participate. It is a critical part of **clinical trial ethics.**

22. What is clinical trial randomization?

Answer: **Randomization** in clinical trials is the process of assigning participants to different treatment groups using a random method, ensuring that each participant has an equal chance of being assigned to any group and minimizing bias in results.

23. What does the Declaration of Helsinki address in clinical trials?

Answer: The **Declaration of Helsinki** outlines ethical principles and guidelines for conducting research on human subjects. It emphasizes the importance of **informed consent, participant welfare,** and scientific integrity.

24. What is the role of the FDA in regulating clinical trials?

Answer: The **FDA** regulates clinical trials by reviewing and approving **Investigational New Drug (IND)** applications, ensuring that trials follow ethical guidelines, and monitoring trial results to guarantee the safety of participants.

25. What is the World Health Organization (WHO)'s role in clinical trials?

Answer: The **WHO** provides global standards and guidelines for conducting ethical and scientifically sound clinical trials, including **Good Clinical Practice (GCP)** guidelines that are recognized worldwide.

26. What is the Regulatory Affairs Professional Society (RAPS)?

Answer: The **Regulatory Affairs Professional Society (RAPS)** is a global organization that supports professionals working in regulatory affairs by offering resources, training, and certification in drug and device regulations.

27. What is the importance of pharmacovigilance in post-marketing drug safety?

Answer: **Pharmacovigilance** is the practice of monitoring the safety of pharmaceutical products after they are marketed, including tracking adverse drug reactions, identifying new risks, and ensuring the ongoing safety of the drug in the general population.

28. How do regulatory bodies ensure that drugs are effective and safe?

Answer: Regulatory bodies ensure drug safety and efficacy by reviewing clinical trial data, inspecting manufacturing facilities, setting labeling requirements, and monitoring adverse events through pharmacovigilance systems.

29. What is the Good Manufacturing Practice (GMP)?

Answer: **Good Manufacturing Practice (GMP)** is a system of regulations that ensures pharmaceutical products are consistently produced and controlled according to quality standards, minimizing risks to patient health.

30. What is compassionate use in drug regulation?

Answer: **Compassionate use** allows patients with serious or life-threatening conditions to access investigational drugs outside of clinical trials when no other treatment options are available.

31. What is regulatory submission?

Answer: **Regulatory submission** is the process of submitting a drug or device application to regulatory agencies, such as the **FDA** or **EMA**, for approval to market the product. This involves providing clinical, preclinical, and manufacturing data.

32. What is labeling compliance in regulatory affairs?

Answer: Labeling compliance refers to ensuring that drug labels meet regulatory standards set by agencies like the **FDA** or **EMA**, including proper instructions, side effects, warnings, and indications.

33. What is a drug recall?

Answer: A **drug recall** is an action taken by the manufacturer or regulatory authorities to remove a drug from the market because it is defective, unsafe, or does not meet the required standards.

34. How do clinical trial phases help in drug development?

Answer: Clinical trial phases help to progressively test the **safety**, **efficacy**, and **optimal dosage** of a drug, ensuring that it is safe for use in the general population before it is approved for marketing.

35. What is risk management in drug development?

Answer: Risk management in drug development involves identifying potential risks associated with a drug, assessing their likelihood and impact, and implementing strategies to minimize these risks during clinical trials and post-marketing.

36. What is the Regulatory Affairs Professional Certification (RAC)?

Answer: The **RAC** is a certification offered by **RAPS** for regulatory professionals, verifying their expertise in drug and device regulations and demonstrating their commitment to maintaining industry knowledge and standards.

37. What is the role of clinical trial monitoring in ensuring compliance?

Answer: Clinical trial monitoring ensures that the trial is conducted according to the approved protocol, **Good Clinical Practice (GCP)** guidelines, and regulatory requirements, ensuring the safety and ethical treatment of participants.

38. What is the FDA's role in post-marketing surveillance?

Answer: The **FDA** monitors the safety of drugs after they are marketed through **adverse event reporting**, **drug recalls**, and post-marketing studies to ensure continued safety and efficacy.

39. How does regulatory harmonization benefit global drug development?

Answer: Regulatory harmonization streamlines the drug approval process by aligning regulations across different countries. This helps reduce duplication of efforts, increases efficiency, and facilitates quicker access to global markets.

40. What is the role of the regulatory affairs professional in clinical trials?

Answer: A **regulatory affairs professional** ensures that clinical trials comply with relevant regulations and guidelines, assists in preparing and submitting regulatory documents, and interacts with regulatory agencies to facilitate the approval process.

41. What are the key principles of regulatory science?

Answer: The key principles of regulatory science include ensuring drug **safety, efficacy, quality, public health protection**, and **scientific integrity** throughout the drug development and approval process.

42. How does the FDA's accelerated approval program work?

Answer: The **FDA's accelerated approval program** speeds up the approval of drugs for serious conditions based on early evidence of efficacy, allowing patients to access promising treatments while additional data is collected.

43. What is a clinical trial protocol review?

Answer: A **clinical trial protocol review** involves assessing the trial's design, methodology, and ethical considerations to ensure that the study is scientifically valid and that participants are protected.

44. What is regulatory documentation?

Answer: **Regulatory documentation** includes all required documents such as clinical trial data, manufacturing information, labeling, and **drug master files** submitted to regulatory agencies for approval.

45. What is the role of regulatory agencies in post-market drug surveillance?

Answer: Regulatory agencies like the **FDA** and **EMA** monitor drugs after approval by tracking adverse events, conducting inspections, and ensuring compliance with safety standards.

46. What is the role of regulatory guidelines in drug approval?

Answer: **Regulatory guidelines** provide a framework for drug development and approval, ensuring consistency and compliance with safety, efficacy, and quality standards to protect public health.

47. What is the fast track designation in drug approval?

Answer: The **fast track designation** expedites the development and review of drugs for serious conditions, allowing for earlier approval and quicker access to patients in need.

48. How does the FDA ensure drug quality?
Answer: The **FDA** ensures drug quality by enforcing **Good Manufacturing Practices (GMP)**, conducting inspections of manufacturing facilities, and reviewing drug quality control data.

49. What are the key ethical principles in drug development?
Answer: Key ethical principles include **informed consent**, **risk minimization**, **justice in participant selection**, and ensuring the **safety** and **well-being** of participants throughout the trial.

50. How do regulatory agencies impact the global drug market?
Answer: Regulatory agencies ensure that drugs meet international safety, efficacy, and quality standards, fostering trust in the global drug market and facilitating the availability of safe medicines worldwide.

About Authors

Dr. K. Nagasree

Dr. K Nagasree earned her Ph.D. in Pharmaceutical Sciences from Jawaharlal Nehru Technological university, Hyderabad. She has earned her PG.D.IPR. from Osmania University Law college, Hyderabad. Formerly worked as Asst. Professor at St.Mary's college of Pharmacy and as Professor & H.O.D. at Aditya Bangalore Institute of Pharmacy Education and Research, Bangalore. Currently working as Associate Professor & H.O.D., Department of Regulatory Affairs at samskruti college of Pharmacy, Ghatkesar, Hyderabad. She is also a resourse person at seminars. Dr. Nagasree is widely acclaimed as a teacher, Researcher, professional and ad mired by her students and well wishers everywhere.

Dr. Konda Shravan Kumar

Dr. Konda Shravan Kumar is a seasoned academic and pharmaceutical professional with over 25 years of experience in the field of pharmaceutical education and research. He currently serves as the Principal and Head of Samskruti College of Pharmacy, Hyderabad, where he has played a key role in shaping the institution's growth and academic excellence. Dr. Shravan Kumar is well-regarded for his contributions to pharmaceutical sciences, particularly in the areas of **pharmaceutical biotechnology, drug delivery systems, and microbiology.**

He earned his **Ph.D. in Pharmaceutical Sciences** from **Kakatiya University**, with a specialization in **Pharmaceutical Biotechnology**. His research has led to several **Indian patents** and has been published in numerous high-impact international journals. Over the years, his work in the development of **antimicrobial agents** and **controlled drug delivery systems** has been widely recognized.

Dr. Shravan Kumar has held prominent academic and administrative positions at various reputed pharmaceutical institutions. His expertise has been instrumental in the **development and revision of academic curricula,** aligning them with industry standards. He is deeply involved in guiding research scholars and students, encouraging innovation and practical application of theoretical knowledge in real-world pharmaceutical challenges.

As a dedicated researcher, Dr. Shravan Kumar has also contributed to national and international **conferences and seminars**, discussing the latest trends in **drug formulation and regulatory practices**. His leadership has not only contributed to the advancement of pharmaceutical sciences but has also helped to foster collaborations between academia and industry.

With a strong passion for **education and innovation**, Dr. Shravan Kumar is committed to advancing pharmaceutical education and contributing to the development of new therapeutic solutions.

Dr. K. N. V. Rao

Dr. K. N. V. Rao is a highly respected academician, researcher, and administrator with over 34 years of experience in teaching, research, and academic administration. He currently serves as the Principal of Nalanda College of Pharmacy, Nalgonda, Telangana. Dr. Rao's dedication to advancing pharmaceutical education has made him a pivotal figure in shaping the academic structure and fostering a research-driven environment at the college.

Dr. Rao's extensive academic journey has been complemented by his remarkable contributions to the pharmaceutical sciences, with a particular focus on pharmaceutical biotechnology, microbiology, and pharmaceutical regulatory science. His research expertise is widely acknowledged in the scientific community, with more than 155 research and review publications to his name in prestigious national and international journals. His publications have significantly impacted drug development, formulation technologies, and the regulatory aspects of the pharmaceutical industry.

In addition to his scholarly work, Dr. Rao holds five Indian patents, demonstrating his innovative approach to pharmaceutical research.

Throughout his career, Dr. Rao has remained dedicated to fostering academic excellence. His work in curriculum development, research advancement, and institutional leadership has earned him recognition across academic circles. He has played a key role in establishing collaborative relationships between academia and industry, creating opportunities for students and faculty to engage in cutting-edge pharmaceutical research.

Dr. Rao is deeply committed to promoting regulatory compliance and quality assurance in pharmaceutical research and drug development. Under his leadership, Nalanda College of Pharmacy has achieved significant milestones in research innovation, academic performance, and regulatory standards